Confessions
of a Dying Thief

Confessions
of a Dying Thief

**Understanding Criminal Careers
and Illegal Enterprise**

Darrell J. Steffensmeier
& Jeffery T. Ulmer

ALDINETRANSACTION
A Division of Transaction Publishers
New Brunswick (U.S.A.) and London (U.K.)

Third paperback printing 2007

Copyright © 2005 by Transaction Publishers, New Brunswick, New Jersey.

This book is printed on acid-free paper that meets the American National `Standard for Permanence of Paper for Printed Library Materials.

Library of Congress Catalog Number: 2004007277
ISBN: 978-0-202-30761-9
Printed in the United States of America

Library of Congress Cataloging-in-Publication Data

Goodman, Sam.
Confessions of a dying thief: understanding criminal careers and illegal enterprise / Darrell J. Steffensmeier and Jeffery T. Ulmer [interviewers].—lst ed.
p. cm. —(New lines in criminology)
Includes bibliographical references.
ISBN 0-202-30760-3 (cloth: alk. paper)—ISBN 0-202-30761-1 (pbk: alk. paper)
1. Goodman, Sam. 2. Burglars—United States—Biography. 3. Burglary—United States–Case studies. 4. Receiving stolen goods—United States—Case studies. I. Steffensmeier, Darrell, J., 1942- II. Ulmer, Jeffery T., 1966- III. Title. IV. Series.

HV6653.G66A3   2004
364. 16'2'092—dc22   2004007277

Darrell Steffensmeier dedicates *Confessions* to Emily Erin and Abbie.

Jeffery Ulmer dedicates *Confessions* in memory of Charles A. Ulmer, Jr., and Virginia Webb Bradshaw.

Contents

First Author's Prologue

Darrell Steffensmeier

> *I do know I am not going to make it. [Doc] gave it to me plain, very Goddamn plain: "Sam, there ain't time for that. Get your house in order, with your grandchildren, with Wanda. I says, "How long?" He tells me, "Give or take a little, six weeks, three months. Maybe sooner." That hit home like a ton of bricks fell on my nuts.*
> —Sam Goodman

Sam Goodman—long-time thief, fence, and quasi-legitimate businessman— died following a four month bout with lung cancer. Sam's criminal career spanned fifty years, beginning in his midteens and ending with his death when Sam was in his midsixties. I had known Sam for roughly twenty years and had written about him in *The Fence: In the Shadow of Two Worlds* (1986). *The Fence* described Sam's criminal career as a burglar, his eventual drift into fencing, and the circumstances that led to his incarceration for receiving stolen property in the 1970s.

Confessions of a Dying Thief offers an updated and greatly expanded case study of Sam Goodman based on continuous contact with him for many years, on multiple interviews with his network associates in crime and business, and on a series of interviews with him shortly before he died. I stayed in regular contact with Sam from the time he was incarcerated in the 1970s up until he died in the 1990s. Toward the end, the contact became more intense, as I visited him frequently during his four month bout with cancer. I also interviewed Sam at length on a Friday-Sunday weekend, five days before he slipped into a coma and eleven days before he died.

A few weeks after Sam's death, I gave Jeffery Ulmer a partial transcript of the deathbed interviews and asked for his reactions. Jeff was a graduate student working with me during the time Sam was alive and sometimes visited Penn State. Jeff had met Sam, heard him speak to criminology classes, and occasionally "hung out" with Sam and me during these visits. Jeff also talked frequently with me during Sam's illness and death, and served as a sounding board for my ideas and emotions.

These discussions eventually led to my asking Jeff to collaborate in producing *Confessions*. I brought him into the project for several reasons. First, Jeff is very familiar with *The Fence* and the material behind it (more familiar with it than anyone except myself), he had met Sam several times, and he had read through parts of Sam's last interviews. Second, Jeff serves as an added check on my objectivity, since I sometimes was concerned with how my friendship with Sam might influence my interpretation of the material. Third, I wanted Ulmer to help with the writing, rewriting, and organization of *Confessions*—in particular to help organize and analyze the massive amount of material collected from in-depth interviews, observations, and other sources. Fourth, Jeff is well-versed in both criminological theory and ethnographic research, and therefore brought additional ideas to the methodological framing and theoretical arguments of *Confessions*.

It was on Thanksgiving day, about five months prior to Sam's death, that I got a telephone call from Sam canceling our plans to attend an out-of-state auction. As recorded in my field notes at the time, Sam complained of "feeling rougher than hell and coughing like a son of a bitch." Sam's tone and the unusualness of this sort of cancellation added to an already strong premonition of mine (never shared with Sam) that he had cancer. A heavy smoker, he had seemed short of breath lately and lacked his usual pep. Roughly six weeks later, Sam was hospitalized for "fluid on his lungs" and subsequently was diagnosed as having advanced-stage lung cancer.

The deathbed interviews were wide ranging—an assessment of Sam's life as a whole and of a criminal career that spanned fifty years; a recollection of criminal and quasi-legitimate associates, of good times and not-so-good times, a reflection on crime and the criminal justice system, on "straight" society, on human relationships, a revelation of Sam's sentiments toward me, "the professor" (moniker often used by Sam and his colleagues), and an intimate disclosure of Sam's showdown with death.

Sam's illness and death are a sobering backdrop throughout the whole book. However, what follows this prologue is not just a dying thief's intimate confessions; rather, it is a rare and penetrating journey into the dynamics of criminal careers and the social organization of criminal enterprise. The journey begins with Part I, which further introduces Sam and *Confessions*, and spells out the book's contributions to sociology and criminology. Part II frames the book theoretically and focuses on the life trajectory of Sam's career in burglary and fencing. Part III focuses on the social organization of criminal enterprise and criminal careers. Finally, Part IV takes stock of Sam's life, and of his confrontation with death. Let the journey begin.

Acknowledgments

We want to thank the following for all their assistance with this project and seeing it through to publication. First, we thank Sam Goodman and his associates for sharing their experiences and perspectives. Next, we thank Paul Blaum and Bill Roddey for helpful feedback and our colleagues Emilie Allan, Miles Harer, John Kramer, Emily Erin Steffensmeier, and Renee Hoffman Steffensmeier for carefully reading and commenting on prior drafts of the document. Their comments greatly improved the quality of this book.

We thank Richard Koffler, Thomas Blomberg, Irving Louis Horowitz, Mary Curtis, Karen Ornstein, Michael Paley, and production editor Mai Cota for their thoughtful assistance in bringing this book to publication. We also thank Lee Carpenter and Mike Solic for their careful and helpful editing suggestions.

Finally, we thank "The Two Edwins," Sutherland and Lemert. We consider them to be the two pre-eminent criminologists of the 20th Century, and we are indebted to their career-long efforts to educate us about the social worlds of crime and deviance.

PART I

Introducing *Confessions*

1

Confessions' Data and Contributions

If you asked I told you. Didn't try to rattle your
cage. [And] wanted you to see for yourself, that
seeing is better than just hearing about it.
—Sam Goodman

This book is an examination of a career in crime and the world of theft, fencing, and criminal enterprise as experienced by Sam Goodman—a long-time thief, fence, and quasi-legitimate businessman who also was the principal subject of *The Fence: In the Shadow of Two Worlds* by Darrell Steffensmeier (1986). Sam died in his mid to late sixties following a four-month bout with lung cancer. Steffensmeier met Sam in the 1970s, stayed in regular touch with him, and visited him frequently in the hospital during the course of his illness. Steffensmeier also interviewed him at length on a Friday-Sunday weekend, five days before he slipped into a coma and eleven days before he died. Hence the title, *Confessions of a Dying Thief.* These interviews with a dying thief are both original and unique. We know of no other instance in criminology where a career thief about to die has been interviewed, much less probed so intimately.

Most of the book consists of two interrelated components: narrative accounts by Sam portraying his life and criminal career, interspersed with our conceptual commentaries that put the narrative material in social science perspective. In presenting *Confessions,* we have "cleaned up" Sam's language (e.g., swear words, ethnic slurs), but not entirely. We have left intact his vernacular at most places, especially when he discusses topics like death and religion, to give the reader a better feeling for Sam and his response to events, people, and life in general. We have changed names, dates, and certain details to protect Sam's associates from identification. We also have edited Sam's prose to remove the false starts and repetitions common to speech, but annoying in print.

Although the narratives in *Confessions* are in Sam's own words, both they and our accompanying commentaries are also based on additional, corroborating information from other sources. In order to establish the validity of Sam's account and recollections, Steffensmeier continually sought information and contacts for verification—for example, by discussing similar matters with Sam's associates, and by securing information from police, newspaper, and other sources. In some instances this process involved *multiple interviews and frequent (even regular) contact* with this or that associate of Sam. In general, these sources confirmed Sam's experiences and accounts and by extension the ideas and conclusions described in *Confessions*.

Especially informative were interviews with "insiders" like Jesse (Sam's one-time burglary partner), Rocky (a thief who regularly sold stolen goods to Sam), Timmy (a warehouse worker who sold pilfered merchandise to Sam), Puddy (a local bookie with whom Sam hung out), and Chubby (a longtime hanger-on), who knew Sam very well and also were knowledgeable about the theft world. The many meetings and conversations Steffensmeier had with them and other insiders could itself be the basis of a companion document. Moreover, as with Sam, the time spent associating with them across settings and over time helped to introduce information that one may be otherwise unable to secure.

If the respondents were willing and the situation favorable, Steffensmeier taped the interviews. Otherwise, he made notes at the earliest convenience or taped his recollections and observations. The interviews were often actually conversations, and like most conversations, jumped from subject to subject, time period to time period. The interviews took place in homes, on porches, at places of business, in cars or pick-ups, in parks, in bars, in restaurants, in offices, in jails, at auction sites, and on the street. Sometimes the interviews lasted several hours, other times a few minutes to an hour. Occasionally the "interview" was an all-day affair or a morning or an evening spent together at Sam's place of business, at an auction, or at another site. Interviews were conducted with a single informant, with two informants together, or with several informants together.

Each of these sources added valuable comparative data, but in the process made it increasingly difficult to handle the material (especially within the printing limitations of a book). As Wright and Decker said, "Perhaps the most challenging aspect of any field-based research project involves reducing what one has seen, heard, and felt 'out there' to written form" (1997:xiv). Given the longevity of the project and the plurality of individuals and sources involved, attempting to come to terms with all the material collected was at times almost overwhelming. Sorting out and deciding which out of an abundance of relevant examples to use at times seemed almost impossible, especially in light of the multiplicity of people and activities with which *Confessions* is concerned. It was especially taxing to address occasional discrepancies (typically minor) in Sam's or an associate's account between earlier and later interviews over several years, or between Sam's account and another insider's recollection, as all viewed an event or activity somewhat differently according to their own lens and interests.

Significance of *Confessions* for Criminology

The document that follows is both a life history of a criminal career *and* a description of the underworld and illegal enterprise, as experienced by a veteran thief and fence who had been engaged almost continuously for roughly fifty years. Sam's account tells us about underworld culture and organization, the social worlds of theft, hustling, and illegal enterprise. *Confessions* depicts the underworld as what Anselm Strauss (1993) called a "social world" of interaction, communication, and (to some extent) shared meaning. In other words, we see the underworld as a *"field"* of mutually recognized goals and organized striving for achievement, to paraphrase Pierre Bourdieu (1977; see also Martin 2003). *Confessions* elucidates the social organization of burglary and of fencing, the criminal social capital necessary for successful criminal enterprise, the importance of criminal networks, the stratification or pecking order of the underworld, and the nature of localized organized crime networks. This major theme in *Confessions* of the social organization of the underworld and criminal enterprise addresses matters only briefly touched on or implied in *The Fence*.

This study of a seasoned thief and criminal entrepreneur makes at least eight contributions to criminology and sociology in general. First, Sam provides a kind of voice from a culture and situation not known to most sociologists and criminologists. *Confessions* is a live and vibrant message from "down there," telling us what it means to be a kind of person most of us have never met face to face. We learn about his view of the world, about the interconnections across individuals and settings that not only shape the underworld but frequently link it to the upperworld, about how the culture of the underworld grows out of and is related to the general culture, about the thin thread often separating the two worlds, and about the need to lessen the distance between underworld members and upperworld academics who report and construct theories about crime.

Second, Sam's confession reminds us that deviants, even persistent criminals, are seldom deviant in all or even most aspects of their lives. Sam comfortably rubs shoulders with thieves, gamblers, and quasi-legitimate businessmen but also courts respectability and pledges allegiance to some major normative standards. His keen eye for the moral loophole and general lack of remorse for all the "rank shit he has pulled in his life" only partly cloak the marginality from legitimate society and the concern for the appearance of respectability that even the career criminal can only rarely overcome. We feel the publicly known as well as privately experienced stigma of a "criminal record" that is difficult to reverse, disguise, or ignore.

Third, Sam's own life and his recollections about his many associates do not support some contemporary views of career development and desistance. We know much about the "careers" of low-level and ordinary offenders—most of whom *apparently* have exited from crime by age thirty or forty. On the other hand, we know very little about persistent offenders like Sam and about the extent and types of crime committed at different stages of criminal careers. From Sam, we learn that many "matured out" offenders still find crime morally acceptable and continue to commit crimes sporadically when the opportunity presents itself and the risks are small, or they regularly moonlight as part-time offenders while holding legitimate jobs, or they operate as background operators. We also learn that some subsets of the larger criminal population—good burglars, dealers in stolen goods, bookmakers, con artists, quasi-legitimate businessmen, local racketeers, and mafiosi—frequently persist in their criminality until they are too old or feeble to do otherwise. The prison samples used in the bulk of existing studies underrepresent the offenders for whom crime is the most remunerative.

Fourth, we witness (through Sam) the complex mix of rewards and motives for criminal entrepreneurship—material gain, excitement, attention, peer recognition, and the enjoyment of simply doing what one is good at. There is also the playing out of the central ingredients for success—integrity, reliability, generosity, larceny sense, and business-sense (including hustling)—in the midst of activities characterized by risk and ambiguity; and the oscillating pattern of involvement and disengagement as entrepreneurs like Sam attempt to balance concerns with safety and desires for fast profits over extended periods of time. There is also in Sam (and in many of his underworld colleagues, and in many blue-collar people in general) a sort of resentment toward the system because of the variability and perceived unfairness in life chances across individuals and groups.

Fifth, the accounts of actual offenders like Sam caution against simplistic views of criminal opportunity. Opportunity is, of course, a venerable concept in criminological theory, but it is almost taken for granted as a given when criminologists study criminal careers. Throughout *Confessions,* we critique existing conceptions of opportunity. *Confessions* directs attention to the notion that there is considerable variation in criminal opportunities, and in *types* of opportunities, across individuals and groups. More importantly, however, *Confessions* illustrates that *offenders like Sam not only respond to crime opportunities, they construct and sustain them.* Furthermore, motivation and opportunity are not easily distinguished in the "real" world of criminal involvement. Being able makes one more willing. What is objectively possible is more likely to become subjectively acceptable, and vice versa. Finally, access to—and how one capitalizes on—opportunities for serious, sustained criminal enterprise is likely to involve matters like preexisting ties, preparatory knowledge, reputation, and whether one is from the "right" racial or ethnic group.

Sixth, inasmuch as *Confessions* is about the *life course* of a career criminal, it has special relevance for the development and assessment of the *life course perspective,* which has become popular in recent criminological writings. Life course perspectives focus on onset, persistence, and desistence or continuation of criminal careers, and emphasize the importance of "turning points" as critical events or decisions that trigger transitions into or out of crime. A focus on the life course and criminal offending is compatible with a variety of theoretical perspectives central to criminology, such as social learning/differential association, social control, opportunity, routine activities, and rational choice theories.

Certainly, *Confessions* contributes to our understanding of crime and the life course, and life circumstances, contexts and turning points that facilitate onset, persistence, and desistence or decline in offending. For example, Sam's narrative is filled with emergent and pivotal turning points that decisively structured his criminal career and fostered his development of criminal capital (such as his poor relationship with his stepfather, his tutelage in theft and hustling at the hands of his uncle, his initial periods of incarceration, his burglary partnership with Jesse, opening his secondhand shop, being invited into the local gambling club attended by organized crime figures, and his conviction and prison stint for dealing stolen goods). In short, *Confessions* amply illustrates the dynamic nature of criminal offending and how offenders exercise agency and choice in the face of emergent constraints and opportunities over time.

By tracking Sam and his several of his associates into their fifties and sixties, *Confessions* also helps to illuminate later stages of careers in theft and criminal enterprise by going beyond adolescent or young adult samples. It is quite remarkable that robust claims about the causes and risk factors shaping the *persistent* or chronic offender expressed by many criminologists today rely almost exclusively on offender samples that cover only the adolescent and/or young adult years (typically up to about age thirty—see the review by Farrington 2003). This reliance and the robust claims are most strongly observed among those writers who espouse a life course or developmental perspective on criminal offending. Yet, following offenders into their twenties or even thirties hardly captures the fullness of the life course. Consequently, we know relatively little about the dynamics of offending and/or desistence beyond the ages of twenty to thirty.

Seventh, we outline an integrative *learning-opportunity-commitment* theoretical framework throughout our commentaries. This framework combines differential association/social learning theory and an extended and refined conceptualization of criminal opportunity with a three-fold theory of commitment to crime versus conventionality.

Finally, *Confessions* is an in-depth life history, but it is also more than that. *It is equally a picture of the criminal underworld and criminal enterprise more generally.* As Sutherland (1937) argued long ago in *The Professional Thief,* crime is socially organized and is a group phenomenon. Sam and his associates provide a unique window on the social organization of criminal enterprise, including organized crime. In other words, *Confessions* is about a *social world* (Strauss 1993) or *field* (Bourdieu 1977, 1985) of local criminal enterprise and Sam's place in it. Through Sam's narratives (corroborated with information from Sam's criminal associates and other sources), we understand the organization of burglary crews, the ins and outs of running a successful fencing operation, the crucial importance of criminal networks, the stratification or "pecking order" of the world of crime, racism and sexism in the underworld, and the nature of localized organized crime networks. As a part of our examination of the underworld as a field, we identify and analyze types of *criminal social and cultural capital* that are necessary for success and longevity in money-oriented crime and criminal enterprise.

The Validity and Generalizability of *Confessions*

Confessions is testament to the value of the ethnographic perspective and its emphasis on understanding the effects of opportunity structures, social norms, lifestyles, stressful life circumstances, and other commonly invoked explanations of behavior, criminal or otherwise, by seeing them from the actor's viewpoint. The strength of ethnographic data, especially when it is collected over a substantial period of time, is that it enables us to understand *processes* rather than just static outcomes of social processes.

Criminal careers research in recent years has taken two main turns. One is the growth in *ethnographic* research that builds on a long research tradition in criminology and seeks to comprehend crime through the eyes of offenders. The bulk of this research has been on street offenders and their pursuits—their lives, routines, and decisions. The other is the much larger growth in *statistical* studies that track offenders using arrest or conviction data or that use data from offenders' self-reported offense history. The self-report data are typically collected in questionnaires or in *one-shot* probes or interviews. As a consequence of these twin developments, there is some narrowing of the experiential distance between criminological subject matter and criminological researchers, but on the other hand, "growing numbers of criminologists know crime and criminals only as lines in electronic data files" (Neal Shover, cited in Wright and Decker 1997:xi).

In our view, one-shot interviews can provide useful information about backgrounds, worldviews, and some dimensions of crime (e.g., strategies and templates for committing crime). However, one-shot interviews are quite limited when it comes to acquiring information (1) about an offender's *own* history of law-breaking and especially his or her recent or current law-breaking, and (2) about an offender's criminal associates and networks. This difficulty in getting offenders to disclose increases with age, as offenders become more circumspect and cautious—middle-aged and older offenders probably require more rapport.

Studying practitioners of crime and vice is a risky business, studded with traps and pitfalls. Interviewing criminals is challenging. If the interviewer makes the offender subject feel pushed, defensive, interrogated, and prodded, he or she is likely to "clam up" and not participate in further interviews, especially in early stages of the interviewing process. We believe that getting accurate and valid details depends especially on the rapport one builds with informants. Offenders have a vested interested in protecting their identities, maintaining secrecy, and keeping outsiders out (Fleisher 1995:21). For these reasons we, like other ethnographers, tend to distrust data gathered in penciled-in questionnaires or in one-shot interviews with informants, especially when minimal efforts at cultivating rapport are made.

To illustrate, Steffensmeier's initial interviews with Sam (as well as with this or that associate) produced some useful information about Sam's life and about the world of crime, but very little useful information about Sam's own criminality. Moreover, while some of Sam's associates eventually revealed their own recent or current criminality (e.g., Jesse, Sam's one-time burglary partner), other associates never did disclose it, but their criminal involvement was divulged by other informants.

Issues of trust and offender honesty therefore lessen the usefulness of questionnaires and one-shot interviews. The latter should not be construed as "life history" interviews, much less as "in-depth." *Furthermore, we note that such data collection methods may be biased in favor of showing much more desistance than in fact is the case.* This is because offenders, especially middle-aged and older offenders, would be less likely to admit or self-report recent or current offending on an impersonal questionnaire or during a one-shot interview. Therefore, researchers who relied on such data would conclude that all offenders eventually desist, or that life-course-persistent offenders are a small minority who are quite different from other offenders.

Ultimately, we rest our claim to validity on the fact that the research reported here is based on *many* interviews with Sam over a long period of time, and on multiple interviews with his associates or network members. Additionally, attempts were made to corroborate information with multiple sources of data whenever possible. Steffensmeier had regular and frequent contact with the key individuals referred to in *Confessions*. *As a rule, gaining rapport or getting informants to "open up" about their criminal activities was simply not feasible in the first interview or two or three.* The only partial exception to this rule occurred when Sam *sponsored* or vouched for Steffensmeier to a new interview subject and facilitated the contact.

This study adopted what Glaser and Strauss (1967) call the "constant comparative method," and can best be characterized as what Burawoy (2003: 668–69) called "rolling ethnographic revisits." This strategy involved (1) *intensive* interviewing, including the ongoing preparation of semi-structured questions or interview protocol and (2) successive visits in which there is a running dialogue between field notes, observations, and conceptual framework.

For all these reasons, we believe that the data presented here have more validity than most studies of criminal careers, which rely on self-report questionnaires, official arrest records, or one-shot interviews. As for generalizability, social scientists have two goals in different kinds of research. One common goal is to generalize from a sample to a population, and this is the typical goal of studies using statistical data. However, another kind of generalization is theory based: the researcher's goal is to generalize from the data at hand to theory and concepts (Glaser and Strauss 1967). That is, in the latter scenario, the researcher is not interested in the statistical representativeness of his or her research subjects, but in the implications the data have for developing and testing theoretical ideas and concepts.

Ethnographic studies data typically pursue this latter goal, and that is what we are doing here as well. This also means that the generalizability of this study is intimately tied to the validity of its data, as discussed above. If we have confidence in the validity of our data, then we can have confidence in their utility for applying and testing general theoretical ideas about crime, criminal careers, criminal enterprise, and the underworld. Ultimately, the generalizability of this study and the theoretical arguments we make from it are empirical questions. We strongly encourage future researchers to put them to the test.

Images of Crime and Criminals

Another theme of *Confessions* contributes to the ongoing debate within criminology about the accuracy of popular images and social scientists' ideas about contemporary criminals—especially about chronic or life-course-persistent offenders. Images of crime and criminals intersect with emotions and sentiments about the essence of human nature and about what to do (or not to do) in order to deal with crime. Two stubborn images of crime and criminals prevail both in folklore and in academic criminology. One might be called the image of criminals as "desperate people in desperate circumstances." The other is the image of criminals as "pathological," "developmentally damaged," or "suffering from personal deficits." Both of these sets of images, we believe, provide a very narrow view of the criminal landscape.

The first of these sets of images views criminal decision-making and behavior as propelled by the desperate circumstances of offenders' lives. Offending results when offenders stumble into crime as a result of their social and geographic proximity to crime groups and situations. This view portrays criminals as leading more or less passive lives, driven by "grim economic or psychic necessity" (Bordua 1961:136). A related set of images portrays criminals as viewing life as one big escapist party, a party that they have to gain illicit income to finance.

The second view is that "criminals" are very different from the rest of us. As Lemert (1951:91) notes, the stubborn folk idea also thrives in academic criminology that "persons leading lives condemned by society must be unhappy, demoralized, and emotionally maladjusted." In this view, criminals, especially those referred to as life-course-persistent offenders, suffer from low self-control or impulsivity, low intelligence, or other biological or psychological deficits. This view often implies that criminals are bad now, have always been bad, will always be bad, and are bad in almost every way.

A related view is that criminals are "outsiders" who profess values and views drastically inconsistent with mainstream conventional values and norms. Relevant here is Bordua's assertion: "It seems peculiar that modern analysts have stopped assuming that 'evil' can be fun and see [crime/delinquency] as arising *only when boys [men] are driven away from 'good'* " (1961:136, emphasis added).

In the late 1980s, the Pennsylvania Crime Commission (PCC) chose Steffensmeier to be the project director and chief consultant for the PCC's 1990 Decade Report, *Organized Crime in Pennsylvania: A Decade of Change* (1991). Jeffery Ulmer also worked on this project and contributed to the report. The PCC did so largely on the basis of their favorable reading of *The Fence.* In many respects the popular images and the social scientists' ideas about contemporary criminals noted above were at odds with *The Fence,* and the criminal investigators and intelligence analysts of the PCC saw it as a more realistic portrayal of criminal enterprise and its practitioners.

The PCC Executive Director and staff shared David Matza's (1964) view that academic criminologists, who profess expertise about crime, appear to have a remarkable reluctance to get close to or gain firsthand knowledge about their subject matter. In fact, they delighted in pointing out what they saw as the disconnect between the "ivory tower" theories of academics and their own, "real-world knowledge" of criminal careers and criminal enterprise.

For the veteran criminal investigators of the PCC, *The Fence* was grounded in "the real world" of crime—it provided, as does *Confessions,* a rich, in-depth understanding of the criminal life and world. They felt that the book showed how crime and criminal enterprise are woven into the fabric of society, and how the line between legitimate and illegitimate is often thin. They saw *The Fence* as offering a more nuanced and representative portrayal of the criminal landscape, particularly the world of theft, hustling, and illegal or quasi-legal enterprise. Also, they saw it as addressing "real crime" because it focused on *adult practitioners of crime and vice* whose criminality impacted hugely on society at large, as opposed to studying delinquency and what they considered "kids' stuff."

The Commission's staff and its director tended to recognize the partial validity of "desperate men facing desperate circumstances" imagery, but felt that criminological views overemphasized this and exaggerated it beyond its statistical reality. As much or more than resource scarcity, they saw crime as a product of one's greed, or as one's niche or "thing," played out in a society where the worlds of business and politics provided lots of moral leeway. They were highly skeptical about pathological and developmental damage views of persistent offenders, and could counter them with example after example. And they particularly saw as gullible the solution of "early childhood intervention" as a panacea that would dent the extent of crime or criminal enterprise in U.S. society and the pathways into such. *Confessions* continues in this mode of calling into question sometimes simplistic or overgeneralized popular and criminological imagery.

We have placed Sam's narratives in theoretical perspective by way of intermittent commentaries that reflect our assumptions and sentiments about human nature, our orientation to what to ask and what kinds of information to collect, and our cognitive abilities (or limitations) in interpreting the data. Our questions and representations clearly do not reflect or contain all of reality. There obviously is plenty of room for alternative approaches and interpretations. We invite the reader to supply his or her own interpretations and view the narrative material through their own lenses, in addition to or instead of ours. Like Sutherland did in his preface to *The Professional Thief,* we offer *Confessions* merely as a basis for further study of particular aspects of criminal careers and illegal enterprise, in the belief that it will provide a helpful, fuller understanding of pathways into and out of crime as well as the social organization of illegal enterprise. Like Sutherland, we are striving for an imagery of the criminal landscape that enlarges our ideas about what might be present in the world we study.

2

Sam Goodman: Homecoming and Farewell

It was during Sam's incarceration for receiving stolen goods in the 1970s that Darrell Steffensmeier first met Sam and subsequently accompanied him on his first furlough trip to American City, where Sam had settled almost twenty years prior and where, in his words, his criminal career "went swoosh." That trip both confirmed other thieves' description of Sam as an "old head who knew his way around" and bolstered confidence in Sam as the subject of a case study. Sam had done a lot and he knew a lot, not only about the underworld but about the nexus between the underworld and the upperworld. Most swaying, however, was (1) Sam's exceptional ability to recall events and approximate dates and to remember names, faces, and identifying details of individuals he had known or encountered, and (2) Sam's openness to both divulge and introduce Steffensmeier to his "business" network.

We begin with the beginning and the ending-the beginning of Steffensmeier's research odyssey with Sam, and the end of Sam's life. The three sections that follow are used to set the stage for the rest of the book. The first section, *Sam's Homecoming,* is extracted from Steffensmeier's field notes describing the furlough trip to American City, including a notable stopover at a neighborhood bar that Sam had once frequented, in which we are given a glimpse of Sam's personality and social world as well as Steffensmeier's decision to study him. The next segment, *I Feel Rougher Than Hell,* also draws on Steffensmeier's field notes to describe the sequence of events (including the discovery that Sam has cancer) leading to the deathbed interviews, beginning with a Thanksgiving day telephone call from Sam to Steffensmeier canceling their weekend plans to attend a large antique auction in an adjacent state. The third section, *The Jig Is Up,* includes excerpts from Steffensmeier's weekend interview with Sam in which Sam speaks about his bout with cancer and appraises his life.

Sam's Homecoming

Setting: Midstate Penitentiary. Sam and Steffensmeier depart for American City. The following account is drawn from Steffensmeier's field notes taken at the time.

I picked up Sam at the penitentiary on an early June morning and we headed for American City where Sam was planning to spend the weekend with Becky, his female companion prior to his incarceration. On the way, Sam pointed out several places—a fire station, an American Legion Club, and an antique shop—that he and Jesse had "clipped" some years ago. On the outskirts of American City, we stopped at a "doll and antique shop" and visited with its owner, who formerly had traded both legitimate and "warm" antiques with Sam. Their shared ribbing was amusing, as their discussion of the current trade in antiques was interesting but "over my head" since I know little or nothing about "good antiques." The high-light of the day trip was stopping at Casey's Pub—a neighborhood bar and thieves' hangout that was once a favorite stopover for Sam, especially on Friday evenings after he had attended one of the local auctions. I guess you could call it Sam's "homecoming."

We arrived at Casey's about 5:30–6:00 (early Friday evening). Casey's is a fairly large place, with a long bar, a row of tables for dining, and an open room in the back with a pool table and video machines. Sam held the door as I entered first. Then jeez, the place went up for grabs when the roughly 30–35 patrons, mostly male, spotted Sam walking through the door. We [he] were greeted with shouts of, "Hey, god damn it's Sam. Sam, you son of a bitch, what the hell you doing here," and so on. I think everybody in the place shook Sam's hand. Many shook mine as well, as Sam quickly told them I was a teacher at Penn State who had visited him in the penitentiary [always Sam's term for referring to a prison]. Katie, the female bartender, rushed from behind the bar to give Sam a big hug. He ribbed her about how flat-chested she still was. She dished it right back, wise-cracking about Sam's bad luck with women. Sam quickly had a half-dozen "bourbon and cokes" in front of him—his favorite drink as remembered by those present. Myself, I sat facing half-a-dozen Budweisers, a result of responding to someone's probe of "What are you drinking?"

A number of people that Sam had talked about (e.g., Steelbeams, Mickey, Timmy) were there, along with several "locals" who lived in the neighborhood and had gotten to know Sam. Very much enjoying the scene and camaraderie, I moved around and chatted with many of those present. One of the neighborhood locals commented how unfair it was that Sam had to do time—"sure, he was a little loose in how he ran his store but he would give you the shirt off his back if he saw you needed it. There are a lot worse ones around who are still walking free." We stayed at Casey's until about 9:00, after which I dropped Sam off at Becky's—where I also met Muffin, Sam's Doberman that I had heard so many stories about, especially about how Muffin "hated cops."

As Steffensmeier looks back today, the spontaneous welcoming Sam received at Casey's marked a kind of "turning point" in Steffensmeier's career choice to document Sam's life and criminal career. Already then, but even more so as the years have passed, that first visit to American City and Sam's reception has taken on a somewhat surreal quality (since Steffensmeier cannot really recall a parallel happening for other acquaintances, much less for himself). The reception also planted the seeds for a more appreciative stance of the often fine line between deviance and respectability in the minds, everyday lives, and practical moral systems of ordinary people, a stance that is reflected in *Confessions*.

"I Feel Rougher Than Hell" (Sam Has Cancer)

Steffensmeier receives a phone call from Sam on Thanksgiving day canceling their weekend plans to attend an auction in an adjacent state. The phone call sets in motion the chain of events leading to Sam's hospitalization and eventual passing, as recorded in Steffensmeier's field notes below (written in first person).

"I feel rougher than hell," Sam coughed, "whatever it is I can't shake it." I phoned Sam a couple of weeks later, hoping to get together over Christmas break, but instead found him still "feeling lousy." A week or so after New Years Sam phoned again: "Hey, Bubba, guess where I am. Motherfucking hospital. They're jamming stuff up my arms, my ass, like you wouldn't believe. Think it's pneumonia. They're running all kinds of tests."

That weekend I visited Sam at the hospital. The results from several tests were in—Sam had lung cancer. It was serious. The cancer had metastasized and spread throughout his upper body. Sam was in pretty good spirits and optimistic that he "would lick it." Over the next several weeks, however, Sam deteriorated rapidly. I increasingly found him heavily sedated, uninterested in food, and barely able to communicate or even recognize me. Lying in his hospital bed, he would greet me in familiar fashion—either "Hey, professor," or "Hi, Bubba." He would squeeze my hand with a grip that, once very powerful, now was feeble and soft. The cancer ravaging Sam had shrunken his body's stout frame, dwindled the muscle tone in his limbs, and thinned his face to a bony landscape. He was too weak to begin chemotherapy and radiation treatment. I, along with Sam's family and friends, felt the end was near.

Then, as sometimes occurs with terminal cancer patients, Sam surprised us. "He just perked up," his daughter Amy told me. Sam's appetite and alertness returned. His spirit rebounded and he talked again about "licking this Goddamn thing." He badgered the doctors to release him from the hospital, to allow him to go home and begin the cancer treatment. They agreed.

Sam's stay at his home lasted less than three weeks. Bedridden, but able to ambulate with assistance, Sam attended a couple of local auctions and visited with acquaintances in the antique trade. But the bulk of his time was spent "putting his house in order"—finalizing his will and establishing a chain of command at his upholstery shop.

I traveled to see Sam during his second and final weekend at home. I had phoned Sam ahead to make the arrangements, indicating that I would probably "do a little taping"—something I routinely did when interviewing Sam or even conversing with him. "Yeah, we haven't done that for a while," he noted, pleased that I was coming. We both sensed that this likely was our last "real" interview. With this in mind, I came prepared with a well thought-out protocol.

I arrived early Friday morning. Sam was in good spirits, telling jokes, and kidding Wanda (his female companion for the past eight to ten years) about going with me to one of the local flea markets. Wanda eventually left for the day, saying she would call later to check if everything was okay (which she did). The Friday and Saturday interviews were punctuated by phone calls and short visits from some of Sam's cronies in the antique business. Sam was quite worn out by midafternoon, although he insisted on continuing.

I returned Sunday morning and found Sam looking tired and weak. His energy soon waned and by early afternoon he had dozed off. I chatted with Wanda while Sam slept, but he awoke as I prepared to leave. "Thanks for coming, Bubba," he whispered. "Bring those chairs next time you come. The boys will get right on them, get them done while we're visiting" (this was in reference to an earlier offer by Sam to reupholster six dining room chairs of mine).

On the return trip I listened to parts of the taping, anticipating that this was probably my last real conversation with Sam. Four days later, on Thursday, Sam was rehospitalized. His lungs had filled up and he was having a hard time breathing. Wanda called on Friday to report that Sam had gone downhill very fast. He was basically in a coma. Unless they keep him on a life support system (which the family had decided against), "It's just a matter of time—he'll just sleep away."

I visited Sam again that weekend, on Sunday, in his hospital room. Wanda greeted me when I arrived but soon left for the afternoon, leaving me alone with Sam. I doubt Sam recognized me, despite some eye contact as well as occasional musings or utterances from him. Some utterances were apparent flashbacks or "nightmares" to his days in prison. Viewing me as if a fellow inmate, Sam's eyes would open wide and with a look expressing fright, he would motion me over and mumble, "Nail the fat one, I'll get the big fucker." Then, with a weak hand gesture and eyes rolling in that direction, he would add, "Over the wall, that wall there." Sam, it seemed, was instructing me to help him escape from prison. Wanda had mentioned these flashbacks, noting how painful it was to see Sam apparently relive his worst days in prison. Those flashbacks were the last "communication" I had with Sam.

On leaving the hospital, I wrote a note to Wanda, asking her to give me a call if there was any change in Sam's condition. I remember squeezing Sam's limp and unresponsive hand, and mumbling, "Goodbye, Sam, goodbye, good buddy" (or something to that effect). Three days later Wanda called—Sam had "slept away." She would notify me about funeral arrangements.

The following is an excerpt from the very last interview with Sam. In it, we see the bluntness of Sam's vernacular and the openness with which he talked to Steffensmeier.

"The Jig Is Up—I Do Know I'm Not Going to Make It"

Setting: Sam's home, Friday midmorning. Wanda departs for the day shortly after my arrival. Day 1 of what will be a three-day weekend of "interviewing" begins briskly. Sam is eager to talk.

I'm going to lick this fucking cancer. Get my legs back, be back at running my shop. Get on Donnie and Benny's asses. They need that. Before I didn't care. Now my mind is on getting fucking better. No doubt I'm gonna get better.

But Fifteen Minutes Later . . .

I do know I am not going to make it. Asked the Doc about seeing another specialist. He gave it to me plain, very god damn plain: "Sam, there ain't time for that. Get your house in order, with your grandchildren, with Wanda. It's too late. If you had started treatment when it was first spotted, then maybe." I says, "How long?" He tells me, "Give or take a little, six weeks, three months. Maybe sooner."

That hit home like a ton of bricks fell on my nuts. Kicked right in the belly is the way it felt. Whew, I am thinking how fast this year went by and bang here it is already. A year ago the doctor told me I had a dark spot on my lung, that we should do some tests to check it out. That was in April. I thought right away, fuck, it is cancer. But I ignored him. Kept right on smoking. I'm thinking, people with cancer live a long time—five, six, ten years. No big deal—have to die sometime anyway. Didn't worry about it, not realizing how quick it can be and what you have to go through. I thought, you get the cancer, take pills and that, and then you just die. But it don't work that way. That year went so awful fast. At that time I didn't care. But as it got closer, god damn, you know you wanna live.

Three months ago about, the jig was up. Found out I had the cancer. Wasn't surprised 'cause I was spitting up blood, coughing like a sonofabitch, no energy. Wanda and the guys at work were worried, really worried. They knew something was wrong. Knew this wasn't "Goodman," 'cause I was always on the go. It got to where I was having a hard time breathing, so Donnie took me to the doctor. Bang, bang, right off to the hospital. Drained my lungs—I think they got a quart, maybe two quarts of fluid.

Tell you what. The doc tells me now, you'd better do this, I'm gonna do it. I nearly died a couple of times the past six weeks. That night after you left, shortly after, I done a flip. My eyes came out and everything. Wanda thought I had died. Doctor said it was a stroke.

I stopped eating and everything. I remember Wanda coming in, saying: "If you don't eat, you are going to die." She made it very god damn plain. She wasn't pulling any punches. I did start eating and my strength kept coming back. That is why I got home last week, got out of that god damn place [the hospital].

Looking back, I did give up. Why, I don't know. Knowing me—what I am like, that is hard for me to believe. I hope I'm not that much of a pussy, to give up that way. Holy fuck that isn't Goodman. I've stared death in the face many times. I hope I didn't get that fucking weak that I gave up that easy.

I was ready to go. I had made my peace. My will and the shop stuff were taken care of. So much goes to my daughter, so much goes to my grandchildren. So much to Wanda and to Donnie to keep the shop going. Benny will get the shop but if he gives it up, then it goes to Donnie and Wanda.

Telephone Rings, Sam Answers a Call from His Former Wife

That was Connie. She has been coming to visit me. Is very religious. Wants her minister to come pray with me. She's a good woman, a good mother. We always stayed in touch. Met her way back in American City, not too long after I got out of the penitentiary for the burglary and then the escape. She worked at a restaurant, a waitress. We was going out—bang, bang. Says she is pregnant, we should get married. Had a little girl, Amy. We only lasted a couple of years together but I was never there anyway. Came and left as I pleased. Actually, that is the only time I was married. The divorce was never finalized until a few years ago.

I really should pray 'cause that is the only answer there is. It is over unless there is some miracle. Maybe there is something to this. One night, everybody left. I can't go to sleep. I'm laying there, my fucking shoulder is hurting like you wouldn't believe. I'm in pain like you wouldn't fucking believe. I prayed. Lord, please help me. Blah, blah, blah. It was like a big fucking black cloud came over me. Boy it scared me. It fucking scared me. This is after I done that flip. What the fuck is going on now?

I start getting better after that. Started eating. Now, is there something to prayer or not? Was that an omen from up there? I cannot tell you what to make of it. It is a hairy subject, very hairy. Is there a god? I don't want to take any chances. Don't want to knock the praying but I don't want to make a mockery out of it.

Wanda is the best woman I've met in my life. Has stuck with me the most. But I don't think I've found that woman yet who meant a lot to me. I've walked out on Wanda a number of times. Dumb stuff. I do not want somebody on my case, telling me what to do. Don't preach. 'Cause all you are doing is blowing wind up your ass. 'Cause I'm gonna do what I wanna do anyway. Only blowing wind out of your ass. Grab my little suitcase, stay at the shop or stay at a motel. Then she'd write a letter. I should come back. "Just come back, everything would be all right." I guess I don't like to be hassled. She would worry about me getting jammed up. That is my problem.

I do think I have a way with women. Of their wanting to come by my shop and rap with me. Not to get in their pants now. Well, sometimes that, too. But because I rap with them, puff them up, make them feel important, that I'm really interested in them. Agree that their husband or boyfriend is a real asshole, doesn't appreciate what he has.

As honest as Wanda is, it's funny how we could stay hooked up this long. Listen to this. Just before I went into the hospital, we're leaving the restaurant and Wanda finds a twenty dollar bill on the floor by the cash register. She picks it up and gives it to the lady behind the cash register, "Here, you musta dropped this." Holy fuck, I could've rung her neck. But that is the way she is.

Was married to a cop. Real asshole. Would spend his pay check chasing other women and running with other cops after work. Wanda told me one time, "Sam, you might have done time for breaking the law but my husband was a helluva lot worse." The way she told it, if the police recovered stolen property, he would help himself. Or, if they found dope money, help themselves. Still, she had to work like a dog to pay the bills in the house. Compared to him, I am a fucking angel. I always got a kick out of that.

I really am not close to Wanda. I don't confide. Not at all. For one, she would not hesitate to tell. She is very honest. I am very careful about that. She would lie a little bit, maybe. But only a little.

Same with Benny who is a partner in some ways.[1] It is my shop but we have a fifty-fifty split on the upholstery and furniture business he brings in. The antiques and my own upholstery business are mine. I watch him. Would not confide in him. Don't get me wrong. I like Benny. He's a helluva nice guy. But he's a shyster. Can't let him think he can get over on you. Then you're in trouble. I would never give him an edge, that feeling. I jump on him right away. I will hammer him but always give him an out. I do that with anyone. Never hammer someone too hard—if tear them down, then build them back up. That is part of understanding people. At the shop, if there's a problem. I would take the person aside, away from others so he's not seen being hammered. Say, "Look, motherfucker. Get your shit together. You're good help. Like to keep you. Don't want to jump on you. But get your shit together."

Had to do that to Donnie a number of times. Has been my main help in the shop for several years now. My foreman, really. He used to be more cocky. Now puts his head down like a little poodle 'cause he knows I'm right and want him to do it right.

My brother stopped by yesterday. Is doing okay but drinking again. Had an ass operation, hemorrhoids. Quit for a while. Tells me, "I have to quit." See his ass was burning, on fire all the time. Even a beer would set off the sparks. Now they're cut out, he can drink again.

We have become buddies, you might say, the past ten or fifteen years. He was a big help when I got out of prison this last time. Gave me a job, a paper job, at his auto shop. So I could satisfy the parole people. All the time I'm out hustling to get my shop going again. I'm giving him money to pay me is what it amounted to, to keep the parole people happy.

I have never been really close to anyone. Especially to a woman. Closest I ever came to anyone was you. As far as revealing anything, even Jesse—all the burglaries we done, what we've been through together—I would confide in only so much. If you asked I told you. Didn't try to rattle your cage. Wanted you to see for yourself, that seeing is better than just hearing about it.

An Undisclosed Murder

I don't know if I should tell you this. 'Cause I have never told anybody. Never, never. Not even Jesse. Never mentioned this to anybody. I had to put a motherfucker to sleep. I did it because I had to. I would've ended up with a lotta time otherwise. I put him to sleep. It was in American City.

Came up twice in my mind since I've been sick. I don't even want to bring it up now, 'cause I don't want to remember it. Afraid I will say something in my sleep or if I'm delirious. All these years I have buried it, has only been a few times it has popped into my mind. Always afraid it might come out. Not that it was painful or that I felt bad about it. But somebody hearing it, then asking: "Hey, you were talking the other night about putting someone away."

I had to snuff him out. Guy I knew from jail. Wanted me to wait in the car while he robbed a bookmaker. Bookie was making the rounds, picking up his money. I should wait in the car on the next street. But the bookie didn't go along with it as planned. Carried a gun and fired shots at this guy when he was running back to where I was parked. Got him in the neck and leg. Bleeding bad, very bad. I was over a barrel. I don't really want to say more 'cause it will just refresh my mind, make me more likely to repeat it when I shouldn't.

Steffensmeier Brought Up the Matter the Following Morning and Sam Elaborates

I did it with my hands. Choked him. Dumped his body in a quarry that had filled with water. Tied rocks, weighted him down. The car I burnt.

They never found him. Five, six years ago, I heard they drained the quarry. I wondered if they had found the body, the bones. But never heard anything.

Wasn't really a decision on my part. Knew what I had to do. He was hurt bad. Needed to go to the hospital, get sewed up. But then questions would be asked. It would come out what happened and I'm back doing time. The other thing was, the bookie was connected, tied up [with the local mafia]. So I'd be on their bad side too.

I don't feel bad about it. Not good either. Know what I mean? Snuffing somebody out like that is accepted. Not by the cops and the ordinary joe blow. But among thieves and them, yes. You have to do what you have to do. I wish there had been another way. There was no hesitation on my part. I knew what had to be done. I snuffed him out with hands. Gag, gaaggh. It was over for him.

Remember when you came to the penitentiary to interview me? You had seen my file and thought I would be a good mark [subject]. At first I was leery and not sure I wanted to be bothered. You asked me about women doing crimes. But mostly we talked about antiques and how easy it is to fool people about them. You pushed a little but I shied away from talking about the burglary and the fencing. The hour flew by. Told you if you wanted to come back, I would try to help you. Then you started coming on a regular basis. I looked forward to that. I remember that like it was yesterday.

Looking back, whew, so damn much has happened. I pulled a lotta rank shit in my life, lotta rank shit. But helped a whole lotta people, too. If somebody needed something, came into my shop, I more or less gave it away. Was very fair that way.

The deathbed interviews were in many ways a shared reminiscence for Sam and Steffensmeier. Knowing that Sam's life was very soon to end, the interviews were also Steffensmeier's last chance to both gain more insights into Sam and the world of theft and illegal enterprise he witnessed, as well as a chance for Steffensmeier to reach some closure for what by now had become a lengthy friendship. Material from these deathbed interviews are interspersed throughout the book, but are the primary source for this chapter and Chapter 20.

What Lies Ahead

Chapter 3 provides an overview and discussion of the major theoretical ideas animating this book. This chapter articulates and synthesizes a number of themes that run through the succeeding chapters. In particular, our theoretical framing of the book focuses on themes and issues that we think have too frequently been neglected in criminological and social science writings on crime.

After our theoretical discussion, we then presents Sam's narratives about his upbringing and early criminal career, along with the apex of his burglary and fencing activities and his conviction and imprisonment for dealing in stolen goods. Each of Sam's narratives is accompanied by a conceptual commentary. Important conceptual themes in Part II of the book include the notion of criminal capital, the importance of networks for successful criminal enterprise, and commitment to crime, desistance from crime, and "moonlighting" at crime. Part III of the book then follows the same commentary/narrative format in addressing the social organization and stratification of the underworld and organized crime, and pathways into and out of crime. Part IV presents the final narrative and commentary, in which we, and Sam, take stock of his rewards and regrets, his life and ledger. A key theme of Part IV is questioning popular and common academic imagery of crime and criminals.

Note

1. Telephone rings. Benny is on the phone: "I got the professor here. He's babysitting me. Call back later. Hey, Donnie told me about Steve got the check from you and you told him to wait until Monday to cash it. I would straighten that out Benny. It isn't good that Steve tells Donnie about this. You should go over, be nice, talk to Steve. Tell him that this is between you and him, not to run to Donnie. You know what I mean. I don't want my employees knowing this. It is bad business to have that. Do you agree with me. Good. Take care of that. I'll be seeing you." We footnote Sam and Benny's telephone conversation to illustrate the sort of call from colleagues and friends that punctuated the weekend interview with Sam. The interviewing was also punctuated by several drop-in visitors.

PART II

Sam's Life Unfolds:
Chronology and Turning Points

3

Conceptual Themes and Tools

We sketch in this chapter the conceptual framework that we use to analyze and interpret Sam's life history narrative and his account of the theft underworld and illegal enterprise. That framework relies heavily on differential association and social learning theory, opportunity theory, and labeling theory (although elements of anomie–relative deprivation and social bonds theories are also applied, along with ideas from rational choice and social exchange perspectives). We also apply life course and criminal career perspectives, which have a long history in crime and deviance writings in sociology and that today are receiving enhanced attention in popular and social science writings on crime. In addition, we develop a theoretical perspective on the nature of criminal enterprise, which we subsequently elaborate in later chapters.

The theoretical perspective we present rests very broadly on the intuitive yet robust hypothesis that criminal behavior depends on the coincidence of being both willing and able (having both the skills and the actual opportunity), on the coincidence of appropriate motivation and realistic opportunity, or, as Steffensmeier described in *The Fence,* on whether crime is subjectively acceptable and objectively possible. While our analysis addresses the matter of motivation in some detail, we especially focus on the notion of opportunity since its treatment in the criminological literature is sketchy and undeveloped.

The concept of *criminal opportunity* is a central element of our theoretical framework. Strongly implicit in the writings of Edwin Sutherland and subsequently rendered explicit by Richard Cloward, the concept remains *largely silent* in many contemporary treatments of crime. This silence is strongly at odds with how social scientists approach legitimate pathways and legitimate work careers, where the role of opportunity (e.g., job skills and openings, educational level, contact networks, gender, race, or ethnic segregation, social capital) is so central to the analysis. As with the legitimate world, we emphasize the notion that key forms of social capital increase success in the criminal world. These forms of criminal social capital include competence and collaborative relationships, criminal resourcefulness, and embeddedness in criminal arenas and networks and the scope of opportunities they bring. The extent of one's criminal social capital (or lack thereof) is a key element leading toward or away from *commitment* to sustained criminal involvement or lifestyle. One major goal of *Confessions* is to develop the notion of criminal opportunity and expand its application to an understanding of criminal careers and criminal enterprise. We posit the importance of variable access to messages and opportunities as key for understanding pathways into (or out of) crime.

Furthermore, the notion of commitment is a key organizing concept for our understanding of persistence or desistance in crime. Relatedly, concepts from the labeling theory and symbolic interactionist literature such as agency, interpretation and reflexivity, drift, interaction process, pathways, and turning points are explicitly or implicitly central to our entire conceptualization of Sam's criminal career and criminal enterprise.

Differential Association/Social Learning Theory

As we see it, the key elements of differential association/social learning theory are (1) that people commit crime when crime is, or they are able to make it, subjectively acceptable morally, cognitively, or emotionally; (2) that prior behavior and experiences in which people are rewarded for criminal involvement positively reinforces criminal behavior; and (3) that having or acquiring access to criminal opportunities and networks and having the criminal resourcefulness to take advantage of them foster criminal involvement. While this latter theme of opportunity may be implicit in Sutherland's differential association theory, it is explicit in Akers's social learning theory.

That delinquent/criminal behavior, like most social behavior, is learned in the process of social interaction is at the core of differential association and social learning theory. In Sutherland's (1947) classic statement, criminal or delinquent behavior involves the learning of (a) techniques of committing crimes and (b) orientations (motives, drives, rationalizations) and attitudes favorable to violation of law. Differential association refers to *differences in association with messages (orientations, attitudes, skills, knowledge) favorable or unfavorable to law violation.*

Akers (Akers et al. 1979; Akers 1998) combines Sutherland's ideas with Sykes and Matza's (1957) theory of vocabularies of motive and crime and with developments in social psychology that postdated Sutherland to articulate a social learning theory of crime that specifies the process of differential association in more detail and specificity. According to Akers, crime is learned through three conceptually distinct—but potentially interrelated—social processes: differential association, differential reinforcement, and imitation. Akers's key addition to this perspective is the notion that differential association includes *differential reinforcement relative to learned or anticipated rewards and punishments (e.g., in pursuing criminal as compared to conventional activities or roles).* In sum, socialization favorable to crime involves learning definitions, attitudes, behaviors, skills, assessments of rewards versus risks, and vocabularies of motive favorable to given forms of deviance, as well as forming relationships with deviant others and self-definitions in terms of deviant identities.

For both Sutherland and Akers, the key principle is that criminality and especially *systematic* or repetitive criminality is learned: "It is learned in direct or indirect association with those who already practice criminal behavior; and that those who learn this criminal behavior are segregated from frequent and intimate contacts with law-abiding behavior" (Sutherland 1940:10–11). Unfortunately, both the specific content of what is learned and the process by which it is learned has not received enough attention in either theory or research. Some prominent treatments of differential association actually hamper its application through incomplete, even inaccurate, accounts of the theory. Such treatments of differential association and social learning theory often see it only as a *subcultural theory* or as a theory of *peer influence.* In addressing these shortcomings, we consider the following as key, often neglected elements of differential association.

The concept of normative or message conflict frames the theory. Normative conflict is simply the notion that various groups and subgroups in society differ in terms of "codes of conduct" or moral systems including their *definitions* of right and wrong, and in their definitions of whether and to what extent individuals are obligated to follow laws (either particular ones or laws in general). These groups can include subcultures, professions and occupational groups, ethnic groups, voluntary associations, religious groups, neighborhoods, and other collectivities. This normative conflict, in turn, is played out at both the individual and group levels.

The structural, group-level manifestation of normative conflict is *differential social organization.* Differential social organization refers to differences between individuals in social or cultural groups, collectivities, or community settings within which they are located or with which they identify. The norms, values, meanings, skills, and definitions found within these groups can be favorable to particular kinds of crime, or to crime in general. In addition, cultural, subcultural, or group messages or definitions can be *supportive, neutral, hostile,* or *mixed* toward crime. Furthermore, many groups draw a thin line between legitimate and illegitimate activities. The thinner this line, the more the potential for criminality, and the line is thinner in some groups or settings than in others.

Groups are organized differently (e.g., in terms of skills, status orders, philosophies of life, vocabularies of motives or neutralizations, and network relationships), so that some are more organized for crime or exposed to crime-favorable messages than are others. The social and cultural organization of various groups or settings can potentially be favorable for crime in general, for specific kinds of crimes, or for specific kinds of crimes in specific circumstances. Therefore, differential association/social learning theory is both a theory of general criminal behavior and offense-specific behavior; of both generalized criminal propensity or *versatility and specialization* in crime. In sum, Sutherland describes the effect of differential social organization this way: "The law is pressing in one direction, and other forces are pressing in the opposite direction" (1940:12).

As we learn from *Confessions,* Sam's career is an illustration of how biography is embedded within differential social organization and association. The nearby gas station hangout, the penitentiary setting, the theft subculture, the local quasi-legitimate business community, and local organized crime networks all provided him with abundant messages and opportunities for criminal enterprise.

It is important to note that differential social organization need not entail or imply *oppositional culture,* as some caricatures of differential association theory argue (Kornhauser 1978; Hirschi 1996). First, differential association theory does not assume an overarching dominant culture characterized by consensus, but instead treats as variable the existence of dominant cultural norms and the degree of consensus around them. Second, while oppositional cultures are possible, they are but one potential manifestation of differential social organization. More accurately, subcultures and their messages vary in the degree to which they contradict legal norms, and how overtly or subtly they may contradict them. Sometimes subcultural messages can be largely congruent with dominant culture, but can contain themes or subthemes that subtly encourage lawbreaking. Furthermore, dominant cultures often contain contradictory messages, as Merton (1938) noted long ago. For example, American culture values honesty and trust, but also values shrewdness and what Charles Dickens called "the love of smart dealing."

Opportunity

Although Sutherland did not spell it out, the notion of *opportunity* is part and parcel of the concept of differential social organization, and is central to his conceptualization of criminal careers (see especially *The Professional Thief,* 1937). In fact, Sutherland admitted later in his life that opportunity was a key missing ingredient in his original formulation (Merton 1997). He was gratified to see that Cloward and Ohlin (1960) produced a theory of criminal opportunity to complement differential association.

In our view, the concept of *criminal opportunity* in criminology is underdeveloped. In *Confessions,* we seek to help build and better understand this important but neglected concept.[1] Many treatments of criminal opportunity, we believe, suffer from several limitations. First, despite Cloward and Ohlin's emphasis that criminal opportunity structures vary widely, it is common in criminology to see criminal opportunity treated as a given, or something ubiquitous that would-be offenders simply stumble across in the course of their routine activities. But this ignores the practical reality that an offender's scope of opportunities is not static but is rather an ongoing process in which s/he (or the group) continuously constructs his or her habits, know-how, and circle of contacts in striving for some immediate goal or extended venture. To recognize this latter reality is also to emphasize the role of human agency in the opportunity—crime relationship. Second, opportunity is often treated as something separate from motivation. Third, criminal opportunity is usually treated as a unitary concept, but in fact there are different types of criminal opportunity, and the distribution of these types has a great deal to do with the stratification of the underworld. Fourth, criminal opportunities are seldom viewed in relation to larger social changes. That is, as society changes, the nature and distribution of criminal opportunities also change. Fifth, the extent to which many people live a life of virtue because they lack the good opportunity to do otherwise is, we believe, a key missing ingredient in theoretical discussions of crime today.

Of these limitations, perhaps the most important is the need to better conceptualize the role of criminal opportunity in shaping or restricting pathways into virtue or vice because of varying access to know-how and social contacts for *achievement in crime* (e.g., pursuing money-oriented crimes more safely and profitably). Depending on one's biography and embeddedness in diverse groups and settings, people differ in their prospects for selection and recruitment (and for being able to recruit other co-offenders), in the range of career paths and access to them (opened by way of participation in these groups), and in opportunities for tutelage, increased skills, and rewards. For example, not only does embeddedness in different kinds of groups, neighborhoods, and communities influence who has more or less criminal opportunities in the first place (differential social organization), but broader societal sentiments such as racism and sexism also profoundly shape both the extent and especially the *types* of criminal opportunities available. In particular, racism and sexism shape criminal opportunity in at least two ways: (1) in blacks and women being excluded from certain crime groups and networks; and (2) in blacks and women being relegated to less-valued or less rewarding roles within crime partnerships, groups, or networks.

Building on Steffensmeier's (1983) extension of illegitimate opportunity, access to crime opportunities entails differences across individuals and groups in access to *civil, preparatory, or technical knowledge useful for committing crime as well as access to (a) places, victims, and suitable targets, (b) tools and hardware, and (c) contacts or networks facilitative for actual crime commission.*[2]

Civil knowledge refers to knowledge that most people in some ways have, to conventional kinds of knowledge that can easily be transferred or "sharpened" for criminal ends. Examples of this kind of civil knowledge are found in Sam's later discussion of his foray into passing checks while a prison escapee and his explanation of the role of the "drop-off" driver for a burglary crew. *Preparatory knowledge* refers to familiarity with orientations and techniques of theft and hustling that is acquired by "hanging around" or being embedded in groups or settings where general or specific forms of crime and vice routinely or periodically take place. For example, a young person simply hanging out at Casey's Pub or at Sam's secondhand store, where "it's only natural you would pick up things," would gain such preparatory knowledge "by osmosis" for varied theft or hustling endeavors. This know-how also would foster their recruitment into theft by its practitioners if they are seeking co-offenders. *Technical knowledge* is knowledge that is mainly or only acquired by way of access to people in specialized locations. As described in Sam's narrative, for example, one learns the ropes of safecracking by tutelage from other safecrackers.

These types of crime know-how can easily shade one into the other, and this is particularly the case with technical as compared to preparatory knowledge. One can hardly pursue criminal opportunities where the accepted skills, styles, and informal know-how are unfamiliar. One does better to look for a line of action for which one has the cultural equipment. Preparatory knowledge is that which comes from familiarity with hustling or theft because of "hanging around," or being around practitioners of crime and vice, or being in settings where such activities occur, or perhaps from being in occupations like policing that provide the learning for general or crime-specific skills. In other words, people gain preparatory knowledge by simply being exposed to the *umwelt* (or "surrounding world") of a criminal lifestyle and its social world (see Adler and Adler).[3]

For example, individuals involved in recreational drug use or the "party scene" may observe drug transactions or come into contact with suppliers from which they acquire some *knowledge preparedness* for drug dealing (that is, they learn about drug paraphernalia, specific skills like "cutting" or "weighting," how to get along with fellow drug hustlers, how to avoid being exploited by customers, etc.). In this way, the learning of attitudes conducive to general or specific forms of theft and hustling may begin long before one actually becomes involved in them.

In turn, crime opportunities can be distinguished relative to whether they encompass (1) underworld versus upperworld forms of criminality, (2) solo, partnership, or more organized forms of criminality, (3) unskilled, moderately skilled, or highly skilled criminal activities, (4) short-term and situational versus long-term, sustained, and self-generating forms and (5) minor, less serious versus lucrative, more serious forms.[4]

In effect, individuals and groups vary in *criminal social capital,* which is the information, skills, habits, role models, social networks, and resources necessary for success in criminal endeavors—in particular, to pursue crime regularly, safely, and profitably. The narratives and commentaries to follow, particularly on the types of thieves and types of fences, the importance of networks and criminal capital in fencing, and the social organization and "pecking order" of the underworld all key off these distinctions in terms of criminal capital and opportunity.

A person's life choices are structured insofar as both legitimate and criminal skills are concerned. In many cases, the range of criminal roles a prospective offender can satisfactorily fill may be small and, for the most part, he or she may not be able to graduate from marginal or petty offender status to a more lucrative, higher ranking criminal occupation. But when one has acquired more profitable criminal skills, acumen, and contacts, a different trajectory is available. Furthermore, the opportunity to acquire criminal skills also may change over the life course. As will be seen later, the nature of skills for theft or criminal enterprise, the great variability in individuals' possession of them, how people acquire them, and how skills and opportunity mutually influence each other over the life course are major conceptual themes illustrated by Sam Goodman's narratives throughout the book.

The availability of criminal opportunities also has a *motivational* side. While analytically distinct, opportunity and motivation intertwine in reality in ways that render them not easily distinguished. Being able to do something often makes one more willing to do it, just as being willing often makes one pursue the ability to do something. As Steffensmeier notes: "The availability of concrete opportunities helps explain why offenders gravitate to those activities which are easily available, are within their skills, provide a satisfactory return, and carry the fewest risks" (1983:1025).

Differential Association

The individual-level manifestation of normative conflict is the *process of differential association.* Criminal behavior becomes more likely to the extent that individuals learn and internalize procriminal norms, values, meanings, skills, and definitions through socialization and social learning processes within the kinds of procriminal group contexts described above. "Whether a person becomes a criminal or not is determined largely by the comparative frequency and intimacy of his contacts with the two types of behavior" (i.e., "criminal or law-abiding") (Sutherland 1940:11).

Procriminal messages will have varying degrees of influence on individuals, depending on the source, emotional intensity, frequency, and duration of the individual's contact with the messages. Associations that occur earlier in one's life (*priority*), occur more often (*frequency*), last longer and occupy more time (*duration*), and involve others with whom one has the more important relationships (*intensity or source*) will have the greater effect or criminal or law-abiding behavior.

Recent discussions of differential association/social learning theory (both favorable and critical) have tended to treat differential association as synonymous with peer influence (see especially Warr's [2002] review of this issue). Literally dozens of articles exist that operationalize differential association theory with some measure or another of peer influence, and treat interaction with deviant peers as the only association of import for transmitting criminal messages, and family, teachers, or employers as the only associations important for transmitting anticriminal messages. We are uncertain how and why differential association/social learning theory came to be identified solely with peer influence.

However, one crucial point that has gotten lost in these treatments is *that procriminal messages need not come from interaction with peers.* Differential association is a theory of *differences in association with criminal messages,* not any particular kind of associate or person (e.g., peers). Thus, association with criminal messages (or anticriminal messages) can come through association and learning at the hands of parents, siblings, or other family members as well as peers; and the association and learning can occur by way of general culture, the media, one's occupational group, or a diversity of other groups or settings. As will be seen later, this point is especially illustrated by Sam Goodman's early criminal career and the messages he learned from some members of his family.

Differential association is also a theory of both criminal *versatility and specialization.* That is, one may be exposed to and learn messages and skills favorable for crime in general or for varied kinds of crime. For example, one may learn to "make a buck" from widely varying criminal activities whenever various opportunities present themselves (as members and associates of La Cosa Nostra apparently do, according to Sam's later narrative on organized crime). Or, one might learn messages favorable to using violence to get what one wants, whether it be settling disputes, emotional satisfaction, or money. Alternatively, one can be exposed to and learn messages and skills favorable to one kind of crime but not others. For example, one may learn messages and skills favorable to embezzlement, taking bribes, or burglary that do not translate into a willingness or ability to deal drugs or pimp.

We make two final points about differential association/social learning theory and its relationship to other popular theoretical ideas in criminology.

Rational choice and social exchange theories that are so popular today see criminal behavior as a decision-making process involving an assessment of costs and risks as well as rewards or profits. The rewards or reasons for committing crime in rational choice models are largely material, i.e., the score, the catch, or payment; whereas social exchange models stress not only material but also immaterial profits or rewards, like social approval, self-satisfaction, and excitement. The key ideas of both rational choice and social exchange perspectives are consistent with and easily incorporated into differential association/social learning as a more general theory of crime and deviance (see Steffensmeier and Ulmer 2003). Contagion models of crime are based on the premise that the deviant behavior (e.g., violence, drug use) of neighbors and peers strongly influences or spreads to the behavior of others (Jones and Jones 2000). Actually, this notion of contagion is simply one element of differential association theory.

As we see it, a key concept of social control, or social bonding theory, *attachments,* is also a key element of differential association and social learning theories. Interpersonal attachments of all kinds—not just peers—are certainly a potential influence on the exposure, intensity, duration, primacy, and adoption of messages favorable *and* unfavorable to crime.

Commitment

Central to several major theories of crime is the task of explaining continuity (and by implication change) in criminal activity and careers. Sociologists have long relied on the concept of commitment for explaining such continuity (see reviews by Becker 1960; Ulmer 2000). In fact, commitment is a term widely used in criminological theorizing (Bernard 1987). It is most visibly central to social control theory, where commitment is seen as a key "stake in conformity." The concept of commitment is also often used in labeling theory, where it is seen as an "investment" that sustains criminal involvement. Furthermore, similar or closely related concepts such as attachment, allegiances, or side bets are often used in criminology as explanations for continuity in crime or conformity.

Despite Howard Becker's (1960) call for more systematic and differentiated conceptualizations of commitment, most criminologists still use the term in a simplistic, undifferentiated manner (see reviews by Johnson 1991; Ulmer 1994). However, different types of commitment can easily be recognized, and different kinds of causes and experiences produce them. It is therefore important to use a differentiated, specified conceptual framework for thinking about commitment rather than a simplistic and unitary one that confounds different kinds of commitment experiences and causes. In our later commentaries, we use a threefold typology of commitment as an organizing framework to explain continuity in Sam's criminal career.

Our use of this threefold organizing framework of commitment combines two traditions in criminology in the usage of commitment. The first is the well-known prominence of commitment as a stake in *conformity* in social control theories (see Bernard 1987), such as in the work or Jackson Toby, Travis Hirschi, and Robert Sampson and John Laub. The second tradition comes from the symbolic interactionist and labeling tradition's longstanding attention to the study of deviance, where commitment is viewed as stakes or investments in *deviant* pursuits, as in the work of Edwin Lemert, Howard Becker, Erving Goffman, Robert Stebbins, Daniel Glaser, and others.

Thus, commitment is a generic concept that applies to both crime and conventional activity. For example, if someone has a reputation and a satisfying self-concept as a "religious person" or a "respectable businessperson," that person knows that he or she places these in jeopardy by engaging in crime. Likewise, if someone has a reputation as a "decent thief" or "tough guy," he jeopardizes these should he abandon theft or toughness. Both a criminal and a conforming life generate potential losses if they are abandonded.

This threefold typology specifies structural, personal, and moral types of commitment, and combines both "objective" or external factors and "subjective" or internal factors that produce continuity in behavior over time. We use this framework as a conceptual tool for grappling with issues of persistence, desistance, or partial desistance in crime across the life course. Our use of this commitment framework aims to explain pathways out of or *not* out of crime, or perhaps pathways into lesser criminal roles (as a example of the kind of pathways between criminal roles we are talking about, see Lemert 1951:336–37). Structural, personal, and moral commitments are also key for understanding *turning points* in the life course.

Differential Association/Social Learning as a Life Course Perspective

Life course perspectives, which have become very popular today, involve the idea of *pathways into and out of crime,* emphasizing biographical elements, life course trajectories, turning points, and developmental sequences (e.g., Sampson and Laub 1993; Benson 2002). The perspectives may draw on the notion of "career" to chart the onset (e.g., early- versus late-starters) and persistence (e.g., deepening commitments to deviant identities and activities), as well as pathways to desistance. Proponents claim that the life course perspective departs from earlier criminology in (1) focusing on the relationship between age and crime; (2) focusing on the relationship between prior and future criminal activity; and (3) adopting a *process* versus static orientation in focusing on the dynamics of offending over age. However, these concerns were also central to the work of more traditional scholars in criminology and sociology, such as Edwin Lemert (1951, 1967), Howard Becker (1963), Donald

Cressey (1953), James Inciardi (1975), John Lofland (1969), Daniel Glaser (1972), Robert Prus (Prus and Sharper 1977), and Patti and Peter Adler (1983).

Furthermore, differential association/social learning theory is very much a processual, life-course-oriented perspective, although Sutherland did not systematize that perspective in the way that life course theorists do today. Matsueda and Heimer (1997), for example, describe how key emphases of differential association/social learning, such as self concepts and attitudes are dynamic across the life course. That is, the perspective is clearly compatible with the notion that criminal propensity changes—sometimes dramatically—over the life course. On the other hand, the kind of differential association/social learning perspective we describe here is also consistent with the possibility of stable or enduring criminal propensity. Ulmer and Spencer (1999) point out how key themes of differential association/social learning theory, such as definitions, skills, self-concepts, commitments, and rewards can produce both change and stability in criminal propensity over the life course.

However, *Confessions* also illustrates some important limitations to life course concepts as they are usually used in the criminology literature. First, they tend to imply much more precision and orderliness in criminal careers than is empirically recognizable. Second, they tend to assume greater differences between offenders and nonoffenders, between persistent and intermittent or occasional offenders, and between early starters and late starters than is plausible. Both of these features of how life course concepts are often used may lock us into conceptual boxes that may mask the variability and complexity of criminal offending and careers. In particular, *Confessions* problematizes concepts like "life-course-persistent offender" and what characteristics they are supposed to have.

Personality, Self, and Stable Criminal Propensity

We also recognize that people may develop relatively stable personality characteristics that emerge by way of dispositions and childhood experiences (priority). This can clearly be seen in the life of Sam Goodman, who exhibits some very stable personality features. For example, Sam was always striving and hard-working, loved to make money for the sake of making money, "enjoyed pulling something," and was gregarious and socially perceptive. We would include such stable personality characteristics as a part of the "subjective acceptability" of crime. Lemert (1951:85–86) referred to the "internal structuring of personality" as an important aspect of the "internal limits" on deviant behavior. Lemert put it this way:

> At any given point in the personality development of an individual there is a definable set of alternative roles which are subjectively congenial to him. . . . This

subjectively delimited area of choice may lie within the range of the external limits or it may fall outside, and while the external limits may be comparable for different persons, the internal limits tend to be much more variable. *Aspirations to status and role arise within the scope of the internal limits; likewise, social pressures upon the individual to accept certain roles and status which fall beyond the internal limits will be resisted, circumvented, selected out, and rejected.* (ibid.:86, emphasis added)

Symbolic interactionism has long emphasized that one's social self is as stable as the relationships within which a person is embedded (see Strauss 1969). While people's self-concepts are certainly never static, they do often exhibit enough stability for scholars to posit the existence of a "core self" with persistent characteristics. Furthermore, dramatic self-change does occur, but it is relatively rare (Strauss 1969; Athens 1995). Stability of self-concept is therefore a key aspect of subjective acceptability of crime and internal limits, and a source of stable criminal propensity.

Labeling Theory

Differential association and labeling theory also have a symbiotic relationship with one another. One basic contention of labeling theory is that sanctions against crime or deviance can inadvertently contribute to continuity in deviant activity and careers. This occurs in that sanctions can potentially (1) restrict opportunities for conventional employment and relationships, (2) open up illegitimate opportunities and access to deviant networks or subcultures, (3) lead to the development of deviant identities and a sense of estrangement from conventional society (Lemert 1951; Lofland 1969; Braithwaite 1989; Ulmer 1994). In particular, Braithwaite has developed the notion of reintegrative shaming, and contrasted it with stigmatizing processes that exclude and alienate the deviant rather than reintegrate him or her. The other contention of labeling theory is an emphasis on *careers and process,* in particular the notion that the original causes of criminal behavior may not be the same as the eventual causes that reproduce or sustain criminal behavior or, as Becker (1963) says, the deviant behavior in time produces its own set of deviant motivations.

Situational Contingencies

We also recognize the value of labeling theory's and more generally symbolic interactionism's situational approaches to crime and deviance, and their emphasis on the interplay of *human agency* with internal and external constraints. The idea that people are endowed with choice and agency within attitudinal limits and external constraints has always been central to symbolic interactionism (Maines 2001). Furthermore, all human behavior takes place in situations of some kind. It is an interactionist truism that larger-scale contexts set the conditions for situations. Situations (and crucially, how they are defined) set conditions for action and interaction. In turn, people confront these situations and exercise agency within them, as they define those situations, make choices, and act (see Ulmer and Spencer 1999). The importance of agency, situational definitions, and emergent contingencies, as well as processes of "drift" into crime, can be seen throughout Sam Goodman's career.

Sutherland's earlier treatments of differential association have been criticized for ignoring the situational level of analysis, but it is not incompatible with labeling theory's more situational focus, and the situational level of analysis has also been incorporated into social learning theory by Akers. The long tradition of interactionist research on crime and deviance is based on the following assumptions (see Lemert 1951,1972; Becker 1963; Strauss 1993; Best and Luckenbill 1994):

1. Situational constraints and opportunities make different types of action more or less likely, and actors' biographies and prior repertoires of action affect the definitions of situations they construct. Situational and biographical constraints can influence people's definitions and actions both with and without their awareness of those constraints.
2. Situational contexts are set by, and actor's biographies are located within, larger arrangements of social structure and culture.

Lemert's cornerstone formulations of labeling theory emphasized situational contingencies, drift, and adjustment. For example:

Much human behavior is situationally oriented and geared to meeting the many and shifting claims which others make upon them. The loose structuring and swiftly changing facade and content of modern social situations frequently make it difficult to decide which means will ensure ends sought. *Often choice is a compromise between what is sought and what can be sought. . . . Each of such actions has its consequences and rationale and leaves a residual basis for possible future action depending on the problems solved or the new problems brought to life.* (1967: 51–52, emphasis added)

Criminal Enterprise

Another major theoretical issue that is central to our examination of Sam Goodman's career is the nature of *criminal enterprise*. By criminal enterprise, we mean "business" crimes pursued on a more or less sustained basis for money. Criminal enterprise refers mainly to that slice of crime and underworld that relies on "business practices," involves *ongoing* criminal ventures, and tends more toward *market* offenses involving consensual exchanges between providers, suppliers, sellers, and customers than toward predatory crimes, like ordinary forms of theft and hustling. Enterprise crime typically involves more supply-related offenses like fencing, bookmaking, loansharking, smuggling, drug dealing, and sex peddling. Obviously, more sustained and organized forms of burglary, auto theft, fraud, etc. (e.g., theft or fraud rings), can shade into the criminal enterprise and market categories.

We especially draw attention to the contours of criminal enterprise and the underworld as a "social world" or "field." *Confessions* depicts the underworld as what Anselm Strauss (1993) called a "social world" of interaction, communication, and (to some extent) shared meaning. In other words, we see the underworld as a "field" of mutually recognized goals and organized striving, to paraphrase Pierre Bourdieu (1977; see also Martin 2003). *Confessions* in many ways maps the field of the underworld of criminal enterprise as a social arena involving both a moral sphere and negotiable realm of opportunities and relations for economic or social achievement. In later chapters of this book, we elucidate the social organization both of burglary and of fencing stolen goods, the criminal social capital necessary for successful criminal enterprise, the importance of criminal networks, the stratification or "pecking order" of the underworld, and the nature of localized organized crime networks.

Sam's criminal activity illustrates the nature of serious crime as work and business, and the similarities and differences between conventional and criminal enterprise. We believe a major contribution of *Confessions* is that it provides a unique and rare glimpse into the social world of criminal enterprise, and enhances our understanding of this field and its ordering. In addition, the book illustrates how conventional and criminal worlds very often overlap both in their social organization and in their normative codes. By implication, Sam and perhaps all of us face *competing moral systems* because of the differing fields and social worlds we participate in.

As participants in this field, Sam Goodman and his associates are uniquely suited to inform us about their social world, giving us a glimpse into a lifestyle, philosophy, and pattern of living ordinarily obscured from our vision. His case study is a statement about one offender's long-standing involvement in crime as well as a narrative about a wide variety of criminal actors, small-timers as well as big-timers.

We believe our theoretical arguments about criminal social capital, criminal enterprise as a social world, and the social organization of that world make contributions to the criminology literature that are at least equal to our contributions to understanding criminal careers. Furthermore, the two themes are closely related. We elaborate these arguments about criminal enterprise in our commentaries in Chapters 5, 7 and 9 as well as in Chapters 13 and 15. Sam Goodman's life history reveals crime and criminal careers not so much as discrete events or series of events, but as a process that can be marked by amplification spirals, shifts, and waxing and waning commitments to crime and criminal others. In turn, all of his activities are contextualized by the field of criminal enterprise and by the interplay between criminal and conventional social worlds. It is to Sam's own narratives that we now turn.

Notes

1. That lack of more than "lip service" about the role of criminal opportunity in crime production is shown in the well-regarded text, *Theoretical Criminology* (Vold, Bernard, and Snipes 1998). The authors' list of characteristics or risk factors for crime as drawn from their review of criminology theory and research does *not* include criminal opportunity.
2. Steffensmeier's earlier treatments (1978; 1980; 1983, 1986) drew heavily on the works of Lemert (1951) and Lofland (1969) and, more recently, on the writings of Prus (Prus and Sharper 1977; Prus and Irini 1980), Cullen (1983), Hagan and McCarthy (1997), Naylor (2003), Hochstetler (2001) Ruggiero (2000), and Tremblay (1993). Some of the ideas delineated here are also compatible with *routine activities theory*. The latter focuses mainly on (a) availability and vulnerability of suitable targets for theft and hustling such as unguarded places and easy-prey victims and (b) how these targets vary across space and are subject to change in response to larger social and economic developments (Felson 1998). While beyond the scope of *Confessions,* we believe that ideas from routine activities theory could be used to help flesh out the criminal opportunity perspective we present here.
3. We thank Miles Harer for suggesting this point.
4. Some other distinctions of access to criminal opportunities also may be useful such as whether the modus operandi involves force, fraud, or both, or whether the victimization is consensual and involves relatively free exchanges between participants; and whether the opportunities center around the commission of *predatory* or *market* offenses (see Naylor 2003). Predatory offenses represent appropriative crimes that lack "fair market value" (ibid.:84) such as robbery, burglary, auto theft, passing bad checks, identity theft, defrauding the government, and a variety of other thefts and hustles. Market offenses involve consensual exchanges between customers, producers, sellers, and perhaps protectors. Besides fencing, market offenses include smuggling, illegal gambling, loansharking, drug dealing, gun dealing, prostitution, extortion, bribery, and other supply-related and "racketeering" offenses. Our notion of criminal enterprise (see below) mainly encompasses the types of crime that might fit into market category, while also including more long-term and businesslike involvements in theft and hustling.

4

Sam's Narrative

Onset of Sam's Criminal Career

How did it all start? It is hard to remember all the twists and turns.

Growing Up

My grandparents mostly raised me. Never did know my real dad 'cause my mom and him split when I was a baby. Moved in with my grandparents, and my mom worked. Then she remarried when I was about seven but mostly I am still with my grandparents 'cause we lived close by. Had a little farm on the edge of town. I always helped out when I was there. No such thing as a free ride. Were really tight with the money, like the old Germans were. Believed in hard work. They were good to me but as far as buying me bicycle and that, no way. I got mine hustling and trading. I'd save a little money, buy an old bike or car, fix it up, and trade for a better one. From little on I was doing that.

I did okay in school. Report card was always pretty good. Not at the top of my class, a little above the middle. I wasn't an angel but not a troublemaker either. If I had to stay after school, I had to answer to my grandpap. He had a willow stick. Not that he overdid it but you knew what was coming. Get the chores and my homework done, then I could go play. Or work on an old car or bicycle, then trade or sell it. Turn the money over.

Couple of my teachers thought I should go on to high school. But my grandparents didn't encourage it. I didn't give it much thought. Already had a job lined up, with a construction company where I'd been working during the summers. Was itching to be on my own. Same with most of my friends, didn't go to high school either. That's the way it was at that time. Except for those with money, the higher-ups, your ordinary joe blow finished eighth grade and then got himself a job. Turn over most of the money they made to their parents, which is what I done. To my mom, even though my grandparents were the main ones to raise me. Except if I worked extra hours, then pocket that. No need for her to know.

I got along with my brothers but they were younger and I'm mostly at my grandparents. Half-brothers, really. Ricky and Herb. See, my mom had two kids with my stepdad. Didn't hate my stepdad, but didn't love him either. Buy my brothers a BB gun, but not one for me. They're only like four, five years old. Really, too young to be having that. I'm twelve, thirteen—at an age where you remember that sort of thing. Know what I mean. Not a lot of contact. Never really kept in touch.

By the time I was fifteen I was running my own life. Am at my mom's or grandparents, just to hang my hat. I was always on the go. Working, trading cars, horsing around. Hustling pussy was the big thing in my life at that time. I'm working six days a week, long hours. After work, I would bum around, maybe go to the skating rink—which was known as a place to find a woman. Or I hanged around the gas station. Always be guys there, maybe some girls too. The gas station crowd was older. When I was sixteen, they were maybe eighteen, nineteen, twenty. Some of them like my Uncle Howie was a lot older. Lots of horsing around, pulling little shit and then ribbing each other about it. Al, the guy that ran the station, got a kick out of it, more or less egged us on.

Like we'd take candy corn or groceries from the town drunk, outta his car when he'd be drinking at one of the bars. We'd get a kick out of it when he'd stop by the gas station and complain to Al about somebody stealing his candy corn. He had a thing for candy corn. That he even hid it under the seat but somebody still swiped it. Never bothered to lock his car, so I'm thinking he just wanted to have something to complain about, someone to talk to. Just guys wanting to be part of something, to show off to each other, and wanting to get away with something.

Uncle Howie helped me learn the ropes you might say. My stepfather's brother. Was maybe fifteen years older than me. Nice-looking guy. Kind of a gambler, hustler type. Did time in the penitentiary for a hot car. He was a lot of fun. Was a "live and learn" thing for me.

Howie always out for chasing women, especially the younger ones. He took me to my first whorehouse, in Cloverdale. That was something. I still today have to laugh about that place. I'm barely fifteen years old. My first experience with a woman, first time I got pussy. Boy oh boy! That was a helluva experience.

Came about 'cause my uncle wanted me to fix him up with a neighbor girl that was really stacked. Big tits. Really stacked. So I got rapping with her and said my uncle wants to meet you. So, she went out with him. I says to him, "Did you score, get into her pants," and all that shit? He said, "Yeh, it was good, real good." I said, "Hey, what can you do for me?" He says, "I'll get you something better."

Took me to a whorehouse. Just a big room with maybe four or five beds in it, and had curtains in between. I got me a skinny one. Didn't even have take my pants off. Just pulled them down, screw and then you leave. Just a sheet in between the beds. I could hear my uncle on the other side. Crummy, goddam, it was crummy. You know how kids talk in school about sex and that shit. Try to figure out what's going on. It's a wonder I didn't get all kinds of diseases. I still today have to laugh about that place.

I think I was more advanced for my age than the girls were who were my age. I could get over on them. Get in their pants. I knew what was happening, especially from running around with Howie. I don't think I was a ladies man, no way. But I've had some helluva experiences with women. And see, I always had a car and that made it easier to pick them up.

I could meet people easy but in many ways I was a loner. I more wanted to go my own way. Looking back, I was mostly out to pick up a broad, get in her pants. That's about all I was. A lot of times I'd sleep in the car and go right to work.

I knew early that you have to look out for yourself. I had to go hustle for myself all the way. If I wanted a bike, I had to go get it. My attitude was I'll go do it myself. I could pull my own way, I really didn't need anybody.

I always had a little larceny in me. Looking for the buck. I don't know how to put this. I always thought I was sharper than the next guy as far as getting over. This goes back. Even in grade school I was in different deals. I would always come out ahead. Even with the guys at the gas station who were older. I just had a head for getting over.

I don't know if you'd call this crime or not, but devious anyway. You know how there are always some girls who will put out. Like at the skating rink, a couple of sisters were known as easy lays. The one, Loretta, had the rocks for me, maybe 'cause I had a car and in her eye that is a big thing. Couple of times I needed gas money, so I would line up Loretta with one of my buddies. This you know 'cause Al has blabbed to you, to rib me. Some of the girls that hung at the gas station would put out. A main one was Millie Street. How it got started I don't know but I got her to charge a dime or a quarter or a couple of candy bars—instead of doing it for nothing. We'd split it. Looking back, I feel a little shitty I done that, but at the time it was an extra nickel and some devilment too.

Drift into Burglary and First Trouble with "The Law"

My first real trouble with the law was clipping the gas station with Ronnie, Marge's cousin. Were my first *real* crimes you might say. Before then, I hadn't really done much. Just kid's stuff—hubcaps, apples from an orchard, knock over mailboxes.

Met Marge at the skating rink. She was a regular. Really stacked. In her eye I was her boyfriend. In my eye I was getting my rocks off. If the opportunity was there, I nutsed with other women. Ronnie and me got to horsing around 'cause he was at her place a lot and he was my age. I'm between sixteen and seventeen at the time. Putting in long hours working for this construction company, driving tractor trailer truck. After work, I'd bum around. Am staying at my mom's but many times I just slept in the car or at Marge's house. On the go all the time. I didn't need much sleep, never have.

One evening, Ronnie and me is driving around. In my 1939 Lafayette Plymouth convertible. Bought it right after I turned sixteen with money I had saved. Got my driver's license—boom, boom, bought this car. I kept it nice. Wish I had it today. Be worth one helluva lot of money now.

I pulls into this place for gas. Ronnie gets out, goes inside the place. Turns out he is looking over the place. We're taking off, he says: "Hey, this would be an easy place to break into, to rob." Words to that effect. "You and me can take this place. Be an easy dollar for both of us. All you have to do is watch and be ready to take off with the car." I remember asking, "Whatta you mean, whatta ya thinking?" He talked some more about how we'd do it and I went along with the idea.

That same night we hit the place, got twenty-five, maybe thirty bucks. It went smoothly. I dropped Ronnie off, waited in the car a half-block away where I could see the place. He comes out, hops in and we take off. The money we split down the middle.

I didn't have much of a reaction. Was a thrill, at getting away with something. On the order of stealing hubcaps, only a little bigger. Some extra spending money but sure as hell didn't get rich. Not that the money didn't come in handy 'cause I'm spending a lot of money—on Marge, the car, just bumming around. Ronnie presented the opportunity and I went along with it. In my eye the risk of getting caught was small. I had no qualms, put it that way. There was no fear on my part.

Next month or so, we hit a couple of more gas stations. Ronnie did the breaking in, I did the watching and driving. Just kick in the door or pry it open with a crowbar, screwdriver, whatever. Clean out the cash register, run back to where the car is parked, and take off. Half-assed jobs. I don't think we got more than twenty or thirty dollars a pop. Pretty pitiful, put it that way. Some little bullshit stuff before, but the burglaries I pulled with Ronnie were my first *real* crimes you might say.

The burglaries with Ronnie ended when me and Marge broke up. A month goes by, the cops show up where I'm working. Arrest me for eight, ten burglaries—the ones I did with Ronnie and half-dozen other burglaries that Ronnie had done on his own. Or maybe with somebody else, that I can't say. Somebody had spotted Ronnie's car, wrote down the license plate number. Ronnie's story was, I was with him on all the burglaries. Fingers me and then testifies in court that the burglaries were my idea, and that I was in the one in charge.

I pleaded not guilty, said I knew nothing about the burglaries. I got sent to a reformatory for juveniles. Ronnie got probation. I think the judge came down hard on me 'cause nobody from my family showed up for the court hearings. Didn't see nor hear a peep from any of them. The only ones to show up were Marge and a couple of guys I palled with. To my thinking the judge also saw me as a wiseass. I didn't show any emotion, put it that way. Looking back, that is one time I should have pled guilty. Say I was sorry, been more penitent. The judge wanted to hear that.

Doing time in the reformatory wasn't that bad. Lots of fights. I took up boxing. I was always pretty strong and with the boxing, I could handle myself pretty well. The "jailbirds," the ones who done time before, were the worst for the needling shit, see if they can get under your skin. They pretty quick left me alone. I wasn't one to pick fights, but I wouldn't back away neither. Sure, somebody can start something, but can they finish it? I never feared getting hurt, and they will take some good shots from me.

See, I wasn't jail-wise but I had already been in jail about two months before my juvenile hearing on account I couldn't make bail. Had to deal with older guys who'd jerk your chain or make cracks on you. Learned how to handle myself—yeah, you can get all you want, but you got to take what comes with it. That, and it don't take me long to make friends. Never did.

It was altogether different with my mom after I got out. Even more with my grandma and grandpap. I would stop by to see them. We would talk but there's no conversation. Words, but it was like we didn't have anything to say. I could see the hurt in their eyes.

I was eighteen when I got out of Morningdale. I'm back living at my mom's place, just to drop my hat. Paying her rent for a bedroom. Right away, I get my old job back—driving truck for this construction company. My life was working, horsing around, picking up broads. Your ordinary joe blow. See, I always worked. But partied a lot too, out for a good time.

Then I got on at the big paper mill in the area. Worked the evening shift 'cause it was better money. The burglary started a year or two later. A group of us—twelve, fourteen guys—would fuck around after work. Ride around, drink beer, up to no good really. It started little—driving across people's lawns, knocking down mailboxes, stealing hubcaps off cars, jack up a car and take off with the tires. Then, it was breaking into empty houses or grocery stores. It was mostly petty shit, more damage than anything.

But it was getting more serious, too. There was starting to be some money in it. Free set of tires, piece of furniture, or a radio. Some of the houses had cash or jewelry. The cash was extra spending money. Mostly, you'd blow it—on women or buy the guys drinks and food. What you stole was mostly used by yourself or spread around the group. But there was some peddling, too. One guy might sell jewelry or a set of tools to his buddy or a neighbor. We didn't know any fences, put it that way. It was more, "Who do you know that can use this stuff?"

Looking back, I was pretty half-assed but I was learning too. If we were going to hit a house or gas station, I was the main one who did the planning. So and so does this, so and so does that. Trial and error, guys talking things over, you know enough to have different assignments, not break into a place in broad daylight with the neighbors watching.

Doing it for fun, the devilment and to bullshit with your buddies about what you pulled, what you go away with. These were still the main reasons. But the easy dollar was pushing me too. The business side of crime was taking hold. Not for making a living at it but extra bucks for chasing women, being a big spender with your buddies, splashing up your car.

Don't get me wrong—I was still a greenie. Didn't know any "real" burglars—not guys who pulled big jobs or made a living at it. Didn't know any fences, didn't know people who gave tips, didn't know any corrupt cops. I sure as fuck didn't know how to open a safe. Really, even how to scout a job. I would just be blowing wind up my ass if I would tell otherwise. And I'm hanging with guys who are dumber than me.

This I can say, I really wasn't part of the criminal element. Didn't know shit about who the local criminals were. Not the penny-ante thief, not the regular thief, not the better thief or the higher-ups in crime for sure. Just blowing wind outta my ass, if I said otherwise. Now, just from bumming around—at the nightspots, the pool halls, the skating rink—it turns out there were guys I bumped into who were into burglary or were clipping in other ways and were pretty decent at it. Met a couple of them in the penitentiary later on. But it didn't register, know what I mean.

This, too, I can say: I didn't think of myself as a burglar at the time. Not as a thief, not as a criminal. Just somebody who liked to have fun, out for a good time. A twenty-year old wiseass who thought he had the world by the tail.

Popped for Burglary Again

Then, shit, we all get popped. A couple of guys were breaking in a place and were seen by some neighbors. Cops had themselves some real patsies. The guys that were caught started talking and one after another the cops are picking us up. Guys are snitching—"Yeah, yeah I did it and so and so was along."

That's how I ended in the county jail. The case went to trial 'cause I pleaded not guilty. Several of the guys testified I was the ringleader, how I came up with the places to hit, did the planning. Sometimes I was a main one but not all the time. No way. Sure, if we were out horsing around and somebody would say, "Let's do this," I'd say, "Solid, let's go."

Their lawyers were trying to pin it on me, on account I was the only one to have a record. Some of the guys are confessing to burglaries they didn't even do, to clear the books for the cops. Tell me this and tell me that, we'll let you go. One of those deals. Public defender who was my lawyer knew what was going down but couldn't do anything. Everybody got probation except me. I am given a one to two-year bit in the county jail.

I can't say for sure but I think my real dad showed up for my hearing, when I am being sentenced. This guy is sitting in the courtroom, the only one I didn't know. See, a few people I knew showed up. Not my mom, not a peep out of her. But a couple of my friends and Al, the guy that ran the gas station. Afterwards I asked Al—"hey, who was that guy? Was that my pop?" 'cause we had never met on account he split from my mom when I was a baby. I just had an inkling. Al wouldn't answer straight out but I could read between the lines— "Yeah, that's who it was." Never saw him again.

Escape from Jail, Life on the Run

The county jail was in between your ordinary jail and a regular penitentiary. Was a pretty big place, held maybe four to five hundred guys. Other counties sent their people to do time there too. Mostly, it was guys who were there for shitass crimes—writing bad checks, assaulting someone, dumb burglaries. Lotta guys had drinking problems. Your ordinary joe blow who fucked up. No lifers or the hardened criminal you might say.

I didn't run into any really good thieves or con men, but there were some decent thieves. They were the ones I hung with. There was a lotta bullshitting about burglary and that, to impress each other. Mostly guys blowing wind outta their asses but there was some learning on my part. And some contacts, too, which down the road would become part of my life, especially with the fencing.

Things were going smoothly. Was doing easy time, really. Knew how to handle myself from being in jail before, the juvenile reformatory. Fuck with me, I will fuck you back. I became buddies with a big Irish guy, Bill O'Keefe, in for burglary. Worked in the warden's office, was the houseboy. O'Keefe was like a trusty for the warden. Did odd jobs, run errands for him. Warden needs something—"hey, O'Keefe take my car and go get this or that." O'Keefe put the word into the warden for me to help out in the office. This was a plum job. The warden was an old Dutchman, ran a pretty loose operation. On the make all the time, looking for something for nothing. O'Keefe and me were getting stuff from guys we knew from before and guys from jail who were now out—cigars, candy, hams, different things. We'd hold some for the warden, to keep him happy. We both had a lotta leeway but O'Keefe had a lot more than me.

Then, the shit hit the fan. I'm in jail almost eleven months, am nearing my minimum and eligible for early parole. This queer is making the rounds I guess. Comes into my cell, wants to blow me. Called him a fucking queer. Told him to get the fuck out.

He leaves but is waiting for me outside my cell. When I walk out, he hits me with a broom, a deck brush, across the side of my head. Knocked me to my knees. We started fighting. He was a stocky guy, pretty stout. I have him back in my cell, in the corner. I keep hammering him but he doesn't fall 'cause he is being held up by trash can that is sitting in the corner. Then I stop and he tumbles on the floor. Broke his jaw in three places. Cracked ribs, too. Was worked over pretty good.

Charged me with assault and battery. I am facing more time. All they had was a hearing. No trial, no lawyers. Bang, bang, the judge gave me another one to two years. This was the routine way—get in fight, somebody gets hurt, no questions asked. You're just given more time. Not that way today—now you got to have lawyers, a trial, and everything. This was a real downer. Had my sights set on getting out of that fucking place. Bang, bang, two more years. Felt like a ton of bricks fell on my nuts.

About a month after the court hearing, my buddy O'Keefe takes a bottle of vodka from the warden's house, which was part of the jail grounds. We are in the back office, the warden's office. Are by ourselves. We're drinking the vodka and decided to take off. Spur of the moment. Took money out of the jail safe and then took off in the warden's car. The safe was open during the day in his office. The warden was pretty slipshod, put it that way. I believe there was eight hundred, maybe nine hundred dollars, in the safe. Went a few blocks, and grabbed a cab. Headed for the next town. Dropped us off at a secondhand shop so we could get different clothing. The taxi guy never asked any questions. Just wanted to know if we had the money to pay him. Grabbed another cab and took off for the next state. Then got a train and ended up in Oceantown. First night, we had a good time. Girls and everything. After that O'Keefe went his way and I went mine.

It's hell being on the run. It's very hard to make it. In the beginning you're always looking over your shoulder. But afterwards you get to feel you belong there. If you wouldn't need a clean social security card and you kept out of trouble, you could make it. Otherwise, your odds will run out on you. I worked construction jobs or at hospitals and places that ain't too careful about who they hire. As a janitor or an orderly. I'd give them a phony name and turn in a false number to start with, and then I'd keep forgetting to bring in the card. When they would ask: "Yeh, I'll bring it in, I'll bring it in." Hold them off awhile and then I'd know the jig was up. I'd quit, get my last pay, and move on.

I lasted several years by moving a lot and by getting tied up with women, mostly older women, in their thirties and forties. The only special attraction I had for the older ones was the money. See, they're out looking for a man so much that they don't ask that many questions. They might ask, did you have any luck getting a job today. That's about it. I would usually meet them at a bar, like a neighborhood bar, or maybe meet them at work. Most of the time it was just to find a place to eat and sleep, you know, but I hustled money off of some of them.

Some of them were real doosies. This one time, I'm brickcoating, and here comes this lady walking down the street. She was short and hefty, maybe thirty years old. I started bullshitting her. My that's a fine looking ass, shit like that. She stopped and started talking and I asked her for her phone number and all that bullshit. I told the guy I was working with, I think I got a live one here. Gonna check it out. She would do anything. You name it, she done it. I used to pick her up at work and take her to the bank, you know, to deposit her paycheck and that. She'd give me maybe thirty-five dollars. It was comical as hell. Then I convinced her that we should buy a restaurant, get married, and I'd run the place. See, there was this greasy spoon place that I ate at quite a few times. So, I asked the owner if he wanted to make an easy five hundred bucks. Just thought I'd take a chance. But I could tell he had been around. So, I told her about this place and told her we ought to buy it, that I had jewed the guy down to a good price. Just have to put down $5,500 now, then pay the rest later. But the guy wanted the $5,500 in cash. So, I took her to the place and the owner rapped with us, that he wanted to get out of the business and how he thought I had the personality to run a place like this. She went for it. She went to the bank and got the money. Told her I'd settle with the guy the next day and then we should celebrate. Next day, swoosh, I was out of town.

The only crime I did was checks and one burglary. The first time I did checks was living with a nurse. Ann Sanders. I would take her checkbook and write checks at different stores. Then I'd leave town. One time, it was right before Christmas, wrote out checks at different grocery stores. I'd buy like forty dollars worth of groceries and write the check for one hundred to two hundred dollars. Now I had all these fucking groceries. So I just started giving the stuff away. I'd say, "Miss, this is for Christmas." Load up her baby carriage with ham or whatever. It was like I was playing Santa Claus. I got a hell of a kick out of it.

I'm on the run now, when I pulled my next burglary. No, I shouldn't say I pulled it 'cause it was more something that just fell into my lap. I am in this little cafe, eating a bowl of soup. I'm broke. Few bucks in my pocket, that's it. This guy comes in, keeps looking over at me. Then he comes over, introduces himself. Asks if he could sit in the booth. At first I'm thinking—is he a fucking cop? I remember we talked about baseball, Joe Dimaggio, Ted Williams. He was a Red Sox fan. He asked me where I done time. I denied it. Eventually, he gets around to saying he has a job to pull, would I drop him off and watch.

Explained to me what would take place and very little risk for me. So, I went for it. He picked me up that evening and I drove his car, a convertible. He told me where to park, to blow the horn in case anybody came. I think it was a cleaning business. Two minutes, maybe three, he was back. Gave me a handful of money—turned out to be sixteen hundred dollars—and dropped me off. Never saw him again.

Has always stuck in my mind—how that guy carried himself, how cool he was, how easy the whole thing was pulled off. How could he tell I was an ex-con. Whew, I'm on the run, flat broke, and this happens.

The FBI finally tracks me down at this hospital. Am now a janitor, on the evening shift. A lady who is working as a secretary at the police station is visiting her mother in the hospital. Recognizes my face 'cause my mug shot's posted on the bulletin board at the police station, that I'm wanted as a fugitive. I'm about to finish my shift, nurse tells me there are some people that want to see me. Two FBI guys. "Mr. Goodman, we have a warrant for your arrest." No handcuffs, no bullshit. They were very professional.

Being on the run, escaping from jail, changed things for me. I had to pull a lotta shit to make it. I got more cockiness, more brazen. Gave me a lotta confidence in myself that I could do what I had to do, to survive. In some ways I enjoyed it because there was an excitement in it, a certain kick I was getting out of it. But you're always looking over your shoulder. No place to hang your hat. In a way there was a relief that it was over. You know eventually the jig will be up.

This time my stay in the penitentiary is a different ballgame for me. On account of all the charges, I know I am going to be there awhile. I had to finish the old sentence and the one for the assault in the jail when I broke the queer's jaw. And I had new numbers for the warden's car, the money in the jail safe, and on the escape. The escape was the serious one 'cause escaping is a piss off for the cops and people working in the penitentiaries. Will want to hammer you.

I ended up doing seven, no almost eight years altogether. First at Highpoint, then I'm transferred to Oldgate. This time in the penitentiary I am hanging with the burglars and the con men, with the good thieves really. Really, I met a lot of people, learned a lot of things in the penitentiary. How to hustle, how to carry myself, how to read people. This I feel was very helpful down the road in terms of being a better thief and a better businessman, too.

I came across some half-decent thieves in the county jail but nothing like you find in the regular penitentiary. You will still meet a lotta assholes but also will be meeting a better class of criminal and some good thieves too. The hardened criminal and a lotta lifers.

The adult penitentiary was a whole lot different from the juvenile penitentiary and the county prison. The code is stronger and you learn right away to pick your group to hang with. This was already at the county prison but at different level. You're meeting guys who are a whole lot better. You got lifers and some good thieves. There's talking but not as much bragging. Just from hearing different ones talking about it, in a way, I learned how to crack a safe.

I was tested pretty quick. Black guy cracked on me while we was playing baseball. How he liked my ass or words to that effect. I popped him with a baseball bat and that shut him up. The guards are looking right at us but said they didn't see what happened. See, the lieutenant was a white guy and the guards hated the blacks there. The other cons saw this, too, and they knew: stay away from that motherfucker, he's crazy. See, I learned that young in life and from being in jail before. Do it now, and get in the first shot. If you're gonna play games, you gotta beat me to it. I don't argue much.

Later on I became a merchant but one who isn't an asshole. A merchant in prison? That is someone who runs a store where other cons can get cigarettes, tobacco, food, coffee, candy bars and that. Blankets, socks, girlie magazines would be on the list. What they can't get, or can't afford to get, from the penitentiary [inmate] store. Is a buy and bargain thing. Being a merchant, you have to know how to hustle and show that you have some toughness. That you can knock heads or get somebody to knock heads for you. What it comes down to, I am learning how to read and deal with different kinds of people, how to get over on them. To beat them but not beat them too bad.

Main thing is, I'm hanging with the burglars and the con men. I met a lot of safecrackers. Guys who were a whole lot better than what I'd seen before. They would talk about different things—how to scout out a job, how to break into a place. That you needed to have a dropoff driver, a good partner to take inside and back you up, a good lawyer, and places to unload what you was stealing. Even how to crack a safe. It sounded easy and it sounded good. Not that there was that much talking 'cause as you get higher up, with the better criminal, you don't hear that much talking, not that much bragging. But matter-of-fact conversation. I'd listen, yeah, that sounds feasible.

From the safecrackers especially, I learnt that crime is a business. You have to do your homework, check things out, take care of the Ps and Qs. Yeah, you can break into a place and walk off with this or that. But what about afterwards—can you unload the stuff, can you keep your mouth shut, can you take care of whatever needs to be done? Is there a payoff or not? What are the risks involved?

Another main thing was, I am working in the furniture factory. This is first at the Highpoint penitentiary. Turns out I am good at it. Then the warden is transferred to the Oldgate penitentiary and wants me to work in the furniture factory there, to show the other prisoners how to upholster. Looking back, this paved the way for my fencing 'cause I learned a lot about different kinds of furniture, different pieces of wood—cherry, oak, maple, walnut. How to fix up furniture, to doctor it so it looks good. It got to where I am even going to the penitentiary library and reading up on the subject.

I am mostly just doing time at Oldgate. I pulled back from the merchant stuff but not all the way. My parole date is getting closer and, with my being in charge of the upholstery, I really didn't need to run my own store to get what I needed. The upholstery was some leverage, put me on the good side of the warden and the guards, and with the other cons too. I didn't get cracked on, nothing like that 'cause the name carries from one penitentiary to another, like from Highpoint. What kind of a con is he? Is he solid or not? There's a helluva grapevine.

I would have to say that when I got out of the penitentiary that time, in a way I was itching to get into burglary. No doubt. Into safes, really. 'Cause I feel I got a helluva education. Not that I'm planning to fall back into crime but more an inkling.

5

Commentary

Doing Burglary

As described in the previous narrative as well as those to follow, Sam's career is a series of acts and turning points in response to changing social situations, including: his stepfather's favoritism toward his own children, the lures of adult life as a young man "on the make," his mother's absence at court proceedings when Sam first got into "trouble," the learning of crime skills and attitudes during incarceration, the expansion of criminal opportunities that came from associating with the "local clique," the shift to "moonlighting" in crime and a background criminal role as pragmatic response to (1) declining physical skills and enhanced legal risks; and (2) evolving self-pride in the conventional stature and local community's view of him as a "legitimate" businessman. We define the significant phases and shifts characterizing Sam's criminal career below.

Juvenile Phase—Midteens. Sam had an uneventful childhood. He was an average student. He was raised mostly by his grandparents, who were strict and financially tight. He had to fend for himself much of the time. As a young teenager, he was involved in some minor thefts and vandalism ("ordinary kid stuff" as he calls it). He typically hung with an "older crowd." Then, he was *an accomplice in gas station burglaries with his girlfriend's cousin.* Eventually he was arrested and incarcerated in a juvenile reformatory.

Occasional Burglar—Late Teens and Early Twenties. Sam worked at a local factory and *participated in "after work" burglaries with work colleagues.* By his own description, Sam was a "half-assed" thief at this time; however, he also recognizes a growing preference for and an increasing "business" orientation toward burglary. This involvement eventually led to Sam's arrest and incarceration, subsequent escape from prison, and rearrest and lengthy reincarceration. In confinement, Sam hung out with the "better thieves" and "good burglars" and acquired a "business" perspective on crime.

Good Burglar, Part-Time Fence—Thirties to About Age Forty. After his release from prison Sam moved to American City, where he initially worked at odd jobs and burgled off-and-on with several local burglars whom he met largely through prison contacts. Within a year or so, Sam opened a small upholstery shop and also hooked up with Jesse, a good burglar from the area. The *partnership with Jesse, which lasted about eight years, specialized in safecracking and theft of antiques,* and greatly elevated Sam's stature in the local underworld. Sam eventually expanded his upholstery business to include secondhand goods and antiques, and he *also drifted into fencing.* Sam and Jesse were arrested for burgling a house full of antiques. Sam served eighteen months of a three-year sentence, after which he returned to American City where, as he put it, "I decided to stop crawling in windows but instead to have someone crawl into windows for me."

Large-Scale Fence, Part-Time Burglar, Part-Time Racketeer—Midforties to Midfifties. Sam *became a large-scale generalist fence but "mixed in" an occasional burglary* (e.g., opening a safe or orchestrating an antiques heist). Sam also became a *peripheral player in the "local clique" that dominated the rackets in American City.* Meanwhile, the legitimate side of Sam's business in antiques and secondhand goods also flourished. Sam was arrested, convicted, and served four years for "receiving stolen goods." (Steffensmeier met Sam at this time.)

Part-Time Fence—Midfifties to Late Sixties. Sam settled in Tylersville (about ninety miles from American City), where he gradually established an upholstery business, which he combined with a small trade in antiques and secondhand furniture. The "shop" eventually employed seven or eight workers and was Sam's major involvement and source of income. However, he also still *dabbled in fencing*—mainly in antiques, jewelry, and guns; and he *occasionally gave tips to thieves about prospective places "to clip."* He *occasionally opened safes* that had been carried from the premises by an acquaintance burglar; and he *"doctored" phony or fraudulent antiques for resale.* In effect, Sam "moonlighted" at crime, but his major source of income and even identity were more that of a legitimate "businessman." Sam was arrested twice for fencing stolen property during this final phase of his criminal career, but neither arrest resulted in incarceration.

Becoming an Established Thief

The most notable starting point in an examination of burglary and criminal entrepreneuers more generally is the influential work of Edwin Sutherland, in particular, *The Professional Thief* (1937) and *White Collar Crime* (1949). The former is one of the earliest sociological studies of career thieves, whereas the latter is the first large-scale sociological analysis of upperworld criminality and the variety of business behaviors that Sutherland described as "white-collar" crime. Thieves and white-collar criminals overlap in many ways, according to Sutherland. Both sets of activities require tutelage and specialized skill, and prestige among colleagues was enhanced, not diminished, because of criminal activity. But they also differ, apparently because they identify with different social worlds. As Sutherland saw it, "Professional thieves, when they speak honestly, admit that they are thieves," while white-collar criminals "think of themselves as honest men," defining what they have done as nothing more malevolent than "shrewd business practice" (1937:95–96). Both studies, moreover, were instrumental in Sutherland's efforts to develop differential association as a general theory of criminal behavior. Since criminality is learned, Sutherland and Cressey (1966) observed, it can be and is learned at all social levels.

The Professional Criminal Entrepreneur: High Criminal Capital Offenders

The research behind *Confessions* provides an opportunity for an ethnographic revisit (Burawoy 2003) of Sutherland's *The Professional Thief*. *The Professional Thief* is a fascinating glimpse into the underworld of professional thieves and con men. The account is based on the recollections of Broadway Jones, alias "Chic Conwell"—thief, ex-drug addict, and ex-con, who worked for twenty years as a pickpocket, shoplifter, and confidence man. Conwell's recollections include details about the roles of members of the *mob* (criminal group), their criminal *argot* (slang), the *fix* (ways of avoiding conviction and/or doing time in prison), and thieves' images of the police, the law, and society at large.

Much of the book was actually written by Conwell, but Sutherland edited it for publication and wrote two interpretive chapters. His analysis concluded that professional thievery has five basic features: technical skill, status, consensus, differential association, and organization.[1]

- **Technical Skill.** Professional thieves (like bricklayers, lawyers, and physicians) possess a set of talents and skills. Some combination of wits, speaking ability, manual dexterity, specialization, and contacts is needed to plan and execute crimes, dispose of stolen goods, and manipulate the criminal justice system in those cases involving arrests.
- **Status.** Like other professionals, the professional thief holds a certain status based on ability, character, lifestyle, wealth, and power. Professional thieves often show contempt for amateur, small-time, and "snatch-and-grab" thieves.
- **Consensus.** Professional thieves share similar values and develop a philosophy or rationale regarding their activities and criminal specialty that aids them in their criminal careers.
- **Differential Association.** They tend to associate chiefly with other professional thieves and to maintain barriers between themselves and members of "straight" society.
- **Organization.** Professional theft is organized in the sense that technical skills, status, consensus, and differential association entail both a core of knowledge informally shared by thieves and a network of cooperation.

Sutherland further concludes that the professional thief is a graduate of a developmental process that includes the acquisition of specialized attitudes, knowledge, skills, and experience; makes a regular business of stealing—it is his occupation or a principal means of livelihood; and identifies with the world of crime. Professional thieves *tend to specialize* on a relatively small number of crimes that are related to one another, although they may *transfer for longer or shorter periods of time from one specialty to another* (emphasis added in light of our later, more detailed treatment of the specialization-generality issue in the study of criminal careers).

However, some contemporary criminologists have criticized Sutherland's depiction of professional thieves (ca. 1900–1925). Some consider it somewhat unreal (e.g., Lemert 1958) and antiquated (Inciardi 1975). Still others contend that the typical criminal lacks self-control and cannot plan, organize, acquire skills, or delay gratification (Gottfredson and Hirschi 1990). Organization among criminals, including organized roles and alternative status hierarchies, Gottfredson and Hirschi (1990) say, is more a fanciful creation of criminologists than a reality.

If Gottfredson and Hirschi are correct in stating that practitioners of crime and vice are inept, incapable of networking and organization, and so forth, then ethnographers are easily duped by their criminal subjects since (despite their intensive interviewing and close-up observations) they almost universally conclude otherwise. Even ethnographers who study street-level offenders, while they may characterize their criminal subjects as hedonistic and spur-of-the-moment, also find them to be fairly skilled or adept in their hustling or theft endeavors (Akerstrom 1985 in particular discusses this issue). Also, drawing from Sam's narrative, Sam (who *hated* "dopers") observes begrudgingly that he "will give them credit, as far as knowing how to steal or how to hustle, they are pretty decent at that."

Other critics note that in sociology, the concept of *profession* refers to occupations that entail esoteric, useful *knowledge* after lengthy training, a *code of ethics,* and a claimed *service* orientation for which they are granted autonomy of operation and various concomitants such as high prestige and remuneration (Hagan 1994:294). In this light the term "professional" may be inappropriately applied to criminal activities and criminals, even very skilled ones.

A final criticism is that Sutherland's treatment restricts professional crime to thieves or hustlers who rely on wit and *nonviolent* techniques. It excludes criminals involved in "heavy" theft such as truck hijackers, stickup men, arsonists, and "hit" men. Excluded, too, are those practitioners of crime and vice who are involved in the "rackets" and illicit businesses such as bookmakers, dealers in stolen goods, drug traffickers, sex merchants, mafiosi, and racketeers and background operators more generally. Many of those involved in these activities fit the elements of "professionalism" enumerated by Sutherland as much or more so than did Chic Conwell.

Part of the skepticism associated with Sutherland's treatment is a failure by some subsequent writers to adequately delineate professionals from other habitual or career criminals, even though Sutherland (1937:4) went to some length to indicate that he was discussing a more *savvy* or upper-level group of thieves—people little affiliated with the ordinary persistent offender. Prus and Sharper (1991:153), two veteran field observers of the criminal world, point out that very few modern criminologists have intimate familiarity with those likely to be characterized as professional thieves by Sutherland's standards— or as described by Sam as "decent or good thieves" and as "this or that guy in the local clique."

We learn the following from *Confessions* about the nature of professional crime today. First, many aspects of Sutherland's characterization of the processes involved in becoming a professional thief, the thief's relationship to the general society, and the larger subculture of theft are largely applicable today. As was true when Sutherland sketched it, Sam describes how one becomes an established thief today through stealing with, and tutelage by, other seasoned thieves. From them, one learns criminal techniques (physical, interpersonal, perceptual, and definitional) and how to manipulate the criminal justice system. "Moreover, in the process of learning all this he will become plugged into a network of criminal and quasi-criminal actors with whom he can establish mutually advantageous working relationships" (Shover 1972:543).

Second, Sutherland used the term to describe a small subset of thieves picked from the very large population of thieves, hustlers, and con men. But as we see from Sam's narratives, the term applies as well, even better perhaps, to a variety of racketeers and background operators involved in activities such as official corruption, the supply of illegal goods and services, and the running of an illicit or quasi-legitimate business. Viewed this way, from the perspective of Sam's and his associates' experiences, even though the category of *thief* that he described appears even rarer today (e.g., "class cannon" or pickpocket, good burglar, con artist), Sutherland's professional criminal is hardly a dying species.

Third, many "skilled" criminals are only slightly better than other crooks at lying, cheating, and stealing; labeling them "professionals" should be done carefully. Some criminologists who have studied career criminals suggest terms like *able* criminal (Mack 1975), *high-level* thieves (Shover 1996), or *seasoned* offenders for those who commit more sophisticated crimes and face a lesser chance of arrest or conviction (Steffensmeier 1986). Still others suggest the term *semiprofessional* (Hagan 1994).

Fourth, the term "professional thief" or "seasoned illicit entrepreneur" recognizes that offenders differ in their criminal capacities: some (perhaps most) are very limited in what they get out of their criminal behavior, whereas others are very experienced, resourceful, and successful, and still others fall somewhere in between. More so than the ordinary thief, professional or good thieves can be characterized as having a lot of *criminal capital.* To be a successful criminal, different forms of capital are required: physical capital (tools like guns and wire cutters, physical strength), human capital (resourcefulness, criminal insight, physical strength), social capital (reputation, networks of useful people), and cultural capital (knowledge of underworld culture, argot, meanings, etc.). Having a lot of criminal capital both reduces the risks of crime and increases the prospects for safer and more profitable crime opportunities, for example, by increasing the offender's attractiveness to co-offenders and crime networks (see Weerman 2003; McCarthy, Hagan, and Woodward 1999; Steffensmeier 1983, 1986). In a commentary accompanying Sam's narratives on fencing stolen goods(and throughout the book), we describe in more detail the nature and importance of criminal social capital in the field of criminal enterprise.

Differences in criminal capital across offenders or criminal entrepreneurs and across types of crime or criminal enterprise are therefore important markers of underworld stratification and career success. Furthermore, it is plausible that criminals pursuing less organized or street-level forms of illegal enterprise will need less social capital (e.g., kinship ties) but more human or personal capital (e.g., conning ability, "larceny sense," ingenuity, violence), whereas entrepreneurs involved in illegalities that entail greater organization and longevity will have to rely more heavily on cultural and social capital resources. *Our point is that the professional versus run-of-the-mill criminal distinction can be recast in terms of having a lot of versus a little criminal capital.* This is a point we elucidate in our commentary accompanying Sam's narrative on the social organization of the underworld and organized crime.

Fifth, though many writers (including Sutherland) use "professional criminal" in their discussions of crime, the term is seldom, if ever, applied by criminals themselves (for further discussion of the use of the term "professional" by criminals themselves, see *The Fence:*279–80). Even seasoned thieves and hustlers do not use the word professional or nonprofessional. Instead, they refer to themselves (or others) as thieves or hustlers; as good thieves, good hustlers, or good people; as aces-in-the-hole, first-class or decent thieves, wise guys, and so forth. Nevertheless, thieves (like Sam) are aware of the word's meaning in the larger society, and may use it as a shorthand way of communicating with members of straight society. Rather than struggling to convey to a "joe blow citizen" the difference between a "common thief" and a "good thief," it may be convenient to say: "He is an old pro," or "He's a real professional." Or, amongst themselves, thieves may say "that was a professional job."

Nevertheless, because of its widespread usage in the literature, professional criminals or *seasoned criminal entrepreneurs* will be treated as a separate category in the material in *Confessions.* But we will use this term somewhat critically. The professional criminal is not truly a professional in the sociological sense, but the term is appropriate in referring informally to those who are skilled, have high status in the underworld, and earn a considerable portion of their livelihood in criminal pursuits. As such, the term applies not only to a small subset of thieves picked from the very large population of thieves, hustlers, and con men, but also includes some dealers in stolen goods as well as many other illicit entrepreneurs, swindlers, racketeers, and mafiosi.

Becoming a Burglar

Sam Goodman's career offers a general picture of the social factors that shape the beginnings and persistence of a criminal career. It also permits us to discern the processes involved in becoming a seasoned burglar, and later a large-scale dealer in stolen goods. This process involves both *being willing* and *being able*—it hinges on whether burgling or dealing in stolen goods is subjectively acceptable as well as objectively possible to an individual.

Both are necessary conditions and may complement one another. Having the skills and available opportunities may contribute to a willingness to steal or buy stolen goods, just as the desire to steal or buy may lead to a search for opportunities. Simply put, one is more willing to do what, in fact, one is able to do.

Willingness to burgle or deal in stolen goods depends on individual perception of such activities as immoral, inexpedient, or both. For the average citizen—due to upbringing, ties to conventional society, or risks to a legitimate career or business—the attractions of theft or trading in stolen goods are offset by moral concerns about engaging in illegal behavior, worries about discovery and getting caught by the police, or fears of exploitation and violence associated with an unlawful setting. The importance of and changes in these concerns and fears are key themes in *Confessions,* and will be examined later (e.g., in sections on "rewards" and "rationale").

Individual ability depends on one's wherewithal to meet certain conditions. These conditions overlap and vary across burglary and fencing. We delineate similarities and differences in these conditions below, here for burglary and then in Chapter 7 for fencing.

The term *career contingencies* has been applied by some criminologists in highlighting key elements of the processes involved in becoming a persistent offender (Shover 1996). These contingencies refer to changes in offenders' subjective schema or in objective circumstances that maintain their crime path, switch them to other crime paths, or change them to noncrime. Identifying significant contingencies in thieves' careers helps to explain why some individuals dabble or are not very successful at theft; why involvement in crime is short term for some individuals while others devote decades to it; or why some individuals stay with a main criminal line while others switch to more lucrative, safer criminal endeavors or vacillate back and forth. Describing the contingencies for becoming a persistent offender is key to understanding variation in criminal careers. Sam's career illustrates these contingencies.

Conditions for Carrying Out Successful Burglaries

The next narrative chapter describes the escalation of Sam's burglary career into full bloom. Traditional common law defined burglary as the act of breaking and entering another's house at night with the intention of committing a theft. Today, burglary is more broadly defined as illegal entry (including breaking and entering) into a building (or analogous structure) to commit a crime therein. The building or structure may be a home, apartment house, business, railroad car, truck trailer, booth, tent, or shop; the crime may occur anytime, day or night. The most common forms of burglary are entry into residences and commercial establishments, and the "hijacking" of delivery trucks. Closely aligned crimes, though they may have different legal classifications, include auto theft, breaking into autos, theft of auto parts, and theft from storage lots or open spaces.[2]

The criminal careers of seasoned burglars embody solutions to a number of demands and fulfill several interrelated conditions. These conditions are more easily determined and better understood following a description of the *stages* that typify a successful burglary (or auto theft, truck hijacking, or breaking into a car or van), each with a specific set of tasks oriented toward getting the target's goods without discovery, selling them, and avoiding subsequent apprehension (Best and Luckenbill 1994).[3]

Stages of Burglary

Stage 1: Planning the Burglary. This typically involves (1) selecting a target, (2) casing it, and (3) tailoring equipment and contingency plans to it.

In selecting a target the burglar typically seeks a location that (1) contains enough cash or valuable goods to make the theft worthwhile and (2) does not pose unmanageable risks of discovery and apprehension. The importance of these conditions varies by type of burglar and level of risk. Seasoned burglars tend to bypass even lucrative targets if the risks are substantial.

Targets are selected on the basis of personal assessments and tips. An offender may "happen upon" or spot a target that may yield a good take; more likely, he discovers targets by scouting or canvassing an area for places that are both lucrative and vulnerable. Seasoned thieves, at least occasionally, also rely on tipsters for information on targets.

Once the target has been selected, the offender is likely to assess risk or "case" the place. In casing the burglar surveys regular and routine features of the social setting with an eye for those that might hinder or facilitate the burglary. These features include the location of the place in relation to other buildings and traffic, the type of alarm system used, and the time when the cash or the goods are both abundant and vulnerable (Best and Luckenbill 1994:175).

Casing can range from a few observations made while walking or driving around the place to careful inspections over a period of days or weeks. The offender may watch the place from a distance or enter it (or send in a girlfriend or another accomplice) to observe. Casing skills involve reinterpreting conventional features of social settings in the framework of the problems of burglary, such as observing various aspects of architecture and patterns of social action that either hinder or facilitate the completion of a burglary.

Planning also involves preparing for the burglary by selecting equipment, positioning the dropoff driver, and developing contingency plans such as the best vantage point for a lookout, the alternative routes if discovered, and arranging for the sale of the stolen merchandise to a "fence." Veteran thieves maintain that planning for "what to do afterwards" is typically more important and difficult than "doing" the actual burglary. The types of tools may include a crowbar or big screwdriver (e.g., to pry open doors or windows), Stillson wrench, pipe cutter, hacksaw, tinsmith shears, chisels, steel punches, small sledgehammer, drill, saw, flashlight, and canvas or cloth gloves to protect hands from injury and avoid leaving fingerprints. Additional tools, especially useful for bypassing alarm systems, may include a voltage meter, wire snips, alligator clips, and a battery-operated soldering iron. Also, a police scanner, walkie-talkie radios, and cell phones may be used for communication within the burglary crew. These and similar tools can be purchased (mostly) in any hardware store.

Stage 2: Entering the Place. There are several techniques for entering a closed place that is secured and possibly equipped with an alarm. Where there is no alarm, the offender may simply kick in the door or pry open a locked window. Places with alarms are more troublesome. In some cases, the offender neutralizes the alarm so it will not go off. In other cases, he might bypass the alarm or enter by an alternative route, such as a hole cut in the roof. Dogs, fences, and security gates may also present additional obstacles

When entering or approaching a closed place, the less suspicion the better. The offender seeks to appear as a person who belongs in the setting at that time. Usually the burglary is carried out during the late night or early morning hours. When the offender works in the daytime or in a busy or heavily populated area, the illegal entry itself also must not arouse suspicion. For example, a burglar can reduce neighbors' suspicions by appearing as a repairman (e.g., plumber) or an employee of a moving company who has been sent to a residence. Vans are favorite sources of transportation for burglars.

Stage 3: Stealing. A number of tasks may be performed once inside the place. The burglar may establish lookout points, locate escape routes to be used if the operation is interrupted, or rig the entrances to prevent intruders from entering. He then locates the goods to be stolen. Whereas large and openly displayed items are easy to spot, some skill for "searching" is required if the offender intends to steal cash or small valuables that may be hidden or kept in an unpredictable place. As Sam notes, sometimes a burglary crew designates one member as a searcher, who locates items of value to steal.

Once the goods are located, the offender must take them. This is a relatively simple matter when the offender intends to steal easily accessible items. They can be taken and carried away in comparatively little time, but they must be removed from the place without observation and later converted into cash, typically by selling them to a fence. Acquisition is more difficult when the offender wants to take money or small valuables from a secure location, such as a cash register or safe. This may call for special skills, special tools, and considerable time.

Safecracking is the most challenging method of stealing cash or small valuables in a burglary. It generally is restricted to seasoned thieves working in crews of two to four persons who use special techniques. Some writings still persist in showing the safe burglar skillfully fingering a combination or listening to the tumblers through a stethoscope; other writings describe the famous nitroglycerine gangs who, with a well-placed charge of "soup," could unhinge the door of the strongest safe. The combination job has always been very rare (even more so today since most safes now have manipulation-proof locks), and the explosives job has almost never been used in this country. In those instances where it is used, it is likely to involve dynamite (a relatively safe explosive) rather than nitroglycerine.

The safecracker's techniques are often more roughhouse than light-fingered. High-speed drills or acetylene torches are used to rip the bottom or back out of a safe. Small sledgehammers may be used to bludgeon the dials on the front of a "square box" or a safe of older build, to punch out the combination (modern safes are punch-proof), and to open the doors. The major techniques today are:

1. **"Chopping" or "Ripping":** Tearing a hole through a part of the safe other than the door such as the top, side, or bottom. Often the safecracker turns the safe upside down to expose its bottom, usually its weakest part. A hole is bored or punched or "pick axed" with a reasonable amount of force. A jimmy also may be used. This method is crude but effective. Many imported safes today, more aptly called "containers," have a sort of plastic alloy material that is light and easily ripped or peeled or sawed.

2. **"Peeling":** The thief may "peel" or pry a poorly constructed safe. A small chisel is used to sheer rivets and make a hole in the safe. Or an electric drill or a hand-held brace is used to make a hole in a corner of the safe. Larger chisels or a steel bar are inserted to enlarge the opening and peel away the outside wall panel. An axe or other sharp instrument is then used to break through the safe's weak inner wall. A lot of cheaply made safes today are easy prey for peeling, although they may require persistence and a fair amount of physical effort on the part of the safeman.

3. **"Punching"**: The safecracker knocks off the combination dial (usually with a ten-pound hammer), revealing a steel spindle that holds the tumblers of the locking mechanism in place. He then uses a hammer and a long steel punch or drift pin, and punches the spindle into the safe. The tumblers fall, and the safe door opens. One disadvantage of the punch is noise. A key advantage for those more adept is that the punch is the quickest method of attack. Newer safes typically have punch-proof spindles or relocking devices that are automatically implemented when the dial is hit or possibly when the safe is pounded on.

4. **"Drilling"**: A time-consuming technique, in which the safecracker uses high-speed battery- or electric-powered drills to drill a hole near the combination dial and then manipulates the tumblers until the lock opens. To penetrate "burglar-resistant" safes typically requires high-torque drills and carbide- or diamond-tipped drill bits of high quality. To prevent movement of the drill and bending or breaking of the bit against the safe's steel plate, safemen may use a "jig" fastened to the safe. The jig helps to locate the bit over the target area (e.g., combination lock) and provides an anchor for the drill (small holes may be drilled for anchor bolts).

5. **"Burning"**: The safecracker may use the burn or torch technique. He applies his oxygen-acetylene torch to the central area of the safe, burning a circle around the dial, which is then removed to permit the opening of the door.

Burglars may use a combination of several methods to overcome the various types of obstacles in modern safes. Also, many burglars prefer removing the safe, often transporting it on a dolly cart to a truck or van, because it allows them to open the safe leisurely at their hideaway. The practical problem here is removal of a safe can be difficult or impossible due to its weight or because it is bolted to the floor or wall or is embedded in concrete. However, some older safes and many newer fire-resistant safes ("containers") are fairly light (75–150 pounds) and can be carried or carted off easily. These lighter safes today are mostly foreign made, relatively expensive, and typically purchased by residential occupants rather than commercial establishments. A skilled safecracker, once the safe is carted out, can also be called upon to open safes that are more burglar-proof. A hernia is one risk of carrying out a safe.

Stage 4: Departing. Once the theft is completed, the offender checks to ensure that no incriminating evidence is left behind and that there are no witnesses to the departure. Additional precautions may be taken to avoid identification. The stolen getaway car may be abandoned, burglary tools thrown away, and clothing worn during the burglary disposed of—since carpet fibers and other particles from the burglary scene or the safe may have impregnated the offender's clothing and would link him to the crime.

Precautions taken both during and after the burglary will depend on the target's defenses—alarms, locks, fences, dogs, safes, lighting, or other security measures—aimed at keeping offenders from gaining access to valuable property. The greater the precautions, the more the burglar will need special knowledge, skill, and equipment to circumvent special monitoring systems and penetrate secure locations to steal the target's property.

Stage 5: Converting Stolen Property into Cash. Most burglars steal both cash and property. Even those burglars who go "strictly for cash" will pick up, at least occasionally, jewelry or other small valuables. The offender therefore needs to convert the stolen property into cash. Seasoned thieves may have a temporary storage place (a "drop") or they may go directly to a fence not only to convert the stolen property into cash but to dispose of additional incriminating evidence. In this sense, the thief's best protection against arrest is the services of a reliable fence or "offman"—someone by whom the thief is able to unload or "get off" the stolen goods in his possession.

Conditions for a Successful Career in Burglary

The work of the thief and/or burglar requires that he complete one and sometimes two tasks without getting caught by the police. He must steal property, and if the property is not money, he must sell the property (Gibbs and Shelly 1982; Shover 1972, 1991; Steffensmeier 1986). To accomplish these tasks with at least some success entails solutions to a number of work demands.

Coping with the technical and legal realities of long-term burglary requires building a personal network with those kinds of people who can support and sustain the burglar by teaching and assisting him in various ways. *To be successful, a burglar must meet five conditions*:

1. First, the prospective professional burglar must learn the many skills needed to commit lucrative burglaries. Since this knowledge is at least somewhat esoteric and generally only known by other seasoned burglars, the would-be burglar must learn the craft at the side of an experienced burglar. This may include learning such techniques as entering homes, commercial establishments, or truck trailers, selecting targets with high payoffs, properly opening safes without damaging their contents, and using the proper equipment, including chisels, cutting torches, electric saws, and pry bars.

2. A second contingency is his ability to team up with or to form a criminal crew. Connecting with trustworthy associates is essential if the obstacles to completing a successful job—police, alarms, watchdogs, secure safes—are to be overcome. Sophisticated burglary usually requires at least two men working in concert. Although one finds a number of unattached burglars who prefer to work alone, the significance of hooking up with a reliable and capable partner is the typical career pattern for most successful burglars. However, even

unattached burglars must build a network of contacts with tipsters and others who can assist them in their work.

Burglars usually work in groups or *crews* of two to four, although some larger *projects* may include as many as six or more burglars. The typical three–four person crew is differentiated by fairly distinct roles or activities that each burglar performs, pragmatically described as: "safeman" (if cracking a safe is part of the burglary), "lookout" or "watcher," searcher(s); and dropoff. The watcher role may be furthered distinguished by "inside watcher" and "outside watcher." Whereas the safeman is typically the more skilled and prestigious position, the dropoff driver is considered the least skilled and is often viewed as less of a "real partner" or crew member than the other roles.

Crew members may sometimes change from job to job, but members are typically selected from a small group of people. Larger-scale or project burglaries, in particular, are likely to require more participants who are brought together to pull off a specific burglary but may not work together again. However, usually a core member or members are likely to be involved in organizing, planning, and going out on these project burglaries. Most crews divide the score money equally among members but this can vary depending on their work and risk taking. Notably, dropoff drivers often receive a smaller percentage of the score money as compared to "close" or "longtime" partners who may divide the money in their favor. The dropoff driver and "fill-in" crew members often receive less than the safeman, lookout, or close or longtime partners.

People who connect with seasoned crews or with better burglars (thieves) are also "learning the ropes" in ways that supplement or add to the learning of skills referred to in contingency 1 above. Drawing from related research on veteran card and dice hustlers (see Prus and Sharper 1977), this learning includes the sharpening of one's larceny sense or "eye for clipping," in Sam's words—i.e., attitudes and techniques conducive to burglary or to theft and hustling more generally. Second, there is learning to get along with fellow thieves—"learning to deal with them as equals and learning how to avoid being exploited by one's co-workers" (ibid.:48). Third, there is role-specific learning in which one acquires skills for particular burglary roles such as dropoff, lookout, searcher, or safecracker.

Two added points are worth noting. One is that these types of learning occur more or less concurrently and more or less continuously throughout one's career. The other concerns the advantages in connecting with more skilled burglars or crew. While burglars or thieves may acquire these same qualities bouncing around in roughhouse burglaries and thefts, the extent and intensity of the learning experiences available in more experienced crews are likely to be so much greater than what otherwise is likely to be encountered. Prus and Sharper write: "Within a single professional crew, one is able to experience a much more diversified, concentrated, and refined set of operations than one might while working with a variety of non-professional crews"(ibid.). (We can see this, for example, in how hooking up with Jesse's crew boosted Sam's know-how and sharpened his larceny sense.)

3. The good burglar (usually) must have advance information about the place he plans to burglarize and what awaits him inside, including whether it will contain something worth stealing and perhaps its whereabouts. Without such knowledge, the burglar can spend considerable time and effort on empty safes and jewelry boxes. Because it may include intelligence about alarm systems or watchdogs, the advance information also may greatly lessen the risk of apprehension. Thus, along with casing and scouting, the professional burglar may employ finders to locate jobs or tipsters to furnish information.

4. Fourth, the burglar must gain access to fences or buyers for stolen wares, and then learn how to sell products for a satisfactory price. Surmounting these economic realities—of cultivating access to a select group of dependable "dealers" who do not openly advertise their trade in stolen goods, and acquiring the wherewithal to negotiate effectively with them—may be even harder than the prior mastery of burgling skills.

5. Fifth, the burglar must learn to thwart the criminal justice system. Because even the good burglar is likely to be arrested at some time during his activities, he must acquire the knowledge and connections to manage the legal realities of a burglary career. Thus, his network must include "resourceful" individuals he can turn to in case of misfortune. Access to a "good" criminal lawyer is a must but the list of helpful contacts also may include a reliable bondsman or loan shark, as well as a corrupt police officer, prosecutor, or judge. The loyalty of a friend or a "good woman" also may be useful, for example, as an information channel during periods of incarceration.

Thus, whether in teams or alone, professional burglars (and thieves) are usually connected with a loosely organized support system of other people. Key "connections" include finding a "good partner"—probably the most crucial contact. Other helpful contacts are fingermen or tipsters, who provide information on lucrative targets. They do not have to be criminals themselves; all that is required is the right information and the willingness to share it with a burglar. Delivery people, service repair people, bartenders, hairdressers, prostitutes, police, attorneys, security-industry personnel, insurance agents, antique or estate appraisers, jewelers, shady businesspeople, local racketeers, and fences, as well as other thieves or ex-thieves, may for a fee or a percentage of the profits pass along tips on possible scores. A third important connection is access to the services of a competent attorney, since a burglar cannot steal repeatedly without at some time being arrested. Some attorneys have better connections and are comparatively more skillful at thwarting the criminal justice system to gain release or light sentences for their clients. To free his client or get a "good deal," the attorney may rely on cash payoffs or political favors, skillful backroom bargaining, or both. Finally, the burglar must know one or more fences who trade regularly in stolen goods.

The significance of connecting with a reliable fence goes beyond the mere buying of stolen wares. Because he often is an underworld veteran and both knowledgeable and well-connected, the fence is in a unique position to provide other support services to the fledgling burglar. These include educating him on how to distinguish valuable merchandise, coaching him on theft techniques and ways to thwart the criminal justice system, providing him with information on potential scores, giving monetary assistance or a loan during periods of inactivity, and putting him in contact with other burglars as well as people in the legal system such as other fences, bondsmen, and attorneys. Coaching by the fence, as well as concluding successful transactions with him, are likely to be important reinforcers to the escalating career of the fledgling thief.

Thus, the process of becoming an established burglar is contingent on acquiring trusted relationships with members of deviant social circles who are careful about whom they allow in. Jesse, a long-term burglar and one-time partner of Sam's, characterizes the important connections as follows:

> To make it, really make it, now, as a burglar—not this penny-ante shit . . . you need someone on the inside to give you information, say, a lawyer, or have a contact with somebody that works in a security agency or a place that sells burglar alarms. . . . Need a good partner unless you can hack working alone, which freaking few can do; a lawyer to get you off and help line you up with the right people; the right kind of fence unless you're going strictly after cash, which is getting harder and harder to do; and a good woman to stand by you but not get in your way.

The objective circumstances of getting "connected," of benefiting from assistance rendered by a network of contacts, and of "being able" in other ways are likely to have important subjective effects as well. The perceived risks of stealing lessen and its rewards simultaneously rise, further drawing the burglar into his criminal activities and strengthening his commitments to them. As success at burglary becomes more objectively possible, it also becomes more subjectively acceptable. How key opportunity and subjective elements are played out in burglary involvement and careers is better understood in the context of (1) categories of burglars and (2) stages of career development that burglars go through—distinctions that some prior writings and *Confessions* help to provide.

Four basic categories of burglars are found in *Confessions*. These categories also inform us about, or coincide with, key stages of development that burglars typically go through. The typology also may apply to thieves and hustlers more generally. The basic distinctions are: greenies or rookies (stage 1), in-between or roughhouse burglars (stage 2), decent or good burglars (stage 3), and semiretired or moonlighters (stage 4). Absent the latter, these distinctions roughly correspond to Maguire's (1982) classifying of burglars into *low-level, middle-range,* and *high-level;* or to Cromwell, Olson, and Avary's (1991) threefold grouping of burglars into *novices, journeymen,* and *professional* burglars.

Stage 1: *"Greenies."* These learn theft and burglary from older more experienced burglars, frequently relatives, neighbors, or coworkers; or learn "hands on" by relying on their own or peers' initiative and ideas in order to scout targets, think up better methods, and make contacts. Their burglaries (or thefts) tend to be somewhat "spur of the moment" and their rewards as much or more excitement and being part of the group than money or financial gain. Many will desist from burglary as they get older and as they feel the pull of conventional relationships and the fear of more severe adult sanctions. Members of this group do not develop connections that allow them to select good targets or move large volumes of stolen goods.

Stage 2: *"In-betweeners."* (Sam also refers to them as "half-assed"). These graduate to searching for more lucrative targets and careful planning, are more likely to develop their own markets (fences) for stolen goods, and to develop reputations as experienced criminals. They are generally a bit older (than juveniles) and may go back and forth between legitimate pursuits and crime. Their take may at times be fairly substantial but they still may lack the connections for partners, stolen goods outlets, or facilitative others (e.g., tipsters, good lawyers) for practicing burglary or theft safely and profitably.

Stage 3: *"Decent or good thieves."* These work in more organized crews, have the skill-level to scout or are connected with reliable sources of information about targets, have reliable stolen goods outlets, and are aided by other outside sources. They tend to carefully plan their crimes, and they can earn a good living from the proceeds of their crimes. They also have high esteem among their peers.

Stage 4: *"Semiretired" or "moonlighters."* These are burglars or thieves who are in the process of "packing it in," or are moving to background roles, though they may engage in burglaries or theft sporadically.

All these themes (e.g., know-how, larceny sense, contacts, rewards, career contingencies) are illustrated partly in the previous narrative chapter and later in Chapter 18 on criminal "pathways," but more particularly in the next narrative chapter, as Sam's burglary career gets into full swing.

Notes

1. The description of these skills is adapted from Beirne and Messerschmidt (1995:387).
2. In strict legal terms, breaking into or stealing from a motor vehicle like a car or truck is classified as a *larceny-theft* for crime-reporting purposes. But many police agencies count theft from a motor vehicle as a burglary, particularly if the modus operandi involved "breaking and entering."
3. Our discussion here builds on Best and Luckenbill's (1994) treatment of burglary stages, along with several key analyses of burglary by Curtis (1971), Gibbs and Shelly (1982), Wright and Decker (1994), Shover (1996), Steffensmeier (1986), and Steffensmeier and Terry (1986).

6

Sam's Narrative

Sam's Burglary Career Escalates

I headed for *American City* as soon as I got out of the Oldgate penitentiary.
I don't know for sure why. Except I'm hitting thirty or thereabouts and was
looking for a place that didn't go around busting the balls of ex-cons. Knew
some guys from prison who moved there. Heard it was a good place to find
work, that the cops weren't hard-asses. So, I took a shot at it. The rest is really
history. My life as far as crime is concerned went swoosh.

First on it was mainly burglary, and then it was burglary with a little fencing mixed in. But the fencing kept getting bigger. Then Jesse and me gets
popped for pulling this antique burglary. Cleaned out a whole house. Pleaded
guilty 'cause they had us cold and the DA is offering a short sentence in the
penitentiary.

After I got out, the fencing becomes the main thing with a little burglary
mixed in. All the time now—well once I got it rolling—my legit business was
doing good. Had a helluva shop in secondhand goods and antiques. Right off
the main drag in American City. Some new merchandise too. With the fencing
and with the legit, I was really doing good.

Career "Goes Swoosh" in American City

Right off in American City I get a job at this greasy spoon place—as a cook,
a short order cook. And am driving tractor trailer, whenever I was needed.
Then I got on at Bailey's, a big furniture factory. Make furniture and sell it to
different places, like to Sears or Montgomery Ward's. Just put different labels
on it. I was a repairman. A load of furniture goes out and some pieces get damaged, I'd repair it. Cushion, leg, inside arm—I'd doctor it up, patch over. I
really learned about wood, how to fix furniture, make it look passable. I had
worked in the furniture shop in the penitentiary but nothing like this.

The greasy spoon place was where I ran across the guy I put to sleep [see Chapter 2]. I'm working there a little more than a month. He stops by for lunch and I see him from the kitchen. Turns out we know each other from prison. Was an okay con. Said he was staying with a cousin until he could get settled. He comes back two or three days later. Would I do a job with him? Rob this book-maker who is making the rounds, collecting and paying on bets. I should drive the car, wait for him. I went for it. Ends up I have to put the motherfucker to sleep.

Was never any suspicion of me, that I was involved in robbing the book-maker. No suspicion either of the guy I snuffed out. He wasn't known, wasn't from the area. His telling me he was staying with his cousin was bullshit. I'm guessing he was passing through to pull a couple of jobs and then skip town. Different names came up in the grapevine, but never his. If the conversation came up about the robbery, I'd badmouth whoever done it—"What dumb motherfucker would rob a bookie that way?" I knew what had to be done [Sam mimics a choking action with his hands.] Very little struggle on his part, then his lights were out. I am barely in American City a couple of months and this happens. Was that an omen of what was to come? I can't say.

I don't remember much else about the greasy spoon place, except later on I met Connie there. This is two or three years later. I would stop to have a bowl of soup or a sandwich, and she was working there. We went out, off and on for a year or so. Then she says she is knocked up, words to that effect. We should get married. I went along with it. Had a little girl, Amy. Very cute, at least I thought so. We only lasted a couple of years together but I was never there anyway. Came and left as I pleased. Still have to laugh about this. I come home one night and everything is out of the house. Except left a paper plate, plastic spoon and fork and knife, potato chips, and couple of pickles. I guess she didn't want me to starve. Actually, that is the only time I was married. The divorce was never finalized until a few years ago. But we stayed in touch. She has come to visit me in the hospital, very regular. Would send her minister to come pray with me. She's a good woman, a good mother.

In the meantime, now, I'm getting into burglary. Mostly from running into other guys I done time with. They were breaking into gas stations, small busi-nesses. Were after cash. These guys were half decent—not good burglars but not penny-ante either. If they needed another guy they'd ask me to go along. I did whatever was needed—driver, lookout, some scouting. Altogether, I'd say over the next year I pulled twelve, fifteen jobs with them.

The burglary really takes off after I met Jesse. Jesse Tate. We became part-ners. He comes into my little upholstery shop I had opened up. Is shopping for a partner. We had heard of each other. Jesse heard I was solid, that I didn't scare easy. His brother or somebody recommended me, that he check me out. I knew his brother from hanging out at the same places. Jesse and I was teamed up for a long time.

Partnership with Jesse

It seems like yesterday. I'm in the back of my shop, upholstering some chairs and Jesse comes in. Tells me he hears I upholster old chairs and sofas, that I'm pretty fucking good at it. Has a sofa chair he wants upholstered. Words to that effect. We kidded around, talked about some of the people we both know. Then, he puts it right out in the open. "I got this jump I want to do. Need somebody to go inside, watch my back while I'm opening the safe." This was Jesse's way of talking, referred to a burglary as a "job" or a "jump."[1]

See, it wasn't too long after I landed in American City that I opened up a little upholstery and secondhand furniture shop. This is fluky, hard to believe. But I was renting a room that didn't have any furniture to speak of. So, I recovered a couple of chairs I bought for like fifty cents at the rescue mission, and the lady I was renting the room from wanted to buy them. She paid me thirty-five dollars a piece. Right away I am thinking, this a good racket. I opened up a little shop, painted a sign on the window—*Goodman Upholstery and Furniture.* I'm running to the auctions and elsewhere to find old chairs, recover them, and sell them in my little shop. They would sell right away.

I had heard of Jesse. That he was good people, a good safeman. Was careful who he worked with. I'd say all the better burglars in that area knew of Jesse, respected him for what he was. But still was surprised when he came in.

He was teamed up with two guys, Dean and Hoyt. Hoyt did the dropping off. Dean would go inside with Jesse, was his main partner. Dean was pretty decent but was losing heart, getting shaky. He would drink sometimes to build up his courage, but it was false courage. We went the next night. A hardware store that was attached to a lumber yard. Jesse and Hoyt had scouted the place. Drove right up to it. Hoyt dropped me and Jesse off. Broke open a side door, found the safe. I am watching the front door and Jesse is punching the safe. A couple of minutes, whew, he was done. We got like $3,200 which that time was split three ways. Later on, me and Jesse often chiseled the other guy.

Right off, we felt very comfortable with one another. The trust grew very quickly. Not just in terms of not snitching but knowing you could rely on the other one to do what needed to be done.[2] It would be hard to find a better partner than Jesse. Not just at opening safes, although he was known for that, but you could depend on him to handle his end of things in a lotta ways. With coming up with places to clip, with the scouting, with what to do afterwards, say, if things went wrong. Another thing, Jesse could handle himself if the police came looking. Knew what to say, be friendly with them, but not let them scare you or con you into revealing something. That is very important because a lotta guys will blurt something out, say something they regret later. Main thing, though, Jesse had lot of contacts—with the lawyers, with places to unload, with different ones for giving tips, and with your better thieves, too. He is good people, very good people.

Some jobs we pulled ourselves but usually we had a dropoff driver. Like a couple of times we were out scouting and the opportunity was there to pull the job right away. A few times Jesse or me had a tip and we'd know there was no need for a third guy. We'd park the car in a field or whatever, walk to the place and break in. One guy would go back to the car while the other waited with the cash and that. Get to the car and signal if the coast was clear. But ninety-nine out of a hundred burglaries you pull, it is best to have a dropoff driver, not let any cars around, 'cause that ties you in right away. Even a stolen car is bad to have around in case a cop is suspecting something, calls it in, it's all computerized now. Boom! Finds out it's a stolen car, and your ass is nailed.

Different ones were the dropoff. When I first hooked up with Jesse, it was Hoyt. Not much of a burglar, was really half-assed, but was solid. Could keep his mouth shut and was dependable to do what he was told. Was in his late twenties. Was on the edge of crime but not into it in a heavy way. Drove a delivery truck for the same company that Whitey worked for and that is how Jesse met him. Whitey at one time was a very good burglar but was getting too old to crawl into windows. Hoyt quit his job and went to work for us, you might say. Lasted a year, a little longer. Then, he got a girlfriend and was losing his heart for the burglaries 'cause we was hitting something fierce. She'd ask, where were you this weekend, where is the money coming from—on account he wasn't working. We kidded Hoyt about being pussy whipped but we were also sensing that he wanted to pack it in and there was some risk in his staying involved.

For a time after that, Jesse's brother dropped us off. The one who first recommended me to Jesse. But we didn't like the way he handled himself— too nervous and afterwards he would show off, throw his money around. We talked about it. Should we dump him? How should we handle it 'cause he was Jesse's brother. Then—this is funny. I don't know how it all happened, but he was involved in a burglary with some other guys, got shot at. Went chicken. Scared him into his fucking retirement. So Jesse and me was rid of him. So what does his brother do? Becomes a cop in a small town, maybe an hour's drive from American City. Then he starts giving us tips on places. Some cop he was.

Next thing, we get a tip on a safe, at a McDonalds. Jesse says, "Bernice will drop us off." I'm thinking, "What the motherfuck you talking about?" See, Bernice is Jesse's wife, and she is good people. Then I seen she had done it before, that she knew what she was doing. She was very dependable, you could put your faith in her, to drop you off and be back at the right time. If we're not there, then go to a spot and wait for us. That's what you want in a dropoff, is he dependable—that they don't fucking run away, leave you sitting there.

Bernice dropped us off quite a few times. Not all the time, now, 'cause Jesse didn't want her to know how much we was hitting. See, Jesse always had some pussy on the side and he needed money to take care of that. Then, we runs into trouble one night, couldn't meet Bernice at the pick-up. If we're not there at such a time, then she should wait in this field not too far away. So, she waits in this field, all night she waits. It was a pitch-black night and there are horses nearby, and a couple of them come up to the car and are going "brrrrhhh, brrrrhhh." Bernice is scared, very shook-up. Next morning she comes back, cusses me and Jesse 'cause she is still shook up. That was it with Bernice 'cause Jesse says: "I'm not going to put her through this anymore. We'll have to go shopping. Find another dropoff."

That's when we got Dwayne, a so-so burglar but solid. He was with us three, four years—until we got popped for the antique burglary. More so than the other dropoffs, Dwayne was a partner but not a full partner. Well, from his mind, yes, but in our eyes, no. Couple of times if it looked like an easy job and the coast was clear, we'd let Dwayne go inside and Jesse or me would be the dropoff. Dwayne was curious and he wanted to know what it was like. Wanted to keep him happy. But, no, normally, Jesse and me went inside.

Burglary Career in High Gear

Once we got rolling it is hard to believe how many burglaries we pulled, how many were on the entire list. First on, we was hitting safes—mostly for cash but also jewelry—and clipping for metals. Later on, we went for antiques. Are mixing all three. Jesse was known for metals—mainly nickel and copper but some bronze. Hit the safes for a while, than lay low and go for metals. Off and on, too, we're hitting houses, cabins, and vacation homes for jewelry and antiques—dolls, glassware, good silver, porcelain figurines, old coins, clocks, guns. Even hit a couple of antique shops.

We clipped metals mostly in the summer, mostly electric companies that would be putting in a substation. We'd load up the copper on a truck, all we could take. Run it to a quarry pit, dump gas on the copper, put sheet metal on top, lit it and burn off the coating. Once the insulation was burned off, we had No. 1 copper which was worth a good dollar. Take it to a foundry in Franklintown, one of Jesse's connections. Jewish guy. Very friendly, treated us fair. Weighed it, paid us cash right there. No hassles.

We also hit some foundries and the trains for nickel. Was a place near Franklintown that made nickel. Loaded it on a train car every Sunday night. Jesse knew the guy that switched the trains and we was paying him to get the nickel car on the one side long enough for us to fill up a small load. The nickel was usually in four-by-four bricks. It's very, very heavy. You had to work like a son-of-a-bitch 'cause you only had so much time. Was good money in nickel.

Very good. Some of our biggest scores came from nickel. Run it right into Franklintown, to the Jewish guy. You couldn't ask for a better outlet. Just call him, "Hey, we're on the way or we'll be there at such a time." The money was always there. So easy to work with.

All this time now, the burglary is changing for me and Jesse. We pretty much had quit safes altogether, except if we pulled a job way outside the area. Jesse wanted to pack in safes on account of all the heat from the state police. They knew we was hitting something fierce. We still clipped for copper or brass once in a while but mainly we was hitting houses, cabins, antique outlets—for antiques, glassware, silver, jewelry, guns, and that. These jobs were coming more from me on account I was dealing legit in antiques by this time, and I had the knowledge and the outlets to go with it. See, I was getting heavier into antiques, legit now. Was a dealer, you might say, and rapping with other dealers and from going to the auctions and different places, I would find out about places to clip.

In the meantime I am pulling some safe jobs without Jesse. By now I know the burglars in the area—from one guy introducing you to other guys and from the fencing, which I more and more am getting into. A couple of them, like Bowie or Steelbeams, came to me 'cause they needed help opening a safe. Bowie is now one of the best safecrackers around but he was very green then. I more or less coached him. This wasn't regular but off-and-on. If they had a good tip on a place, yeah, I'm available.

Burglary Skills and Pecking Order

By now I am getting to be a pretty decent burglar. No doubt. Before I hit American City, I would say I was a half-ass thief. That's my looking back. But when I was twenty-two, twenty-three, I didn't say I was half-assed. I probably thought I was pretty good, in a way I was pretty cocky and the guys I was pulling jobs with were even bigger assholes. In those days, knocking around with those guys after work, I didn't know nothing about good thieves. I was *green.* Not a rookie, but damn near. Terms like good thief, good people didn't mean a damn thing to me. We were more like *roughhouse.* More like raising hell. As thieves we weren't nothing but assholes. This I learned in prison, from hanging with the better thieves, and from watching all the assholes. I found out what an asshole thief is, and what a *good thief* is.

In my eye, a good thief is trustworthy, has heart, awareness, and luck. I think being brazen has a lot to do with it, too. Myself, I had no fear at all. No fear of the cops whatsoever. And I'm very brazen, say, about going into a place or just doing whatever needs to be done. This partly came from my being in prison, and from when I escaped from jail and was on the run, and just from doing the burglaries, too. I don't scare easy. In fact, I don't scare at all.

The good burglar has more contacts than the ordinary thief, too. A good thief always has the best lawyer. Like in American City, the good thieves had the top lawyers in town. Ones like Stanley Cohen and Walter Gleason, and Lenny Savelas. Same way with the guys in the local clique, had the best lawyers. Even more so.

Then have places to unload. Unless it's strictly cash you're taking. But even the guy going for cash is going to pick up good jewelry or even good antique pieces if that is what he comes across. Will need an outlet like the foundry guy or someone like Rosen for the jewelry. Or have a connection with an Angelo or a Louie [local mafia guys].

Something else, Jesse and me always got a lotta tips. From bartenders, insurance guys, different salespeople, contractors like someone who has a carpet cleaning business, even hairdressers and a few women who would hustle a guy and then give us the inside scope on what he had. Lotta tips from guys who more or less had packed in the burglary and now had jobs, like driving a delivery truck or doing maintenance work. Main one was the guy who broke Jesse in on burglary, Whitey. Had pretty much quit the burglary, then is driving a furniture delivery truck and would give us tips on places to clip.

We always got a lotta tips from lawyers. See, your lawyers handle a lot of wills. And many times they know the house and the people exceptionally well. It's too bad, really, that people trust a lawyer that way. We also got tips from mafia-connected guys, like Angelo and Louie. We got tips from some cops, and some auctioneers. Main one was Cooper, main auctioneer in the area. Did appraisals and that for a estate if somebody dies. We have known each other a long time. Is a pretty long list of different ones we got information from.

We would watch the newspapers for ads and that, too. To find out, say, if the Legion or VFW was having a dance or if a fire company was having a fundraiser. Maybe a carnival or a barbecue. Or, say, a business was having a grand opening. This would be a good time to hit, early the next morning, on account the place would have more cash and just waiting there, too. Usually over the weekend. The money would usually be in a safe that was really a tin can, it was so easy to get in. They wouldn't be taking it to the bank until Monday morning.

Next thing, we'd scout some of the places. Check out the vicinity. Maybe have lunch in that town, get a feel for the place. Many hours we spent just driving around, spotting and looking for places and then scouting and planning how we would clip the spot.

It would be like eating cake for us, it was so easy, if you had a good tip on a place. You can't imagine how nice it is, unless you went through it the other way. When someone can tell you, so and so is going on vacation for two weeks. Even knows that someone two doors down the street checks the place twice a day. And when you get in, the money or whatever is always there, where it's supposed to be. Now that makes you feel wonderful in itself.

And opening a safe is an excitement. As soon as you see the money, you feel wonderful. It's just like coming. Not that type of feeling, but a good feeling.

I don't know if you'd call Jesse a pro or not. In the newspaper and in the cops' eye, he'd be a professional. But not in my eye. No, 'cause that is not our way of talking but is a law enforcement word. Maybe hear that so and so is an "old pro." Or "we have a professional thing, we have a good skill." That's about it. Now, some of these kids, mostly asshole thieves is what it comes down to, might be talking and say so and so is a professional, or that they are professional. On account of they read that in the papers, see it on TV. But they wouldn't call themselves that around the better thief or the old timers. Is a cop word, mostly to build themselves up. Like, catch this guy and claim he's a professional thief and that. Shit, the guy's probably an asshole thief. Maybe way back, "professional" burglar and that was used. I can't say. Not in my lifetime.

All I can say about Jesse is that he knew his safes. That he was solid and had the connections, like with a good lawyer and with people for giving tips. A very good safeman. Actually anybody with any kind of knowledge can crack an old type safe, the old square boxes. They're easy to punch out or you can peel it. The old round ones, the niggerhead safes, that are set in concrete you can pretty much forget about. Same with the newer safes today, not the cheap ones that are really crackerboxes, but the ones that are better built—unless you know the combination or can work the dial, you're dead. Can drill or burn a safe but I never really got into that side of it, except have been with Bowie a few times. What I didn't know from prison about safes, I learned from Jesse and from doing it.

Techniques of Burglary and Roles in Burglary Crews

Being good at burglary? Different things are important. That you are good with your hands. That you have a good eye—a good eye for clipping. That you can plan—put together who will do what, what to do if this should happen, what to do afterwards. What tools will you need, that you can't leave any of those things behind. You want your main partner to have this knowledge, too, otherwise you have to compensate. But if there is a third or fourth guy along, no, it ain't necessary they have all of these. Except want to make sure the watcher, the lookout, can carry his end, to make sure everything is going all right.

It helps to be good with your hands. To have a knack for fixing things, maybe know something about wiring, about alarms, about getting into places, at working with locks. But then there is someone like Steelbeams, who couldn't pick up a screw and put it in. But he is very solid at breaking into safes and has a good eye for finding places. Even more so, for what to pick and what not to pick out once inside. Like he was put on earth for that.

You don't need that many tools, really. Many times for a house job, just a big screwdriver, bolt cutters, flashlight, and a pair of gloves will do. Maybe a hammer and a chisel or a punch if you're after a safe and it is too heavy to carry it out. Screwdriver is to break into the place, pop out the door, but often you can just kick in the window, turn the lock and you're in. Is as simple as that. Depends on what you are hitting. If the place is wired and it is a decent safe you're after, then may need to bring the works—drip pins, twelve-pound sledge, whatever.

You're not expecting too many safes when you hit a house. Unless you have a tip that has told you so. Lotta guys today like Rocky and Andy, even Steelbeams, will carry the safe out, open it later. That is why Rocky got a hernia, from carrying out a fucking safe. May take a hand truck along, just slide it underneath and wheel it out. A house usually has a two-by-two safe. Just a little thing you keep in your closet, to keep stash in. You can open it just like a can opener. You're talking about paper thin metal. After you get past that, what's inside is yours.

If you're hitting a business it is altogether different. You know there is going to be a safe in there and it won't be a two-by-two can. Many times it's going to be too big, you can't carry it out. Or it is set in concrete. You're going to have to take all your tools with you. You're thinking about the hammer, the crowbar, the tape, the chisels, the big drawbar.

If it's a tip job, you know exactly what you're getting yourself into. What kind of a safe it's exactly going to be. If it's going to be an eagle-head or a round-face sitting on the floor. Eagle-head is the old square safe. There are many different ones. The smaller they are, the easier to get into. Can carry them out but Jesse and me opened them right there. Most guys today I think just peel them. Peel them back. But Jesse and me would usually punch them. It is faster if you know what you are doing. The round-faces are a lot harder to get into. May have to use a torch—acetylene torch—and oxygen. Or drill it but that is something Jesse and me never did.

When Jesse and me was hitting, worried some but not that much about bugs and security systems. Now that is the first thing you check. If they have a box, a bell, you know the place is bugged. Usually on contacts, so when you go through the door or the windows, it will go off. The contacts usually aren't on the basement windows, so you go through one of them. If it is, now you go up two stories. Climb on top of the roof or get a ladder from the garage and get into a second-story window. You know damn well the contacts won't be there, unless they have a motion detector inside. But if it's going to be all that, you might as well skip it and hit another place.

It is possible sometimes to unhook, defuse the alarms. Especially if it is a tip job. Clip the wires, then nothing else can go off except the place may have a little "fuzz-buzz" they call it. When you get inside the house, it will go bz-z—z-z-z-z. It gives you thirty seconds like to get in and get out or if you can get to the switch, turn it off. Then you can go through the whole house with no problem. Or you can go on top of the house and snip the wires.

Most business places are wired today. Are tough to get into. But depends on what kind of a business, what they hold. If it's an insurance company, you know it's going to be a sensor or a beam. Same with jewelry stores. Are usually on at certain times. Has a clock alarm. Maybe goes on at 5:00 when they quit. Next morning they come in, click it back off. For a while you had some guys pulling stickups in the morning when the help showed up 'cause the alarm isn't on.

A lotta business places like McDonald's make nightly deposits now. Have alarm systems. I'm talking about sensors and a lot of beams and contacts on the safes. Contacts is two pieces of metal. Like two magnets together with wire running to a transformer box and it has an alarm system with a whistle or a big horn attached to the side of the wall. You can hear from the outside very well. Or it is a silent alarm, maybe goes to a Wells Fargo system. You don't know it's going off.

Beams aren't wired. It's like a flashlight beam. Sensors is a sound system. As soon as any sound happens in the building it would automatically set the sensor off. Goes into a computer bank at a Wells Fargo place and tells them that somebody's in the building that isn't supposed to be. Lotta places like drugstores have sound and eye beams, not just one but a whole bunch of beams. Now more places have cameras, video cameras. Don't know how you get around them but assume you can.

A big worry for a lot of burglars is dogs. Can be a headache if you let them. Myself I have no fear of dogs. Have a way with them really. Maybe take along some treats like caramel popcorn or beef sticks. But if need be, put him to sleep. Snap his neck or whatever. But a lot of burglars are afraid, will walk away if there is a dog, especially a Doberman or a Shepard. Jesse knew if there was a dog, it was my worry. Would be taken care of.

Burglars like Rocky and Steelbeams will hit houses or different places for antiques, silver, sterling, and go after jewelry and diamonds. Cash, too, that is a given. Bowie and Gordon would hit for that, too, but they can go for bonds, certificates, and stuff like that on account of their connections with the mafia, who can handle that. And can go for the better antiques and higher class paintings. Lotta their tips come from mafia people—to clip not just local places but more places outside the area.

They is today what Jesse and me was back then. Only more so. Bowie is the best safeman I know of. Learnt punching and peeling from me but has gone beyond that. Can do the torching or the drilling if he has to—which more and more is the case 'cause the safes are whole lot better today. May take longer but most safes can still be opened. Gordon handles the breaking in, takes care of the alarm systems, does more of the scouting.

Now Bowie has returned the favor, has gotten me to go along with him a few times when he has opened a safe for another crew. Said he felt more comfortable if I would be inside with him on account Gordie wasn't involved. There is a lot more to drilling or burning a safe than if you are only popping the rivets [peeling] or are punching it.

If the safe can be punched, that is usually the best. Is the quickest if you know what you are doing. One or two swings of the sledge [ten- to twenty-pound sledgehammer] and you have knocked off the dial. Then insert your center punch or your drip pins, to drive back the locking mechanism, to knock loose the tumblers—then click, you will hear the tumblers roll and fall to the bottom of the safe, and you can open the door. May only take a couple of minutes. But other times may take a while. But have to know what you are doing 'cause if you bend the dial or botch it in other ways, then you can't punch it.

Fewer burglars today know how to punch a safe. Mainly I guess because there are fewer old-timers to teach that and because the newer safes pretty much can't be punched. Will have a metal plate behind the dial to keep the punch from pushing through, or there will be device in the locking mechanism that keeps the tumblers from falling when you knock off the dial or pound on the center punch.

So you will have to peel it or drill it. Most safes you can still peel, in some ways even more so today on account of the cheap, import safes that people are buying. Are made of what is almost a plastic type material that you can dent with a hammer, it is so flimsy. Can protect what you have from a fire, but not much good as far as keeping a burglar from opening it. Are easy to peel. Or drill into one of the sides or even pound a screwdriver into a side, then work in a pry bar or whatever. More tear it apart than anything. Lotta guys will carry the imported safes out on account they are so light. Then take all the time you want to open it.

The cheap imports sure as hell aren't like the old Mosler safes.[3] That has always been a good safe. Diebolt is a good safe, Gardall makes a good safe. A Sentry safe is a crackerbox, cheaper made. What you'd like to come across. A safe will have a number, a rating, for how much fire it can stand or how hard it is to break into. Higher the number [e.g., TL15 is a pretty decent safe, a TL30 is a good safe], the longer it would take the decent burglar to peel or drill it. Can't punch the newer safes the way you could a lot of the older safes, and some of the newer safes are better built. Will have layers, say, of steel and copper. Will have to know what you are doing to penetrate them. But most of safes that are sold today are cheap crackerboxes, can break into them as easily as the old square boxes. And are lighter, so guys today usually just take them, something Jesse and me would seldom do.

If have to peel a Mosler safe, may take a long time and can be a lotta noise. Or you will have to drill it. Maybe do both. Peeling is hard work. Start with a chisel to make a crimp, or drill a hole, in the corner of the safe away from the door. Keep banging and working the chisel until you get a bite, a little opening. Then keep going along the seam and hammering with chisels to shear off the rivets. Once you get it started good and work in bigger chisels or maybe a crowbar, then "pop, pop, pop"—the rivets are breaking and you can hear them popping. Is a helluva good sound. The (steel) cover will peel back like a sardine can, except you are busting your ass a lot more. Next, you will have to break apart the "firebrick" that the safe is lined with to protect it from a fire. Is like a concrete insulation. This is messy, can take awhile. Finish that, and what's in the safe is yours.

Here is something else I learnt from Jesse. Check the safe handle first, see if it is unlocked. You'd be surprised at how many people use the safe but don't bother to turn the dial when they close the door. Another thing that came from Jesse was to turn the dial backwards very slowly and keeping pulling on the handle, very gently—in case the person that used the safe last didn't bother to turn the dial past zero. If that has happened, then every so often you will find the (safe) door isn't locked on account the locking mechanism inside hasn't been triggered. I'm not talking about what you see on television about somebody turning the dial and then he listens for clicks and that in the locking mechanism. Or seeing (on television) somebody using a doctor's stethoscope to do that. If there are safecrackers like that, I have not run across them.

If you hit a house, usually the jewelry is in the master bedroom. Look for a jewelry box, look through the closets. Check if they have a safe there. If they do, if it's carryable, take it along. You figure on some jobs it takes no more than five, six minutes to do a burglary. That's the max. Then get out. But other jobs there is no hurry. Take the whole evening if you need to.

With the crews today, usually you have a lookout or watcher, and two searchers. Maybe have a dropoff driver. The watcher usually stays inside because if he stays outside there is no way in hell you can hear him if anybody comes along. He's inside and looks outside the window to where they're going to park. Usually it will be the driveway, which you will know from seeing oil stains there. Check that out, find the best spot for watching. By that time, one of the searchers goes up and searches all the bedrooms, makes sure everything is clean, that nobody's in there, and then from there, the man gets his post and stays there until the job is done and the searchers come back out.

It is best if the crew has the same guys. But it many times don't happen that way. Depends on the job, how much is involved, how many guys do you need. Bowie and Gordon will have guys they pick from different crews or pick up a guy who is working alone or just has one partner. Maybe even bring in an ordinary joe blow who is solid and has a little larceny in him. Same as what me and Jesse would do when we was clipping. Sometimes another crew would contact me, they needed another guy. If I thought it looked okay, I would do that.

Rocky over the years has done that quite a bit. Doesn't have his own crew, even really a regular partner. But different ones will contact him to be a lookout or a dropoff, or maybe to help with the alarm system and that. On account of Rocky is pretty decent all-around.

In some ways, the watcher is the most difficult because he is responsible for two lives really. When you're searching, that's all you do is search. You don't worry about what's outside and who's outside. But in the long run, the searchers have to know what they are doing. Can't be missing anything. Because you never go back in the place twice. Never.

You really should have a dropoff driver but Andy and them sometimes have the watcher be the driver, too [Andy is a thief Sam bought from during his last period]. Stays in the car and watches from up the street. I have cautioned them on that. The driver is more an accessory. Not that important that he have a whole lot upstairs. Except that he show up at the right time. Someone like Bernice or Dwayne was just fine. You wouldn't want to take them inside but they were dependable to handle the drop off and pick you up at the right time.

Jesse and me always made it clear to the dropoff. Your job is, you do the driving. Get out of the area and keep clean. Don't worry about what is going on inside. Don't be driving by the place. Leave us alone until we get back to the appointed spot, or a back-up spot if there is any trouble. If you can't meet us there because the cops are around, meet us up here at two miles. If we're not there, head home and wait.

Main thing is to have a good partner—one guy in whom you have a good deal of trust, have faith in. A good partner is somebody who is solid and has the knowledge of burglary. It is even better, if he has some connections—with a fence or a good lawyer, or for getting tips. Then stick with that one partner and shop for the other guys when you need to pull a job.

It is best if the partners get along. But Bowie and Gordon don't really get along, personally. They would both bitch to me about the other one. Don't like each other. That is unusual. In my eye, they are both whiners and get on one another's nerves. Most burglary partners like each other, are comfortable with one another. Me and Jesse was. Normally, that is what you want.

If the guy is *green,* is a rookie, you have to bring him along gradual. Give him a small part. Check out how he does. Guide him. It is only natural he will want to do more, that he thinks he is better than he is. Even if he is an *in-betweener,* more *roughhouse* than good at what he does, will have to bring him along. If he is solid, that is the main thing.

Are rules, understandings, that burglars and thieves have, at least the better ones. Not to be a snitch is a main, main one. And don't be a blabber puss, running off the mouth, to your buddies or girlfriend about the clipping you are doing 'cause then the whole world will know. Settle things amongst yourselves, with your partner or the guys you're are working with. Don't be whining and carrying your grief to others. Are other understandings, too. One is that everybody on the job should get the same, except it don't always work that way. The main guys on a job will split it evenly amongst themselves but may chisel the dropoff or if somebody is not a regular but is just brought in for this job. Generally, you don't wanna break into a place if you know the people are there. This is common sense, you don't want to risk that there is now a witness who has seen your face. And what if the fucker has a gun and starts firing. Another understanding is, say, you come across another crew operating—then move on and let them be. It is first come, first served.

I'd say for most burglars—I mean the decent ones, if they come out with a couple of thousand or so, that would be satisfactory. From their point of view. Now, Bowie and Gordon, the amounts would be bigger. But, no, guys like Rocky or Andy or the oldest Beck boy, they are doing okay but are not getting rich. There will be some bigger hits, but lotta smaller ones too.

It is the big hits the thief will remember. Take Rocky, the one he likes to tell about is when they hit this wealthy home, on a tip from a contractor who gave the lay of the house. Six guys involved—one did the dropoff, two guys did the lookout, one guy took care of the alarm system, the other two went inside. Cash and a lotta jewelry. Couple of very nice diamonds. Carried out the safe with a handcart. Bing, bing—so many minutes to get in and get out. Several hundred thousand all together. Very big. But that was unusual. Rocky hasn't had that many big hits. But a thief will remember the big ones, play it over in his mind, and dream it can happen all over again. This you have heard Rocky tell—how when he got his cut, dumped the money on his bed, the bills, and laid on top of the bills. Shit, he makes it sound like he came he was so pleased with himself.

A burglary, actually doing it, is fairly simple. Might sound difficult but it really ain't. Can be a lot of work. A bitch, really, especially if the weather is nasty or things don't go right. Jesse and me went one time, it was snowing up to our ass. We got the safe, had to peel it and are sweating like a son of a bitch. Then out into the fucking cold and had to go across a couple of fields to get to the dropoff spot.

But it is afterwards that is the hardest part. Can you keep from blabbering. Can you handle the tension, say, if you get pulled in by the cops. Ninety-nine out of a hundred jobs, no one knows something unless someone tells them something. That was always Whitey's theory. Cops don't know anything until someone tells them.

Someone like Rocky is better now at the looking ahead, at the organizing part. At being able to see the things you should see and being prepared for the unforeseen. Just comes with time and experience. Still, when you do so many, the law of averages is there—that you will get careless when you shouldn't or the burglary takes a wrong turn on account anything can happen.

Popped for Antique Burglary

This part of my life I am a thief, and a pretty good thief. A good burglar, really. But I am always running my shops, had my businesses. I am getting to be a half-assed fence, too. And Jesse is pulling back. The first few years especially, after first settling in American City, I was a thief all the way. Then, the burglary is slowing down but the fencing and the legit side are both growing. My time is being split different ways.

Jesse and me had quit safes pretty much altogether. There was a lot of heat from the state police 'cause they knew we was hitting something fierce. Jesse in particular wanted to pack in the safes. If had a really good tip, then maybe we'd go. But mainly we are hitting houses, vacation homes, cabins, and antique places. For antiques, glassware, silver, good porcelain, coins. You name it. Then we gets popped for stealing antiques out of this rich lady's house. Me, Jesse, and Dwayne. Cleaned out the whole house—chandeliers and everything. Were at it from early in the morning into the evening. Took our lunch, our ice tea, and everything. We had to pay the lawyers something fierce but then we didn't get much time.

How it happened was, Jesse gets a tip from a main security place in town, that this couple was vacationing. Be out-of-town for a couple of weeks. They were private collectors who had good antiques in the house. So, we take my big truck, the twenty-two footer, and park it back in the hills. We take my little truck and made it look like we was carpenters or plumbers. We drive right up to the place—this is in the broad daylight, now. Break in, open up the garage door, and back the little truck in. Load up the little truck, then Jesse would drive to where the big truck is parked. He and Dwayne would unload. And Dwayne is staying with the big truck and watching it. I'm at the house, packing and getting all the stuff ready for the next loading. Figurines, glassware, and that stuff had to be wrapped and packed carefully. Chandeliers, doll set, dishes, just about everything.

My plan was to run the load up to Oceantown, to Scottie and some dealers I knew up there. But what happens is some guy is hunting in those hills and spots the big truck and gets suspicious. Calls the police. It's night now and Jesse and me are coming out with the big truck. We hits the main road and half a dozen cop cars sirened us in. It's the state police and they made a really big deal out of it. Handcuff us, walk me with a gun in my back, pictures in the paper. Big bullshit, you know, lotta show.

We was wanted in two counties. We did the burglary in one county, transported the stolen antiques and was caught in another county. With what the antiques were worth and the damage to the place, and with the owners and insurance company blowing it up, it was listed as a $250,000 job. Gleason and Cohen handled the case, and they also worked with two good lawyers in the other county. It cost me alone $24,000 'cause I had to pay off. Well, really more than that when you add everything like the bail and the court costs. And during this time while we're out on bail, we're pulling safe jobs to pay the lawyers. The lawyers done their job, I'll hand them that. Got it arranged to have us tried in only our home county where our lawyers knew the judge and the DA. The other county wanted to bury us. Dwayne and Jesse each got six months to a year. I got one and a half to three, on account of my record.

I ended up doing about fifteen months. At the Hartsford Penitentiary. The penitentiaries were beginning to change at that time but it was still pretty much the old type prison. Pretty bare bones. No TV in your cell like today, no shrinks doing the psychological bullshit. It was pretty easy time 'cause I knew I wouldn't be there that long. I skated by. The big change for me was now I'm an older con and the younger thieves are looking up to me on account of my being a safecracker and that I was known as good people.

Burglary Career Diminishes

After I got out of jail on the antique burglary, the fencing and running my legit shop were basically it. I am getting tired of crawling in windows but if Jesse hadn't quit, it might have been different. I can't say, but maybe I would not have gotten into the dealing so big.

Getting popped for the antique job made up Jesse's mind. Decided he was going to pack it in. Was already wanting to slow down and had pretty much quit safes. Now, pack in the burglary all the way. On account of our reputation, how known we were, it was time to go legit, was Jesse's thinking. One of Jesse's contacts knew the county supervisor and landed a job for Jesse. Very good job. With the county, as all-around maintenance guy. Jesse's mind was decided. No more clipping. We didn't discuss it no more.

But I am only blowing wind outta my ass. *Turns out, Jesse didn't pack it in.* This is something that is still hard for me to admit—Jesse admitting to you that for all these years he has been pulling jobs by himself, going it alone. Doesn't tell a soul. Not me, not Bernice. Only ones that knew were the ones he was getting tips from. Then he tells you.

After Jesse quit [or so Sam thought], I have never really clicked with another partner. The trust, the faith in the other guy, wasn't there like it should be.

Myself, I am staying more in the background. The only burglaries I did was mostly some safe jobs. How many I can't say. With a couple of pretty decent burglars who wanted me to open the safe or maybe just wanted me to tag along, to help with the planning. Maybe my tagging along was a security thing for them, that I was an old head who'd been through a lot. Off and on I'd give tips to burglars. To Bowie or Steelbeams, mainly. Sometimes I'd guide one of the younger guys like Mickey or Timmy. I would want a cut. It all depended on the job. We'd talk beforehand, then work it out after the job was pulled. Say, it was a safe but there was also a coin collection in the place. I'd say, you can have what's in the safe but I get the coin collection. If it was cash or jewelry, I'm gonna get 10, maybe 20 percent.

I was never that greedy. You can't be with the better thief. A so-so thief, yes, you will want a bigger cut. These past years—this is in Tylersville now—I would give tips to the Beck boys or to Andy, and I am shooting for a third or maybe a half. There is more risk on account they are half-assed and you will have to guide them. Most times I got at least a half, 'cause I would chisel them.

It would depend on my involvement. A couple of times I had someone knock off an antique place. This would involve my telling them the right time to clip it and what pieces I especially wanted. Drop the antiques at a dropoff place or take the truck to such and such a spot. A lotta detail 'cause I know the guy that owns the place, what he has. Have been in his shop. Then, too, I am picking up the antiques and running them to my connections. Lotta involvement on my part. It was more or less a fifty-fifty deal. I got half, they got half.

Other than the safe jobs, though, I pretty much had packed in doing the actual burglary. If a safe was carried out, yeh, I'd meet the guys and open it. It wasn't that I had lost my heart. But more that I would be spreading myself too thin. I didn't have the time to put into it, to do the scouting and the planning. On account I am getting busier with the fencing and my legit business was doing good. See, I was never just into burglary.

Notes

1. Other thieves' slang often used by Sam and Jesse include (in Sam's words): "*Score* is when you pull a job or how much you get from the job. *Spotting* is finding a job and may involve some casing. *Casing* is checking out a job, sizing it up, figuring out what you want to do both as far as clipping the place and then what to do afterwards. *Scouting* is spotting and casing both, some of each."
2. In *The Fence,* Jesse said this about meeting Sam and selecting him as a partner: "I was looking for a man, a guy I could trust. Sam was recommended to me. What happened was that the guy I was working with was pretty decent but was getting shaky. Losing his nerve. I wanted to get rid of him. . . . Looking back, this is fucking funny 'cause the first time I met him was in that damn little shop. . . . My brother knew Sam 'cause he had nutsed around with him a little. Said Sam was solid, which was the main thing for me. Then we talked about the jump we were going to do. . . . [I] seen he wasn't scared at all when we went into a place, and to me, that meant an awful lot. . . . Once him and me got together, why, you could really lay your faith in him. . . . I knew automatically he would do what had to be done" (p. 46).
3. Veteran burglars like Sam often mention Mosler safes (and Diebold). Mosler safes have been around a long time and have a reputation for being a well-built safe—i.e., as being more burglary- and fire-resistant than most other safes. The Mosler "Safe" Company stopped producing safes a couple of years ago, apparently because of strong competition from more cheaply produced "import" safes.

7

Commentary

Trading in Stolen Goods

Fencing, the crime of buying and reselling stolen goods, is one of the links that bind theft into the larger social system. Without someone to dispose of stolen goods, thieves would have to rely on their own connections, and the costs and risks of crime would increase substantially. For the rest of society, the fence provides an opportunity for interested people to buy something at less than market price.

As we noted in Chapter 3, fencing is a key form of illegal enterprise. It remains relatively neglected in criminology, probably for two reasons. First, it often wears the cloak of legitimate business and is carried out in a rational, businesslike manner, so that it has few of the qualities associated with street crime. Second, because fencing is a crime with low visibility that is conducted in secrecy, researchers have directed their attention to more visible crimes such as theft, drug trafficking, and violence.

Crime As Work and Business

Criminal and conventional domains are in many respects alike. The factors and processes that operate in one domain influence social behavior in the other domain. Concepts used to investigate the conventional world can also be employed to provide insight into its criminal counterpart, and vice versa. Similar to conventional occupations, for example, criminal work is stratified by prestige and stereotyped by gender and race. Whether in criminal or legitimate roles, all persons are subject to the influences and shaping of various work-related factors and contingencies. As is the case in criminal subcultures, a considerable amount of risk-taking is built into conventional business culture. Tastes for risk and risk taking are highly valued orientations of both the business and the criminal culture. The success or incomes of legal as well as illicit entrepreneurs depend on the scope of operations and the operator's skill at marketing. Both need people who can be trusted, remain loyal, keep secrets (or be discreet about what they say), and be on time and dependable. So, too, reputation and network ties enhance opportunities in illicit enterprise as they do in legitimate entrepreneurial settings. Also, one can develop commitments or acquire investments that bind one to either illegal or legal work, or vice versa.

A number of criminologists besides Sutherland have analyzed crime as work. Maurer, a linguistic scholar, focused on con men and pickpockets in *The American Confidence Man* (1974) and *The Whiz Mob* (1964). Polsky (1967) later wrote about pool hustlers and their work situation, Shover (1972, 1983, 1996) studied the skills and contacts of "good burglars," the careers of aging property offenders, and lifestyles and worldviews of ordinary thieves. Letkemann (1973) examined the work methods of robbers and safemen in *Crime as Work,* Prus and Sharper (1977) concentrated on the careers of professional card and dice hustlers in *Road Hustler,* and Conklin (1994) analyzed art thieves and dealers in *Art Crime.* Akerstrom (1985), in *Crooks and Squares,* described the work methods of types of thieves and drug addicts. Wright and Decker (1994) analyzed the decision-making processes of burglars regarding choice of target and other work-related roles. Adler (1993) examined the networking and business skills of upper-level drug dealers, and Klockars (*The Professional Fence,* 1974) and Steffensmeier (*The Fence*) further extended this type of analysis by examining the skills and work habits of professional fences or large-scale dealers in stolen goods. These are only a few of many other worthy examples we could cite.

All these studies emphasize the lifestyle and work habits of criminals as much or more than analyzing the reasons or motivations for their criminal activities. They address questions such as:

- What problems are faced by criminals, and what strategies do they use to solve them?
- What are the pros and cons of a criminal lifestyle in comparison with a more conventional one?
- What skills are involved in a criminal lifestyle?
- How are contacts made?
- What is the mix of rewards and motivations?
- How does aging affect crime skills and rewards?

Many of these studies also view illegal enterprise as a business activity having many parallels to legitimate enterprise. Planned theft, racketeering, running a bookmaking operation, and fencing stolen goods involve in many respects the same laws of supply and demand and the same fundamental assumptions that govern entrepreneurs in the legitimate marketplace. In this way, too, the same questions can be asked of both illegal enterprise and legal businesses (Haller 1990), for instance:

- What are the sources of capital for starting or expanding the operations?
- How are the goods or services advertised to customers?
- How are prices set?
- What financial arrangements exist between the entrepreneur and others who participate in the enterprise?
- What are the similarities and differences in running a legal as compared to an illicit business?

Indeed, the similarities appear sufficiently strong, as *Confessions* documents, that it is common for seasoned thieves, racketeers, and illicit entrepreneurs like Sam Goodman to view themselves as "businessmen," and to perceive little difference between their actions and the behavior of legitimate entrepreneurs.

Task Environment of Crime: Uniqueness of Criminal Enterprise

The semblance between legitimate and illegitimate businesses can be easily exaggerated, however, as can the parallels between criminal and conventional careers (see Lemert 1972; Steffensmeier 1983). To survive or do well in the world of crime entails dealing with at least two major threats. One is the threat of arrest and imprisonment, or other sanctioning actions by the authorities. The other is the threat from other criminals who may betray one another to social control agents, cheat in their dealings, attack one another, or take over the other's scams

The dangers posed by officials and by deviant associates or rivals profoundly alter the work environment to which the organization and culture of an illegal business must adapt. Depending on the permanence or size of the operation, illegal entrepreneurs or networks will seek to regulate their relations with other criminals on the one hand and to protect themselves from legal intervention on the other.

An important additional factor also shapes the running of an illegal operation. Illicit businesses typically adjoin or at least straddle the larger subculture of theft or the underworld more generally. Broadly, the underworld includes the culture, setting, or social organization associated with criminal activities and more general rule-violating behavior. The underworld is not necessarily set off from the legitimate world, but the two worlds are analytically and empirically distinct in their crime opportunities and practices.

Thus, although influenced by many of the same conditions that apply to legitimate businesses and legal markets, the work and business of crime differ in other important respects. What difference does it make that the enterprise is illegal, or that many illicit businesses have an underworld dimension to them?

In comparison to legal businesses, illegal entrepreneurs are handicapped in several important ways. First, they must establish safe, predictable relationships in a hazardous environment where there are special impediments to trust and communication. Because security or well-being is so jeopardized by officials or deviant associates, involvement in criminal enterprises creates a higher price for mistakes. Goffman writes: "What is special about criminal enterprise . . . is the narrowness of this reserve and hence the high price that must be paid for thoughtlessness and bad breaks" (1967:166).

Second, they must deal with the lack of court-enforceable contracts. Criminals lack many of the protections and institutional supports provided by the law, such as enforcing of rules and mediating of disputes. Third, illegal operators need to restrict knowledge of participation in the enterprise. For instance, partners and associates (including employees) can provide information leading to arrest, the seizure of assets, or the takeover of the enterprise by other criminal entrepreneurs. Fourth, they must deal with the lack of external credit markets. Financial transactions typically involve payments in cash; "deals" are frequently negotiated on a "pay later" basis. Credit (but not credit cards) is extended in many circumstances, including bail, lawyer fees, gambling debts, ripoffs, and sharing the proceeds of a "score." Fifth, the would-be illegal operator faces the problem of acquiring the skills and abilities needed to run a racket or illicit business. These are not available through conventional channels (at least not entirely), such as schools or books, but are mainly acquired through illicit and cumulative experience. Sixth, he faces the problem of gaining satisfaction from his work or business in the face of high risks and a hostile environment. The rewards of fencing or racketeering must compensate for time and effort as well as for sanctions and exploitation. Finally, the illegal operator encounters the problem of rationale—how to justify, make sense of, and refer to his/her particular world. That is, he must contend with the invidious moral evaluation and pejorative attributions "putting down" those engaged in illegal, immoral, and disapproved behavior.

The remainder of our treatment of fencing focuses first on types of dealers in stolen goods and then on key aspects of running a fencing business. Running a fencing business involves confronting a number of *economic* and *legal* obstacles or contingencies that handlers of stolen goods must cope with, such as connecting with thieves, perhaps other fences, and buyers, setting buying and selling prices, and a variety of tasks necessary for covering the fencing business from law enforcement attention.

Types of Fences and Stolen-Goods Handlers

Those who handle stolen property are a diverse group, ranging from professional criminals with ties to organized crime, to respected citizens such as businesspeople and lawyers. Building on prior writings on the trade in stolen goods (Colquhoun 1800; Hall 1952; Klockars 1974; Walsh 1977; Cromwell et al. 1996; Sutton 1998; Steffensmeier 1986, 1993), we can differentiate criminal receivers of stolen property and other buyers of stolen goods by (1) whether they deal directly with thieves, (2) the frequency with which they purchase stolen property, (3) the scale or volume of purchases of stolen property, (4) the purpose of purchase (for personal consumption or resale), and (5) the level of commitment to purchasing stolen property.

On the basis of Sam's narrative and these criteria, we distinguish below *four major groupings* of buyers of stolen goods that can be elaborated into ten more detailed types of buyers.

1. **Amateur or "joe citizen" buyers:** In Sam's words, this refers to the "ordinary joe blow who once in a while buys stolen goods to use himself or to peddle to one of his pals."
2. **Occasional or part-time dealers:** In Sam's words, the "in-between" dealer, the guy who buys off and on and then peddles it out of his store or maybe on the street or at an auction . . . is more a sideline thing."
3. **Professional fences:** In Sam's words, the "regular" or "bigger" dealer, whose buying and selling stolen goods is "a main part of what he does." (Professional fences overlap with so-called master fences, what Sam characterized as "referral" or "go-between" operators who do not deal directly with thieves but instead stay behind the scenes.)
4. **Online buyers and sellers:** Fencing stolen goods through Web sites has accompanied the rise in popularity of online auctions (like eBay.com) and is a fast-growing distribution path that emerged after Sam's passing. Indeed, one police investigation of online auctioning of stolen goods subsequently targeted several thieves and a secondhand dealer Sam dealt with.

Expanded Typology of "Criminal Receivers"

These four groupings can be further refined into a more complex differentiation of ten types of handlers of stolen goods. We include a variety of actors who buy or sell stolen goods in the typology below in order to reflect the complexity of fencing and the broader trade in stolen goods. It is worth noting that among thieves and the underworld more generally, the terms "fence," "dealer," "off-man" are usually used in a somewhat restricted sense to refer to buyers who deal directly with thieves and who also buy fairly regularly (i.e., they are *reliable* purchasers). Viewed as such, amateur fences, business buyers, and private buyers (while still legally liable) are arguably not bona fide fences in the sense that professional, referral, and proactive part-time fences are. Following Sam's descriptions, we consider only referral fences and professional fences, and to a lesser extent part-time fences who are proactive receivers (like Sam in his later career), to be "*true*" fences—which is why we put them in italics.

Professional fences are those whose principal enterprise and source of income is fencing. These receivers establish a reliable and persistent flow of merchandise, buy regularly, and on a large scale.

Referral or contact fences regularly and knowingly buy stolen goods from other fences and then resell them to other outlets, where the merchandise is then sold to the consuming public. These referral or contact fences thus do not deal directly with thieves. In a sense, referral fences are "the fence's fences," or "master fences." They are almost strictly "background operators." Referral fences often tend to be all-around criminal entrepreneurs or "racketeers," with extensive criminal networks. For them, fencing stolen goods is usually part of a larger criminal portfolio. They tend to have a high commitment to crime and quasi-legitimate activities, but they may not necessarily be highly committed to fencing (it may depend on the significance of fencing for their overall criminal portfolio). They are in contrast to other professional fences who buy directly from thieves, as Sam mostly did. In Sam's narratives, Angelo was a major referral fence.

Part-time fences/in-between dealers are those whose main livelihood is not fencing, and who do not buy as regularly as professional fences, nor in the same volume. Fencing is something at which they "moonlight." Part-time fences may vary in their level of commitment to fencing, but typically display less commitment than the professional fence. Furthermore, some part-time fences are *passive receivers* (those who do not actively seek or solicit stolen goods, but only buy when offered, and may often buy stolen goods for personal use) and some are *proactive receivers* (those who mimic professionals but on a smaller scale—actively seeking to buy stolen goods for resale only).

Associational fences are those whose legitimate occupations place them in close contact and interaction with thieves. Examples might include police, bail bondsmen, bartenders, or defense attorneys.

Neighborhood hustlers are those for whom fencing is one of several "hustles," or small-time criminal activities. They are often as apt to buy stolen goods for personal use as for resale.

Drug dealer fences barter drugs for stolen goods. In addition, other suppliers of illegal goods and services are also known to sometimes fence stolen goods (e.g., gambling operatives, pimps).

Amateurs or "joe citizen" buyers tend to exhibit the lowest level of commitment and experience in buying stolen goods. They tend to buy goods for personal use directly from thieves, or else to resell them to friends or acquaintances. Most commonly, amateur receivers have developed a relationship with a thief (a relationship that usually does not initially involve buying stolen goods) and may buy fairly regularly from them.

Private buyers are merchants or collectors who deal directly with thieves, but only with a small number of select or established thieves.

Merchant or business buyers do not deal directly with thieves, but buy stolen goods from other, perhaps more professional fences or referral/contact fences. For example, the merchants who bought from Sam and resold such goods to (probably unsuspecting) legitimate customers would fall in this category.

Online fencing: Since it opened in 1995, eBay has exploded into the world's most expansive online marketplace for the sale of goods and services by a diverse community of individuals and businesses. Today, the eBay community includes many millions of registered members all over the world. There are, of course, other property auction sites besides eBay. People come to these sites to buy and sell all kinds of items, from antiques, coins, and collectibles to cars and boats. The online auctioning of these items is appealing to individuals or organizations wanting good prices on hard to find goods and the convenience of shopping at home by computer. Meanwhile, the online auction is also an attractive marketplace for those interested in selling stolen or fake merchandise of nearly all types to interested buyers. While many of these buyers may not suspect the goods are stolen, others will purchase auction items preferring not to know and proceeding on the basis of "no questions asked."

Selling stolen goods online allows thieves and receivers of stolen property to reach a broader market and to dispose of stolen goods quickly. Relative to traditional paths for selling stolen goods, one risk is that it creates a paper trail that can be traced, since a user must be registered to buy or sell on eBay. To counter this, perpetrators may use public computers in libraries or Internet cafes to advertise stolen property, making it more difficult to track them down. The risk in large part is offset by the sheer amount of traffic. An online auction site like eBay.com has millions of items up for bid each day, which generate millions of dollars in daily sales. Not only do shoppers have little reason to suspect that a particular item up for bid was stolen, but with that amount of traffic, it is difficult, if not impossible, to police that much commerce. Within days or a few weeks, stolen property can be sold and shipped anywhere in the country, making recovery difficult.

Although this may change as law enforcement and prevention security better respond to this expanding form of cybercrime, the ease with which stolen property can be sold online provides an attractive criminal opportunity for a wide range of prospective offenders, including "ordinary joe citizen" thieves and regular thieves, as well as dealers and fences. In this sense, *online fencing overlaps and may be a facet of the other types delineated above.* While it likely will dent the volume of stolen goods handled in other distribution paths, it is unlikely to put local secondhand places and fences like Sam out of business.

In terms of this tenfold typology, at the height of his career Sam Goodman was obviously a professional fence (or what Sam sometimes called a "dealer" and what some thieves referred to as "my offman"). As we describe later, after he was released from prison for the last time and opened up his legitimate furniture shop, one could view Sam as a more or less proactive part-time fence.

Distribution Paths

There is no way of knowing at the present time which of these criminal receivers get what proportion of the traffic in stolen property. From Sam's narratives we learn that not all stolen goods are fenced: some thieves keep the goods or sell them directly. In other cases, thieves may peddle their stolen goods on the street, in bars, at flea markets, or online. Nevertheless, professional fences like Sam are probably the characteristic outlets for serious, i.e., "professional" or "good" thieves. They also are likely to be the major outlets for moderate to large quantities of merchandise (e.g., hijacked pallets or truckloads of food, cigarettes, or liquor) as well as low-quantity but high-value goods (e.g., gems, precious metals, high quality guns).

The various paths by which stolen property passes from thieves to eventual customers can be direct or indirect: direct, as when the thief sells stolen goods to an acquaintance or coworker; less direct, as when the thief sells the stolen merchandise to a dealer like Sam, who then resells the merchandise to customers in his store or to patrons of an auction he regularly attends; even less direct, as when Sam channels the stolen goods to local businessmen or to other fences, who then sell the stolen goods to consumers or perhaps channel them along additional distribution paths. In light of its growing prominence, we include online fencing as a distribution path.

A thief can do the following with the stolen goods:

- use them for himself
- trade them for legitimate goods
- trade them for other contraband (e.g., drugs)
- sell them directly (face-to-face) to others
- sell them online directly to others
- sell them to a go-between, who sells them to the public or to other go-betweens and middlemen

We diagram the different paths of the sale and distribution of stolen property from thieves to eventual customers in Figure 7.1. The paths by which Sam distributed stolen goods varied from relatively simple (thieves to Sam to public customers, auction patrons, or private collectors), to relatively com-

Figure 7.1
Common Distribution Paths for Stolen Property (——→ = **sells to**)

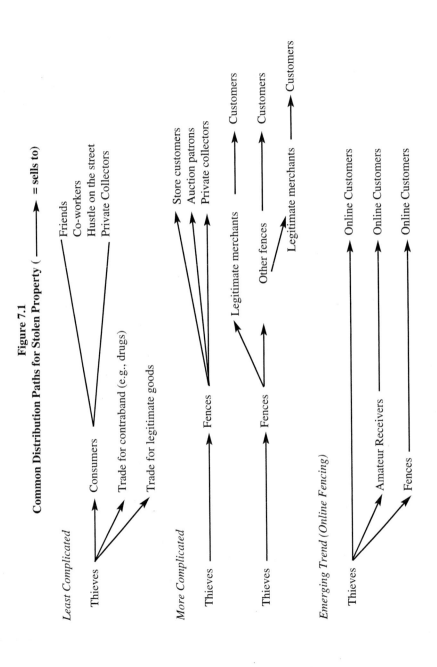

Least Complicated

Thieves ——→ Consumers ——→ Friends
                              Co-workers
                              Hustle on the street
                              Private Collectors

Thieves ——→ Trade for contraband (e.g., drugs)

Thieves ——→ Trade for legitimate goods

More Complicated

Thieves ——→ Fences ——→ Store customers
                        Auction patrons
                        Private collectors

Thieves ——→ Fences ——→ Legitimate merchants ——→ Customers

                        Other fences ——→ Customers

                        Legitimate merchants ——→ Customers

Emerging Trend (Online Fencing)

Thieves ——→ Online Customers

Thieves ——→ Amateur Receivers ——→ Online Customers

Thieves ——→ Fences ——→ Online Customers

plicated (thieves to Sam to one or two layers of intermediaries to public customers). Some of the more complicated paths involve Sam selling to legitimate business merchants, who then sell the goods to the public. Other paths involve Sam selling to wholesale buyers, who sell the goods to legitimate business merchants, who in turn sell them to the public. Still other paths lead from Sam to other fences, who may then resell the goods to their own public customers, or else to other merchants, who then sell them to public customers.

Other Distinctions

We can further refine our classification of "true fences," such as professional, referral, and proactive part-time fences, with other important distinctions. Fences can be distinguished according to the kind of cover they use to conceal their fencing, the scale of their fencing operation, and their relationship to the larger criminal community. In terms of these distinctions, Sam was a business fence, a partly covered fence, a generalist fence, and a fence with extensive ties to the criminal world (see the more detailed discussion in *The Fence,* Steffensmeier 1986:19–25).

First, all true fences are businesspeople: they are middlemen in criminal commerce. Most fences are also *business fences,* or proprietors or operators of legitimate businesses that provide a cover or front for the fencing. Businesses most advantageous for fencing are those that have a large cash flow, such as coin and gem shops, pawnshops, secondhand stores, auction houses, or bars and restaurants. The flexibility to set one's own hours is also an advantage. For some fences, the stolen-goods trade is central to their criminal portfolio, and their major source of income. For others, fencing is a lucrative sideline to their legitimate business, or just one of a number of criminal enterprises they are involved in. Sam was a business fence in that he bought and sold stolen goods under the auspices of his legitimate secondhand and antique shop (and later, furniture shop).

Second, fences can be distinguished by their *cover,* how closely the stolen goods resemble the legitimate goods they sell. In this way, fences can be *fully covered, partly covered,* or *uncovered.* Sam's fencing was *partly covered* by his legitimate business, rather than fully covered or uncovered (uncovered fences are probably rare among business fences). That is, the ordinary transactions, traffic, and merchandise of Sam's businesses provided partial cover for his fencing, but he also fenced some kinds of items for which his legitimate business provided little cover, such as guns, liquor, cigarettes, food, lawntractors, and computers. If Sam had been caught with ten cases of stolen whiskey, for example, it would have been very difficult for him to pass it off as legitimate merchandise he had acquired for his shop.

Third, fences also vary in *product specialization*. Generalists will buy and sell almost anything, whereas specialists handle only one or a few kinds of items (e.g., jewelry, guns, auto parts, food, liquor). Finally, Sam was a *generalist fence*. As Steffensmeier (ibid.:25) noted, Sam was a specializing fence early in his career, dealing mainly in antiques, silver or coins, and guns. However, in the thick of his fencing career, as well as during his later "moonlighting" period, Sam would buy or sell almost anything (one exception was clothing) if he felt it was safe and profitable to do so.

Finally, fences can be distinguished on the basis of *their relationship to the criminal and legitimate communities*. This dimension has two aspects. The first concerns how "public" the fence is. That is, how widely it is known among thieves, police, and others acquainted with the criminal community that one is a fence. Not only will thieves know about the fencing operation, but many customers will too, and because of bargain prices, the police will begin to suspect as well. Second, fences vary in how "respectable" their legitimate operations are, and their affinity with the criminal community. Some fences operate establishments that are seen by the larger community as "clean," others operate businesses that are seen as clean but somewhat suspect, and still others operate businesses that are widely seen as only quasi-legitimate. Furthermore, some fences are more disreputable than others, in that they come from thief of hustler backgrounds, or have a fairly extensive affinity with the underworld.

Although some commentators (e.g., Walsh 1977) have described the typical fence as essentially a "respectable businessman," the available evidence suggests otherwise. From what we surmise from Sam's narratives, the typical fence is probably characterized by one or more of the following: (1) prior criminal contact or background in criminal or quasi-legal activities; (2) operation of a quasi-legitimate business, and (3) some degree of affinity with the underworld. In fact, it is quite common for organized crime members and associates to be involved in fencing (Pennsylvania Crime Commission 1991).

Buying and Selling

As we noted earlier, criminal enterprise shares some similarities with legitimate enterprise, but exhibits some key differences as well. Fencing is similar to legitimate business in that both buyers and sellers of stolen goods are willing participants motivated by self-interest. When profits are unsatisfactory, the participants can negotiate to change the terms of exchange, or else quit dealing with each other. On the other hand, fencing is unlike legitimate business in that connecting with both sellers (thieves or other fences) and willing buyers (customers) is more problematic and fraught with risk. Both suppliers of stolen goods and fences can exploit each other, and also can inform on the other to law enforcement. These constraints mean that typical economic rationality does not fully fit the fence–stolen-goods supplier relationship. In legitimate business, price and profit are typically the major determinants of to whom one will sell one's goods—a businessperson will sell to whoever will pay the best price. However, ready money and reputation for trustworthiness and dependability, and perhaps constrained options, account more for the thief's choice of outlet than the price he or she receives alone.

The key to profitability in fencing is setting the price at which one buys from stolen-goods suppliers and the price at which one sells the goods, and a variety of considerations go into these determinations. The price paid to the thief will depend on factors that at least minimally include the following: (1) whether competing fences (if any) would pay a higher price; (2) the experience and skill level of the thief, which influences what the thief considers a fair price and his knowledge of the value of the goods; (3) the nature of the goods, the demand for them, and the hassles involved in storing or transporting them; and (4) the risks the thief took in stealing the goods.

On the other side, the fence is constrained by the need to sell at a price low enough so that potential buyers will buy. That is, potential buyers are unwilling to buy unless they believe they are getting the goods at a sufficient discount compared to legitimate outlets to warrant the risks of "buying warm." Of course, the fence's buying price from the thief and the selling price to the buyer are inextricably intertwined. In general, Sam would try for a 100 percent markup over the price paid to the thief. He might try to sell at an even higher price, depending on some of the same factors listed above in buying from thieves.

When dealing with thieves, the fence usually has the upper hand. That is, the fence's greater capacity to reward or punish the thief rather than vice versa means that the fence is usually the dominant trading partner. In addition, the fence is under no pressure to buy from the thief, whereas the thief is under real or perceived pressure to get rid of the stolen goods quickly. When fences buy from or sell to other fences, however, dealings are more equal. Fences will usually buy from or sell to each other at lower prices than they would thieves or the public.

In general, *normal economic dealing involved in legitimate commerce better characterizes fence–buyer than fence–thief transactions.* Thieves and drivers may know little about their products and may be under strong pressure to sell what they have. Those selling stolen goods will also be more choosy—selecting buyers on the basis of trust and loyalty rather than simply economic payoff. As long as the thief does okay financially (i.e., does not have to take too low a price), he will opt for a smaller profit for the sake of selling safely, particularly if in the past the fence has been a reliable market for the thief.

In contrast, those who buy from the fence—upfront store customers, auction patrons, antique dealers, wholesalers, retail merchants, and other fences—are able to buy the goods elsewhere and are able to shop around. They also will be much less concerned, if at all, about the fence's trustworthiness since his "middleman" role pretty much guarantees buyers that he will not jeopardize their freedom. Consequently, the fence's prices and dealings with those to whom he sells will bear considerable resemblance to conventional market descriptions, driven largely by market demand and the threat of competitive buying among his customers and buyers.

Covering One's Back

Whereas buying and selling stolen goods for a profit is at the economic core of running a fencing business, "covering one's back" to do so safely is at the legal core. To convict a person of receiving stolen goods, the prosecutor must prove (1) the receipt or control of the goods, by the individual in question; (2) that the goods were indeed stolen; and (3) that the individual knew the goods were stolen. These are the three legal requirements for successful prosecution of fences, and provide the legal context for a fence's "covering" activities as the fence manages the threats from law enforcement and from conventional society.

As mentioned earlier, Sam was a partly covered fence, meaning that the stolen goods he handled partly overlapped with or corresponded to the legitimate goods he sold. The fence who can "cover," or mesh and intermingle, his stolen goods with legitimate merchandise enjoys quite an advantage in avoiding prosecution. In fact, at the height of his career Sam adapted his legitimate business to roughly parallel his diversified trade in stolen goods.

In addition to his covering of stolen goods under the guise of legitimate businesses where the stolen goods did not look out of place with the legitimate merchandise, Sam used a variety of other techniques at one time or another, depending on the situation, to avoid prosecution including:

1. not asking explicit questions about the origins of goods;
2. being extra careful with goods known to be stolen locally;
3. telling thieves not to "clip" too often, thus attracting attention to the theft and the goods;
4. having "drops" or secure places to hide stolen goods (e.g., a concealed space under the floor in his American City shop, or an old abandoned railroad car);
5. moving/selling stolen goods as quickly as possible (while still making a profit);
6. creating vague or false receipts for goods; and finally,
7. gaining the complicity of law enforcement through outright corruption, giving bargains to police, or else occasionally helping to recover stolen property (as long as it did not involve snitching).

Beyond these covering devices, Sam deplores another way of gaining police immunity often relied on by large-scale fences like Louie—*snitching* or "turning in thieves" as a major strategy for acquiring a "license to steal."

That Sam achieved at least some immunity from prosecution during the time he was a fence in American City rested partly on the larger network of mutual favors, corruption, and exploitation characterizing American City's underworld and elements of its local criminal justice system. This network perpetuated itself through relationships of interdependence and mutual support, and mutual interest in covering up illegal activities. However, despite Sam's resourcefulness at "covering his back," as Sam (still smarting) recounts in Chapter 12, his "license to operate" was far from an absolute one, and he was convicted of receiving stolen goods. He attracted the attention of state (rather than local) police, and to some extent federal law enforcement. These agencies were not enmeshed in the local network of corruption, were eager to take down Sam and Louie, and had their sights on even "bigger fish" such as Angelo and Nicky.

In the next three chapters, we present Sam's narratives and our commentaries on fencing. In Chapter 8, Sam describes getting started, buying and selling stolen goods, and covering his fencing operation. Our commentary in Chapter 9 then discusses the conditions for successful fencing and the kinds of criminal capital needed by the would-be fence. Then Sam's narrative in Chapter 10 details the skills, character, and connections necessary for successful fencing. Our commentary in Chapter 11 addresses the shifting commitments Sam experienced in his criminal career after he "takes a fall" and does time in state prison for receiving stolen goods. His career enters a "moonlighting" phase, which his narrative in Chapter 12 details.

8

Sam's Narrative

Running a Fencing Business

Sam's Drift into Fencing

The fencing started small, then grew to where it got to be my main thing. Guys I knew—other burglars—are coming into my shop at first just to kill time. This goes way back to a year or two after I came to American City. Then this or that one started bringing antiques and guns to me, to see if I could get rid of them. These were pretty decent burglars who knew me from being in prison and from being hooked up with Jesse. Now, in the meantime, I am running to antique shows and to the auctions fairly regular, maybe two or three times a week. I would sell chairs, furniture and that, which I had upholstered. This led to meeting different antique dealers and different ones asking me to work on their antiques, repair them and doctor them up. It got to where I'm starting to buy and sell antiques with these dealers, and I'd mix in some of the stuff from my burglar buddies.

It is funny how this all started—in a way from renting this room when I first hit American City and upholstering those chairs from the rescue mission. Saw I could peddle them, so opened up my first shop. Which was a good front for the burglary, too. Later on I moved to a larger place and took on lamps, end tables, sofas, and other kinds of furniture. And the antique side keeps growing. I am learning more, feeling more comfortable with what they are worth. Eventually I am operating a used furniture and secondhand shop that would handle almost any goddamn thing. Hire a woman looking for work or have somebody like Chubby mind the store and wait on customers. That way I was free to come and go. But I still spent a lot of time at the shop—mostly working in the back 'cause that's where you'd find me if I wasn't scouting or clipping with Jesse, or if I wasn't running to the auctions.

Jesse and Louie were the two main contacts that helped get the ball rolling in American City. Jesse with the burglary, Louie with the fencing. Both had heard of me, that I was solid. See, the name carries, from prison and that. You might say my name hit American City first, before I did.

There's like *three periods with the fencing*. The *first period* was in the sixties, right before Jesse and me got popped for the antique burglary. I was rolling pretty good in the fencing, but nothing like later on. The first period I am pretty careful who I bought from. Mostly I am buying from the better thieves and I pretty much stayed with guns, coins, antiques. Small pieces, mostly—like figurines, cut glass, porcelain dolls. I was more into burglary than fencing. I was leery of dealing, and I was learning. Let me tell you, it's a helluva education.

The *second period* is after I did the bit for the antique burglary. Then the fencing really takes off. It becomes a main thing for me. I'm in all the way. Guys pushing on me, but I'm pulling, too. Really, I am buying anything and just about from anybody. Even doper thieves and asshole thieves. It is very wide open. Most things I was covered on but on a lotta stuff I wasn't covered. If you brought me shit wrapped in paper, and I thought I could make a buck, I'd buy. More or less thought I had a license to steal.

Then I got popped for dealing stolen goods and ended up at the Midstate Penitentiary. Where I met you. That was my last fall. Some close calls but was the last time I did time.

The *third period* is the last twelve to fifteen years, after I get out of the Midstate Penitentiary. First on I settled in Boonesboro and set up shop there. Then I moved to a bigger place in Tylersville. I did buy warm stuff and peddle it. But not like the way I was before. This time [in Tylersville vs. American City] it was off and on. Nickel and dime, really. It never got to be big thing.

What is a "Fence"

In the cop's eye—yes, I was a fence this last period. On account of I am dealing in hot goods. But not in my eye. To me, the dealing has to be more an all-the-time thing [to say someone is a "fence"], that one is doing it regular and is making a good dollar. May lay low if the heat is on but otherwise it has to be more than off and on, more than just the nickel and dime stuff. Say, a couple of your students are stealing computers from the college—you buy them, peddle them to your daughter and her friends. That don't make you a fence. The cops are very loose with that term.

Calvary Harry, you know about him. I always get a kick out of telling this. It shows what I mean about cops thinking everyone who touches warm stuff is a fence. In the cop's eye he was a big fence, but they are only blowing wind outta their ass. Harry wound up with a bunch of World War II guns one time that were hot as hell. Harry wasn't a fence at all. He was just a half-assed hustler and gambler. He got the guns from a couple of guys in a crap game who ran short of money and unloaded the guns on Harry. Remember, they're hot as hell. Harry stores them in an old garage. Meantime, the cops find out about this, on account of the whole fucking world knows about it. They confiscate the guns, but couldn't pin it on Harry. But he got taken so fucking bad on them guns he got the name, "Calvary Harry." He was the laughingstock of the town. The cops always thought Harry was this big fence. He was a fucking joke. That was about the only hot stuff he ever bought and he couldn't unload it.

A lotta guys that run secondhand shops will buy off and on, when the coast is clear. That is mainly what I did this last period. I'm pissing around but not taking a full leak. Off and on the fencing might shoot up, but mostly it was smalltime. Geez, nothing like before—I had burglars then that were bringing in stuff every week. Guys driving truck or working on the docks knew I would pretty much handle whatever they brought.

The same with a guy who runs a store, legit now, but he buys from a dealer like me—who is buying direct from the thieves. He is keeping a layer between himself and the thief, so the chances of hassles with the police are small. And he doesn't have to put up with the thieves. To me, this store guy is a business-man looking for an easy buck. Nothing more than that. He ain't a fence.

That don't mean you always have to deal direct with the thieves, with the ones stealing the stuff. Someone like an Angelo in American City or an Amato here in Tylersville will deal with regular fences, like with me. If I came across cigarettes, liquor, guns—I would contact Angelo and he would tell me where to drop it. A person on that end would take care of it. A few times Angelo would have the guy contact me to make the arrangements. Angelo's hands would never touch it. He had the connections for unloading. Or he might deal with a good thief like Jesse or Bowie. But always stay in the background. This was a regular way for Angelo, to be the contact man, the go-between. More or less be the referral.

In my eye Angelo is a fence 'cause this is pretty regular and is on a pretty big scale. Ain't nickel and dime shit. But normally a fence is someone who is dealing direct with the thieves. I guess you could call someone like an Angelo *a "go-between" or a "referral" fence,* but no, I don't think I've heard those terms used.

A main thing is, can the thief depend on you to take whatever it is you are handling? Can he count on unloading what he steals? Someone like Rosen—if you're hooked up with him and bring him jewelry, he will buy. Same with the foundry guy. Jesse and me would bring him copper or nickel, he would buy. Louie was pretty wide open—not just the thieves he regularly dealt with but many times he would buy from the walk-in trade. And whatever they were bring-ing in. Silas, Ben Silas, is Lebanese or something like that. Big operator here in Tylersville. Is a big fence. He can handle truckloads, he is that big. If you're tied up with him, he is an outlet you can depend on. That is what the thief means when he says so-and-so is my "offman," that he can unload what he steals.

I don't know what you'd call someone like Willie, Willie Swopes. Is the main pimp in Tylersville. Is a piece of work. Has like five or six brothers, a couple of sisters. Part of a black family that is well-known for being into different things. Willie's uncles were involved at one time. The one is still alive. Willie is the main one now. Will buy warm stuff and pretty regular, too. Doesn't have the good outlets, so peddles the stuff in the bars or right on the street—mostly to the ordinary joe blow. May peddle to dealers like me if we'll buy or maybe even go to someone like Silas. In my eye, ones like Willie are more hustlers than anything 'cause they're dealing in dope and in girls, too, and other hustling bullshit. That is their main thing, the fencing is just sideline.

It's hard to be fence and not be known to the police. Maybe if you just buy from a handful of thieves, not many will know. But if you're at all wide open, the police will know. This or that thief is gonna give them a name—"Tell us where you're unloading the stuff, and we'll let you go." Myself, it was very widely known I was buying hot things back in American City. But not this last period. A couple of cops may have had an inkling but, no, it really wasn't known that I was dealing. The cops are seeing me as similar to most secondhand dealers or pawnshop guys, as somebody who may buy warm stuff off and on but not regular.

The fences I've known in my life were more or less like me. Not that they were into burglary at one time or that they had done time. A lot of them haven't done time, or very little time. But they were shady in one way or another. If not into crime, on the edge of it. Most will own a legit business. Would be hard to be fence and not have the legit side. 'Cause if you're handling much stuff, your chances of getting popped and the charges sticking are more, whole lot more, without that cover.

It goes both ways—the legit helps the fencing, and vice versa. The two go hand in hand. Your equipment, your trucks, the guys working for you, the warehouse. Your overhead expenses, really. Like the trucks and the storage I had with the legit business helped to make the fencing go. And the contacts—the contacts from one can help the other. The money you are making from one can help build the other side. It would be hard to be a fence and not have the legit side. It's covering your back, but more that.

What it comes down to [being a fence means]—there is turnover, there is doing it regular. There is dealing with the thief, there is dealing with the guy who is an outlet, and dealing with the cops. The dealing in warm stuff is a main part of what the guy is about. Hustling and making contacts, and dealing with people from all walks of life, not just the illegit side. Before in American City, yes, I was a fence, a dealer all the way.

Getting Started in Fencing

I just fell into fencing, you might say. See, I was never just into burglary. I was always working, too. Running my shop. The shop at first was a front for the burglary, but still was doing okay. I always hired somebody to look after the store, and I was free to come and go. But I spent a lot of time in the store when I wasn't clipping or scouting or running to auctions.

A big boost came from Brubaker, local guy who was very big in antiques. I am running to the auctions and elsewhere to find old chairs and sofas—to recover and doctor them up. Sell them in my shop or peddle them at this or that auction or even at some antique shows. Brubaker sees my work 'cause by now I am moving into other furniture pieces like old chests and kitchen tables. He buys a rolltop desk I'd done repairs on. Then asks if I would do his antiques. Now other dealers are seeing my work, that I was good at repairing, at doctoring antiques. This led to my buying and selling antiques with these dealers, and I'd mix in some of the warm stuff from my burglar buddies.

But Scottie was my first really big contact as far as the fencing goes. Contact came from Brubaker, who recommended my work to Scottie. Very big second-hand dealer from Oceantown [a large city several hours away]. Lived in American City at one time and now comes back to buy and sell with the local dealers. We hit it off. He knew about my background and I am knowing from the grapevine that Scottie was on the shady side. Two peas in a pod. Scottie is legit but pretty heavy into the fencing too. First on, he's bringing antiques to me that are warm—antique furniture, sofas, chairs, rolltop desks—to upholster and to doctor up so they'd sell better. And to cover his back. He tells me, "If you run into anything, Sam, pick it up and ship it on up to me." So I said, "Solid." Now I could buy more and different things. I could buy local stuff that was warm and sell it out of the area. Meant, too, Jesse and I had another outlet if I came across good antiques or if I got a tip on place that was waiting to be cleaned out.

Louie was the main fence in town at that time. Really, he was into a lot of things—gambling, shylock loans, a big used-car dealership, and was a slum landlord. Off and on, he'd run a flea market. He was very well connected. Not a member of the mafia but ties with them. He was my main outlet for stolen goods until I got rolling. Louie and me palled a lot yet we was always trying to outdo each other, too. Louie put me in touch with a lot of people, especially the local clique that more or less ran American City. Being hooked up with Jesse and palling with Louie put out the message that one could do business with Goodman.

The other big fence was Angelo, whose old man, Mario, was very high up in the mafia. Angelo was a big spoke. Angelo was big, very big in the "rackets"— that is your [Steffensmeier's] term now—until he got popped a couple of years ago. Angelo had a helluva spider web, could put in you touch with a lotta different people. As a favor for you but then you owe him back.

The other two main fences were Ray Weinstein, a Jew tied up with the Jew mob and the Italians. At that time, the Italians and Jews worked together more. Still do, but not as much. Weinstein dealt with the better thieves. Then Weinstein packs it in and Rosen becomes a main one, especially for the jewelry.

Rosen and his dad had a lot of connections with the police and the good lawyers, and with the Italians. Dealt with the better thieves or with dealers like me.

There were other big spokes—Phil and Grasso. Cooper, the auctioneer guy. And Woody later on 'cause he had a big auction house in Southstate where I could unload almost anything. Duggan was a big help, who was a helluva corrupt cop. Would be quite a few that could make the list. But Angelo, Louie, and Jesse were the biggest. You need a few good spokes to get the wheel rolling. To get a decent spider web. Then can lose a spoke here and there but no big deal.

All the time now I'm getting a helluva education, from dealing with Scottie and the other dealers, from palling with Louie, and just from running to the auctions. I always thought I had a head for business and getting over on somebody but now I am seeing for myself and getting the confidence I can handle whatever needs to be done.

The big change in the fencing comes when I get out of the penitentiary for the antique burglary with Jesse. Before that, the fencing is building and building but in a way I am holding back. The burglary and my legit business are what I'm mainly into.

Is still hard for me to believe how the fencing takes off. For one thing, Jesse decided to pack it in—get out of the burglary altogether. And in some ways I am thinking, too, that I am getting too old for crawling in windows. Maybe it's time to have somebody crawl in windows for me.

Another thing, the local clique in American City is more and more opening its doors. I am pulling but in many ways they are pushing on me. Angelo and me is doing a lot of business. He doesn't want to be out front anymore, so I'm handling the warm stuff for him. I would deal with the thieves or whomever and have the stuff taken to such and such a place. I am a layer in between 'cause Angelo wants to stay in the background. A lot of Angelo's connections came from his old man who was in the mafia. I mean really "in." Angelo was always someone I could go to if I needed a contact or for quick cash if I was short.

The local clique was a clique of guys who each has his fingers into something. Like a gambling club. Get together to play cards and craps every week or so. You have to be invited in. Nicky Moretti was the main organizer. Was mafia, always came with a bodyguard. Charlie Ciletti came, Angelo, Phil, and that whole crew. Different businessmen would be there. The two main pimps in town, Stokes and Cain, were usually there. Would blow their money and run out, round up their girls, come back in, and blow their money again.

Another strange one was Jerry Gucci. Ran the vending machine business in town, big drug dealer, too. Jerry wasn't in the mafia really, but was connected with them. He'd show up, say, at 9:00. Then it was bang, bang, a couple hundred bucks a roll. Go around the table once, maybe twice, then he'd leave. If he won, he won, if he lost, fuck it. He did it quick. We all got a kick out of that.

For a crap game there would be as many as thirty or forty guys, but sometimes they'd bring in fresh money from the outside, say a salesman or a businessman that was visiting town. We'd start around 7:00 and if it was poker, there were times some of us played till morning. It was a friendly game but we wanted to beat each other. It was a way of relaxing for me and finding out what was going on. Just by listening and watching you could get a good notion of what was going on. It more or less put me in touch with a lotta people and helped me get hooked up with the police, too.

In my eye, the local clique and different ones have more confidence in me. On account of me doing very little time for the antique burglary. With my record and then "bang," I'm back on the streets. That, and nobody went down with us. Knew I was solid but even more they are feeling they can do business with me. That I could handle my end of things.

The fencing just goes "swoosh." It gets to where I am buying from anybody and everybody. Carried it too far. Was getting careless. Too many people knew my business. I got too greedy. It got harder and harder to walk away from a deal. I got to liking being the center of things, people knowing who I was, coming to me for deals—the local clique, the better thieves, this or that businessman. Even some of the local cops were coming to my shop for good deals. I thought I couldn't be touched, that I had a license to steal.

Buying Stolen Goods

My bread and butter was always the in-between thief, between the good burglar and the walk-in thief. Off and on I might buy from the penny-ante thief or a doper thief but I was leery and didn't want the hassle that comes from dealing with them. The good thief was my preference and there was always some of that but they have other outlets. I seldom—very seldom—bought from kids.

I always did a lotta business with this or that guy that works in a store, in a warehouse, or drives a truck—who clips off and on. This is a surprise to the public 'cause in their eye a "thief" is the shoplifter or the burglar or the doper thief.

Here's another thing, quite a few times I have bought from your ordinary joe blow. Isn't really a thief, but runs out of money and clips somebody he knows. His girlfriend or his neighbor or somebody he pals with. Checks me out to unload. Not just guys now 'cause I've had women come into my shop wanting to sell furniture or jewelry that's in their apartment. Turns out they are living with a guy and want to split.

In fencing the general rule is, the thief gets paid on the spot. Then and there. But there's a lotta leeway. I usually paid the thief right away. But many times

I would pay them after I unloaded, especially this last period and especially with the Beck brothers. It all depended on who I was dealing with. If the thief has faith in you, he'll wait.

I always carried a lot of cash in my pocket but if it was something half-big, I would need a little time to raise the money and I didn't want to be empty-handed in case another deal came my way. So, I would tell the guy, here's what I'll pay but I got to unload it first or I need a little time to get the money. Many times a regular thief would call ahead if he has items that are worth a good dollar. That way, I have an idea of the dollar amount and will have the bread there for him. Or, I'd say, "Hey, I'm a little low on cash—give you so much now, come back tomorrow for the rest." This is not a big deal for many of your thieves, especially the better ones and the ones you're dealing with regular. You work things out. With the walk-in thief, yes, he'll more want his money then and there, and you will want to pay on the spot 'cause the amount will be small and you don't want the hassle of his coming back for his money.

It worked the same way when Jesse and I was clipping. The foundry guy that was our outlet for the copper or nickel was loaded, full of money. But a couple of times he didn't have the money. Come back a day or so later and the money would be there. We had no problem with that. Knew his word was good. Oftentimes we called ahead, just to give him an idea of what he'd need. That way you didn't have to make another trip 'cause we're talking about three-hour drive. Same with the jewelry guy and other ones, too, that we were doing business with fairly regular. There was no big rush if they were short of cash. But, say, we unloaded with a guy we didn't know or we were a little shaky about, no, then we had to have our money right away.

Is a lotta bullshit you hear from the cops, and you see this on TV—that the fence pays the thief 10 percent of retail, maybe less. The thief isn't going to steal for nothing. Say a thief steals three CD players, that is each retailed at two hundred dollars or six hundred dollars all together. He steals them, lugs them over, does all that and you pay him only sixty dollars? Maybe a doper thief would do that but a half decent thief? No way.

The ordinary thief is figuring like one-third of retail. Not that he gets it, but that's his rule of thumb. Whereas the good thief is thinking about wholesale or about a percentage. That he should get half of wholesale or half of what the fence can unload the stuff for. Thereabouts. The fence wants to double his money or triple it. Or, at least make a decent dollar.

There's a range in there that has to be worked out. Depends on what the merchandise is. Say it is a carat diamond. You tell me you want four thousand dollars for it, that's what you have to have. There ain't no flaws, no bubbles, no carbon, no nothing in it. If I am unsure what I can get, then I will want to bid low. But many times I would say, OK, leave it here, give me a day to see if I can peddle it. I would contact Rosen, see what he will pay. If I can get six thousand dollars, I might pay four thousand dollars. I want to make 50 percent or thereabouts. Now Rosen knows he can sell it for ten to twelve thousand dollars. Is a good profit for him—no record, no paying Uncle Sam. If someone like Steelbeams or Andy or Rocky went direct to Rosen and he was willing to deal with them, they are going to get more than what I'd pay. But still not that much more. On account of Rosen can buy the jewelry legit at a big discount and he will want to have a layer in between, which is where I would fit in.

The fence is gonna get it as cheap as he can so he can make more money, same as any businessman, but not be too greedy. Most thieves are not hard to satisfy. The better thief, yes. It's more a business for him. But your ordinary thief has nothing but his time invested. He don't wanna be caught peddling the stuff, does not want to shop around. But you got to be fair, can't cut off the hand that is feeding you. My rule of thumb is to get it as cheap as I can but not beat the thief too bad. I am paying a fair price, in his eye. Am an okay guy.

Really, there ain't no set rules for how much the fence will pay. Different things have to be figured in. What is the risk factor? How sure am I of my outlets? Does the thief know what he has? Can he peddle elsewhere? Do you want to do business with the thief again? What will keep him happy? How much hassle, how much work is there for me?

Most thieves are pretty sharp about prices and pretty much know what they have. Even your dopers and walk-in thieves will have a ballpark idea, just by checking the store prices and what they hear from street talk. Depends on what they have. The ordinary thief don't know shit about the secondhand stuff and the antiques, so you can chop the price down on that. Same with jewelry—the knowledge the ordinary thief has is very superficial.

Take watches, if your ordinary burglar is grabbing jewelry, he may pick up a handful of watches. Chances are he doesn't know what they are worth. Most of the time, they will be junk, penny ante. But, say, it's a pocket watch that has an open dial face or is a hunting style with a covered dial face. A good watch like that is worth a hundred to two hundred dollars. Or take what is called the Dollar Watch. These go back fifty to seventy-five years when they were produced, at one time could be bought new for a couple bucks or even less. Today these are worth a hundred, couple hundred bucks depending on how many jewels it has. Another is the old Railroad Watches that can go back eighty, ninety years. They will bring a very good dollar today. It will depend on the engraving, how many jewels it has, what shape it is in—but pocket watches can bring a pretty good price. Your ordinary thief don't know that, so you can beat him bad and in his eye you are still treating him right. So, I'd say, here, I'll give you so much for the jewelry—say, five hundred dollars. Here's another fifty dollars for those fucking watches. Next time he comes in, I might throw another fifty his way—to keep on his good side and encourage him to clip more of them.

I would usually want the thief, the ordinary thief, to tell me what he thinks he should be paid, what he has to have. That way I will know if they know what they have, what they think is a fair price. If the price is okay, we can deal. If not, and we can't work it out, he has to peddle elsewhere. If he's a regular thief, I might say: "Okay, let me unload, see what I can get." If my price is off too far, then throw them a few extra bucks. They were happy with that.

With the better thief, you don't play the head games. The bargaining is mainly with the ordinary thief. Even on antiques, the good thief will have a working knowledge of what they're worth. You will pay him a fair price to begin with. If he don't want to set a price, you will make an offer. I didn't mind paying a fair price, especially if a man knew what he had. I respected that.

Most of your thieves can be reasoned with. Once you explain how you got to ship it out, how there has to be a cut for the next guy, and all that, most of your thieves will take that into account. Same with the warehouse thief and truck driver, once they get it through their heads how the fencing works, there is very little haggling about prices. Really, I had very few hassles about prices. My thing was, don't cut off the hand that is feeding you. I would always come across as pretty decent guy.

A lot depends on who I'm doing business with. Does he know what he's got, do I want to keep him in my pocket, how much hassle is there for me. Actually, I was the cheapest on prices I paid the thief this last period. I wasn't thinking so much about keeping the thief in my pocket. Another thing, I didn't have the places to unload. Nothing like before. Phew, it is hard to believe all the shit I was buying then 'cause I knew if I made enough calls I could unload the stuff. So back then I'm going overboard, catering more to the thief, just to keep him in my pocket.

Take the Beck boys this time, and some other ones too. I would chop them pretty bad, especially on antiques and even jewelry 'cause many times they didn't know what they had. Not in their eyes now—they are still thinking that I am paying a fair price. I didn't go for finagling. Well, maybe a little, 'cause that is part of the enjoyment—for me and many times for the thief. They expected that, otherwise would think Goodman was getting soft. But mainly, if I could make a buck and not have any hassles, then, yeah, here's what I can pay. I didn't put up with the bullshit like I might have before. I didn't wanna hear any fucking whining or crying about what I'm paying 'cause then you and I can't do business anymore. The fencing wasn't a main thing this last period, so I could take it or leave it.

Really, my aim has always been to make a good dollar, and make it quick. From going to the auctions and knowing what this or that outlet would pay, I pretty much knew what I could get on something. Sometimes I would double or triple my money, but other times the percent would only be 50 percent or less. My cut was not that important. As long as there wasn't much work or hassle on my part, I might buy even if I'm pocketing only a few hundred bucks. Now, if there is hassle or much risk on my part, then my edge will have to go up.

With someone like Angelo, my cut was like 25 percent. I was happy with that 'cause, say, it is liquor—I'm still making three or four grand and very few hassles on my part. Call him up, "I've got such and such." Would park my truck at this or that spot. His boys would unload it, take it from there. Go back and get my truck. Very little work on my part. Settle up later. Angelo pays me, I pay the thieves or the drivers that peddled it to me.

This goes way back. Bought a load of whiskey from Bowie and his partner, Rudy. Bowie was just getting into safes but mostly was into heavy stuff. Bulk. Take the whole truck. I gets this call. "Hey, Sam, we got a load for you." From a whiskey factory. Drove off with the truck, a 16-footer. Took my two trucks—Chubby is driving one, I am driving the other. Put the cases right on my trucks. In touch with Angelo right away. Met his boys and they took the whole shebang. At that time, Angelo owned the Friday Club, a bar room. The rest of the cases I am guessing he peddled to other nightspots in town. I gave Bowie five thousand in cash and five thousand more the next day. I think I got twenty-two thousand from Angelo, so doubled my money easy. That load shoulda been worth around fifty-sixty thousand, so Angelo did all right too.

Especially with your truck driver or warehouse thief, I was content to make a decent dollar but not be greedy. See they're safe, 'cause the police don't expect it. Just have to make sure they don't grab too much or clip too often. It's altogether different with most ordinary thieves. They are known to the police. If something goes down, they will be suspected. So, I have to make a better dollar.

I was cheapest with the joe citizen thief who is trying to sell something quick 'cause I am knowing I will never see his face again. This happened a month or two before I went to the hospital [for the cancer]. A guy comes into my shop, has a station wagon stuffed with Walkman radios and cheap cameras. In boxes and paper bags. Said somebody owed him money, this was their way of paying him. I'm figuring these are stolen from a warehouse or a delivery truck, by him or somebody else. He was jittery, not a real thief. I'm asking "What do you have to have?" Says he isn't sure but was figuring two, three thousand was reasonable. I mentioned a couple of auctions in the area and suggested he try selling them there, one at a time. Would take awhile but maybe get his money that way. Would take them off his hands, but best I could do was eight hundred bucks. Lotta nuisance for me to unload them. Pulled the bills out of my pocket. He gives me a blank look, then says my offer is too low. Walked out. Forty, fifty minutes later he is back. Yeah, he'd take the eight hundred dollars. Loaded the stuff on my truck. Could tell he felt very relieved. Never saw him again. Shot down to Southstate and got rid of them for like ten dollars apiece for the Walkman and twenty dollars for the camera. Sold like hotcakes. A couple hundred Walkmans and maybe fifty cameras, so I made a pretty nice dollar.

Even more so I would chisel your crybaby, your whiner, the hustler types. Set a price and they keep finagling. Come back later, cry about what you paid them. I would chop them bad or put a shoe in their ass. Never want to see their fucking face again. This last period I wouldn't deal with them at all 'cause I didn't want the hassles.

Some things are easy to unload, some things are not. Guns and good jewelry are easy to peddle, so you are willing to pay a fair price for it. But what if it's something unusual? One time in American City I got a load of canned mushrooms. Another time it was a van full of musical instruments. These are hard to get rid of. So you are going to pay a lot less and the guy you're dealing with will accept that.

Razor blades, got a whole shitload one time. Lying loose in big boxes. Came out of a warehouse. Guy calls me, tells me what he has. I'm thinking, what the fuck would I do with them. So, I calls Louie and he says, "Yeah, go for it." But even with Louie's contacts we couldn't peddle them. Stored them for a couple of years in an old school bus that Louie had. Then had them packaged and Louie was finally able to unload them. But it was a losing deal and a lotta hassle. A lesson, really.

Another thing, what if the stuff is really warm, hotter than hell? The thief knows he has to unload it quickly but you're leery of touching it. Can be a lotta heat on some pieces, especially antiques or a piece that's been in the family for a long time. So hot your outlets won't touch it. The police will be feeling the pressure to do something and will be watching dealers like me. The temptation is to buy 'cause it's worth a good dollar and you can get it cheap. But there can be too many hassles.

One time I got some good antique pieces. Baby highchair, rocking cradle, and a couple of French baby cribs. Worth a very good dollar. But at that time I didn't have the contact with guy down south who was more willing to handle the antiques that were really warm. Ran the stuff by Scottie but he wouldn't touch it. Even contacted Angelo, thinking he could put me in touch with an outlet. But no play. Then I hear at this one auction that some insurance people are nosing around, are on the lookout for those cribs. I scooted back to where I had them stored, set a match to them. This still makes me cry.

Selling and Marketing Stolen Goods

How much I am getting for the stolen merchandise depends on different things. How covered is my back? Is it a very warm item? Do I have faith in the buyer? Will there be any hassles for me? Is it somebody I've been dealing with for some time? Do I want to do business with this guy again? Is there a big dollar involved or is it nickel and dime? Am I selling local or outside the area?

In my eye, the selling end of fencing, getting rid of the warm stuff, is more like the legit side of a business. More so than the buying part. The thief and your drivers may not know what they have and may not have another outlet. Are anxious to unload. But the people the fence is selling to will know. Same with the guy who shops at my store, he wants a good price and a good product. If not, can go elsewhere. Same with this or that dealer, or this or that merchant. They will buy if they can get it more cheaply than buying elsewhere. Can't get over on them like you can the ordinary thief.

Whether the guy is solid and can handle his end of things—sure, that is important to the people the fence is selling. But how solid is the fence? That's a lot more important to the thief. On account of the risks are different, are greater for the one who does the stealing than the guy who buys the warm stuff from a dealer like me. Say it is a store customer, a merchant in town, or guy who runs an auction—I am a layer between him and the actual stealing. Maybe he knows or should surmise the stuff is warm, but the law will have a hard time proving that 'cause how is he supposed to know.

I let go the cheapest on stuff I wasn't covered on. Like batteries or razors or musical instruments. Or, if I was to handle laptop computers—that is a good item today. I'm not covered, so sell it cheap to unload quickly. Another one was food products. Make a profit and be content with that 'cause you can get jammed up on that easier. Now these can turn out to be good deals 'cause the thief has to unload too and I am paying less to get the stuff.

Same way with an item that is very warm, maybe an antique piece or a namesake piece that's been in the family. These can be traced easier, may even be registered. You know the police will come looking. Will post different places—like antique shops and auction outlets—on what's been stolen. They should be on the lookout for this or that item, this or that thief. Even this or that dealer. Those times, I'd unload real quick, wouldn't even think about making top dollar. Make a quick dollar and be satisfied with that.

A lot would depend on the buyer. Do I have faith in him. If it was a fence I hadn't dealt with or if he wasn't recommended to me by somebody else, I covered my back more. Would offer a take-it-or-leave-it price. If he says no, be done with it. Move on to another contact. But if it's somebody I've been dealing with and he's an okay guy, we can dicker over the price.

You can't be too greedy when you deal with another fence. Maybe he can't run it through his store, and has to ship it out. Same with the local secondhand dealers. The more ways it has to be cut, then the less there is for each one. Has to be room for the other guy to make a dollar, too. It is that simple.

In the long run, now, many times you are coming out ahead when you deal with another fence. On account of you can turn it over fast and chances are I'm buying from him, too. I did a lot of buying and swapping with other dealers. Like Woody, Grasso, and Scottie. This last period with Ollie and Lennie.

"Have you got anything for me?" "I'll give you these pieces for that." Or, it'd be so much for this and so much for that. Then total it all up at the end. We would both know what we had in it, what we could get at our end. Is good business, really, 'cause some items I could move better and vice versa. Take Woody, ran a big auction in Southstate, he could move tools, lawnmowers, bicycles, shit like that. Furniture, antiques, and that I could move better. Even with the legit stuff we could help each out that way. Another thing, if I can come back with a load for myself, legit or shady, I'm making up for time and gas.

It was friendly business. We'd try to outdo the other, get over on each other. Then laugh about it afterwards. Have a cup of coffee, buy the other one dinner. We wouldn't beat each other too bad. More or less helped each other. Price-wise, maybe I could make more if I peddled this or that elsewhere. But there are fewer hassles this way, fewer worries. We were content as long as we could both make a good dollar.

The warm stuff in my store I would sell a little cheaper than the regular merchandise. This is in American City now. You could bargain on prices in my store. Not just on what is warm but on the secondhand stuff and the new stuff as well. I always done business that way. Some people would bargain, others would pay the price on the tag. I would drop the price more on the warm stuff 'cause I would rather get rid of it. But not too much 'cause my prices were already low. The person shopping in my store got a good deal whether the stuff was hot or not.

At the auctions I was never sure what I'd get. The prices are very variable. Sometimes the prices are dirt cheap, other times I would do okay, and other times you can hit "auction fever." Then you can really clip. It helps to have the auctioneer on your side 'cause he can help keep the prices up and mix in the warm with the legit. If the auctioneer works the crowd, gets them going, they will pay top dollar for junk. Make a bundle by mixing in junk with this or that piece. All the more so if they think the stuff is a little shady. It would be same as you going to a flea market or wholesale place 'cause you think the prices are cheap, and the price tags are showing big discounts, especially on some items. But, really, the prices aren't any better than you'd get at a regular retail place. People are very funny that way and can get taken very easily.

With the guy running a store, your local businessman, I would sell for less than wholesale, maybe 25 or even 50 percent less, just so there is a good dollar in it for him and a good dollar for me. There's a range there you both have to operate within. Keep in mind, his take will be greater than buying legit 'cause many times there won't be a record of the sale and he won't have to pay tax. Uncle Sam doesn't need to know. This can be a big savings. Take Burdette, big TV and appliance place in American City. I sold him a lotta TVs. Never any hassles. He would let me know, "Hey, I can take more of those TVs." My price for him will be cheaper than for someone else 'cause there are no hassles and I don't have to ship them out.

If you know ahead what somebody needs, then you're all set when the thief comes peddling. You're got the outlet in place and know what price you're gonna get. There were different ones, this or that dealer, this or that store owner, I would know what they were in the market for. Maybe they'd stop by my shop or we'd bump into each other over coffee. "Give me a call Sam, if you run across such and such." Or I'd ask, "What are you running short of?" The prices were roughly understood.

It is a two-way street. The fence will want to know what the thief can get his hands on. Same as the thief will want to know what the fence will handle, what he will pay a decent price for. That's only natural. Same with the businessman or another dealer, the fence wants to know what they are in the market for, what they need. Just easier for everybody.

You play it by ear. There are no hard and fast rules. I could make more money selling piecemeal, say, if I shopped around and sold to the one paying the best prices. On some things, like cameras, I had several places I could peddle. Most of them, like the smaller secondhand place or a camera shop, might buy a few but not twenty-five or fifty. Whereas, another secondhand place or another fence might buy the whole shebang. If I spread it around, I can get fifty dollars each but only forty dollars each if I sell them all at one shot. But I'm taking a chance on getting busted every time I'm selling to a different one. Usually, I'd unload it all on one person. I'm making a little less but you also got to figure the risks of peddling and your time. It depends, may want to spread the warm stuff around just to keep up your contacts.

Mixed State of Competition in Stolen-Goods Market

There's more competition in a legit business than there is in fencing. In a legit business, you're gonna buy from whoever you get the best price and you're gonna sell to whoever pays you the best price. That's where the competition comes from. But it don't work that way in fencing. Not as much anyway. The trust and how you carry yourself, what kind of guy you are, is more there with the fencing. Is the guy an asshole or not. The thieves knew I would treat them fair and the cops could never come to me to help them out. Once the goods were in my hands, it was my problem.

I bothered very little about whether the guy could peddle elsewhere or what other dealers were paying. I worked harder trying to outdo the other secondhand dealers on the legit side than I did on the fencing. Ask Jesse, he will tell you—if you like the guy and you trust him, that is more important than anything.

I wouldn't go overboard just because another dealer was paying more. Now, if a decent thief comes my way and I'm thinking he is shopping around, I'd pay a better price than usual. Try to get him to give me a shot at what he's stealing. Once he is coming regular, I wasn't worried he'd go elsewhere 'cause my prices are in the ballpark of what others are paying and he isn't gonna go to somebody he doesn't know or is leery of, just for a few extra bucks.

Not that I didn't try to outdo Louie or some of the smaller secondhand dealers. There was some of that. But you also help each other, work together in some ways. Say I can't handle something or need an outlet, I might send the guy to Louie or call him for a contact. Louie and me did play games with some thieves, the younger ones who hassled and hassled over price. I would bid low, figuring they'd go to Louie next. Call Louie, to chop down the price even more. Was more to put the thief in his place than anything. I'd laugh with Louie about it afterwards. I've done that a few times with other dealers, too, that he can buy it at a good price. That way he owes me a favor. Or, if it's piece I really want, ask him to buy it for me.

But this very seldom happens. You ain't gonna get one dealer to beat a thief or work against him 'cause the other dealer sent him or calls ahead. The fence wants that thief's business and isn't gonna pass up a good deal or risk this guy's not coming back on account of another dealer. They're too greedy and there ain't that kind of honor among fences. There's more honor among thieves—well, among your better thieves anyway.

Covering One's Back, Coping with Legal Obstacles

If you're careful, do what needs to be done, it is hard to catch a burglar, even harder a fence. To pop him and then make it stick. To have the evidence to put a guy away. If you do your homework on a burglary, keep your head together, don't get sloppy, and nobody snitches, even today your chances are good.

Even more so with the fencing. If you're looking ahead, if you're careful about covering your ass, it is hard to prove that someone is dealing stolen goods. Hard for the police and hard for the prosecution to get a conviction. They got to show the fence had them in his hands, that he actually handled them. Then, that he *knew* they were warm, were stolen. Not just surmising now, but proving it.

Main thing is, the less anybody knows about your business, the better. Actually knows now, not just surmising. That, and having the money to pay the lawyers when you get popped 'cause the law of averages will work against you if you're clipping regular. Be able to lean on somebody if it should come to that.

My legit business was always my best cover. My shop in American City handled damned near anything—not just secondhand stuff but a lotta new stuff too. Once I got into antiques, this was even a better cover 'cause what the hell is an antique? Could be anything. I am learning about antiques and building an interest from going to the auctions and that, but I'm also doing it 'cause I wanted a cover for the fencing. Once the legit side of antiques got going, it carried on by itself and became a main thing. It was enjoyable and good money, too.

In American City the legit and the warm was pushing each other. One was helping the other. Both kept getting bigger. If I was handling this or that warm stuff, then that became a bigger part of my legit business. Because I'm handling furniture, antiques, and that on the legit side, then naturally I am more likely to deal in that. It would be hard to find a better cover than the kind of legit business I had then. Very hard to know, to suspect the warm dealings from the legit ones, the hot goods from what's clean.

This last time [in Tylersville] I didn't have as much cover. I am still handling antiques but the secondhand side of my shop is small. Mostly, I am doing upholstery work and handling used furniture and pissing around with small collectibles. I have some cover 'cause even on goods that don't match your legit line, it helps. Is loading and unloading, and different people coming and going, so there is less suspicion. Really, my best cover has been my being an antique dealer. Thirty some years now, I have been handling antiques.

No Questions Asked

Generally you don't want to know if what you're buying is warm or not. You can surmise it is warm but you prefer not to know. Same with many of the ones I sold to. They don't want to know. Just as soon turn a blind eye. Don't want that facing their conscience and are figuring what they don't know won't hurt them.

It will depend on how warm it is. What I am buying from another dealer isn't really hot. Strictly speaking, yes, but the chances of getting caught are so small on account there's a layer between me and the thief. It would be hard for the prosecution to prove there was knowledge on my part, to put the blame on me. Even what I am buying from outside the area is not as warm as my buying what is stolen from local places or from local thieves on account the risk is small. The chance of the police finding out and pinning it on you is a lot less. Isn't that much cooperation or working together among the police, especially if goes across state lines.

Coaching and Managing Thieves

If it's a thief or a driver I'm buying from pretty regular, then I would want to know where the stuff was coming from. What did come from local residences or from a burglary of a business where there was a pretty decent take, I would ship this out very quickly. Run it to one of my outlets or warehouse it. You can get jammed up on the local stuff very easily especially if you are dealing with a known thief, somebody the police is watching. Different ones over the years, I would tell them, "Let me know where it's from, don't fuck with me when it comes to telling me that." If I find out they bullshitted me, then can't do business again. Not the small stuff, now, that comes out of a department store or somebody's car. Things like radios, lamps, CD players, cameras, binoculars. That you just put on the shelf or run to an auction.

Sometimes, too, you want to slow down the thief. Don't clip so often or clip a different product, to keep the heat off. Not just your thief but the warehouse guy or the guy that works on the dock. Clip too much, it will be noticed and can lead to an inventory check. Like I would have to tell Danny, the tow fork guy getting me those grandfather clocks from the docks. "Danny, don't break into the crates so often, will raise somebody's eyebrows." Same with the Beck boys for breaking into cars: "Take a rest, hit a different town."

Unload Merchandise Quickly

You want to get rid of the stuff quickly, not have it sitting around. But this depends on how much heat there is and on whether I could make more if I held it. If it is local stuff or something the police will suspect is coming to me, I would ship it out right away. Move it out real fast.

If there's a lotta risk, the pieces are really warm, then you don't even want to warehouse it. What if the police have a tail on you? Otherwise you can warehouse for a few days, or even longer, 'cause the police don't act that fast. What I'd do, say it is appliances or furniture or tools or maybe small antiques, I'd store it for a week or so, get enough for a load, maybe mix in some legit stuff. Then I'd make a trip to one of my outlets.

On some items there is no point to holding them 'cause the price isn't gonna change. Like liquor and cigarettes, I knew that was going to Angelo and what he'd pay. Would move that quickly. Call him, make the arrangement where to meet his boys. It was bang, bang. Louie was different. He would sit on things, even store them for a year or so, looking for a better price. I didn't like to do that. I would take a lower price to get rid of it.

It depends on your cash flow, too, and how much protection you have from the cops, from the law. I needed to turn the merchandise over to keep the cash flow going. Louie didn't need to do that. His pockets were a lot deeper than mine. And Louie was very connected. Had been operating a long time. Was popped a few times but he always walked. Louie didn't fret about the extra risk from sitting on the warm stuff. Was cocky you might say.

Hiding Places and Drops

Most of your bigger fences I am surmising will have a place to store things, a place where burglars and that can drop the warm stuff. Maybe have both.

Myself, I have used garages, an old railroad car, a barn, even an old country schoolhouse. One guy I knew had a cabin with steel bars on the windows. Louie had an old school bus. That's where we stored that shitload of razor blades—hell, for a couple of years, until we finally peddled them.

Another thing, I always had a place in my shop to hide things quickly. Small items like jewelry or small antique pieces. First shop I had in American City, I put in a fake ceiling in the john. The big shop later on, had a trap door that opened up into a stairway to the basement. Kept it covered with a rug and my desk on top of that. Has been some close calls. One time I had picked up a couple of rare guns. Very valuable. The police had a tail on me. I headed right for my shop, into the john, and shoved the guns into the fake ceiling. Another time, the police came into my shop with a search warrant, were after some coins that were stolen. Tore the store apart but never found them. All the time, the bag of coins is under the trap door, right under their noses. This last shop, Tylersville, is an elevator at the back. Goes to the second and third floor but will only go to the basement if you use a special key. Is the only way to get down there. Any jewelry, any guns, or good antique pieces I'd keep down there.

I always had a Doberman or a Shepherd, to guard the place at night. To scare away a thief but just in case the police come barging in, they would have to answer to him. This would give me a few minutes. Still hurts me I had to put my last Doberman to sleep on account Wanda and some of the help were afraid of him. He could get nasty. I don't think you liked him very well either.

Altering The Merchandise

I never altered merchandise that much. Never bothered to change serial numbers. Who keeps track of them anyway? A few times I'd tear off a label or exchange backs on a TV or appliance. But didn't really bother doing that. Never had any hassles either. Think about it. My shop in American City was so full you could hardly walk through it. I'm buying and selling all the time, legit and illegit. I'm running back and forth to the auctions. Somebody dies, I might buy out the house. This place goes out of business, I'm buying from them. People are coming in off the streets, selling and buying. I've got new stuff and used stuff, this brand and that brand. Some of the stuff is junk, some isn't. Who is gonna be able to tell what is warm and what isn't?

I did try to have receipts on some items. I might buy junk at an auction—TVs, furniture, whatever. Buy it cheap, then get the receipts so I had this piece of paper in case I got jammed up. Maybe get the guy at the auction to give me blank slips, so I could fill them out whatever way I wanted.

Some merchandise I would alter, especially this last period. Take antiques that come out of private homes or from a dealer whose shop has been clipped.

If I was leery, I would "doctor" them. Maybe break off a leg, or upholster part of a chair. Take the stain off and refinish it. On the wicker, I would usually repaint it. Put doubt in the person's mind that this piece was theirs, and it had been stolen from them. Something like mountain bikes, switch the tires or change a fender. Make it harder for the cop who investigates and also give him some leeway if he wants to give you a break.

On things I was covered on, many times I would get a sales slip which says I bought this or that from so and so. If it was a thief, I might have him sign it. But more likely I'd write up a bill of sale and have somebody in the shop sign it, a hanger-on or one of the guys working for me. Didn't care what name was put down. Just get a signature. Then, if somebody comes in my shop and can identify their property, I got that piece of paper. May lose the merchandise, but that will be it.

Keep in mind, the sales slip won't help that much on stuff you're not covered on. Take when I bought the van full of musical instruments, even with a sales slip I would still have a lot of explaining to do. Another thing, if you buy from a thief that is well known to the cops, the cops and a jury aren't gonna believe that piece of paper. They will figure you know he's a thief and know that what he's peddling is warm, paper or no paper. Same as if you buy something that is a worth a good dollar or a truckload—the best cover is to get rid of it quick. Don't bother with the sales slip.

In many ways you don't want to keep good records. Know what I mean? Make them dig for whatever they get. My thing was to be contrite with the police. Tell them, yeah, I know I need to keep better records, take the time to write everything down, and keep a file on what I bought and from whom. But I was only blowing wind outta my ass.

Protect Yourself against Snitching, and Keep Thieves from "Jerking Your Chain"

If you're buying regular, you got to face the law of averages, that somebody is gonna turn you in to save his ass. Especially if you're buying from the ordinary thief. Even more so the doper thief. He will get popped and start talking. Police will have a patsy. The more times your name comes up, the more pressure on the police to do something. More chances for them to get something on you, to make a case against you. The fence has to be able to manage that. I had to pay more attention to this in this last period [in Tylersville] on account of I didn't have the contacts with the police and the magistrates, and with the really good lawyers.

My thing was to limit the snitching by being a "nice guy" and their knowing you can get rough. The thief has to know you can play hardball. I was always a firm believer of that. If he snitches, then we can't do business again. A shoe up his ass or kick in his nuts if you want to send a message to anybody that is watching. But whack him, no.

Need Some Slack from Law Enforcement

If you're a dealer like I was in American City the police are gonna know. One way or another they will have to be taken care of. You can't operate without getting some slack. Mostly, the fence needs a break now and then.

How much slack will depend on how wide open the dealer is, how regular he is dealing, who he is buying from. If he is buying regular from the ordinary thief, the walk-in trade, the police for sure are gonna know. If a fence is careful about who he deals with and has good outlets, the police may know but not know enough for doing much about it. Take the foundry guy Jesse and me sold the nickel and copper to, he dealt only with the better thief, with someone who had been vouched for. The police can surmise he is dealing but not really know.

Say a thief does snitch. Is he telling the truth? Can the cops get enough evidence to go after the fence? The cops can spend a lotta time for nothing-checking it out, then come up empty. Ordinary cop doesn't have the time and doesn't have the know-how "up here" [Sam points to his head]. Except for this or that detective, the police mostly don't wanna be bothered.

It depends, too, on how shady the cops are, and the DA and the magistrates. Once I got in with the local clique [in American City], I had more leeway from the local police and the local magistrates than I really needed. American City has always been pretty loose. As far as the local cops and the district attorney go, and then throw in having a good lawyer go to bat for you, different ones have a license to operate. In gambling, in the fencing, in the higher-up drug dealing, in the shady land deals. It is all joined together. Are quite a few involved. There's something in it for everybody.

Tylersville is pretty corrupt too. Cops aren't as shady but the magistrates are just as bad, maybe worse. Has been a couple of investigations about magistrates taking kickbacks and one of them letting prostitutes go if they will blow him. Which there is a video of. The local clique, like Amato and the Lebanese guy, pretty much have a license to operate. State police might interfere but the local cops pretty much look the other way. Not with me, I'm not protected that way anymore. My attitude these past years in Tylersville has been—if you keep it small, watch who you deal with and cover your back, the risks aren't that great the police will have anything that will stick.

It is hard to get a conviction for the fencing. Rosen, the jewelry guy, has been at it for long, long time. Now his son is involved too. They have been my outlet for jewelry all these years. But they are careful, very careful. Just deal with the better thief and with a dealer like me. Would have to get somebody like Bowie or a dealer like me agree to set Rosen up. Even then, the cops would have their hands full to get a conviction. Rosen isn't in the gambling club but is hooked up with different ones in the local clique. Very shrewd, very connected.

From what Phil has told me, state police and the feds are putting a lotta heat on Rosen. Lotta surveillance, tapping the phones, bugs, the whole works. When Steelbeams got picked up last year, the state police were pumping him about Rosen. Are trying to build a case against him. But he has a good cover and is careful who he deals with. And has the bread to pay off, and he has Savelas, the best lawyer in the area. Don't forget that. So, I don't think they will nail him. Harass him, yes, but convict him, no.

There are different ways for a fence to get some slack from the police. My approach was to be good guy with the police. Give them good deals on merchandise in my shop. Not badmouth them, like Louie did, but show some respect. Appreciated they have a job to do. Maybe help them out in doing their job when that is possible, say, if they are really under the gun to track down stolen property that has led to a lot of fuss. Myself, I would help the cops on certain things. Not be a snitch like some fences will do. But if a detective came to me, "Hey, these people had a set of china stolen that's been in the family for generations, give us a break on it if it comes your way or let us know if you hear anything." The detectives appreciated that. If push comes to shove, then fall back on a payoff, mostly through your lawyer. Don't make it easy for them—cover your back in little ways and take them to a trial if it comes down to that.

I had some slack in American City but nothing like an Angelo or a Phil or even Louie. Angelo and Phil had the local cops and the magistrates. And the DA wouldn't buck them. Angelo is smooth, very smooth. Was connected something fierce. Even had some connections in the state police. Another thing, the good lawyers would take my case but they wouldn't pull out all the stops, the way they would for Angelo or Phil. At one time, Louie had just as much in the way of protection but he made a lot of enemies that hurt him in the end.

I do know some fences, more than you'd think, who will snitch to give themselves some slack. Especially will snitch on a bottom-barrel thief or a doper. Are helping the police look good, keep their arrests up. This doesn't mean the fence has to set the thief up or testify against him. Just identify whether this or that thief or burglar was involved or stole such and such. Then the police know they have the right guy and can turn the heat up. Or maybe the fence knows who is dealing drugs or is mugging people, 'cause those are crimes the police want to solve. The fence can help the police out 'cause he hears what's going on in different areas.

Louie would snitch, especially on the penny-ante thief, the dopers, and the black thieves. The better thief was leery of Louie. But Louie's slack just didn't come from the snitching, now. Louie was very connected and he did favors for the police, same as me. Ran a used-car lot. Would give the police old cars for their driver training or sell a car dirt cheap, say, if the cop was buying a car for his kid. Louie's place was kind of hangout. I would stop by and this or that cop would be there, having coffee, seeing what Louie had on his lot. Same thing with a flea market Louie would put on once in a while, different cops would drop by.

Another thing, Louie played dirty with some of the smaller dealers. It was well-known that he had tipped off the police about this or that secondhand guy who is buying and even that this or that thief would be coming in. Lot of the little dealers feared Louie that way, 'cause they didn't have the connections with the police. See, the police can give one fence the slack to operate and screw over another dealer so he can't operate.

This last period I didn't have the slack like before. Had a decent lawyer in Tylersville but doubt he had the connections. If he did, I couldn't count on him to pull out all the stops for me. I knew guys in the local clique but wasn't part of it. Enough to say, "Hi," and did a little business with some of them, but not much more. Same with the magistrates and the cops. Knew some of them, even did some upholstery work for this or that one. Can't say if they'd give me a break or not, but they sure as hell wasn't in my pocket.

A big help for me has always been that I made a good living from the legit business. If there is slack in the fencing, the legit side can pick you up. If the heat is on, you can't always depend the fencing. If I needed cash, I could always take on more upholstery work or run legit stuff to the auctions or run a sale in my store. Raise some extra bucks. And what if you get popped? Your legit business can be collateral and help you put up bail or pay the lawyers. Can help you ride it out if you have to shut down for awhile.

9

Commentary

Criminal Capital for Illegal Enterprise

In Chapters 3 and 7, we discussed several themes surrounding criminal enterprise. This chapter continues with this enterprise focus by describing how criminal social and cultural capital, in the form of attitudes, skills, networks and ways of thinking is necessary for long-term viability in criminal enterprise.

The "job" demands facing any prospective dealer in stolen property involve managing the economic and legal realities of running a fencing business. On the economic side, the would-be fence must confront and solve the problems that present themselves to any business: capital, supply, demand, and distribution. On the legal side, he must cope with the dangers posed by control agents and the potential disruption of his fencing business. The material here, along with some prior writings on the trade in stolen goods (see review in *The Fence*), suggests that *successful fences typically must engineer five demands or interrelated conditions.* These conditions—which shape whether fencing stolen goods is *objectively possible*—must be more or less continuously and simultaneously met, but for descriptive purposes each may be considered separately.

1. *Keep up-front cash.* Most deals are cash transactions, so an adequate supply of ready cash must usually be on hand. Several factors contribute to the general rule in fence–thief dealings: the fence must pay on the spot or within a relatively short time frame. These factors are the need for secrecy, inability to call on the law to enforce agreements, and, frequently, the thief's need for money. More so than in legitimate commerce, running a fencing business requires upfront cash, or at least the ability to raise cash quickly.

2. *Display knowledge of dealing–knowing the ropes.* Learning to become a dealer of stolen goods revolves around four themes. The first is the sharpening of one's *larceny sense or "eye for clipping,"* that is, learning skills and attitudes conducive to general forms of theft and fraud. Second, there is learning

how to "buy right"—to buy and sell stolen property profitably while maintaining the patronage of both sellers and buyers. Third, there is learning how to "cover one's back"—to buy and sell regularly and routinely without getting caught. Fourth, intertwined with the other learning experiences, is learning how to "wheel and deal"—to exploit one's environment, to *make* one's opportunities rather than simply buying and selling stolen merchandise when the opportunity presents itself.

3. *Maintain connections with suppliers of stolen goods.* Persons engaged in certain occupations, such as pawnbroker, jeweler, secondhand dealer, salvage yard operator, and auctioneer, are likely to be approached to purchase stolen property because of the similarity between the types of property commonly stolen and those routinely handled in their occupations. Likewise, bartenders, bondsmen, drug dealers, criminal lawyers, gamblers, and established thieves or hustlers (and many ex-thieves) also are likely to be invited to buy stolen property because of the types of people they routinely meet. Indeed, many ordinary citizens are likely to be approached at one time or another to buy stolen property.

The professional dealer differs from such persons by his ability to generate and sustain a steady clientele of suppliers in order to buy stolen property regularly and routinely. Creating a steady stream of willing sellers may not be difficult if the prospective dealer is willing to buy from the thief with a low level of sophistication. But building up a clientele of thieves who steal merchandise of good value and with whom it is also relatively safe to do business is a quite different matter. In this regard, the fence's suppliers of stolen goods may include not only burglars, shoplifters, car thieves, and other criminal types, but truck drivers, warehouse workers, shipping clerks, salesmen, or corrupt police.

4. *Maintain connections with buyers.* The successful fence must have continuing access to buyers of stolen merchandise who are inaccessible to most thieves. Some fences with legitimate holdings may sell stolen goods to their customers but many fences also must rely on other outlets. Many, if not most, fences rely on outlets other than their legitimate business for disposing of the stolen merchandise they purchase. Thus, in what is probably a more difficult and complicated matter than making connections with thieves and suppliers, the prospective dealer needs to establish contacts with merchants or other secondary purchasers as markets for selling the stolen property he has bought.

5. *Gain the complicity of law enforcement.* By buying and selling stolen property on a regular basis, the fence is likely to acquire a reputation as a "dealer" not only among thieves but among the police. He must, then, contend with the prospect of aggressive enforcement efforts targeted at him. The fence can handle this problem in one of two ways. He may corrupt the authorities with favors, such as good deals on merchandise or cash payments, with the latter paid directly by the fence or made through the services of a well-connected

attorney. Or the fence may play the role of informer, and supply criminal intelligence to the authorities in exchange for being permitted to operate. He may aid in the recovery of stolen property that police are under special pressure to recover, and he may facilitate the arrest of thieves or other criminals. Many fences employ both strategies—bribery and informing. Also, some fences may discourage thieves from informing or testifying through a threat or reputation for violence that serves as a halo for the fence's activities. The actual threat ("leaning on" people, as Sam says) may be applied directly by the fence or is handled through the services of the fence's connections. Finally, although official complicity is a protection for many fences, all employ procedures aimed at frustrating attempts to prove illegal conduct by making their fencing activities indistinguishable from those of the legitimate business world.

Particular dealerships may require different solutions to the economic and legal realities of running a fencing business and the five conditions above, as illustrated in the shifts and oscillations characterizing Sam's fencing involvement. Some fences may need only a modest amount of up-front cash because they deal with thieves who are willing to give them short-term credit. Some fences may have extensive legitimate holdings or may deal in only one or two product lines, so that they have less need to develop outside markets for disposing of the stolen property they buy. Still other fences who deal with a handful of carefully selected thieves may manage to keep their fencing involvement more or less secret. They thus will have less need for complicity from law enforcement than the fence who deals with a wide array of general thieves, many of whom are prone both to police arrest and informing.

The conditions for successful fencing and the necessity of developing solutions to the various demands of the enterprise require definite skills and criminal capital. Just as Sutherland (1937) emphasized the importance of acquiring skills and social resources in *The Professional Thief,* we explain the skills, character traits, and types of criminal social capital necessary for fencing and perhaps other criminal enterprise.

Criminal Capital for Criminal Entrepreneurs

> *Entrepreneur or "capitalist"—someone who, in*
> *the pursuit of profit, takes the initiative in order*
> *to manipulate other persons and resources.*
> —Darrell Steffensmeier, *The Fence*

There are differing views in the criminological literature about the talents and attributes of criminals and career thieves, including professional thieves and illegal entrepreneurs. One view emphasizes the professionalism and the acquired criminal capital of at least some categories of career thieves and depicts them as being highly skilled (e.g., Sutherland 1937, 1947). The other common view is that criminals are relatively unskilled and inept. The "anyone can do it" view is held by many criminologists. In this popular view, it is conscience, fear of sanctions, and self-control, rather than lack of criminal skill, that keeps noncriminals from committing crimes (see Gottfredson and Hirschi 1990; Bennett, DiIulio, and Walters 1996).

This view of ineptitude is not shared by ethnographies of crime, nor by most criminals themselves. Sam's narrative suggests that not only con men and other elite criminals, but thieves, drug dealers, and others who support themselves through crime manifest a portfolio of skills, and some exhibit considerable entrepreneurship. This can be said even of many habitual thieves, in spite of Sam's typically derogatory stance toward them.

Sam's narrative supports a middle-of-the-road position on the skill-level issue: most career thieves are not exceptionally talented, as Edwin Sutherland (1937) tends to portray them; but neither are they as inept and slothful as contending views hold. Some criminals are much more skilled than others, and some may not be very skillful at all. Importantly, those who possess a fuller portfolio of crime-relevant skills are more likely to be respected and successful criminals and criminal entrepreneurs.

In a general sense, a mix of interactional, social, perceptual, organizational, technical, and even perhaps physical skills are needed to survive and to succeed as a thief or illegal entrepreneur. Errors of judgment and poor performance or effort, especially early on in one's career, can end it. The fullest complement of these skills, obviously, is not required of every professional criminal, and some talents are more required of some criminal specialties than others. The skills required of the seasoned burglar may overlap to some degree but will be different in many respects from the skills required of the dealer in stolen goods. Craftsmanlike skills are prerequisites for successful burglary, whereas ingenuity, business sense, and "people skills" are more required of successful fences.

Further, the talents and attributes that are prerequisites for involvement may vary within a criminal specialty. The successful safecracker, for instance, who commits burglaries for cash must have technical skills that are not necessarily required of the burglar who specializes in antique theft—which may require specialized knowledge about the value and marketing of antiques. Likewise, the successful dealer in stolen automobiles must be able to do different things than the dealer in jewelry, furs, or guns. On the other hand, the specialist fence who only deals in stolen goods that match his legitimate trade does not have to do the vast number of things required of the generalist fence.

What are the necessary talents and attributes for being able to support oneself through crime or to be relatively successful at it? The specific attributes of criminal capital described next are helpful, if not required, qualifications for becoming an established thief or illegal entrepreneur. However, some offenders may be able to compensate in one area for what they lack in another.

Heart: "Nerve" and "Coolness"

"Most people could never hack it" is a common statement of seasoned thieves, in reference to the dangers, risks, and physical demands inherent in a criminal lifestyle. To gain respect or to recruit associates, the thief or illegal entrepreneur must demonstrate that he has "heart." "Heart" is a set of traits, a combination of physical and mental toughness, of courage and coolness. To have heart is to be someone who does not scare easily and who is able to perform at one's best when the stakes are high and the risks great. The ability to keep cool, remain in control, and exercise fast-action judgments in situations that are unpredictable and suspenseful are highly valued work skills. Having these skills contributes to status and respect in the underworld for those who possess them. As with most work skills, they can become something that one is proud of.

The chief basis of heart is courage and tenacity. These qualities are not easily acquired; one either possesses them or one does not (unlike, "coolness," which can be partly acquired). Heart implies mental toughness, the capacity to endure pain if necessary and an ability to see a task through in difficult situations. It also implies the ability to "get rough," should the need arise. Physical toughness and some "muscle" are essential for dealing with security safeguards (e.g., watchdogs) and for managing criminal associates.

Too much nerve can be a drawback, however, since it can lead to carelessness. Being brave to the point of being "crazy," to the point that the freedom or safety of oneself and that of one's criminal associates are jeopardized, is not helpful. Instead, nerve should be coupled with "coolness." Coolness refers mainly to the ability to keep one's composure in the face of difficulties encountered on capers and/or during illegal transactions; it is staying calm and circumspect when the action is heavy. Coolness also may refer to the day-to-day living of the thief—that he is careful not to draw unwanted attention and "heat" by bragging about his criminal exploits or by living in a high-profile manner (see also Irwin 1970:9–10; Akerstrom 1985:21).

Heart, nerve, and coolness are important for choosing associates, and for being recruited by other offenders. Someone who scares easily, who cannot keep his nerve, or who caves in when the "going gets tough" may put his partner or associates in a "tight" spot and therefore is not to be trusted. Losing one's nerve is one main reason for quitting at least those criminal activities that require courage (e.g., burglary). Also, using either alcohol or narcotics before committing crimes in order to get the needed confidence or "false courage" is a strongly disapproved but fairly common practice.

Inventiveness, Scheming, Ingenuity

The criminal activities and/or lifestyles of many thieves and illegal entrepreneurs require a lot of inventiveness and ingenuity. This inventiveness is
seen in various ways. First, it is seen in "the ability of property criminals to
view everyday surroundings—buildings, situations—in the light of crime
potential" (Akerstrom 1985:25). Second, inventiveness is required because of
the difficulties in establishing contacts, the non-automatic process of tutelage,
the lack of possibilities for realistically "rehearsing" criminal acts, and the difficulty of "beating the system" for success and profit.

The way thieves and criminal entrepreneurs learn their work has often been
described as a tutelage process, i.e., older or more skilled ones train their
young or less skilled companions. However, this implies a recruitment process
that is too automatic and uncomplicated. The reality involves a good deal of
effort by the prospective thief. Established thieves are often not open or
friendly toward newcomers—who may draw attention to the group or talk too
much. A certain amount of testing and worry (and even competition) always
exists. Instead of being open and diffuse, the tutelage process is one of "learning as you go" by watching, by asking others, and by experimenting or "trial
and error." Criminals often have to figure a lot of things out themselves or
improvise, since nobody has ever told them what to do. This also implies that,
at least to some extent, thieves and illegal entrepreneurs must be hardworking
and energetic.

Strategies also need to be developed for outwitting the system and for showing that one can exercise control. One of the main strategies is having a front
for the authorities. For example, Sam used his legitimate business as a front,
and earlier in his career, had a phony job lined up in order to get parole. Other
fronts can include use of welfare or unemployment as a front for illegal
sources of money, and part-time jobs and live-in girlfriends as fronts for stability and sources of alibis.

Successful illegal entrepreneurs such as large-scale fences and all-around
racketeers need to be able to *wheel and deal.* They require what the fencing literature refers to as *ingenuity*—the ability not only to discover or act upon
opportunities but also to *make* them. One must actively exploit his environment
in order to create and control his opportunities, rather than relying on chance
opportunities. This is reflected in terms such as "operator" or "schemer," which
are often used by acquaintances to describe illegal entrepreneurs.

The "wheeler-dealer" or professional fence, for example, in a kind of free-
floating fashion, is required to make success happen by buying and selling
stolen property in ways that appear to be no different from what others in his
environment normally and legally do. That is, he must hold his own and not be

outhustled by thieves and other trade partners; and he must make the contacts and gain the confidence of lawbreakers, law enforcers, and all others on whom his success as a dealer ultimately depends. Wheeling and dealing is a combination of cunning and resourcefulness, and *it is an ongoing creation of the dishonest possibilities of the entrepreneur's environment.* It builds on his knowledge of the suppositions of the underworld, the conventions of his business environment, and the discretionary workings of the law.

Practical Knowledge of Things, Language, and People

Whereas modern society puts a premium on knowledge that is associated with theoretical and reasoning skills, the underworld rewards practical knowledge—the ability to implement in a practical way a project or task, not just theoretically knowing how (Akerstrom (1985:24;*The Fence* 1986). Even though many criminals may not need specialized craftsmanship, they do need a lot of practical knowledge about things, language, and people: how to break into a house or store, how to gauge the value of what they steal, how to acquire information about would-be associates or the police, how to handle people, how to judge potential buyers. This kind of knowledge is not easily learned from books, if at all, but must be experienced and lived.

The practical knowledge required of seasoned criminals builds on their street knowledge described below; it also complements and extends the sensibility of knowing how to do practical things that characterizes many blue-collar and lower-strata members of society who—like thieves—need comparatively more practical knowledge than other groups in order to get by in the world. Whereas theoretical and reasoning skills are considered superior among professionals and academics, criminals and working-class men value practical knowledge.

That the emphasis on the existence and importance of practical knowledge is even greater among criminals stems partly from the lack of protective institutions for appeal if they are cheated, partly from the lack of traditional sources of information such as certificates or licensing for acquiring knowledge about people, and partly from the free-floating and happenstance work environment they face. Criminal pursuits are characterized by less specialization and routine performance than noncriminal pursuits. Consequently, making a living through crime requires much more in the way of individual decision-making and, perhaps, greater judgment and knowledge about a wide range of things. Learning how to get that information through trial and error, through associates, and through underworld grapevines is crucial, and often involves inventiveness and effort as well as the developed ability to "read" others and discern good from bad information.

Street Smarts

For many thieves and illegal entrepreneurs, practical knowledge is anchored in a heavy dosage of street smarts. Being "streetwise" means knowing the underlife of society; what is going on in it or how to find out; knowing what to say or not say to the police. It also means having the angles and not being easily duped by thieves and others who are both prone to and skilled at hustling. Furthermore, because things can change quickly in the underworld, being streetwise is an ongoing process and requires that one stay on top of things or have easy access to those who do.

Worldly-Wiseness

In addition to street smarts, a more far-reaching kind of practical knowledge—worldly-wiseness—is often required of illegal entrepreneurs. Being "worldly-wise" refers to a kind of all-around knowledge that blends together the suppositions of the theft subculture, the business community, and the society at large. Because they deal with so many different types of people and in a wide variety of situations, the generalist fence or all-around racketeer must "know a little bit of everything" and also be socially skilled enough to handle himself in different crowds and in different situations.

Social Skills

As in many legitimate occupations, the need for social skills and managing people is prominent among many successful thieves and criminal entrepreneurs. Seasoned thieves, hustlers, and illegal entrepreneurs exhibit social skills in many areas, including identifying and "sizing up" others, "passing," making contacts, and managing other people. Regular hustling, wheeling and dealing, and thwarting discovery or arrest foster the development of a specific sensitivity for "reading" others in order to take advantage of them. This sensitivity is apparent for successful con artists, but other criminals—burglars, fences, drug dealers, even serious shoplifters—both need and often possess this role-taking proficiency.

Seasoned thieves believe they are adept at identifying others—another crook, an undercover policeman, a prospective customer, or accomplice. Exactly how this is done not well-defined or articulated by thieves, but apparently it is based on outward appearances, gestures, language, and so forth that give the thief a "feeling" or sense of "just knowing." Often, it is not just identifying others that is important, but being able to "read" them, especially their character (what is the individual "made of," can he be trusted, does he pose a danger, is he a "bullshitter"?) The ability to ferret out phony talk or behavior is especially valuable. Since contacts and trustworthy relationships are so important for criminals, it is not surprising that they emphasize its importance, and that they believe they are more able to determine whom to trust and mistrust than most people. These skills are learned or developed situationally, observing other thieves, and often via prison experience (as was the case with Sam).

In some situations, such as being caught in the act, criminals need to "act normal" or to "pass"—such as the safecracker's need to "act natural" when someone enters the room where he is in the act of opening a safe. How one carries himself and plays the part that one impersonates is obviously important (see *The Fence:*125). Criminals get a lot of practice at passing, since they encounter a lot of "strategic moments":

> Here, then, is a standard for measuring presence of mind, one involving the ability to come up quickly with the kind of accountings that allow a disturbing event to be assimilated to the normal. . . . Thieves, of course, have a special need to construct false, good accounts at strategic moments and have a word, "con," to cover ability in this sort of covering. (Goffman 1972:263)

Fourth, criminals also develop social skills for managing or manipulating people. That is, criminals become skilled at social dramaturgy and presentation of self (Goffman 1959), and they need knowledge about others and what others consider normal. They often are "operators" who consciously calculate and adapt to take advantage of a situation. This may entail using deference and showing respect to the police, acting incompetent or stupid, or perhaps puffing up a counselor or parole officer to impress him or her favorably. Thieves have also usually acquired some practical legal sense of how to present themselves in the best light by showing remorse and conventionality (e.g., getting a regular job, or bringing a tearful mother or pregnant fiancée to court).

Finally, social skills are essential both in judging who of one's associates is reliable and for establishing a reputation of being trustworthy. Thieves and others are more likely to do business with someone they trust, and as discussed later in this chapter, the one trusted is also likely to actively cultivate such a reputation.

Larceny Sense—"Eye for Clipping"

What criminologists label as "larceny sense"—the ability to perceive and capitalize on the opportunity to make money in less than legitimate ways—is required of thieves and illegal entrepreneurs. Larceny sense is partly attitude and partly acquired knowledge. In the underworld, it is the ability to read one's environment with an "eye for clipping," as when one thief says of another, "He has a good eye for clipping."

To have larceny sense means, first, that one has "larceny in his heart," or is willing to steal or swindle. He is unconstrained by conventional beliefs about what one is supposed to do. "A second and more subtle aspect of larceny sense is that one be observant and sensitive to circumstances and opportunities for illicit gain, and know when to take advantage of them or to desist" (*The Fence:*190). As Sam recounted in *The Fence,* "It's being able to see the openings, to pick out the right information, to have a good eye for a score; it's also knowing when to pick your spots or when to back away if the risks rise" (ibid.:191).

By relying on commonsense interpretations of society, the average citizen also has the ability to perceive favorable theft opportunities, such as when police surveillance is greatest in a neighborhood, or when residences can be seen to be vacated because of newspapers left lying around. However,

> It is the more specific socialization, such as that which occurs in early hustling experiences or in association with other criminals, that forges in the seasoned offender a complex series of visual cues not readily observed by the layman or the average businessman. Seasoned thieves and illegal entrepreneurs (like Sam) may be ignorant or unmindful of many social conventions but they are criminally sensitive to subtle social expectations and routines. (ibid.)

Business Skills and Knowledge

Successful criminal entrepreneurs must possess at least rudimentary knowledge about the product that is being sold or traded, its pricing, and its marketing. Acquiring such knowledge may require some inventiveness on the entrepreneur's part but can generally be acquired by trial and error or coaching from one's associates.

Illegal entrepreneurs (and some seasoned thieves) must also be knowledgeable about business practices and conventions, such as those utilized by the small business owner. Some knowledge of technical regulations and practices may also be required. And some illegal entrepreneurs must also possess technical or craftsmanlike skills pertinent to their particular trade or specialty (such as Sam's skills at furniture refinishing and repair, antique restoration). They also must be sufficiently skilled at money management to maintain an adequate cash reserve to be able to purchase illegal goods and services in an unpredictable market. The particular kinds of business knowledge required will depend on the entrepreneur's criminal specialty.

Trust, Being Solid

For those with whom the thief or illegal entrepreneur does business, reliability and trust are highly valued. Will the other person deliver? Is he dependable? Does he keep his word? Would he increase risks of trouble with the law? Established thieves and criminal entrepreneurs like Sam place a great deal of emphasis on being "solid." In fact, they often consider it a prime reason for their rise and eventual success as a burglar, dealer in stolen goods, racketeer, or whatever. A "solid" person is one who is reliable and trustworthy. He keeps appointments, honors agreements, and seldom contributes to another's trouble with the law. Some degree of trust is generated by the shared recognition that "we're all doing things we're not supposed to," but concerns about trustworthiness are maximized when trouble arises with victims or with the police. Snitching is the most visible violation of being solid.

Because of its importance for acceptance in the underworld and for making connections, acquiring a reputation for solidness is often an active pursuit of established criminals (see also Pistone 1987). In this sense, too, the *appearance* of being solid—which is as important as its reality—will depend partly on the entrepreneur's skills in convincing others of his trustworthiness.

Concerns about reliability and trustworthiness are greatest among established thieves and illegal entrepreneurs. This does not mean, however, that they are always paragons of integrity. Many, if not most, are at least occasionally prone to "pull the rug out" from under or "bury" a crime partner or associate by absconding when the action gets heavy, or by informing to the police. Some fences and racketeers, for example, compromise with the police and gain immunity from the law by informing on thieves or by assisting the authorities in other ways, and some illegal entrepreneurs set up other fences and racketeers as a way of eliminating or sabotaging competition.

> Nonetheless, even though it is often violated, the rule of not informing is generally respected, if for no other reason than that general compliance with the code "honor among thieves" is essential for expediting ongoing transactions and sustaining an illegal business. (*The Fence:*203).

Acting as an informant can lead to loss of prestige, loss of business, or possible reprisals—as well as loss of self-respect, because of the loyalty and identification that many thieves and illegal entrepreneurs have with the criminal community, growing out of the common experiences that they typically share with other underworld members.

When they do inform, moreover, established thieves and illegal entrepreneurs usually do so selectively—meaning they are more likely to inform on the "riffraff," the garden-variety thieves and hustlers who lack status within the criminal community. Sam's narratives in *The Fence* (see pp. 148–51) as well as here illustrate this tendency. Established criminals are much less likely to inform on a good thief or another established criminal unless they are under very strong pressure to do otherwise. This evasion of the rule against informing is at least partly accepted in the underworld, in the sense that "creeps and assholes" are less deserving of protection from the police.

Seasoned thieves and good burglars apparently violate the rule against informing less frequently than most other underworld types. Fences are more trustworthy than garden variety thieves but less trustworthy than some other illegal entrepreneurs or racketeers. The latter may have considerable protection from arrest because of extensive connections with the police and other public officials. Moreover, although "honor among thieves" is easily and frequently violated by many ordinary thieves, the average citizen or legitimate businessperson who finds him- or herself under pressure from the police is probably most prone to snitch.

Being solid also entails honesty in living up to agreements, paying debts, and not "ripping off" associates. However, considerable finagling and "getting over" are also customary in transactions among underworld operatives—for whom hustling and sharp trading are taken for granted. It is also important to note that honesty here also means honesty within one's own group. To not cheat or steal from citizens or legitimate businesspeople, if the opportunity presents itself, is to be a sucker.

Muscle

Sustained involvement in crime is physically demanding both in the sense that physical prowess is often required to execute crimes and because the potential for violence and/or protecting oneself from getting "pushed around," "ripped off," or "snitched on" is ever-present. Strength, prowess, and muscle are useful for the successful commission of crimes, for protection, for enforcing agreements, and for recruiting and managing reliable associates. Physical strength and speed are obviously useful for committing crimes such robbery, burglary, breaking into autos, and many kinds of cartage theft; and, depending on the merchandise handled, may also be useful for dealing in stolen goods. Less obviously, they are important in theft and hustling activities (including drug dealing) in which the potential for violence or need for quick getaway is considerable. The criminal entrepreneur has to rely on his own or his associates' ability to protect, threaten, retaliate, or inspire respect among crime associates (and perhaps others as well, such as victims or law enforcement).

For many illegal entrepreneurs and racketeers, then, violence or its threat is a critical resource for inspiring respect among one's associates. However, the need for "muscle" does not mean that illegal entrepreneurs have to be "toughs" or heavies. As explained in *The Fence*:

> Indeed, within the criminal community, persons thought too reliant on physical force for doing business or resolving difficulties tend to be distrusted. While it is

fairly common in the underworld to hear persons expressing threats to injure or kill others who have violated their notions of fair play, these threats are carried out infrequently. A more likely response is that of slandering or blackballing the offender and encouraging others to avoid dealings with him. (p. 202)

Variability in Stock of Skills Across Types of Offenders

The skills required of seasoned criminals and illegal entrepreneurs are diversified, depending on the criminal's specialty or range of criminal involvement. Some of the skills are at least partly common to all members of society but they are systematized and sharpened by the criminal who consciously uses them. These skills cannot be learned (at least easily) from books but must be experienced and lived. The combination of skills and distinctive stock in trade that make up the "working personality" of a seasoned *thief* will overlap with yet differ somewhat from those required of an illegal *operator*. The large-scale fence or all-around racketeer, for example, must possess or acquire a fuller complement of skills to effectively exploit his environment in large part because his activities blend together the underworld, the business community, and the society at large; and because he interacts with a much wider range of people, from thieves to businessmen and from the police to the public. Often, therefore, the talents of illegal entrepreneurs such as fences or racketeers are a mixture of the stock in trade of seasoned criminals as well as successful businessmen and salespersons.

The Fence as a Special Case of Networking: The Importance of Making Contacts

We described above key skills or qualifications that contribute to success as a criminal entrepreneur. Such skills are an important element of having or acquiring what, broadly speaking, can be referred to as *criminal social capital* (see also Uggen and Thompson 2003). A crucial element comprising criminal capital is contacts and supportive relationships or networks for criminal endeavors. In Sam's view, "getting the connections" is the hardest obstacle for building and sustaining a criminal career. As Sam put it, success in crime requires "contacts, contacts, contacts."

Though the importance of "connections" for success at theft or illegal enterprise is widely recognized in the criminological literature, there is very little description about the forms and dynamics of how contacts are actually developed and sustained. We learn from Sam's narratives in the previous chapters that the process of making contacts in the underworld is similar in many respects to that in legitimate endeavors. But there also are qualitative differences, such as the greater importance of "trust" and "word of mouth" that characterize the underworld. Even more so than in legitimate commerce, contacts within the underworld derive from mutually beneficial exchanges among persons who trust each other (at least somewhat) and whose skills and resources are mutually supportive. They also often depend on the compatibility of the individuals involved. Typically, trust and connections are based on a preexisting tie or acquired through third-party mediation.

The relatively stable arrangements or partnerships a thief or an illicit entrepreneur develops may be characterized as his *personal criminal network*—a comparatively fluid and negotiable set of relations or working associations subject to considerable vacillation, even termination, as the varying parties attempt to come to terms with their lives and the relative payoffs they associate with one another. For the thief as well as the illicit entrepreneur, the process of building a personal network involves overlapping networks and an ongoing appraisal by prospective associates of one's character and skills.

We can gain further perspective on the notion of contacts and networking as important criminal capital for the illegal entrepreneur by taking a closer look at the dealer in stolen goods, especially the generalist fence (like Sam) whose trade is characterized by diversity both in the kinds of products handled and the types of thieves dealt with. Our analysis here examines in more detail the nature of crime networks and networking skills, which were evident in the previous chapter's narrative ("Running a Fencing Business") and are further expressed in Sam's next narrative ("Skills, Character, and Connections").

As explained in *The Fence* (pp. 160–64), there are three general ways of making contacts: word of mouth, existing contacts introducing one to others, and one's own active recruiting.

Word of Mouth

*Word of mouth is your best advertisement 'cause
there's a helluva grapevine out there. Really,
there are different grapevines.*
—Sam Goodman

Since the illicit entrepreneur cannot advertise publicly, he must rely on informal channels of communication to locate prospective partners with whom to hustle, burglarize, or buy and sell stolen goods. "Word of mouth" grapevines are probably the most common method of making contacts. Each grapevine mixes rumor and fact, and some grapevines provide more reliable information than others. Access to grapevines also varies. The "street grapevine" is accessible to almost anyone acquainted with the criminal community. Other grapevines may interface with it but are more narrowly confined to individuals in specialized locations. The latter grapevines tend to be almost personalized information channels linked both to specific cliques of offenders and to particular kinds of criminal enterprise.

Third-Party Referral: "Being Recommended"

Referral of one party to another is another way to bring thieves or criminal entrepreneurs together. Unlike word of mouth through the underworld grapevine, third-party referral is less diffuse and the information is more reliable. More established offenders and those not associated with the underworld (e.g., businesspeople, joe blows) are likely to link up with criminal entrepreneurs on this basis. For example, one businessperson may tell another of services provided by a particular criminal entrepreneur, and then also offer to "vouch" for him. Further, the grapevine and third-party referral may work in tandem, as when an established burglar hears through the grapevine about a particular fence and checks it out with a trusted associate before initiating contact. Or, the burglar may have a fellow thief recommend him to the fence.

Third-party referral is more than a one-way process in which one party acts as an intermediary for the other. Seasoned offenders will come to know a variety of "contact-men" whose assistance they solicit on an impromptu basis to make a timely connection. Almost anyone can be a contact-man, but they frequently are drawn from the ranks of lawyers, late night bar and night club operators, fences, and local organized-crime members.

Importantly, establishing contacts by way of referral or recommendation increases trust and confidence among parties as compared to contacts through grapevine information. Moreover, the referral process tends to be an outgrowth of friendship networks and business or work associations. By contrast, the street grapevine derives mainly from peer relations and involvement in specific criminal subcultures.

Sponsorship

Closely allied and overlapping third-party referral or being recommended is having "sponsors" who actively vouch for and make connections on one's behalf. We see this in previous chapters, for example, in how Louie, Scottie, and Woody *proactively* introduced Sam to a variety of contacts. In return, the sponsor may expect payment in kind such as a kickback or a share of the profits, or the favor may have to be returned in some other way. (Relatedly, see our discussion of *patron–client* transactions among criminal entrepreneurs in Chapter 15.) The significance of sponsorship will depend on one's longevity and visibility within the local underworld. By comparison to "locals" or established criminal entrepreneurs, newcomers or "outsiders" cannot rely on childhood friendships, kinship, or ties with the local "clique" or syndicate as a source of contacts.

Recruitment

The process of making contacts also involves the criminal entrepreneur's active role in developing and sustaining connections. He must "work" his environment by encouraging and soliciting referrals and sponsorships, and by personally hustling and recruiting associates. *We see this throughout Sam's narratives, for example, in how he subtly "worked" and cultivated auction contacts, truck drivers, warehouse people, business buyers, and others.* The recruiting process may be a spinoff of largely accidental or fortuitous encounters; a result of going to the "right" places for prospective associates or partners; an outcome of checking out someone known or suspected of being a little shady; or a consequence of "opening up" people not necessarily linked to the theft subculture and baiting them to defraud or steal. Successful recruiting is enhanced by a reputation for being "solid" and a "talking ability" that minimizes risks and moral concerns among those being recruited.

There is considerable overlap among making word of mouth contacts, third-party referral, and sponsorship—each in practice may blend into the other. The emphasis for word-of-mouth networking is on the process whereby a would-be thief or associate hears about a particular criminal entrepreneur and seeks him out. In referral, someone already linked to the entrepreneur sends him an associate, either as a favor to the criminal entrepreneur or to the associate. Sponsorship also involves third-party recommendation, but usually the sponsoring individual has a stronger tie to the criminal entrepreneur and acts on his behalf on a sustained basis.

Spokes in the Wheel

However they come about—by third-party referral or by individual active recruiting—certain contacts typically play an especially important role in fostering one's career as a seasoned thief or a wheeling-and-dealing criminal entrepreneur. Some contacts become key "spokes in the wheel" to use Sam's metaphor—designating someone who has helped in a major way to overcome the obstacles (e.g., legal, economic, technical) associated with a particular criminal specialty or illicit business. Probably more so than in legitimate occupations, one or a few "spokes" can strongly shape a criminal career. Examples of crucial spokes in Sam's American City wheel were Jesse, Louie, Angelo, Rosen, "Fat Charlie," Woody, and Cooper. As described in later narratives, key spokes in Sam's *diminished* Tylersville wheel included Phil, Lenny, Ollie, and Rosen.

Contact-Making Differences Across Offender Types

The hardest thing is getting the connections,
'cause [to be a dealer] you have to have the con-
tacts with all different kinds of people.
—Sam Goodman, in *The Fence*

The description so far has been on the general processes by which offenders develop contacts. The processes that come into play, in certain ways, will depend on the type of thief or illicit entrepreneur, and on who is connecting with whom. The paths bringing offenders together will vary both between and across ordinary thieves, seasoned offenders, fences, racketeers, and quasi-legitimate businessmen.

When thieves seek to locate fences, for example, some learn about fences through word of mouth and the underworld grapevine. Others through a third-party referral—perhaps from a thief-associate, a drug dealer, or another illicit entrepreneur. Still other thieves discover fences by checking out "suspect" businesses to see if the proprietor will buy suspect goods.

Drug addicts and less established thieves rely heavily on street talk and contacts, whereas good thieves and more seasoned offenders view the street grapevine as unreliable and also prefer not to associate with dopers and "penny-ante thieves." Instead, seasoned thieves are likely to connect with a reliable fence through another established thief, another dealer who cannot handle the merchandise the thief is bringing (for example, see the account of how Rocky, a key burglar in Sam's network, was introduced to Sam by way of Louie, in *The Fence*:168), or perhaps a lawyer, quasi-legitimate businessman, or member of the local syndicate.

While the paths leading criminal and employee thieves to dealers in stolen goods overlap, there also are some differences. Truck drivers and warehouse thieves are less aware of the underworld grapevine and of ways to locate a fence. Moreover, because their stealing is usually an individual rather than a group activity, they are less likely to spread the word to fellow employees than is the case with full-time thieves. Also,

> Since the theft activities of employee thieves tend to be sporadic and their theft careers short-lived, there is rapid turnover among them. As a result, the self-generating effects of word of mouth and third party referral are less operative among employee than among criminal thieves. This also means that, more so than with full-time thieves, a more sustained recruiting stance is required of the fence if he intends to maintain a steady supply of driver and employee thieves as suppliers of stolen goods. (*The Fence:*168)

Initially attracting thieves is somewhat fortuitous and partly beyond the fence's control, but maintaining the connection is a matter he can considerably influence.

The two processes obviously intertwine in that satisfied thieves are a major advertisement for attracting other thieves. And factors like trust, money, and camaraderie
which contribute greatly to recruiting thieves in the first instance are at the core of
sustaining their patronage. (ibid.:170)

As Sam's previous two narratives show (Chapters 6 and 8), a fence may
offer a number of incentives to encourage thieves to keep doing business with
him, especially in comparison with some of his competitors. These incentives
include:

- paying a reasonably decent price for stolen merchandise, at least in the
  thief's eye
- paying cash immediately for what is purchased
- being a dependable outlet for the thief's merchandise
- being conveniently located
- offering advice on thievery and the criminal justice system
- being a "nice" guy who is amusing and generous; and
- providing perks such as bail money, a temporary job to satisfy parole
  requirements, or a short-term loan.

Together, these foster feelings of loyalty and reciprocity in the thief and
incline him to avoid the risk of "shopping around." However, the perks will be
mainly effective with in-between and younger thieves, who are more easily
swayed by extra services and a friendly atmosphere. Older, more established
thieves are more influenced by profit and safety.

The fence's contacts, of course, must extend beyond thieves and other suppliers of stolen goods to include buyers or purchasers of goods bought by the
fence. As with thieves, word of mouth and third-party recommendations are
important paths for connections between merchants, wholesalers, and other
business buyers and large-scale fences. More so than with thieves, however, the
fence is likely to seek and recruit business buyers, although in some instances a
merchant may seek a known fence and let him know what his needs are.

However they develop, the recruitment and the contacts are likely to be an
outgrowth of the fence's legitimate business activities, particularly when the
stolen merchandise matches his legitimate product line. This match provides
both him and the would-be buyer with a cover for, as well as an "opening" for,
illicit trade relations. As Klockars (1974:174) notes, a fencing operation may
need as few as a "dozen different businesses" as buyers to be profitable.

In general, the grapevine linking merchants and other business buyers to
dealers in stolen goods is much less self-generating than that among thieves—
although similar snowballing effects may exist among some types of merchants such as antique dealers, private collectors, secondhand dealers, and auc-

tion houses. The latter frequently will meet at common meeting places. They also share with fences a "larcenous heart" and a readiness to buy or trade stolen goods "no questions asked." Not surprisingly, fences who themselves (e.g., Sam) are antique or secondhand dealers will find it easier to develop contacts among them than among ordinary merchants. It is worth noting here, moreover, that almost any thief or part-time criminal receiver can, as some certainly do, sell stolen merchandise at flea markets, auctions, and similar "open trade" settings. But to do so regularly and in volume requires contacts with key individuals associated with these operations.

Complicit contacts between illicit entrepreneurs and law enforcement officials require a special trust and loyalty. These contacts occur in several main ways: through prior friendships linked to work or leisure activities; through association with the local syndicate; through well-connected attorneys; and through the active "grassing" (offering bribes or deals) of some police or court officials. Association with local "racketeers" or syndicate group may be particularly important, since it signals that one is safe to do business with. Where the latter practice is prevalent, it also suggests a broader political and legal corruption in which some individuals, but not others, receive special treatment. "The officials not only accept but sometimes solicit 'favors' from illicit entrepreneurs if they can do so safely. In some ways, it isn't so much that the criminal entrepreneur has corrupted local officials as that he has become part of the group able to corrupt them" (*The Fence:*180).

Networking: "Building a Spider Web"

Criminal networks, like conventional ones, are forms of social organization made up of actors who pursue exchange relations with one another of varying duration (Podolny and Page 1998), though unlike conventional networks, they lack a legitimate organizational authority to arbitrate and resolve disputes that may arise during exchange. We would also note that the ability to operate effectively in a network (what Sam called his "spider web") is a skill that must be learned. As Podolny and Page argue, "the ability to exploit the substantive knowledge gained through network relationships without killing the proverbial goose can be viewed as an important capability in its own right" (ibid.:72).

The network map in Figure 9.1 depicts the varied individuals linked to Sam's trade in stolen goods during his *peak* fencing period (i.e., in the early 1970s prior to his incarceration for "receiving stolen property").

The map suggests both the importance of the fence's reputation and the need for contacts in maintaining his career. As characterizes the underworld more generally, Sam's contacts derive from mutually beneficial exchanges with persons who "trust" each other and whose skills and resources are mutually supportive. The exchanges also often depend on the compatibility of the

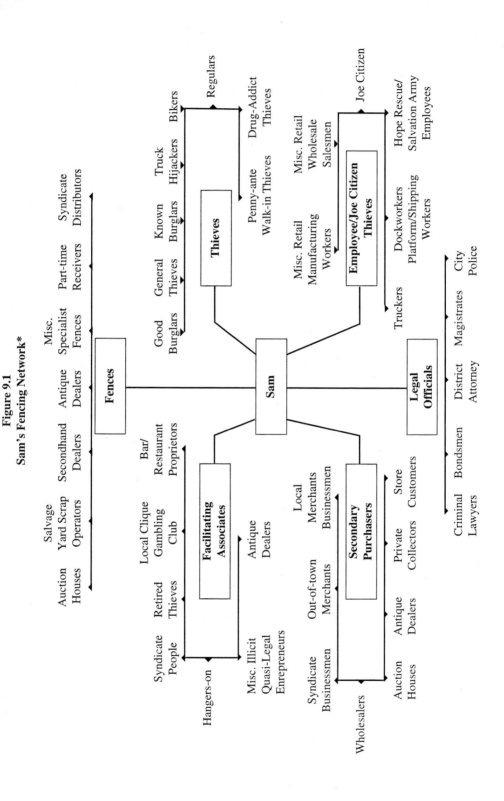

Figure 9.1
Sam's Fencing Network*

individuals involved, especially when they develop into relatively stable arrangements or partnerships. Typically, the trust and the connection is based on a preexisting tie or develops through the mediation of a third party who introduces the participants and vouches for their reliability.

Earlier, we noted the divergent views in the criminological literature about the talents and attributes of criminals and career thieves, including professional thieves and illegal entrepreneurs. One view emphasizes the skills and attributes of professionalism that characterize at least some categories of career thieves and criminals (Sutherland 1937, 1940). The other common view is that criminals are fundamentally unskilled, unintelligent, inept, and/or lacking in self-control (see Gottfredson and Hirschi 1990; Bennett et al. 1996). Sam's narratives, and our discussion above, have suggested that a number of skills and character attributes are crucial for *successful* property crime and criminal entrepreneurship.

Furthermore, network relationships and social bonds between thieves, fences, and other criminal entrepreneurs are not necessarily "cold and brittle" (Kornhauser 1978). While we do not view such relationships through rose-colored glasses, it is clear that trust, reliability, and reciprocity, at least within one's own group, appear to be crucial for *sustainable* burglary, fencing, and other forms of criminal entrepreneurship. In turn, as we elaborate in Chapter 11, network relationships and social bonds in the work of burglary and fencing appear to be held together by a variety of structural, personal, and/or moral commitments.

Such networking brings several advantages for sustained criminal enterprise. First, networks are not coercive; participants are willing members who choose to associate with each other. This is in contrast to some other kinds of work-related or business relationships in the legitimate world, which may be more constrained in that one's coworkers and business associates are often chosen for him or her, or dictated by circumstance. Voluntary network associations may in turn facilitate easier exchanges of information and assistance.

Second, the mutual selection process in voluntary network associations makes it more likely that participants will be (or become) comfortable with one another's work habits, work styles, commitments, and culture. This feature of networks, in turn, provides opportunities for long-term bonds and mutual respect.

Last, we propose that the size and diversity of one's criminal network or "spider web" is an important marker of underworld status. In a manner similar to one's prior criminal record, the nature and extent of one's criminal ties is also an indicator of the "seriousness" of one's criminal career.

As Sam's narrative and our commentary strongly demonstrate, networks, as well as other forms of criminal social and cultural capital, matter a great deal for sustained criminal enterprise and for pulling off more lucrative and more organized kinds of crime. *A successful criminal enterprise of more than minimal size or longevity is simply not possible without making and maintaining contacts.* We believe this fact is insufficiently recognized by many criminologists today. Understanding criminal networks and the activity necessary to build and sustain them is a significant gap in the criminological literature, and *Confessions* helps to fill that gap. Furthermore, a variety of criminal and conventional business skills, as well as leaerned habits and ways of perceiving one's world, also contribute to success and longevity in fencing, and likely other forms of criminal enterprise as well.

10

Sam's Narrative

Skills, Character, and Connections

Skills and Character

It was a helluva education for me, all the way along. Not from books now, but from doing it. From doing the hustling, from doing the burglary, and from the dealing itself. And from being around Jesse, Louie, and Angelo. From watching and listening, like at the auctions and in the penitentiary, too.

Burglary is knowing physical things, being good with your hands, knowing how to see an opening, and knowing the value of things like jewelry, so you pick up the good stuff and leave the junk behind. It is finding a good partner, and having some contacts with fences and tipsters. Hooking up with a good lawyer, not a half-assed one. On account of if you're clipping regular, the law of averages is you will get popped. Jesse would add, having a good woman. That she is there for you and helps out in little ways but have to be sure she will keep her mouth shut. Be careful not to put her through too much.

Fencing is knowing about people and knowing how to clip, and knowing how to sort out the good information from the bullshit—'cause there's a lotta gossip about the cops and that, especially from the thieves. It is knowing how to handle yourself in different crowds and in different situations. Having the business knowledge is important, but more so being world-wise on account of dealing with so many different people. You have to know where different ones are coming from, what they're thinking, what their angle is. Otherwise, you can't get over on them and can't get the contacts you will need.

You have to have an eye for clipping. I don't care if you're a decent burglar, a fence, or a guy in the rackets. That is a must. Have to see the openings and cash in on them when they come your way. And know when to pull back when the opportunity isn't there and the risks are too high. It is an outlook, really, a feeling to be leery or to go ahead. My mind would just click that this is a good time to knock off this place, that this guy will buy hot stuff, or that I needed to do such and such to cover my back. It's not this or that thing, but where the straight person is seeing or hearing one thing, I am seeing something else.

Over the years you pick up on little things, without even thinking. It isn't like you're always looking for the opening but more like it becomes second nature. Like when I'm at an auction and another antiques dealer mentions that another big antiques dealer is having his place remodeled. Or say a liquor store is moving to a place down the street, means they aren't set up yet when they move in. Just like that, it comes to me—this would be a good time to knock it off. Pass that information on to Steelbeams, and he would hit the place. It's knowing little things about how the police operate, too. Like the time I came back from Smithfield with all them guns. I just had a feeling I was being tailed, so I skidooed. Found out later, sure enough, there was a tail.

I still do it, almost automatically. Say when I walk into a place. This is right before I went to the goddamn hospital [for the cancer]. I stopped at an American Legion to play the poker machines. My first time in the place. I knew right away, this is a cracker box place that has a cracker box safe. Just knew where they had the safe on account from watching where they went for the money. Would be like a carpenter walking into a building—boy, that's a sloppy panel job.

Most dealers in an area will know one another, will bump into each other here and there. Same is true of burglars and guys in the rackets. It's only natural that you will rap about things. Not that you say, "Hey, teach me about burglary or about fencing." But you can watch how the guy handles himself and some things will come up in conversation.

Goes without saying, you have to be a little shady, have some larceny in your heart. Be willing to clip or get over on somebody, not worry if it's crooked or not. Say you're a fence—you are a thief, you're stealing but you don't call it that. Your ordinary joe blow and even more your ordinary businessman have some larceny in them, too, 'cause that is part of everyone's environment. But not have enough larceny [in the heart] to really clip, to really get over on others. Your burglar, your con guy, your fence, your guy in the mafia, this or that one in the local clique will have more larceny in them.

You don't become a fence out of the blue. The fences I knew generally had a background that was shady. If not shady, then they're free spirits like Woody and Ollie and Ciletti. Were raised with the hustling and clipping or maybe were hooked up with the rackets in one way or another. I don't mean they were strictly into crime but had their fingers into different things, if not illegal then on the borderline. Somehow they got the street knowledge and the eye for the easy dollar, and got some contacts with the criminal element—say, with thieves and other fences, and maybe with the cops, too. Some of the Jewish guys and the Italians especially were more or less raised with the gambling, the shylock loans, the shady business stuff.

Depends on the kind of legit business the person has or what he does for a living. A guy who is a private collector or runs a secondhand shop or is an auction guy—will come across people who are clipping and will get some contacts and some know-how. The guy who is a bondsman, and some of your lawyers, get the contacts and the street knowledge by handling bail and dealing with the thieves. Learn the ropes that way.

Your ordinary businessman couldn't make it as a fence, just as your ordinary thief couldn't. Especially if you're talking about dealing on a regular basis, not the off and on dealing that almost anyone can do. Your ordinary store guy would have the business knowledge, would know the prices and that, but he ain't world-wise. Not in the sense of knowing the criminal element and of having to deal with people from all walks of life. Not just thieves now—but your auction people, other dealers, the lawyers and the magistrates, truck drivers, warehouse guys, your ordinary joe blow who is looking for an easy dollar.

For one, your ordinary store guy doesn't have the street knowledge to deal with the thieves and the cops. For another, he wouldn't have the heart, would be too shaky. Couldn't lean on somebody, which is something the fence will sometimes have to do. Main thing is, the ordinary store guy isn't known. Others wouldn't have confidence in him. Who would do business with him? Would be very hard for him to get the connections, except maybe with the dopers and the assholes who will deal with anybody. But then he will have the bums and riffraff hanging around, which will affect his legit business.

This or that good thief would have a shot at it but not your ordinary thief. The thief has the street knowledge and has the larceny in his heart. But he won't have the business know-how and he ain't world-wise either. Couldn't deal with the businessman and with the public. Would have a hard time getting the good connections, say, with the police or other dealers. Another thing, most of your thieves don't work, and fencing is long hours, can be very hard work.

A Jesse, yes, could pull it off. But even a Bowie or a Steelbeams, as good as thieves as they are, it would very dicey. To get the contacts, to get the knowledge, to put up with all the hassles.

In my eye, the fence is a go-getter, more so than most people. Not so much in Tylersville this time, but my fencing in American City was a ball buster. I was always on the go. Getting calls two, three o'clock in the morning from this or that thief, "Hey, I got such and such, can you handle it?" On account that is the time when most burglars are hitting. Then shipping the stuff out, running to the auctions, having to be at the store. I didn't sleep much. And you got to be on your toes, with the cops, with your thieves, and different ones.

It isn't easy to be a fence, not by a long shot. Will depend on the kind of dealer one is—what he needs to know, how much he has to cover his back. In my eye, a fence has to be world-wise, has to have heart and be trusted by those he's dealing with. Especially his outlets and the better thief have to have that trust, and that he can deliver. That and he has to make his own openings, be a good schemer, which can only come about if he's world-wise and has the heart. The street knowledge and the eye for the easy dollar must be there. But not be too greedy. Has to have the confidence in himself, that he can get over on others, and others have to have confidence in him, that he's not an asshole. Helps to be likable, but more so that you can be trusted—leastwise to have them thinking you are.

The strictly business side of fencing is not a big thing, especially if you're running a legit business already and handling the same products. Will already know the prices and the profit margin. In some ways the fencing is easier 'cause you don't have to figure in the business tax. Don't have the hassle of people returning merchandise like in a legit business. Your time and the costs in handling and shipping are less with the warm stuff. A bigger worry with fencing is getting stuck with it on account it's too hot to unload. Or having to sell it too cheaply 'cause when you bought it you were thinking you could sell it for a better price than you can actually get.

A dealer like myself who is pretty wide open will need to know at least a little about many things. Not an expert, now, but ballpark prices. This was hard at first, learning the prices and knowing about the different kinds of merchandise. Especially with the antiques and because of all the stuff I handled. Even on the legit side it can be hairy with antiques on account of all the reproductions and because the prices can change so quickly. I think I have a good head for figuring out what something is worth, what it will sell for. This goes way back, even when I was a kid I followed the price of things. Going to the auctions helped a lot 'cause they handle almost anything. For antiques and that, I always kept up-to-date books on what different pieces were worth. I always got along with the secondhand dealers and with different businessmen, too, so I could check with them if I needed to know what something was worth.

The business knowledge I feel I had. Where I fell down was not having the cash in hand. That's where someone like Louie and Angelo, or Phil today, have an advantage. I never saved my money like I should of. This hurt, but not as much it could of 'cause the thieves trusted me more than someone like Louie. Would give me a day or two to come up with the cash. Give me a chance to unload the stuff, then pay. Sometimes I would go to Angelo for a shylock loan. Or go to Ciletti once we became buddies. Pay him back in a few days, don't worry about the interest. Just don't let Angelo know.

The biggest things are knowing how to deal with thieves and knowing how to sort out the good information from the bullshit. The thieves are on the front line—they know who's solid, who the cops are after, who's clipping, who's lying low or who just got popped. But you got to know how to sort out the good information from the bullshit. Different dealers get that in different ways, but being in prison helped me a lot. And having been a thief, I knew where they were coming from.

In American City I knew just about everything that happened from my contacts with Louie and the local gang and from knowing the thieves. Don't have that same knowledge in Tylersville on account my contacts are less and my fencing is a different ball game. I have a general knowledge and know where to go to find out but not on top of things like before.

In my eye the fence has to have a lot of personality. Maybe not every fence, but those who are more wide-open. You have to able to mix with all kinds of people and relate to them at their level. The people have to like you, find you interesting, and have confidence in you, too. The personality side was a very big thing for me, that I could talk to anyone. That I have a knack for remembering names and faces, and little tidbits about someone. I always had the gift of gab. If somebody wanted to talk antiques, I'd talk antiques, If they wanted to talk sports, I'd talk sports, if it's women, I'd talk women. Not just bullshitting my way around but getting others to reveal themselves to me. Give me something I could maybe use later on.

Main thing, you have to be able to open people up, figure them out, let them read between the lines about what you do. You can't just come up and say, "Hey, I buy stolen goods!" They got to figure it out themselves, pick up on it.

And not letting it go to your head, not become a big shot and come across as better than you are. I was always very careful that way, not to act cocky and not to badmouth one thief to another thief, behind his back. You do that, you got to figure the guy is thinking, "Hey, if he talks about this guy this way, what the hell does he say to others about me?" I was always very careful not to run somebody down that way.

It takes a lot of "heart" [Sam touches his chest[1]] *to be a fence, a lot of heart.* What I mean is you have to be a nervy son of a bitch, not scare easy, not fall apart when there's a search warrant on your shop or when the police pull you over. It's the same in dealing with the thieves and the other dealers—you got to be tough in little ways, or they'll take you to the cleaners. Fence can't be a pussyfoot but has to take charge. You do it and do it now, or you can kiss it good-bye.

Can't be a pushover, that is for sure. I would say it would be very hard to be a fence, say, like me or Louie, and not have that side of you, roughness or whatever. That you can do it yourself or have a backup do it for you. Louie was a very big man, very powerful, and he had "ties," which itself scared a lot of people. Same with Phil today, not a muscle man but has "ties" and is a pretty tough guy. You'd be leery about messing with him.

There were just a few times I had to get rough. Am pretty easygoing, but it was well-known I could be very nasty if I had to. Mostly I handled things myself. A few times, yes, shot to the guy's nose or kick in the balls. But mostly get in his face, push his ass out the door and tell him I never want to see his face again. But a couple of times, this is back in American City, it was more serious and I had Angelo's boys give me a hand. The one time was when I got jammed up on account of Lemont Dozier—lied to me that he had stolen these

TVs outside the area and then this woman walks by my shop and sees her TV in the store window. Lemont got worked over pretty good—more than just a kick in the balls. Even the police didn't have to worry about Lemont stealing for awhile. This helped to get the word out, too, 'cause I really had very few hassles with thieves.

Same thing this last period, had to get rough a few times. First time goes back to when I had that little shop in Boonesboro, to when I got popped for buying warm merchandise from the younger Beck boy and his buddies. The Beck boy held up but the other ones were snitching, so had them worked over by the older Beck boy and a couple of his pals.

This just happened a couple of years ago. It is early evening, I'm just back from the auction and am unloading a few things. Two Hispanic kids, eighteen, nineteen year olds, are watching me. I am suspicious. Then the one says to me, "Hey, old man, hand it over." Something to that effect. I opened the door to my cab like I didn't hear him. Then he says it again, wanted my wallet. Could see out of the corner of my eye, they were moving toward me. Reached in the cab and grabbed hold of a big crowbar, turned around and swung at them. Nicked the one. Called them motherfucking punks, "Hey, you can have what I got but you got to take what comes with it." They took off running.

But it doesn't end there. I am fired up and I didn't want them or another ass-hole in the neighborhood thinking they could pull that shit. Hops in my truck and down the street looking for them. Sees them run into this one apartment. I drive right there and bang on the door. The lady answers, the one kid's mom I guess. I push my way in and am yelling for the motherfuckers to come out, that if I see their faces again, I will blow their brains away.

Turns out that Wanda is looking out the office window and sees this all happening, and me hopping in my truck. She yells at Donnie, my foreman in the shop. So, now I am coming out of the apartment and Donnie shows up. Wants to know what is going on and to settle me down.

You wouldn't think a thief would steal from a fence he is doing business with. But it happens and more than you would think. This one morning I stopped by to see Tinker. Runs a little secondhand place. Turns out the night before a couple of thieves Tinker's been buying from broke into his shop. Robbed him. They know who they can pull that shit on. Same with the snitching, you can't stop it all but you can make them think twice.[2]

That little suspicion that you can lean on someone helps with your thief and even with your businessman. Even with your ordinary joe blow. Think about it. You're dealing with thieves and shady businesspeople. Maybe with dopers and real assholes. It's the snitching but more than that. What's to keep them from stealing from you, from ripping you off? Sure as hell can't run to the police. All the way down the line, really, that little suspicion helps 'cause there are quite a few assholes out there.

Normally, no, I didn't carry a gun. Never with the burglary. Sometimes with the fencing. As a precaution if I was transporting some good antique pieces or good jewelry and am leery of some assholes stopping my truck and cleaning me out. A gun can bring you headaches. Pull a gun and there will be heat from the police and from the public too. Can get lot of extra time if a gun is involved.

You usually would not want to hurt someone that way [with a gun], put someone's lights out. A gun can help, can be some protection. But you can't rely on it—you're only blowing wind outta your ass if that's all you have to back you up. It is more how a guy carries himself.

The fence has to get the confidence of those he is selling to, even more so than those he is buying from. Can he be trusted? Is his word good? Whether it is the ordinary business guy who is buying for his store or I'm peddling to another dealer like myself, have to get his confidence.

Most fences are pretty solid that way. Like Angelo and Scottie, I would trust all the way. Other ones I dealt with, if they got jammed up, I would be leery they couldn't stand up. Another thing, there are fences who are snitches, regular snitches, that is how they get their license to steal. Turn in thieves to save their own ass and make the police look good, help them clear their books.

Like Louie, he was protected in other ways, but he would snitch to keep the police happy. Was a main way he got his slack. But he was careful who he snitched on. Would turn in the shitass thieves and the dopers. And he would snitch on some of the other dealers, the smaller secondhand guys, to have the cops slow the guy down or knock him out of business. A lotta thieves would overlook Louie's snitching 'cause he had the cash and the thief is figuring he just turns in shitass thieves but won't snitch on me. Still the suspicion is there and this hurt Louie 'cause the better thieves shied away from him. I never feared Louie that way but I was watchful.

It depends, too, on how covered the guy is, how protected he is. Take Angelo or the lawyer who handled the coins for Jesse and me, they are very cautious and very protected. Very little worry that they will get jammed up. Same with the foundry guy and Rosen, the jewelry guy, you could lay your faith in them. They were so covered and you had confidence in the way they handled things. It is easier to trust someone like that.

Most fences if they snitch will not take down anybody that could hurt them— say, if they [the fences] are leery of getting roughed up or if it will cut off their business. You can get worked over pretty good for snitching 'cause some of the thieves can get pretty rough. That's what happened to one of Angelo's cousins, ratted on a couple of guys and they busted him up, and good. Louie got his due, too, when he was doing time for the fencing [see Chapter 12]. Couple of guys he snitched on, stabbed him in prison. Had to transfer Louie to another prison but he still had to watch his back.

The big thing for me was, my word was good. Once I had the goods, the thieves didn't have to worry about it. It was my worry, and if something happened, it was on me. If I said I'd pay so much, or set it at this price, they knew my word was good. It was known I would handle my end of the deal, be there at such a time, do this or that. All the way down the line, they knew they could depend on me.

That doesn't mean I didn't try to get over the other guy or clip some of the people I dealt with. Take Norm Hirsch, he and his mother were very big antique dealers and importers. I did a lot of business with them, mostly legit but some on the shady side. But I did arrange for a burglary of one of their shops, and I would clip them on the docks, like on the grandfather clocks

The clocks happened this way. I'm at their shop, talking to Norm. And I asked about Sarah, his mother. Tells me, she's in Europe buying dolls, grandfather clocks, and other items. My mind just clicked, that I'd have the guys I knew that worked on the docks watch for her crates to come in. Break into them, and clip a few of the dolls and the clocks. Off and on when Sarah made a trip, I'd post the guys at the dock, "Hey, some crates are coming in." Just make sure they didn't clip too much.

The burglary was a pretty decent haul. Norm's wife tells me that her and Norm are going on a trip out West, to celebrate their wedding anniversary. Their daughter and Sarah will run the main shop but will close down the little shops they have in Salem and Montrose. I'm thinking, this might be a good time to clip one of those places. Don't have to be in a hurry and would be a while before it was discovered. Got Steelbeams and Mickey to hit the place in Salem. From my being in that shop, I knew the layout and how the alarm system worked. Guided them on what pieces to take. Like what dolls to take and what not to take on account some would be too hot to unload and was leery that my outlets might know where they came from. Even scouted the place with Steelbeams and Mickey.

The fence has to hustle, but it is different than the street hustling, what the dopers and street types do. They will do anything to turn a buck, really lower themselves and beat anybody. How can I say it? There's more honor in the hustling a fence does. It is more like that of a businessman or a salesman. Playing on the greed of the person looking for a bargain. Being shrewd, being a shyster. Getting over on somebody to make a buck, to give you information or make a contact. *A good conman, really.*

I especially pulled a lot of shit with antiques. I'm talking about selling what people believed was an antique, but wasn't. Many times I would buy a reproduction and doctor it, maybe upholster or even scratch in an old date. I fooled antique dealers already. It's funny. If it had been legit, they would check the piece out very carefully. But when it's hot, people are too eager.

With antiques especially, I know how to take care of what I'm buying—that has always been big help for me. Even with appliances and TVs when they were a good item, I'm enough of a handyman to repair them if they come in damaged. But with the video cameras, the CD player, the laptop computer—it is a different ballgame. Don't know shit.

The fence is really a schemer, an operator. There is hustling, but it's more scheming. Has to take the openings that come his way, but *he's got to make his own openings,* too. It's more like what Angelo or somebody in the rackets does, 'cause they are schemers, too.

The fence has to make the adjustment if something comes up, but the big thing is to stay one step ahead. Say, I was at the auction, I might buy some junky TVs, furniture, or whatever, just so I'd have the receipts and have my back covered in case things like that came my way. Covering your back, setting up a deal, whatever, you're always thinking down the road. This is more true for fencing than for the guy in burglary.

As far as buying and selling, I did more hustling on the legit secondhand side than with the fencing. The fencing is more scheming, know what I mean. The difference is the fence has to hustle harder to keep up his contacts and has to be more on his toes not to be outhustled 'cause your other dealers and even many of the dopers and street types are pretty sharp. Fence has to watch more carefully so he doesn't get ripped off 'cause who is he going to complain to? Call the cops? They would get a laugh out of that.

Contacts, Connections, and Networking

Getting the connections is the hardest part. For burglary, too, but especially for the fencing. This will depend on the kind of dealer one is. Operating the way I was in American City, whew, you have to have contacts with a lotta people, and different kinds of people. Not just with the thieves now, but with other dealers, with the local clique, and with the legit business guy. And you will need some slack from the cops. Don't forget about that.

I had a helluva spider web in American City. Helluva spider web. *And it connected with other spider webs*—with Louie's, with Angelo, with Cooper, with Scottie, with guys in the local clique. This time in Tylersville, not sure you'd call it a spider web. Pretty half-assed. Enough for me to operate but the comparison would be like night and day.

Some of the contacts just fell into place, others I had to work at. Main thing is to get a couple of good spokes, to get the wheel rolling.

Ways of Making Contacts

Word of mouth is the best advertisement 'cause there is a helluva grapevine out there. One buddy to his buddies, one dealer to another dealer. *Not one grapevine, now, but different grapevines.* There is the street grapevine, there is the grapevine the better thieves have, the grapevine the businessman has, and your fences and secondhand dealers have their own grapevine. Same with your truckers and warehouse guys, they may hear from the street grapevine or from a better thief, but they will have their own grapevine. Is some overlap, but less than you would think.

The walk-in trade and the penny-ante thief will know from the street grapevine but the better thief will not use that. He will have his own grapevine, with other thieves who are decent. The word of mouth that brings a good thief to a fence is not the same as the one that brings the walk-in or the doper thief. Even the in-between thief, like Rocky or Andy or the older Beck boy, won't rely on the street talk. Sure as hell not Bowie or Steelbeams.

Myself, when I was into burglary, I didn't know the street grapevine. Didn't bother with it. My grapevine was with other burglars and with the higher-ups like Angelo or Louie. Here's the thing, your good thieves and even many of your ordinary burglars, pretty much stay to themselves. Won't advertise where he's unloading, except may tell another decent thief or a buddy. Another thing, if they hear somebody's buying, say, from the street talk or from an in-between thief they know, they'll ask another decent thief: "Hey, what's he paying? Is he solid?" Or, they'll check it for themselves. Be cautious, but if they feel comfortable then give the guy a shot. But the rule for the better thief is the recommendation of another decent thief or somebody else they have confidence in—maybe their lawyer or maybe even a businessman he is getting tips from.

Being recommended or having someone vouch for you is a main thing. You need a hookup, somebody who will bring you together. Take Steelbeams, he had heard from the street talk that I would buy. But he didn't pay it any mind. Then, he is talking to Bowie and Bowie tells him check me out. Once I knew he was okay with Bowie, we was set. Your better thief will usually have a number of places he can go, to get rid of his stuff. But sometimes he has to go shopping, too. That's when he is gonna check with his buddies or look for himself.

Even Jesse and me had to shop around a few times. One time we clipped an antique place and headed straight to Scottie in Oceantown. Got there when his place opened up in the morning. But Scottie isn't there, gone for the day. This is a three-hour trip, now, and I didn't want to haul this stuff back. Jesse was leery but went along with checking out the secondhand places in the area. Felt comfortable with a couple of them and decided to unload the antiques. You are pretty safe doing this but there is still too much risk. Jesse was right about that. You should always know the man you are selling to.

Lotta thieves, especially the younger ones, don't know much about what is going on. May run with just a few other guys or a clique. Unless he's done time, been in jail, won't know many people. Take Rocky. The guys he was operating with were selling to Louie. I was already pretty wide open but Rocky never heard of me. They were content with the price Louie was paying and stayed to themselves. Then Louie sends them to me 'cause he couldn't handle the antiques they had picked up. Rocky was a greenie. Knew something about burglary but otherwise didn't know nothing about nothing.

Louie *paved the way* for me, you might say. Introduced me around and brought me into the gambling club. Same with Woody. Paved the way for me and I paved the way for him. Was a two-way street. I had several ones who did that for me in American City. Were good spokes in the wheel. Didn't really have that in Tylersville this time, except maybe could still rely on Phil or Scottie.

The gambling hookup was a big help. One time Louie just asked me if I wanted to come to their card game. Some nights they play cards, other times it'll be rolling dice. Send out for food, any liquor you wanted, bring in girls sometimes. But mostly we gambled and gave each other the business, lots of ribbing back and forth.

Not anybody could come. It was only if one of the main ones—like Louie or Angelo or Nicky—invited you. Were about twenty guys that were part of the regular gang but others would come. It was like a clique and everybody had his fingers into something, were connected with city hall or with the money downtown. I wouldn't say all the main operators in town were part of the club. Some of the Jews weren't. But they were still connected with the Italians and others who were. I already had some connections with the local clique—the gambling hookup just cemented that.

Hooking up with Jesse was a big boost 'cause he was well-known, but getting in with the local clique was an even bigger step. They threw a lot of openings my way. If something came my way I couldn't get rid of, or I needed a hookup with somebody, I could check with one of the gang. And just people knowing I was doing business, say, with Angelo, opened a lot of doors. It helped, too, with the magistrates and some of the police. Most of those in club were getting police protection one way or another. The fencing was starting to roll before Louie invited me in, but it really took off after that.

In American City, yes, I did *put out the word out* I would buy, encouraged that. But not this time [in Tylersville]. Very little anyway. Same with building up the outlets. Then [in American City], if I surmised a businessman or an auction guy might chisel, thought there was some play there, I would feel them out, give them an opening. Not come out and say, "Hey, I deal in warm stuff," but let them know about my shop. That I could handle almost anything, that if they ever needed something or ran across something, I'd appreciate getting a shot at it. It would be pretty plain, they could read between the lines. This time [in Tylersville], I did some of that but was more careful and was more content to stay with the contacts I had.

Contacts with Thieves and Drivers

With the walk-in thief and the doper, you don't have to put the word out. Not as much anyway. They will keep checking out the secondhand places, especially if they hear on the street that so and so is buying. For a long time in American City I shied away from the general thief, from the shoplifters, and the half-assed burglars. Was choosy what I'd buy and who I bought from. Then, I started buying more and different things. Soon, it went "swoosh." Different thieves, like Danny Turner and Lemont Dozier, put out the word that I would buy and pay an okay price. Danny was an all-around thief but mostly a shoplifter. Very good at it. Can go out and get the stuff. Lemont was a black thief, a half-assed burglar and breaking into cars. They were known on the streets, especially Danny. A real talker, likes to brag. They were peddling to Louie, to the other secondhand shops, and to their friends. Once I started buying regular from Danny and Lemont, it spreads quickly in their kind of crowd.

This last period I dealt very little with the walk-in thief. Off and on, yes. If somebody came in with something I couldn't pass by, I might buy. But if the thief started coming back, I'd cut it off. Say, "Hey, can't handle that stuff anymore." If kept coming back, then make it very clear "Don't want see your fucking face again." I didn't want the word to spread. Had to be careful it didn't get out of hand. Would pull back if I was leery of hassles from the police to make sure my name doesn't keep coming up.

I always preferred to deal with the good burglar, and with the truck hijacker or the warehouse guy. I am guessing most fences would. But the better thieves have other outlets. And with them, it's more strictly business. "What can you pay?" "Can you be trusted?" You can't get the better thief in your pocket that way, except they will want to feel comfortable with the guy they are selling to. I always did business with some of the better burglars, especially if they came across antiques, but not as much as I would've liked.

My main business was with the in-between thief, the younger guy who is easier to keep in your pocket. Not that I financed them. But would help them out. If a guy needed bail, put a call into Phil or another bondsman, tell him this guy is okay. If a guy is in jail and needs a job to get out, I'd sign the papers to get him out. Be a job sponsor. Hire him for week or so, then tell the parole officer I can't use the man no more. He no longer works for me. Not just any thief now, but some of the regulars. Like Denny and Mickey back in American City, and the Beck boys this time. If they were short of cash, I'd help them out. It is easy come, easy go for the ordinary thief. Even the good thief can spend money something fierce. Next time around when they are peddling, just take off what they owed me. Just little debts to keep them in my pocket. Nothing big.

This is something I frequently would do, to make the thief think I was really doing him right. Say, you sold me a gun or an antique, and I give you a hundred dollars for it. Next time you come in, I say—"here's another fifty bucks, that gun you sold me was worth more than I thought." You're gonna think I'm a pretty great guy 'cause I don't have to do that. The thief is like anybody else, he more or less thinks he owes it to me to give me a shot at what he has on account of my treating him fair, and just from being his outlet in the past.

In a way you have to be a good sport, not be a tightass. 'Cause a lotta thieves are looking for a handout, a free meal, round of drinks. This can be an aggravation 'cause you know what kind of a moocher someone like Rocky is. But you can play on that, too. With the in-between thief, I came across as a nice guy. Had them a little in my debt. If not on a money basis, then more or less a feeling of guilt if they thought of peddling elsewhere.

Another thing, a lot of your burglars and thieves have a lot of time on their hands. Don't work or if they do work, want a job that won't tie them down, or a part-time job. So, are looking for a hangout, a place to kill time. My shop in American City, I'd be in back working, they'd come back, bullshit, horse around. Somebody got a new motorcycle, they would want to show it off. Maybe see what was on the shelves today. Give Cletus or one of the help a hard time. There was always something going on at my store. I don't know how to say it, *I guess you want to be where something is happening.*

This last time, I didn't allow the thieves to hang around. Not as much anyway. Take the Beck boys, would stop by fairly regular. I'd chat, maybe send Wanda out for sandwiches—for them and for the guys working in my shop. But, I wouldn't let them drop their hat. Didn't want my shop to become a hangout. If you start letting that happen, it can get out of hand. Get more losers than you can imagine.

More so than with your regular thief, it is harder to keep up the connections with your truck driver and warehouse thief. There is more turnover and they usually aren't hanging with other thieves. Are mostly an ordinary joe blow who steals off and on, when the coast is clear. Not part of a clique or a party crowd like your ordinary thief is. So, you got to put the word out yourself, and keep working at it or that trade can dry up.

There are different ways it can happen. Some of your truck drivers and warehouse people will know this or that thief 'cause these are the kinds of jobs that ex-cons and the burglar is gonna get. Take the big tire place in town, and does a lot of service work on cars. Who works there? The ordinary joe blow and ex-cons. Maybe they're hanging at the same taverns or eating places. Or know each other from the same neighborhood or old school days. The flea markets and the auctions are good meeting places. If the thief thinks the driver or the warehouse guy is solid, it may come out in their conversation—"Yeah, this guy at Goodman's will buy what you're hauling or what you are picking up."

In American City I would stop at the truck stops in the area. Rap with the truckers and let them know what kind of a shop I had. Maybe the guy isn't even chiseling yet, but next time when the chance is there, he's gonna be more interested. His mind is gonna click 'cause he thinks he can get rid of it. Then, too, one guy can tell his buddy. Especially with your truck driver, there's a trust between them.

With the warehouse guy, it is funny all the ways it can happen. Take Tommy Willadson, he was working at Hilary's, the big truck and freight terminal place [in American City]. Huge transfer and storage place. I am stopping there pretty regular to pick up furniture, appliances, and different things for my shop. Legit now. And to see if there is damaged merchandise. I would kid with the help, the guys working there. Let them know about my shop, that if they ran across something that was damaged or unclaimed, I'd appreciate their giving me a shot at it. Pay them a fair price and no headaches for them. Let them know that this was hard work they were doing and probably weren't getting paid enough. That the big shots in the office were making all the money. I was pretty direct. Different ones would bring me stuff but Tommy was a main one. Typewriters, tools, radios. Couple of times a month, Tommy would bring me stuff. He worked there a long time and passed the word to some of his buddies, that I'd buy and there'd be no hassles. As long as they didn't clip too often, the risk is very small. I may have to remind them to slow down, not get too greedy. But your hookups with drivers and the warehouse and shipping people come and go. You have to make a lot of little things add up to keep that side of the trade going.

Another time I'm seeing this woman and she is working at a large department store. Picked her up after work a couple of times and got to know her supervisor, the main guy that worked in the shipping department. I started buying used refrigerators, stoves, shit like that—trade-ins. He was giving the stuff to me for a few bucks, rather than throw it away, and pocketing the money for himself. Then I moved on to better stuff, even new stuff. Once I got my foot in the door and he saw the dollars coming in, it got to where he was approaching me. Not just appliances, now, but lamps, chairs, mattresses. Pull my truck right in and load up 'cause he was covered, could say it was used or damaged.

This is funny, how one thing can lead to another, 'cause that is how I met Becky—from this guy. Turns out, he lives across the street from Becky and he is telling her she should check out my shop on account of my prices. So one day, this is like a year after I got out of jail for the antique burglary, she stops by my shop [in American City]. Attractive lady. Dark hair. Had a way about her that caught your eye. Came in with her three kids, two girls and a boy. The boy was the oldest, about ten. Buys a bunk bed for the two girls. I could tell she was having a hard time making it, so I chopped the price way down. Month or so later, she is back and buys a couple of more pieces. *Decided to check her out, so I delivered the pieces myself.* We get to rapping, it turns out she is divorced and is working at Bailey's Furniture, which is where I worked when

I first came to American City. I am leaving, so I tells her, she should come to the auction with me sometime on her day off. You can get good bargains and I could help her pick out the better stuff from the junk. She went for it, and we ended up becoming a couple.

She was married to a real asshole. Left her with the three kids, wasn't paying support or nothing. They was going hungry when I met them. First on, I helped Becky pay the bills and that. Then we bought a house together. I was more or less a dad for the kids, especially the boy 'cause I would take him along in the truck or I'd have him do little odd jobs in the shop, give him a chance to earn some money. I was good to Becky but it was tough for her in some ways. I was always on the go, spent very little time at home. Saturday nights and maybe Sunday afternoons were our main times together. Saturdays, I'd usually take Becky out for dinner. Maybe take the kids along, then go roller skating. Might pick up Amy, too, if her mom would let her go [Amy is Sam's daughter]. The kids got a bang out of that. I enjoyed it, too, 'cause I used to skate when I was a kid.

Becky knew, but didn't wanna know that I was dealing in warm stuff. She more or less went along with it, pretended it was all legit. Some of the regular thieves would stop by my house or call me, "Can you handle this?" "Where should we drop it?" If I wasn't home and Becky knew where I was, she'd call and leave a message for me.

Just running a secondhand place helps. A lot of people surmise that a place like mine is dealing in warm stuff—not just thieves but your truck drivers, your ordinary joe citizen. Even some of your businesspeople, your store people will surmise that. It helped, too, I got along with the different secondhand places. Stay on a friendly basis with guy running the place and even with the help. Stop at each other's shop, to razz one another and see what the other was up to. If a warehouse or a truck thief is shopping around, chances are this or that secondhand guy would send him my way. This is even in Tylersville, but not near as much as in American City. In both places, too, some of the secondhand guys are selling to me what they are buying direct from the thieves. The money is less when you operate that way, but especially this time in Tylersville I many times wanted that layer in between.

I had very few warehouse or truck thieves this last time. Nothing like before. Didn't work at it, which is what you have to do. A main warehouse thief the last few years has been Chet. Works for a big, big wholesale furniture place in Oceantown. In the shipping and delivery department. The foreman is a slacker and more or less has Chet run the department. Chet was at Scottie's place when I was there, asking about art deco. Had come across a sofa and a couple of chairs, and wanted to know what they might be worth. Scottie bullshits him, "Hey, we got the country's expert right here," referring to me. Turns out Chet dabbles in antiques and we hit it off. One thing led to another, I could help him and he could help me. Off and on there'd be a message at Scotties when I'm in Oceantown, that Chet has some boxes for me—lamps, chairs, coffee tables, whatever. This is stuff I could run right to the auction on the way back to Tylersville.

Another good one has been Glenn. At the airport in Franklintown. Knew him from the penitentiary and ran into him at one of the auctions. Him and a guy he worked with would clip, then meet me at a fishing cabin this guy owned. Glenn was very cautious. Very leery of doing time again. Just clip every now and then but clip stuff that is worth a decent dollar.

One guy knowing another guy from being in prison has always been a big source for me. A guy will come into my shop, or calls me at home: "Joe so-and-so sent me or told me to give you a call." In American City that was usually enough for the connection to be made but this last period I was more cautious. I might check back with joe so-and-so or meet with the guy, see if we felt comfortable with one another, or see if there were other people we both knew.

I'm not talking only about the regular thief, now. But guys who have done time, are legit really, but are now driving truck or working on the docks where they might clip a little. Or take guys like Andy or Ronnie, say, they are pulling back from burglary or are lying low for awhile, they will find work driving truck or working in a warehouse. If they come across something at the warehouse or if there was an extra piece on the truck when they delivered, they would keep it. Call me and I would meet them at storage place I had. A few extra bucks for them and for me, too.

Contacts with Business Buyers

Hooking up with a store owner or a businessman who will buy warm stuff is tricky. When I was operating in American City I would go to different places in town and the towns nearby, like the furniture and carpet places. See if they had seconds or damaged items. That was a big part of my legit business and wanted them to know I handled what they have. I am feeling them out, to see if they will bite. This is a good entry. Can build up a relationship by buying their seconds or damaged merchandise and they can see I am pretty decent guy to do business with. Not just that I would buy but can sell to them for a good price, too. Let it be known without saying it that on different items I am covered and can deal with them as if it's strictly legit. It may end up they don't buy warm stuff from me, but the opportunity for them is there.

Once it got around that I was buying, some of the store people would stop in my shop, look around and see what I have. A main one was Winnie Burdette. Had the biggest TV and appliance place in American City. Started buying my TVs that were a year, two years old. Would stop by and pick out the ones he wanted. Turns out that he is selling them as new, as demonstrators. Now, I am knowing I always have an outlet for TVs, as long as they were in decent shape, weren't too old. I could still run them to the auction or to a couple of dealers in Southstate but also have a local outlet. Less hassle, save on time and gas, too. If you were to ask me to pick one thing I handled more than anything else [in American City], it would probably be TVs. Was good money in them then, which is not the case today. I peddled a lot of them, whole lot. Some were legit 'cause I'd buy seconds, but most were warm.

Another hookup with some of the local businesspeople came from my being part of the gambling clique. I got to be buddies with some of them. If I needed an outlet for something, I could go to one of them 'cause you're running in a circle of free spirits and guys that will be at least a little shady. Have their own businesses and know other people in the business world, legit now. Could they recommend somebody?

This is how I met "Fat Charlie," Charlie Ciletti, the food importer. We hit it off, became pals. Charlie would stop at my shop almost every day. Maybe go for coffee or a sandwich. He was a big help 'cause he knew everybody. I would ask him, is so-and-so strictly legit or will they close an eye? Take Ziefield that handled the truckload of lobsters. Ziggy had a big seafood place in town. I ate there a lot and met him. Surmised he was out for the extra dollar. So, when I got the call on the lobsters, I checked with Charlie, "What about Ziggy? Will he take them, is he okay?" Charlie said he thought it was worth a try. I called Ziggy and he grabbed them. You have to figure Ziggy knew very well I was dealing. 'Cause he didn't hesitate. Really, the risk is small on his part—how in the hell are you going identify lobsters as belonging to somebody else.

I would say overall that getting contacts with your businessman and store people is about the hardest connection for the fence to make. But once you get it going and get in with the right crowd, once different ones have confidence in you—that they can deal with you and not have to worry about hassles—then you will have all the outlets you will need. Really, you don't need that many store people, especially if you have a couple of auctions that are good outlets. Couple of furniture places and antique outlets, TV and appliance place, place that handles building supplies, auto parts and that, maybe a restaurant, a good jewelry shop.

This last period I didn't have the contacts with the local businessmen or the store people. [Except for contacts with local secondhand places and antique dealers.] Five, six years ago I get a call—guy has a load of shingles. Did I have an outlet? I was tempted 'cause I did know the owner of a big building supply place right outside of Tylersville but I was leery. Tried calling Phil but he wasn't around. Figured he'd want too big a bite anyway. Thought about Lenny but at that time we were still feeling each other out. So I passed it up.

When I was operating in American City, it would have been "bang, bang"—a couple of calls and the deal would be done. In fact, I did handle shingles in American City. Maybe half a dozen times. It even crossed my mind to contact the guy I had done business with back then. But we're talking fifteen years. You can't go back to the well that way. I am no longer part of that scene. It would be hard for him to have confidence in me. And could I still trust him?

Contacts with Auctions and Antique/Secondhand Dealers

Making contacts with the auction people and the antique dealers is a lot easier than with your ordinary businessman. The auction people are shadier and they're not as afraid of taking a little risk. Know the ropes better. They don't ask many questions. Are figuring, what they don't know won't hurt them. Another thing, your antique dealers and secondhand people hang at the same places, run in the same circle. If you stop at one secondhand place, you might bump into other dealers. Who is gonna know is it warm or not?

When I was operating in American City and taking stuff to Scottie in Ocean City, I would run into dealers there. Just killing time and talking business. This last period I would stop to see Log Cabin [moniker for a man who converted a log cabin into an antique shop] and you'd find other dealers there. It's the same thing with the auctions, you will bump into other antique dealers and second-hand people. You get to know them that way first, then later on it might develop into something more.

That's how I met Woody when I was operating in American City. I'm at this one auction and have bought a shitload of furniture and antiques that were sold that day. This guy comes up and says, "You must have a helluva shop to be buying all that stuff." We chatted and I told him to stop by my shop, see for himself. Couple of weeks later he does stop by, looks over what I have. Tells me that he and his dad run this auction place in Southstate, and that he comes into this area to pick up stuff from the auctions here to sell down there. Says he can get furniture at a good price and what did I have for him. We was both reading between the lines that we was handling stuff that could be a little shaky.

This last period I met Ollie almost the same way. He is at an auction and is buying all the wicker. Including the pieces I'm selling. Afterwards, he comes up to me and asks if I handle much in the way of wicker. Turns out he runs an auction in Bordertown, right across the state line. Bring a load down some-time, he tells me. Which I did. We hit it off, you might say. Felt very comfort-able with each other. But I still started slow. Gradually let it be known to him that, hey, sometimes in this business you pick up things that can be a little shaky. Then, more and more it was out in the open. He introduced me to the people working there, the auctioneers and the ticket people. Normally, I wouldn't broadcast whether what I was bringing was warm. But if something was maybe too warm, I'd let Ollie know. Not blabber out, "Hey, this is stolen," but just say, "The guy selling this to me is a real screwball, so this stuff could be a little shaky." To protect him in case he preferred I peddle it elsewhere and to make sure he doesn't just sell it to anybody, and then everybody gets jammed up.

Ollie has been my main outlet for warm merchandise these past years. Except for small antique pieces, guns, jewelry, few things like that—an awful lot of what I bought that was warm I'd run down to his auction. Very few people know, even have an inkling, that this has been my main outlet. The police never found out. The Beck boys and different ones I was buying from, even Rocky and Steelbeams, I never let them know. A couple of guys who work in my shop have gone down with me, to help with the loading and unloading, and to give them a break from the shop. They might surmise what is going on but don't really know.

Almost anyone can peddle this or that piece, small stuff, at an auction or flea market. But if you're clipping regular or if its pieces that are worth a good dollar, then you will need to know some of the main people at the auction—guy who runs it, the auctioneer, the ticket people, maybe some of the pickers. Need them to help you in little ways, move you ahead in the line, look the other way or give you a break. The police, especially the state police, can watch some of your auctions pretty closely. The ticket guy can give you a heads up, can put you ahead of the line so you get in and get out. I always shot to get on the good side of the auctioneer and the ticket people. Not paying them off now but being a nice guy, buy them a sandwich or cup of coffee, bid up this or that piece of merchandise. If the guy puts you ahead in the line so you can unload first, leave him a twenty or a fifty—"Here, this is for you."

The auctions were always a place I would meet a lot of different ones I had done business with over the years. You'd be surprised who you'd run into. Not just dealers, secondhand people, private collectors, and that. But this or that joe blow or businessman who has some larceny in his heart. A lot of burglars and truck driver types. Maybe looking for a bargain but it was enjoyment for them, too, a way to pass the time.

Another thing, I always met a lot of dealers and collectors from working on antiques, repairing and doctoring them up. I was well known for that. It started small, really, way back in American City. Is how I met Norm, one of the biggest dealers in the area and handled what was worth a very good dollar. Comes into my shop and asks me to work on some antique pieces—a loveseat, chairs, and a grandfather clock. I ended up doing a lot of work for him, and he put out the word that I was very good at the upholstery and working on antiques. We'd stop at each other's place. Got to be very friendly. I didn't know if he was shady or not but one time I got my hands on some good porcelain pieces that I couldn't unload 'cause they were too hot. Included a French punch bowl that your eyes were just pulled to look at. Handpainted in gold and very bright purple. Turns out it went all the way back to 19th century, it was that old. The state police had already checked with some of the local dealers and had checked my shop, too. I called Norm and told him that I had bought some porcelain, some very nice pieces, that "I think are legit but I am still leery they could be hotter than hell. Not sure what to do with them." I didn't know if he'd take a shot at them but he did.

Then, another time I got what turned out to be a Louis XIV cabinet and china set. I surmised it was valuable, so I grabbed it. Ran it by Norm and he told me what I had, only a few of its kind in existence. But said he didn't want to take a chance on it, that he would rather put me touch with a dealer who could handle better what I had. As a favor for me. I ran it down to that guy the same day. Now I had really good contact who could handle the really warm stuff.

But it's different with someone like Brubaker [main antique dealer in area]. He was a important contact for antiques, but he was strictly legit. No need to give an opening. I knew there wasn't any play. *I think I have an eye for that, can sense who has larceny in their heart and who doesn't. I could always do business with both types.*

Even more so this last period, my contacts with antique dealers and private collectors came from my being able to repair and doctor antiques. Has put me in touch with different dealers and forms a bond, too, where you are more likely to trust the other person and they have more confidence in you. I would do the repairing as favor for this or that one but didn't want to make it my main business.

That's how I met Benny and got involved with the art deco. He was buying art deco furniture to furnish hotels in Oceantown. Heard I did upholstery work and was good at it. *Comes by my shop and we ended up becoming partners.* He does the buying and selling, and I do the repairing and doctoring. Benny is a shyster, has some larceny in him. But this side of my business is legit—if not all the way, very close.

Contacts with Other Fences

My best fence contacts were mostly ones where we was brought together by a go-between, by someone we both knew. Like Woody hooked me up with Tex and other dealers in Southstate, Scottie with some of the antique and second-hand dealers in Oceantown, and Cooper hooked me up with private collectors who would take the really warm stuff. Louie and Angelo put me in touch with this or that fence or buyer. Phil has been a big help, especially these past years. And Lenny is becoming a bigger spoke, from the Orchard Grove area. He isn't mafia but is part of a whole clan that has their fingers into different things.

But I did find a couple of very good fences just by playing a hunch. Like Frankie Grasso, dirty little Italian. You wouldn't think he could pour himself a cup of coffee but he was shrewd and had a way about him. His name came up a couple of times in conversation that he had a big secondhand place in Glendale, half-assed town about eighty miles from American City. But I didn't give it any thought. One time I'm in the Glendale area and his name popped into my mind. I just had a suspicion about him 'cause it was odd I wasn't getting any business from this area. I decided to check it out. Were some hangers-on there and a couple of guys who I'm figuring are burglars. His place was like mine, only twice, three times bigger. I told Grasso about my shop, what I handled, and he showed me around his place. I just knew he was dealing. I bought a few items, legit now, and when I was leaving, Grasso tells me to keep in touch. If I have extras or an overflow, I should bring up a load sometime. I said that was fine but if you have a secondhand shop like mine, you never know what might be a little shaky. He says back to me, "Yeah, yeah. You never know in this business. It is something what some people will pull." Just the way he said it. You could read between the lines, was an opening for both of us.

One spider web can overlap with another spider web. In American City some of the people I am doing business with are doing business with Angelo and Louie. Same with Scottie. We knew a lot of the same people, helped make contacts for each other. If I couldn't handle something I would send the guy to Louie, and he was sending people to me. Louie and me palled together, had lunch or saw one another almost every day, went to Vegas together. Same with Woody, when he was in town we had dinner or met at an auction.

Many of the good thieves, especially the older ones, at one time were selling to Angelo. He pulls back, now they're selling to me. The in-between burglar is switching from Louie to me but Louie is now the main one for the walk-in thief. *Is an ebb and is a flow.*

Another thing, Angelo is pretty much packing in the fencing and at the same time I am pulling back from the burglary. He is shying away from buying up front and dealing direct with the thieves. And is getting bigger in the gambling and that, taking over from his old man. So, Angelo is more operating in the background. With the fencing, too, he wants a layer in between. *This was an opening for me 'cause he is pulling back and even pushing on me.*

Contacts with "the Law"

I really did have it good with the police in American City. Dagget was the first cop to help me out. Paul Dagget. Nothing big. Would let me know if my name came up at the police station. Knew each other from the skating rink when we was kids. He was a little on the wild side, drove an old blue ford, a ladies' man. Married a girl from American City, moved here and became a cop.

Another one was Hershel Dokes, a detective. Black cop. He would look the other way or, if somebody was fingering me, he'd tell the other cops there ain't nothing here. Dokes and me worked together at Bailey's Furniture when I first moved to American City. Got to be buddies. I did some upholstery work for them and gave them good deals on stuff in shop, but I wasn't really buying them off. They were both pretty straight cops. They would give me a break as long there wasn't too much heat. You don't need more than that most of the time.

Then, later on I got in with the chief. Big Polish guy—Melvie Pulaski. Met him through his son who was at the auctions a lot. Sometimes the chief would be there, too. I would rap with them, advise them on antiques, little shit like that. Turns out the chief and his son are into guns. Were gun collectors. I could help the chief out 'cause I was getting my hands on some good guns. It isn't too long, the chief's son is under suspicion in a shady gun deal. The state police are pressing him hard—where'd the guns come from. I more or less took the heat for it, that I bought the guns from a gun dealer at an auction. Had a receipt but hadn't seen the guy since. This cemented it even more with the chief. I had no worries from the chief.

My big boost with the cops came from my getting in with the gambling club. That was a message overall to the local cops to go slow. Really opened the door with the detectives. With Lieutenant Duggan and his buddy, Lieutenant Lorenzo. Duggan's brother was in the gambling club and must've passed the word to his brother 'cause he was in my shop almost like the next day. Week or so later, Lorenzo is with him and has his hands open, too. Didn't pull any punches. "Hey Sam, what are you selling cheap? I need a TV, need a refrigerator, can you help me out? Got any snow tires coming in?" Other cops would stop by my shop, too. To kill time but also to see what they could get for nothing. If I saw they were interested in something, I'd tell them, "Can't let it go for nothing but I'm tired of looking at it. Pay half the price that's listed and it's yours." I don't know if you'd say I was buying them off, but I knew I had my foot in the door. Dokes and Dagget more looked the other way, which was a big help. But Duggan and Lorenzo had their hands out. They were really, really corrupt cops.

Most cops will take a handout. If not a big handout, a little one. Some of the same ones who were in my shop stopped at Louie's when his flea market was open. Or run into them at another secondhand place or at junkyard for cars. Guy that runs a junkyard has an in with the cops on account he can provide damaged cars and that for driving practice, for test driving. Very few cops are clean all the way. Some cops like Duggan and Lorenzo are corrupt all the way. Having their hands out with Louie and myself was the tip of the iceberg 'cause they had their hands in the pockets of other guys in the local clique.

The state police wanted Duggan something fierce. The suspicion was that he would pick up jewelry or pocket cash if he investigated a burglary. In

Jesse's eye some of the tips on places to clip that we were getting from a couple of lawyers are coming to the lawyers from Duggan and Lorenzo. Duggan was pretty sharp on antiques. Would ask me did I know where he might buy such and such. As if he wanted to buy. I'm leery that instead he is looking to peddle antiques or a coin collection that came from a burglary. I didn't want to go that route with him, so I introduced him to a couple of dealers but not any of my main outlets. Wanted him on my side but keep some distance between us.

All those years, when Jesse and I was into burglary, Wally [a main lawyer in American City] was a main one for tips—and good tips on safes and on coins. On the safes, he would want a percent. With the coins, he was our outlet. What he did with them I don't know. This kept on when I was in the fencing. If I came across coins, they would go to Wally. Even today I am surmising Wally is the main one for giving tips to Jesse 'cause they are very tight. Is a trust there. Wally is in with the right crowd and maybe has been in their homes, know what I mean?

Another thing, Louie was tight with some of the magistrates in town. They could be bought off, as long as there wasn't much publicity. I eventually get hooked up with them through Louie and from being part of the local clique. Not all the way like Louie was but enough to be a big help. If you get popped, the case has to go through the magistrate first, before it can go to trial. He can throw it out, say, on a technicality or just say the evidence is too soft.

This is something. When I was into burglary with Jesse, we knew our lawyer was paying off. Didn't know to who. Turns out, it is usually the magistrate. Now that I am hooked up, I can go directly to them. I was surprised, very surprised, at how little it cost. Few hundred bucks each time. As long as it was something minor like a thief fingering you but no recovery of stolen property, "Hey, is this all you got?" Was a lot cheaper than paying the lawyer who is jacking up the price but is having you think the people he is paying off are greedy. You are going to pay 'cause you have no way of knowing.

All this time, too, the district attorney is someone that Angelo or people in the local clique helped put in office. First, it was Cummings and later on it was Abbott. I wasn't paying them off, nothing like that, but as long as the state police didn't push too hard they [local DA] pretty much looked the other way. They were hard-asses on the dopers and muggers but not the gambling and the fencing.

Without a doubt, yes, it helps to have good lawyer. Is another backup. Is good in the courtroom but has the connections to pay off is the main thing. I pretty much always dealt with Cohen. This connection came from my burglary days, from Jesse. Later on, I used Gleason or Savelas. Were junior partners with Cohen. Cohen was connected something fierce, was owed a lotta favors. If he went to bat for you, there wasn't much he couldn't get you out of.

Someone like Cohen gets his connections from being associated with the local clique or helping a judge or a prosecutor get elected. A judge and a lawyer can scratch each's back in a lotta ways. Will often run in the same crowd, have business connections. And usually the connections stay in the same law firm. Like Gleason and Savelas got their connections from Cohen, when he took them in as partners.

But I would never leave it entirely to the lawyer. Say a thief is going to testify against me, the state police or whomever is making him promises. I am going to lean on the guy, either myself or have someone do it for me. Do whatever needs to be done.

Looking back, it's hard to for me to believe all the ones that were involved—how big the spider web got to be, how it came about, how this led to that. But still not big enough. The state police surely weren't a spoke in the wheel. Were a helluva thorn, is what it came down to. If it had not been for them, I'd still be operating in American City. Have to hand it to them, how they built a case against me and against Louie, how they put us both away.

Notes

1. Sam used to tap his chest by his heart with the back of a thick fist. Now, weakened by cancer, he slowly touches or brushes his chest with thin fingers.
2. Steffensmeier was actually with Sam on this occasion. Tinker was more chagrined than angry and took in stride Sam's enjoyment and ribbing about the incident.

11

Commentary

"Moonlighting" Phase of Sam's Criminal Career: Shifting Commitments to Crime versus Legitimacy

Sam's "wheelin' and dealin'" involvement in the stolen goods trade in American City ended with his arrest and conviction on charges of receiving stolen property. The subsequent imprisonment marked a turning point in Sam's life and criminal career. In the next chapter, Sam first describes the sequence of events leading to his "last fall" and then his life after being released from prison, when he eventually settles in Tylersville and where his criminal career enters its "moonlighting" phase. That is, Sam becomes more of a "part-time" or "moonlighting" fence, though one with extensive experience and underworld contacts. Sam runs a legitimate business full time, but still engages in criminal activity.

Shortly after Sam's release from prison, Steffensmeier asked Jesse whether he thought Sam would fall back into fencing. Jesse mused: "Sam ain't happy unless he's pulling something. If the risk ain't that high, if the opportunity is there, he'll go for it. Without a doubt." Jesse's words proved prophetic.

Sam's narrative in the following chapter, as well as the commentary and narrative in Chapters 17–20, show that Sam's career after his last imprisonment was characterized by his longing for some legitimate respectability, on the one hand, coupled with his continuing affinity for criminal activity on the other. In other words, Sam experienced competing pushes and pulls toward and away from theft, fencing, and coaching or tipping off thieves. The scale and frequency of Sam's criminal activity would wax and wane as Sam would dabble or "moonlight" in fencing on the side, and then would start getting "sucked into" the game more. At times his level of fencing would almost rival his days in American City. Then he would become wary of getting too deeply involved again, put the brakes on, and pull back. Thus, there were other periods in Sam's career (especially toward the end of his life) when Sam was mostly a legitimate businessman, and he was hardly involved in fencing at all.

After his release from state prison for the last time, Sam becomes a part-time fence or, as he sometimes said, an "in-betweener" dealer, though a skilled and connected one. Sam becomes mostly a legitimate businessman, but "moonlights" at fencing and sometimes other illicit activity. Sam becomes and remains in some ways a "background operator" in the underworld, though he experiences sharp temptations to expand his fencing operation to its former glory and even beyond.

We question the sometimes dichotomous conceptualization of desistance found in much writing on criminal careers (one either desists from crime or not) in favor of a more nuanced and complex approach. In this discussion, we delineate the strong personal and structural commitments to crime and the underworld life that made it difficult for Sam to terminate criminal activity entirely.

In the criminal careers literature, desistance is usually taken to mean "successful" disengagement from criminal behavior. Offenders either desist or not. However, many criminal careers, like Sam Goodman's, are marked by shifts and oscillations (Adler and Adler 1983). That is, many offenders enter and exit criminal activity repeatedly, or escalate and de-escalate their criminal activity, or shift from one kind of activity to another, or all three of these, over the courses of their lives.

Thus, one lesson from the life of Sam Goodman is that the focus on complete desistance is too narrow. Some offenders do not so much terminate criminal activity, but may instead (1) reduce or slow down the frequency of offending, perhaps even "moonlighting" in criminal activity to supplement their legitimate income, (2) reduce the variety of offending, that is, specialize more, (3) reduce the type or seriousness of offending, or (4) switch to less visible forms of offending, to become more of a "background operator." Sam Goodman's later career exhibited all of these patterns. Also, the causes and processes of desistance are likely to vary across distinct offender categories and levels of skill. That is, the desistance process (if there is one) for a professional thief and fence like Sam may be quite different from that of the "bottom of the barrel" thieves Sam describes. Sam's extensive commitments to criminal activity, fencing, and the underworld way of life made a total exit, or a "clean break" from his criminal career very difficult.

Commitment as Key Concept for Understanding Criminal Careers, Pathways, and Transitions

In Chapter 3, we mentioned the centrality of the concept of commitment to the explanation of consistency in lines of activity, and how continuity in criminal careers can be analyzed as dynamics of structural, personal, and moral commitments. Since commitment is an important concept for sociology in general and criminology in particular, then it is important to understand the possibility of different types of commitment and determine whether distinct sources produce them. In other words, we agree with Johnson (1991) that commitment is not a unitary construct, because scholars and laypeople alike use the term to mean several different kinds of experiences (e.g., "I can't get out of this now, I'm committed" vs. "She has a strong commitment to her religion").

Broadly speaking, we see sources of commitment in terms of "valuables" and costs. That is, some sources of commitment are valued resources, opportunities, relationships, or identities that individuals accumulate based on prior decisions and involvements that they would risk losing if they terminated a line of activity in which they consistently engage. Other sources of commitment represent potential costs or penalties to be paid if one terminates a consistent line of activity, such as missed opportunities, foregone rewards, or negative social reaction from associates. It makes sense to us to conceptualize commitment in all its variation, complexity, and implications.

We draw on Howard Becker's pioneering work on commitment and primarily on Ulmer's adaptation of Johnson's (1991) threefold commitment framework to criminology.[1] As noted in Chapter 3, the framework integrates the differing ways in which scholars have seen commitment as being produced by constraints on one hand ("forced behavior" in the words of Stebbins [1971]) or as a product of personal desire or determination on the other (Kanter 1972; Burke and Reitzes 1991). This framework elaborates the commitment concept into three distinct types: *structural, personal,* and *moral.* These commitment types can produce continuity in criminal behavior either by fostering a *desire* for criminal activities and choices, or by *constraining* individuals from terminating criminal careers.[2]

We use commitment as a conceptual tool for explaining the observation that offenders, like people more generally, often follow consistent lines of activity for a variety of reasons. An example of a consistently engaged-in line of activity would be a twenty-plus year career in fencing, like Sam Goodman's. The threefold typology of commitment helps to outline the mechanisms by which *past actions* create interests and allegiances that link to constraints and desires shaping current decision-making and more long-range life choices. This incorporates a key theme of Becker's work that *engaging in a line of behavior (e.g., deviance) in time produces its own set of causes* and of Lemert that the *original causes of the behavior may not be the effective or sustaining causes.*

We also reiterate Ulmer's (2000) argument that many commonalities exist between commitment to conformity and commitment to deviance, and differential association and social control theories depict two sides of the same coin. Just as breaking the law may jeopardize "valuables" such as reputational, economic, occupational, interpersonal, or emotional investments in conformity, so desisting from lawbreaking and turning away from crime may jeopardize those same "valuables" staked to crime. Thus, the commitment framework integrates two theories often seen as opposed, differential association/social learning and social control (see Ulmer 2000 for an extended discussion).

We call an individual's accumulated and valued interests and allegiances, as represented by his or her structural, moral, or personal commitments, an individual's *commitment portfolio*. It is also critical to understand that commitments are not static, but *dynamic:* they wax and wane, shift and change over the life course.[3]

Furthermore, both Becker's work and the threefold framework recognize that people often have *conflicting* commitments. We see this, for example, in Sam's desiring and being pulled toward both crime and conventionality. This pattern is vividly illustrated in the following chapter and in Chapter 20.

Structural and Personal Commitment to Crime in Sam's Later Career

Structural commitment is mostly what Becker (1960) was talking about in his foundational piece on commitment. It represents sources of continuity in criminal careers flowing from opportunities, knowledge, resources, and network ties to useful and trustworthy contacts. These opportunities, resources, and network ties are therefore important components of the kind of *criminal social capital* we talked about in Chapter 9.

As we mentioned in Chapter 3, structural commitment involves what Lemert (1951) called external limits, or what we (see also Steffensmeier 1986) called *objective availability* of criminal and conventional lines of action. Structural commitment is characterized by external constraints of two kinds: (1) those that structure and influence choices between lines of action and (2) those that restrict the termination of a given line of action. Structural commitment is defined by the perception or experience that one "has to" pursue a line of action. It has four sources: (1) the availability and attractiveness of alternative lines of action, (2) hard-to-retrieve investments in current lines of action (what economists might call "sunk costs"), (3) difficulty of processes necessary to terminate a line of action, and (4) social reaction to termination of a line of action.

Structural commitment emphasizes (1) the manner in which *objective circumstances for achievement* or "doing well" (e.g., availability of opportunities for legitimate versus illegitimate endeavors) *shape the decisions and life choices people make* (both with regard to strategies affecting the general contours of their lives and often in specific situations); and (2) *how prior concrete actions or involvements produce an individual's commitment portfolio.* That is, objective circumstances that produce structural commitment include "valuables" like know-how, earnings, contacts, and reputation that are products of prior actions and involvements.

Personal commitment, on the other hand, involves the subjective acceptability of criminal or conventional activity, and is defined by *choice driven by internal desire* to continue a line of action. In other words, personal commitment refers to individuals continuing a line of action because they define it as desirable, something they *want* to do. Personal commitment is thus the proper concept to explain circumstances where people continue to engage in a line of activity because they find it enjoyable, emotionally rewarding, exciting, etc. When people are personally committed to an activity, they may even overcome significant practical obstacles in order to continue in it.

Personal commitment flows from three sources: (1) positive attitudes toward lines of action, (2) positive attitudes toward others with whom one engages in a line of action, and (3) self-definitions in terms of identities mobilized by lines of action. For example, Sam enjoyed theft, fencing, and scamming and their rewards; he enjoyed the company of other thieves, hustlers, and underworld types; and he valued his identities as a "good thief," skilled fence, and a "somebody" in the underworld.

Sociologists have long recognized internal as well as external constraints as important influences on decisions and action (Durkheim [1897] 1951) and as potential factors producing continuity in deviance or conventionality (Lemert 1951; Lofland 1969; Reckless 1973). *Moral commitment* is a particularly important type of internal constraint, and thus is also highly relevant to the subjective acceptability of criminal vs. conventional activity. It is characterized by the perception or experience that one *ought to* continue a line of action regardless of whether one wants to or has to. Moral commitment has three sources: (1) perceived moral obligations to others with whom one participates in a line of action, (2) internalization of action-specific norms discouraging termination of a line of action once one has already gotten involved in it, and (3) internalization of general cultural values that encourage consistency in lines of action. We discuss moral commitment and its distinctiveness at greater length in Chapter 19.

The differential association/social learning process described earlier potentially entails developing all of these kinds of commitments, and the concept of structural commitment also embeds the individual in contexts of differential social organization such as neighborhoods, families, friends, and other affiliations that influence moral orientations and criminal involvement (these influences, moreover, are dynamic forces that may vary over time and across contexts). While most of our emphasis in this book is on Sam Goodman's types of commitment to his criminal career, continuity in conformity over the life course is also explainable by the dynamics of structural, personal, and moral commitment to conventional activities, relationships, or institutions.

As in legitimate careers, the building of criminal valuables or commitments tends to be cumulative. These commitments also tend to be interdependent and reciprocal. For example, having one source of structural commitment or investment to crime will tend to increase other sources of structural commitment to crime.

Furthermore, objective factors like criminal opportunity and structural commitment, and subjective factors like criminal motivation, skills, and personal commitment to crime can obviously feed and complement each other. This was certainly the case for Sam. Critical here is the interplay between Sam's structural and personal commitment to crime. Sam retained a lot of criminal capital or investments in crime in his later career: skills, resourcefulness, favorable attitudes, a good reputation, opportunity structures, and network contacts. Because of this criminal capital, fencing remained very subjectively attractive and rewarding to him, preserving a strong personal commitment to crime.

Sam's later life also provides a good illustration of the interplay between criminal and conventional commitments. On one hand, Sam Goodman markedly reduced his offending frequency, roles, and seriousness. His later career therefore shows some support for contemporary portraits of desistance (see Benson 2002; Shover 1996; Sampson and Laub 1993). That is, stable conventional work, a stable domestic partnership, transformation of identity, aging, and tiring of the "wear and tear" or "hassles" of criminal life all built sources of structural, personal, and perhaps moral commitment to conventionality, and thus contributed to his criminal slowdown. On the other hand, Sam never fully desisted from crime, but instead consistently dabbled at it, sometimes at a slow pace, but other times at a fairly fast pace. The continuing pushes and pulls of structural and personal commitment to fencing and the underworld versus conventional life seem to be particularly at work in his later career, with the ebbs and flows of his fencing activity. In other words, Sam experienced competing pushes and pulls: the desire for a conventional life as a respectable businessman versus the lingering opportunities, attractions, relationships, and investments surrounding fencing and the underworld.[4]

Our discussion here focuses on structural and personal commitment. In Chapter 19, we further examine the importance of personal commitment for Sam's rewards and preferences for crime, and discuss the role of personal and moral commitment in terms of Sam's apologia for his criminal career.

Structural Commitments

Structural commitment is about the objective availability of crime. Two of the four sources of structural commitment seem especially important and intertwined in keeping Sam "moonlighting" at fencing in his later career: (1) the availability and attractiveness of criminal vs. conventional alternatives, and (2) hard-to-retrieve investments or "sunk costs" in crime. Sam's particularly important investments included knowledge, reputation, contacts, and earnings.

We argue that differences in access to crime opportunities, especially safe and profitable ones, play a key role in explaining desistance or continuation in crime. The greater the criminal opportunities that become or remain available, the greater is the inclination to continue in crime. In other words, if older offenders like Sam continue to have attractive criminal alternatives presented to them, they are likely to pursue them, even if they do so intermittently or on a smaller scale than they once did. From the time he was released from prison for the last time until his cancer hit, Sam had ample, relatively lucrative criminal opportunities available to him, often with relatively few risks. From his perspective, it was simply foolish not to take advantage of them.

Relatedly, Sam had invested considerable time, energy, and even money throughout his life acquiring the skills, building the networks, and attending to the business of being a profitable criminal entrepreneur. He had learned the burglary trade inside and out, he had learned what it took to become a successful business fence, and had put in long hours making the contacts and building up the business to make his enterprise work (and rebuilding it after imprisonment). His active investments, in turn, opened up attractive criminal alternatives, and *kept them open.* Given his personal commitment to crime, which we discuss next, Sam would have thought that it was *just plain stupid* to waste all his prior experiences and efforts by failing to pursue attractive criminal opportunities when they practically fell in his lap.

This quote from Sam captures these key elements of his structural commitment "pulls" toward crime:

> Many times I have wished I was back in it [in Tylersville], all the way like it was before [in American City]. To tell you the truth, I would've liked to have gotten a younger guy to be the fence but I would be in the background, more supervising. Say Rocky or Kevin 'cause he has a good head on his shoulders. My knowledge to somebody is worth quite a bit. I put a lot of hours in getting the contacts, running to the auctions and meeting people. Just like if you'd say, "Fuck it, I'm gonna quit teaching. I want to be a fence." Well, I'd be a great help to you. The contacts, knowing how to get the confidence of someone, to read people. It takes hours and hours, a lot of time consumed to get all that.

On the other hand, the range of roles, legitimate or illegitimate, that some offenders like the Beck boys, a Lemont Dozier, a Danny Turner, or a Chubby could satisfactorily fulfill are limited. They lacked the requisite skills, contacts, and knowledge to execute more exacting forms of thievery or criminal enterprise, and they also tended to be excluded from professional or organized criminal pursuits. Their conventional occupational roles are also reduced because of a stigmatizing criminal history and because of their lack of conventional education or skills. However, such offenders *may* exhibit continuity as petty thieves, hustlers, low-level drug dealers, errand runners, or hangers-on.

The "valuables" in their structural commitment portfolios do not augur well for success in either legitimate or illegitimate pursuits. Instead, their structural commitment circumstances may contribute to "default" life choices, and a survival strategy characterized by fluctuations between less lucrative crime and low-level legitimate jobs.

Structural commitments from opportunities and investments may thus go a long way in explaining continuity in crime among offenders like Sam, and less sustained careers among others who lack such opportunities and investments. For example, some people may very much want to become or stayed involved in particular theft or hustling or racketeering activities, but unless they have been or are able to make contacts with the "right people," their chances of realizing their ambitions are diminished considerably. Sam encountered any number of thieves and burglars who wanted to make the "big time" through criminal activities. They did not, however, have the criminal capital necessary for involvement on a more sustained and lucrative basis. Prus and Irini (1980:247) found a similar situation among thieves and hustlers. Many of them did not really "make it" in crime, but instead sought the lifestyle they desired and then settled for what seemed the "best available approximation."

Personal Commitments

Personal commitment is about the subjective availability of crime, including both the willingness and/or the desire to commit it. In short, fencing and the underworld life remained subjectively acceptable, even desirable, to Sam throughout his life. He never lost the "larceny in his heart." We single out here how Sam's personal commitment to crime had three continuously reinforced sources. We later return to Sam's personal and moral commitment to crime in Chapter 19.

First and most important, Sam maintained positive attitudes toward fencing, burglary, and skilled criminal entrepreneurship throughout his life. These attitudes were partly the product of the differential association—or criminal socialization—processes he participated in earlier in his life. His later life experience perpetuated and reinforced these attitudes. He continued to enjoy fencing, antique fraud, and various scams. Moreover, he was quite good at these things, which further contributed to his enjoyment, since one enjoys what one is good at. He also enjoyed the material rewards—the money and the idea of making and having money. In fact, in Chapter 20, Sam expresses sincere regret that he did not take advantage of the opportunity to "go really big time" and make even more money from criminal enterprise.

Second, Sam maintained ties with and positive attitudes toward other criminal actors. His continuing relationships with people like his burglary partner Jesse, as well as Rocky, Steelbeams, and dozens of other thieves, underworld figures, and semilegitimate businesspeople, were not only network ties that provided and facilitated criminal opportunities, but they were also friendships or at least positive relationships that Sam valued. Furthermore, Sam was proud of his contacts with local organized crime or mafia elements. He held respect and not a little envy for such men. These positive attitudes toward and even friendships with other criminals were also a source of continuity in Sam's criminal career.

Finally, in his later life, Sam's definition of himself was still partially tied to a criminal identity. It is true that he did increasingly nurture and value his identity as a legitimate businessman in his later years, but his sense of self was still partially wrapped up in his image of a "good thief," a successful fence, and an "operator" in the underworld. These remained salient, valued identities to Sam, and they fostered continuity in Sam's criminal behavior. After all, a reputation as somebody who is "solid" or is a "good safeman" or is a "wheeling and dealing" fence is difficult, if not impossible, to transfer to a conventional world role.

We do not want to overstate Sam's involvement in crime in later life. We do want to emphasize, however, that he never fully desisted. Relative to earlier years (e.g., his thirties and forties), his criminal activity did drop off substantially. But relative to a standard of conformity, Sam was quite criminally active. We suspect that hardly a week went by that he was not involved in at least some criminal activity: fencing, antique fraud, giving tips to thieves, etc. Furthermore, there were weeks here and there in Sam's later life when he was *very* active, running several deals or schemes at once.

Indeed, Sam was hatching schemes while lying in bed with cancer or right up until he died (see the passage in Chapter 20, where Sam bakes porcelain salt & pepper shakers in his oven with coffee grounds to make them look like antiques not long before his death). Several key sources of structural and personal commitment inhibited his full desistance from crime and perpetuated his criminal career, even though it continued at a lower level and smaller scale than in his prime. Overall, Sam's career and our discussion encourage a more complex view of continuity and desistance in criminal careers than the dichotomous view found in some of the criminal-careers literature. We also propose a useful set of conceptual tools, structural, personal, and moral commitment for probing that complexity.

Contributions of the Commitment Framework

In conclusion, we briefly suggest seven ways that sociological criminology could capitalize on the contributions of this commitment approach:

1. Properly understood, commitment is a processual, dynamic concept. It thus can provide useful keys for understanding criminal-career variation, especially the contingencies, transitions, and turning points involved in maintaining

criminal pathways, in changing their criminal behaviors (e.g., slowing down or switching to another crime), or turning away from crime.

2. Commitment helps us better understand how past behavior conditions future behavior. In this regard, commitment dovetails nicely with social learning theory's notion of criminal reinforcement. Past actions lead to weaker or stronger commitments or "stakes" in criminality (or conformity). Furthermore, commitment helps to explain the old observations of Lemert and Becker that involvement in criminal activity itself may in time produce its own set of causes.

3. The commitment framework we use here recognizes explicitly the individual's *agency* in making decisions and life choices (as opposed to a view of people as overly determined by "outside" or "inside" forces, or that they simply respond to associations and events). It can help us better understand criminals' decisions about their lives and activities, especially in the face of aging and time. The framework views people, including entrepreneurial offenders, as actively involved in transforming their relationships into social capital and their experiences into human capital (conventional or criminal).

4. The commitment framework also helps to integrate concepts from seemingly disparate theories, like social learning/differential association, opportunity, social control, or labeling. Such theoretical integration is something many criminologists see as desirable because it leads to greater parsimony in our concepts and theoretical explanations. That is, the three types of commitment and their sources encompass or imply the ideas indexed by a large array of concepts that are used to explain continuity in crime or conformity, such as path dependence, cumulative advantage or disadvantage, allegiances, stakes, opportunities, attachments, investments, side bets, strategic interests, or incentive structures.

5. The commitment framework is very much a *sociological* approach. It positions the primary causes of continuity in behavior squarely in social structure, culture, and social interaction, and not stable individual traits. It therefore leads away from models of crime that emphasize pathological individuals, and that thus avoid confronting how crime is woven into the fabric of our society. In fact, one could say that the commitment framework rests on a fairly optimistic view of human nature.

6. Commitments can also be seen in the context of *achievement*. That is, assessments of potential payoffs or rewards are influenced by the degree of achievement one has enjoyed in either conventional or criminal pursuits in the past. At issue is whether one goes upward, downward, or stays on an even keel. Criminals, like ordinary folk in general, are often motivated (and particularly as they age) not only or so much by greed and the desire to attain more money or status but also by fear of falling below their current positions.

7. We believe this framework provides the seeds for a general theory of crime and desistance. We would call this a "learning-opportunity-commitment" conceptual framework, in that it blends themes from social learning and opportunity theories of crime with the three-fold commitment typology.[4]

We turn now to Sam's account of his life following his "last fall" when he grappled with "falling back into fencing in a much deeper way."

Notes

1. Johnson's work in turn builds on and integrates the conceptualizations of commitment by Howard Becker (1960, 1963), Erving Goffman (1967), Amitai Etzioni (1964), and Rosabeth Moss Kanter (1972).
2. The framework incorporates symbolic interactionist conceptions centering on the dialectical relationship between choice and constraint, or agency and structure. It is thus compatible with Giddens' theory of structuration and his notion of "duality of structure," as well as Bourdieu's (1977) conceptions of "field" and "habitus." As Hall (1997 and Martin (2003) describe, interactionism, structuration theory, and field theory view structure (whether at the micro-, meso-, or macrolevels) as both constraining and enabling. Furthermore, all three theories hold that actors' decisions and actions are constrained by external structures and internalized norms, but they also emphasize that human agency constructs, reproduces, strategically manipulates within, and changes those constraints.
3. In addition to linking with explicit uses of commitment in the criminological literature (e.g., as a "stake in conformity" in social control theory, or as entrenched involvement in deviance in the social learning and labeling traditions), the framework we apply here also implicitly incorporates or links with many related concepts bandied about in research and theory on criminal careers, such as investments, path dependence, strategic interests, or social capital (including criminal social capital). The concept of continuity in behavior over time and factors that explain it are also of obvious relevance to life course perspectives on criminal involvement [see Ulmer (2000) and Ulmer and Spencer (1999) for extended discussions].
4. Another intriguing possibility, but one beyond the scope of our discussion to explore, is to examine the potential relationship between the threefold commitment framework and rational choice theory. Additionally, it would be equally useful to explore the mutual contributions between the commitment framework and the sociology of emotions. Research should investigate the likely important role emotions play in different kinds of commitment, and their sources, and in decision-making about whether to persist in or terminate a line of action. Johnson's work has briefly explored these points in the context of research on personal relationships, but so far no one has done so for criminology.

12

Sam's Narrative

Continuity or Desistance After Sam's "Last Fall"?

Sam's Last Fall

I was arrested six, maybe seven times in American City. By the state police usually, once or twice by the local cops. But these didn't go anywhere, didn't get past the magistrate or the DA. *I thought I had a license to steal as far as handling the warm stuff. Turns out I didn't.* Got popped for buying from a couple of in-between burglars and from Dorothy Ford snitching on me. Ended up doing about four years in the Midstate Penitentiary. *The only good thing to come out this was, this was my last time in the penitentiary. My last fall.*

As wide open as I was, my name would come up with the cops, this or that thief would finger me, hoping to get a break. And my shop had become a hangout for the in-between thief, like Rocky and them. So, the state police were watching. See the same people walking in and out. Lotta surveillance. Would spot-check my shop, write some things down. Poke around, look at the shelves, and leave. Other times they'd go through the whole place. Can't even guess how many times the state police came in with a search warrant.

The one state cop, Kuhn, came in fairly regular. We would joke back and forth, but I knew he wanted to nail my ass. Would sit in the coffee shop across the street, sit there for hours watching my shop. Nervy son of a bitch. Knew how to handle himself. Would've liked to have had him as a burglary partner.

Looking back, I could say it was the law of averages. When you're dealing as much as I was, and that wide open, the chances are you will slip up or the cops will get a break. There is something to be said for that. Jesse and different ones warned me but I didn't listen. My undoing was I got too careless. I trusted too many people. Too many people knew my business. Left the door open for the state police.

I still shake my head that I got popped and they were able to put me away. But I got to hand it them, especially to Kuhn. Was some luck on their part, but the guy does have a pair of balls and found himself a couple of patsies. The one patsy was Dorothy Ford, a decent-size antique dealer in the area. Mostly legit, but she would buy off and on from somebody she knew, if the coast was clear. Would mix in and sell with the legit stuff, and peddled the rest to me. We got to be friends more or less, her and husband, Albert. I'd stop by her shop or see her at the auctions. Couple of times she went with me to Woody's auction in Southfield. That was my undoing.

What happened is, the state cops pop a couple of guys for breaking into houses and stealing antiques. These are cousins of Dorothy. They confess to the burglaries and that they are selling the antique pieces to Dorothy. Police haul Dorothy in and she fingers me. Kuhn is pumping her, suspected she was selling stuff to me. Squeeze her more and she blabs that I am unloading stuff at Woody's in Southfield. But not a peep to me from Dorothy that she has blown the whistle. This is the break Kuhn is looking for. Knows my outlet and I'm not suspecting. The state police here contact the state police down there, to be on the watch. They are working together.

Week or so later, Kuhn is watching my shop. Sees Rocky and Reggie come and go [in-between burglars who regularly sold stolen goods to Sam]. Kuhn is figuring it had to do with a couple of house burglaries that had just happened. Has a list of what was taken and notifies the police in Southfield that I might be coming. The next day I run a load down to Woody, mostly legit but also the warm stuff from the burglaries—tools, couple of TVs, cameras, and some antique pieces. The cops there are watching. Soon as I leave Woody's, bang bang—have a search warrant and gather up everything. The stuff matched up—the people could identify what had been taken, especially the antiques. The next morning I come to my store and the cops are waiting. They're all over the place. Made a big thing of arresting me.

Same day the cops pick up Reggie and Rocky. They're hammering them, playing off one against the other. Telling them bullshit—somebody had seen Rocky's van at one of the burglaries, their fingerprints are on some of the pieces, and that the other one had come clean. Even showed each other what is supposed to be a signed confession.

Reggie caved in first. Admitted he had done the burglaries with Rocky, and sold the stuff to me. The police keep pumping Reggie: "What about other burglaries, was he involved? Just come clean, he will get a break." Reggie starts blabbering. Not only on me but that a few days before they had sold warm guns to Louie. Next thing, Louie's place is searched and the cops find the guns. Louie gets busted, too. Was blown up in the papers, first me but especially Louie 'cause he was supposed to be mafia and all that shit.

My trial was first. The prosecutor was very shrewd. Had the antiques and the tools spread out on a table and the people testifying, "Yeah, this belongs to us, is our stuff." Put Woody on the stand, "Yeah, he did buy these pieces from me." Then Reggie takes the stand—says him and Rocky broke into the houses and sold the stuff to me. I could've blown Reggie's head away. Prosecutor brings out that Reggie has a record for burglary, is a known thief you might say. Next, Rocky is called to testify. Prosecutor brings out that he's been found guilty for the burglaries 'cause Reggie has already testified against him in an earlier trial. Rocky didn't snitch, claimed that Reggie was the main one and was in charge of getting rid of the stuff, didn't know where he was unloading the stuff. But the jury could put two and two together.

I knew it didn't look good, but I still thought I had a fifty-fifty chance of walking. In my eye, the jury was made up of the ordinary joe blow, the guy who shopped in my kind of shop and probably bought warm stuff at one time or another. Would have some sympathy for me and be less likely to take the word of an asshole thief. But it didn't work that way. The jig was up. Found me guilty and the judge hits me with a three to six.

Rocky held up, never did talk. But it was touch and go. The police are offering him a deal. On account he had a clean record, could walk if he'd testify against me and Louie. Reggie was shaky, was doubtful up to the end that he would testify. But he ended up blabbering all the way. See, Louie and me worked it out that he'd take care of Reggie and that Rocky was my responsibility.

Rocky had his van blown up, as a warning. Reggie was supposed to be taken care of but Louie didn't carry out his end. A good warning and then put him to sleep if that was needed. Louie had the contacts for doing that. But Louie had gotten soft. His hard-on didn't come up no more. At one time Louie was rough. The guy doesn't show his face again, leaves town or is done away with.

Week later, same jury finds Louie guilty. Which surprised him 'cause Louie is still thinking he will walk. All these years and the cops couldn't nail him. Is thinking he can work out a deal with the state police by snitching on other thieves and also figuring he won't have to do much time. Louie had buried a lot of people over the years to save his ass in more than one tight spot. But the police aren't taking the bait and the papers were blowing up our cases something fierce, especially Louie's. There wasn't any wiggle room, even for our lawyers to work out a deal behind closed doors. That, and once Louie started sinking, the local gang was glad to see him out of the way. Louie had made too many enemies, on account he was too greedy and could be a snitch. The local gang was leery, too, 'cause the feds are poking around. Everybody was running for cover.

To this day, I still think I should be operating in American City. I still shake my head. It all fell into place for Kuhn and the state cops. Too many people knew my business. Was getting too careless, buying from anybody and everybody. Jesse, Ciletti, and different ones warned me about buying off the street and letting some of the assholes hang around my shop. Jesse warned me more than once to "stick with the better thief, stay with your kind."

I thought about appealing the verdict. My lawyer was pushing for that. More money for him. Would bleed me dry if he had his way. But my view was, "Fuck it, do my time and get it over with."

I ended up in the Midstate Penitentiary. That is where I met you. You asked me about female crime. Remember? "What kinds of crimes were women into? Did I ever do crimes with women?" I told you, "Hey, I don't know much about female crime but if you want to talk about fencing or antique fraud, then I can help you out." You started coming around every couple of weeks. I looked forward to that, helped to break the monotony.

I didn't plan it to happen this way but, still, I did have an inkling in jail that I'd fall back into the fencing but at a smaller level. But I'm also telling myself—I'm gonna quit this fucking shit altogether. Get the fuck outta here, open up my business but be strictly legit. I saying that but am also in the penitentiary library—reading up on antiques, on furniture, on glassware, on coins. *It was like I was telling myself to go strictly legit, but if I was ever to fall back into the fencing, this is how I'd do it.* See, guys in the prison are always thinking, "Hey, I'm gonna pack it in. This is it." But, in the back of your mind, you're shaky on this 'cause you don't know what you'll do on the outside, when the opportunity is there.

Remember my first furlough? The superintendent let you take me back to American City for my first furlough. That is as clear to me as yesterday. We stopped along the way. Showed you different spots me and Jesse clipped. Stopped at Casey's Pub and many of the old gang was there [See "Sam's Homecoming" in Chapter 2]. I got a kick out of seeing your reaction. Then you dropped me off at Becky's. Met Muffin, my German shepherd that hated cops.

Becky knew, but didn't wanna know, that I was dealing in warm stuff. She more or less went along with it, pretended it was all legit. Some of the regular thieves would stop by my house or call me, "Can you handle this?" "Where should we drop it?" If I wasn't home and Becky knew where I was, she'd call and leave a message for me.

She was shaken when I got popped for the fencing but hung in there. Was faithful about writing and coming to visit. But she was pulling back, too. The letters were fewer and she wasn't coming as often. Then, when I was home for the furlough, she overheard me on the phone, talking to Steelbeams about some warm antiques he wanted me to look at and recommend an outlet. Heard me telling Steelbeams I would call so and so, and would meet him at such and such a place to look them over.

Becky didn't say anything at first. Sends me a letter a week or two later, saying she overheard my conversation with Steelbeams and heard me making other calls. That I was seen over at Phil's place, visiting with him. Spent more time that weekend with some of my old buddies than I had spent with her. Blah, blah, blah. Really running her mouth. Ends up saying, she didn't think

I had reformed but would get right back into crime as soon as I got out. Tells me we should end it between us, go our separate ways. A "Dear John" letter was what it was.

See, we didn't get along that well that weekend. There was an edge to her after she overheard the phone conversation. Had a real bug up her ass. Another thing, I'm finding out that my shop and everything I had built up before going to the penitentiary is gone. To pay the lawyers and 'cause Becky has spent it. The shop was closed less than a year after I was sent to prison. Mickey and Sal, couple of friends who worked there off and on, were going to help Becky keep it going. But they were over their heads and the shop buried them. Sold everything and closed the doors. Becky eventually even sold my tools, all my upholstery tools, all the equipment. I didn't get on Becky's case for it but I did raise with her, "Why the fuck did you sell all my tools?" 'Cause they were worth a lot more than the price she was paid. Deep down I could understand why she did it, to pay the bills and buy things for the kids. But there was a tension there between us.

My reaction first was to say, "Okay, let's end it. If that's where you're coming from, no skin off my ass." But then we talked on the phone and decided to give it another shot. Told her I was reformed and looking forward to her and me getting a little place, maybe out in the country, open up an upholstery shop and she could help out. We'd work together. Part of me believed what I was saying, another part is knowing I am only blowing wind outta my ass.

Sam's Life in the Eighties and Nineties

When I first got out of the penitentiary, I would go back to American City. It was a longing, like I was being pulled back there. Saw some of the guys I did business with. To say "Hi" but also to let them know I was back. On the one side, I'm telling myself not to get involved again but still wanting too. Angelo approached me early on. Whatever I can do, Sam, to help you out, get you started again, let me know. Angelo owed me one 'cause I protected his ass. The state police and even the feds wanted Angelo bad. They would give me a free ride if I'd jam up Angelo. Angelo's offer was a temptation but I didn't want to owe somebody. Then, too, I was leery. I'm past fifty years old, maybe it's time to stay legit.

I'm going back to American City to see Becky, too, and her kids 'cause I was pretty close to them before going to the penitentiary. But it wasn't the same. The kids had grown, were into their own things now. I made a play for Becky but she was leery. Had I changed or would I fall back into fencing? We would argue about little shit, so she tells me she doesn't want to see me anymore.

Couple of weeks later I called, "I'm coming down." I get there, two local cops are waiting. The one tells me, "Look, Sam we'd sooner not be involved but the lady called us. Show your face again and your parole officer is gonna know." See, part of my parole was to stay away from American City.

I said, "Fuck it." I didn't need the hassle anyway. A month later, phone rings. It is Becky. She is sorry about what happened. Could she see me again, blah blah. This shit went on for five, six years. Might not see or hear from her for two, three, five months. Then, bang, we're at it again. I would get in her pants. But more and more it got to be she just wanted to cry on my shoulder, have someone listen to her grief. That I don't need.

Back into Business in Boonesboro

My brother [Herb] was a big help when I first got out of prison this last time, at his auto shop. Gave me a job, a paper job, so I could satisfy the parole people. All the time I'm out hustling to get my shop going again. Found me a garage in *Boonesboro,* a little fucking town maybe ninety miles from American City. Remember that place? No heat, no nothing. Wrapped my feet in blankets to keep upholstering. Running to the auctions, buying junk chairs, sofas, wicker. Fix them up, then peddle them at auctions. What it amounted to is I'm paying my brother to pay me, to keep the parole people happy. I had a little cash saved from before, but mostly I was broke. What it boils down to is, *now I am having to start from scratch.*

For many years never had much contact with Herb. Then our other brother is killed in a car accident, like twenty-five years ago. Helped Herb clean out the house and arrange for a sale. We hit it off you might say. His auto shop was in a small town on the way to one of the main auctions in the area. I would stop to see him on the way back from the auction. Or, sometimes he would stop by my shop in American City or now he stops by my shop in Tylersville. We have become pretty good pals. Can get a little rough when he is drinking but basically he is a good guy.

Then I got me a bigger place in Boonesboro. A place right on Main Street. Five and dime store at one time. Built a bathroom, a little kitchen area, and a couple of rooms in the back. Am getting my upholstery business going and by now I am back into antiques and secondhand stuff. Sell it in the shop or peddle at the auctions.

At the same time, I am working regular hours at a place that makes furniture. That's where I met Lisa. She was maybe twenty, twenty-two years old. Into drugs pretty heavy. Mostly pills and pot. Ran with a bad crowd. I got her off dope. She moved in with me. She would look after the shop if I was running to the auctions or if Chubby wasn't around.

Chubby has been a hanger-on at every shop I've had. This goes way back, thirty years, to my first shop in American City. He just shows up. Heard from one of the auctions that I was back in circulation. It's Sunday morning, I'm in this fucking garage painting wicker. In walks Chubby—"Hey Sam, how you doing." He is something else.

Lisa and me was together about a year and a couple of months. Then she quit work, went back to hanging around with the same losers she knew from before. One thing led to another, back into dope. So I run her out but Chubby lets her back in. I let her stay but it was never right no more. One day she could work like a fucking dog, help out in the shop, the next day she wouldn't do a thing. She was all fucked up.

My big mistake was I bought her a car. She's supposed to run the shop 'cause I'm still working at the furniture place and running to auctions. She's running with the car instead. Hanging out with her old friends. So I come home from work. She ain't around. About 6:30 she comes popping in, all glassy-eyed. She says I want to go to Texas to see some friends. Get away from my friends here, straighten myself out.

No, I said you ain't getting no money off of me. You can go get the hell out of here. So I didn't bother with her. Next night I come home from work early 'cause its auction night. A couple of times she came around to me to make up. I said get the fuck away. Then I went to lay down for a few minutes. Something just told me to get up. Here she's back in the kitchen with a knife. When I seen that I am thinking, she wants to put me out of my misery. I thought she was going to fuck me up with the knife. So I didn't take a nap. When I'm ready to leave for the auction, she wanted to go along. I said, "No, go out with your fucking bums, you ain't going with me."

When I came back from the auction, the back door was locked. So I went around to the front. Go in, turn the corner and push open the door that goes into the room I built, where we basically lived. Boom, there she is. Hanging there. From a ceiling pipe. She had taken a rope from the shop. I said, "What the fuck."

I tried to lift her up which was dumb when you think about it. I said, "Fuck it, her time is out." I called Teddy, the chief [of police in Boonesboro]. Watched her for about a half-hour waiting for Teddy to show. Tongue was hanging out, eyes open and like they were looking right at you. She had the most frightful look on her face you ever want to see in somebody. Was very spiteful. Just mean.

Her feet was still on the ground. Teddy said she tied the rope around her neck, got up on the chair, misjudged the distance to the floor. That little snap was all it took. She was going to scare me, I think. That's how it was. I still think she was thinking of putting an end to me because I later found a big knife over by the desk—a real big one, like the one I used to cut foam rubber.

The coroner said it definitely was suicide. When Teddy was here we found a note. She wrote it on a tablet, left it on the desk. A lot of dumb shit in it. That I wouldn't talk to her. That she never fucked around on me. Her dad didn't want her. Her mother didn't want her. Now, I didn't want her. She didn't want to live.

The district attorney was brought in to do a review on account there was a death and I am guessing on account of my record, that I had done time. Nothing came of it. DA agreed there was no foul play. Teddy, the chief, came over. Said, "Sam, you didn't do anything wrong." The chief and I were pretty good buddies. He liked to play the poker machines and I'd be playing too. Shoot the shit, buy him a beer or a sandwich. Another thing was I helped him build up his gun collection. He was into guns. Lotta cops are. Teddy told me not to worry about it.

I was on a hell of guilt trip. Well, you came up to see me and we rapped about it. I appreciated what you had to say. I am figuring if I would have taken her along to the auction it wouldn't have happened. Then I found out later it runs in the family. See, her mother tried to help her old man put himself out of his misery. Her aunt tried to cut her wrists a couple times. I didn't know nothing about that at the time. I had her off dope good. I really cooled her down. Then she started fucking with the dope again.

Wanda helped out a lot. She was working at the same furniture place where me and Lisa worked. Taught Lisa to sew and she talked about me. So, one time Lisa points me out and Wanda tells her, "He's old enough to be your father, almost your grandfather. He's too old for you." Wanda was like a mom to her.

Wanda did a lot of sewing for me 'cause I was pretty much in charge of the upholstery. "Can't blame yourself," she would tell me. "Lisa did it, not you." I saw that Wanda had a good head on her shoulders. Was a nice person. I saw that right away. But I really didn't pay her any mind. Didn't hit on her. Know what I mean. Then, fuck, we started going out. We have pretty much been together since—shit, ten, maybe almost twelve years.

This is funny. The first time we went out for lobster, Wanda talked so fucking much, it drove me crazy. Wanted her to eat another lobster just to keep her quiet. No, no she had enough. Just kept on talking. Then her friend comes by and asks us to go to a party with her. I said, no I have to see my brother. I just wanted to get away from her. Her fucking mouth drove me crazy. Turns out she really isn't that big a talker. She was nervous and she just talks when she's nervous. She knew I had been to jail.

I did pull a couple of burglaries that helped me get on my feet. With Steelbeams and a couple with Rocky. One was a gun shop. A very nice haul. The other times were some residences we clipped for jewelry. I had done some upholstery work for a couple of the people, before I went to the penitentiary. Knew the layout of the houses and knew they were "snowbirds" who headed south for the winter. Got jewelry and a horse figurine collection. Forty-five, fifty horses all together. Some in jade, some in crystal. Very nice collection. Another tip came from Rocky's friend, a contractor who had remodeled one of the homes we hit. *The burglaries were a big help as far as getting my business going again but I didn't feel that comfortable doing it. I don't know how to explain it. Like I didn't belong there. It wasn't me.*

To this day [*however*]*, I would open a safe if it was carried out and the guys wanted me to handle that.* But as far as going on a job, it has been—whew, those were the last burglaries I pulled, where I actually went along and had an assignment. Except a few times Bowie contacted me for a safe job, wanted me to go inside with him, I would do that.

I lie like hell, I'm only blowing wind outta my ass. This has happened a few times. Like a couple of years ago I ended up going out with a guy and his part-ner I am buying from and am giving them tips. Was a place I wanted clipped that had a lotta clocks and small pieces carved from different kinds of wood, like a Christmas scene. Were lotta so-so pieces but some were worth a very good dollar. I am explaining to the one guy what pieces I wanted but it got too complicated. So, I said, fuck it I'll go along. *But mainly I am staying in the background as far as burglary and that. A lotta tips. Some coaching, too, on what to look for, how to scout and cover your ass afterwards.*

Am doing a little fencing in Boonesboro. For a couple of local guys who are clipping and if someone like Rocky from American City contacted me. But I am careful not to branch out. Then, a guy I know from prison calls my shop in Boonesboro. Is an older guy, in his forties. "Is Sam there?" he asks. Tells me, he has these guns, that "there is a good dollar in it for you, but can't be a peep I'm involved." Described what he had, like a Mauser-Werks pistol and differ-ent Smith-Wesson revolvers that were both .22 caliber and .357 magnum. Ernie was on parole and was leery, thought the cops were watching him and his parole agent, too, who was a real hard-ass. I'm figuring Ernie's been sitting on those guns all the time he was in the penitentiary.

Whew, what should I do? Wanted some time to think it through, so told him I'd get back to him, that I had some contacts that were safe but needed to check them out. I'm thinking, this will pull me into the fencing deeper and deeper. That night I'm at an auction and this is tossing around in my head, I runs into Wally. The lawyer that Jesse and I peddled the coins to. We visited, so then I said, "Hey, I got some guns, are really nice but I got to unload them out of the area." Said he knew this guy who handled guns, that he was safe. Wally called me back the next morning, had talked to the guy and gave me his number. Ernie told me where to pick up the guns and I shot them over to the guy. It went off without a hitch.

I am still not itching to get back into the fencing, not really, but am knowing the temptation is still there. If the good opportunity presented itself, maybe take a shot at. Mainly I am content to get my legit business going. See, all the time I'm building up the upholstery business. Was getting more work than I could handle. And the antique side is really picking up. My thinking was, quit work at the furniture place, take Wanda and another guy from work with me, go into business all the way. I'm figuring I could keep my customers in this area and move to a bigger area at the same time. I knew this was the thing to do. Was outgrowing the place in Boonesboro.

Sam Settles in Tylersville

Then I found me a bigger place in Tylersville. Decent-sized town, maybe forty miles from Boonesboro. Where I'm at now. Old manufacturing building. Has three floors. Big elevator in the back to haul stuff up and down. Place had been vacant for awhile except for the first floor where a guy made kitchen cabinets and that. He went out of business. So I rented it. Just what I needed. Big fucking place. Lots of room to spread out and could store things on the other floors.

I still had a lease on the place in Boonesboro. Landlord wouldn't let me out of it. I'm thinking the hell with this. I load up the good stuff, run to the auctions and peddle what I can. Fucking place has a fire. [Sam laughs.] Not a big one but smoke damage so it was unfit to stay there. This was a break for me. I'm out of the lease and got a little insurance money too.

There was suspicion that I set the fire. But no proof. Fire department questioned me. I bellyached about what I had lost, having to find a new place, what this was gonna cost me. Insurance guy nosed around. I said I was tired, fucking tired, of all the hassles. He could talk to my lawyer. It wasn't long the check arrived.

Two, three years after I moved to Tylersville, this Jewish fellow, Benny, keeps dropping off old furniture for tearing down and having it rebuilt and upholstered. This is very regular. One day, he says to me. "Sam, I got a proposition. How about you and me becoming partners?" Then he lays it out. He is from this area but has lived a lot in Oceantown. Has business in other big cities, too. What he does is furnish hotels with furniture—chairs, sofas, coffee tables, you name it. But it must be old furniture, antiques and that. A big thing is art deco. He has pickers who go to auctions, flea markets, hotels, and different furniture places. Go all over looking for art deco furniture. Then he has it repaired, upholstered and that, and sells it to hotels and some business places, too. Maybe a old hotel is closing down, have a liquidation sale, the pickers would buy everything. Benny would ship it to me.

This is a good racket, he tells me. He would do the buying and selling, make the arrangements with the hotels. I would produce the furniture, work with the people from the hotels on fabric, color, design, whatever. Be a fifty-fifty deal. I could keep running my own business but I had to get the work done he would bring in.

I went for it. It has worked pretty well. Some hassles. Benny has some of the shyster in him. But he knows I will put a shoe up his ass if he jerks my chain.

That knowledge is always there for him. I would say over the years maybe half my time goes into the partnership with Bennie, the other half into my own stuff. My own upholstery business always done good. The local trade has kept me hopping.

This is how I got the name, "sofa doctor," on account of Benny. He was wanting to puff up our business. So he got a newspaper to do a story on how we took old furniture, especially the art deco, redone it, and furnished these nice hotels. The writer called me a "sofa doctor" and then the guys at the shop and different antique dealers I know would call me that. Razz my ass. I more got a kick out of it than anything but it did make me feel good. There was a satisfaction in being called that, in the recognition that somebody would say, "Hey, this fucker does good work."

I'm also buying and selling in my shop—wicker, ornamental gates, used furniture, some antiques, lotta glassware, the trinket stuff, and small collectibles. I handled a pretty wide range but nothing like it was in my shop in American City. I always kept a booth at this one auction, that had a big flea market too. Damn near everything can be found there. I'd peddle small stuff at the booth and stuff that wasn't worth a real good dollar. Old jewelry, watches, music boxes, Mickey Mouse toys, cameras, coins, old Zippo lighters. Could be almost anything. Sundays I might bring furniture pieces or wicker. Keep it open most weekends, some evenings. If I couldn't make it, then have Chubby watch the booth for me. I was always on the go. Besides Wanda, there was always five, six, seven guys working in the shop. Donnie is the main one now. He's my foreman. He was just a kid when he came to my shop in Boonesboro. Maybe eighteen years old at the time. Would hang around looking for something to do. I put him to work and saw that he had a knack for the upholstering and working with furniture. Has a good feel for wood. He is still learning, more now about how to deal with people. But I don't have to put a shoe up his ass anymore. Can take him aside now, say, "Hey, Donnie, there is a better way to handle that." *I took him from scratch, turned him around. I feel good about that. He would of been a delinquent, a real bum, if I hadn't brought him along.*

Fencing as a Sideline Involvement

There was always some fencing mixed in, especially in Tylersville. A little fencing and some antique fraud. *Were times the fencing would build up, kick up a few notches. Would have to pull back so it didn't become a main thing.* I would buy from different ones if I knew them. If you came recommended, then maybe yes. No walk-in trade. Would not buy from someone coming in off the street.

The main ones were the Beck brothers—are five of them. All were into smoking pot, using dope. They all pulled different things—shoplifting, sell dope, but mostly breaking into cars and burglary. I met Jimmy, the second oldest one, at my shop in Boonesboro. He would hang around, so I put him to work moving furniture or hauling things. He was sixteen, seventeen years old at the time.

When I moved to Tylersville, his brothers would show up, too. How it started I don't even know. I think first it was jewelry. The oldest one, Davey, ran some pieces by me. Then it was car radios, cameras, small stuff. Branched out from there to where a lot of different items are involved.

The jewelry I took to Rosen or to Skip. These connections go back to American City. Skip is one of the biggest jewelry and precious metal people around. Will only deal with you if he knows you or if you have somebody good that vouches for you. I would like to show you that place some time but I don't think he would go along with that. You have to call ahead of time. Let him know you're coming and when. Go out to his house. Place is surrounded by chain fence. Has a big Doberman. He sees you coming, he opens the gate. Is very cautious. But he is good to deal with. No hassles, fair price. I don't know what he does with it. I surmise he runs some of the stuff into Oceantown but I wouldn't know that. That is his business. Has a son who has set up his own business. Him and the old man had a falling out, so I can peddle to either one. The old man is good people, very solid. His son is more of a prick. Is solid but I would still be leery of him.

Off and on I bought from guys I knew from American City—Rocky, Steelbeams, Bowie, Ronnie, Mickey. I'd run into them at the auctions or wherever. Shoot the bull. Every so often would call or drop by, especially if they had picked up antiques. But my main trade was local, with the Beck boys and different guys from the area. It was word of mouth but not the street grapevine. If somebody vouched for them or I felt good about the guy, I'd buy.

This time around I was more careful in what I handled. Mostly it was antiques, furniture, and jewelry. Guns was another good item. I wasn't covered on the jewelry, nor on the guns, but I had good outlets to unload, and quickly. Car stereos were good auction items, which I got a lot of, 'cause the Beck boys hit a lot of cars and vans. If I made a list of all the things I bought this last period, it would be pretty long. Even handled some four-wheelers, the all-terrain ones. But the fencing never got to be anything like it was in American City.

A few times, yes, I did handle appliances. Mostly were taken from construction sites—houses, apartments. Builders put in the appliances—refrigerator, stove, washer and dryer, whatever—just before the people move in. The place is locked but no real security. Is a good time to be clipped.

I got on to this from a guy that worked construction. Him and his buddy were hitting construction sites and making off with different appliances. First on, were peddling them to some of their buddies. But then it got to be more serious and they needed an outlet. They stopped by my booth at the shop, are feeling me out and dangling about getting their hands on new refrigerators and that. Told them to come back that weekend, we could talk some more.

In the meantime I check out a place that I am surmising is handling warm stuff. Place called "Low Cost, Quality Outlet." Big place. Had new and used stuff. Tell the guy about the shop I have and that I sometimes run across "seconds"—could be furniture, could be tires, could be appliances. "Yeah, he'd be interested." I started slow with a couple of items, then saw it was okay.

Was hit and miss with this construction guy and his buddy. Would not hear anything, then I'd get a call, "Hey, we got a washer and dryer." Solid, drop it at my garage. Come by my booth and we'll settle up. Then, it just petered out with them.

By now I am seeing that this is a good racket. So I passed this on to the one Beck boy and to different ones. Is a decent profit in this and is safe, as long as they don't clip too often. Can scout on their own or sometimes I would scout a construction site, let them know what to expect. Just watch when the appliances are delivered, then you got a few days before the people move in. Take a van like you're a plumber or electrician, break in, open up the garage door, back the van into the garage, and load up.

I didn't pay upfront cash as much either. With a couple of the better burglars, yes. But the Beck boys and them, no. We'd agree on a ballpark figure. I would give them some cash, but not the full value. I would owe them until I unloaded. That way I didn't tie up my cash and I could chisel them a little on the other end. Now, sometimes I gave them more than what they expected, just to keep them on my good side. They never complained.

My bread and butter this time was mainly guys who were pretty decent thieves but they used dope, partied a lot. Not your drug crowd but into smoking pot, using coke. Were pretty solid but I would not trust them all the way. *Some were regular thieves but others would steal off and on. When they needed money to party, to buy a car, get some dope, they'd clip.*

One would be Andy and some of his buddies. Andy was mainly into burglary but his buddies were mostly hitting cars and vans, and would do some shoplifting. Met Andy at my booth at the auction. Came by a couple of times. Small talk. Good-natured guy. Had an inkling he was fishing, shopping around for an outlet. Then he asks am I in the market for dolls. Tells me his girlfriend has a doll collection she wants to sell. The dolls represent different countries. I am figuring he is blowing wind outta his ass, that the dolls are warm. Went to see them the next morning, after his girlfriend left for work. Yeah, I would take them. Could pay him so much now, then he should stop by my booth next week and pay him the rest.

Headed right for Scottie's and unloaded them. Paid the rest to Andy that next week but gave him a little extra to keep him coming. He wants to know— what else might I be interested in? Told him, I can take whatever I can sell easily. Words to that effect. Here's my number if you want to reach me. Was a while, like six weeks, he's back at my booth. Tells me he has a couple of guns, some jewelry, and a stamp collection. Right off I ask, "Are they warm? I can take them off your hands, but don't fuck with me—are they warm?" Nods his head, has a little smile. It was comical.

Every so often, I'd buy from another antique dealer who had a piece that was a little shaky. He didn't want to take any chances, so he'd contact me. This is very safe because you then have a layer in between. Same with some of your secondhand people, I off and on would buy from them.

This almost got me jammed up, six-seven years ago. I'm buying from Mookie, black guy I knew from the Midstate Penitentiary. Was a good con. The counselors would use him to help run some of their programs, same way they did with me. Is now running this little secondhand shop in the black area. But is selling dope, too. If a doper owes Mookie money and can't get the cash, then Mookie would take stuff they're stealing. Mookie is peddling this stuff to people he knows but that is risky and can only peddle so much. So, comes to me to peddle the stuff the dopers are bringing. Mostly, I'm buying jewelry—rings, gold chains, you name it. But also are some guns, VCRs, some antique pieces, even a couple of laptop computers. Cops find out about Mookie from a couple of the dopers who are snitching. Police are checking around to see where Mookie is unloading the stuff. Question me and a couple of other secondhand places. Nosed around my shop. Nothing really came of it. Told them I knew who Mookie was but didn't have any contact with him except to say "hi." I was leery Mookie would finger me, but he held up. Down the road, I heard Mookie weaseled his way out of it and that he stopped messing with the dope shit. Never had any more dealings with him. Really, it was dumb on my part to take that kind of a chance with Mookie. But you could make a good dollar on what Mookie was bringing 'cause he didn't know much about what things are worth and how to get rid of them.

What I needed this time in Tylersville was a place that would handle both what is legit and what is warm, so I could mix them. A place out of the area, in another state. So I went shopping. I ended up with two places, one right across the border [Bordertown] and the other in the apple orchard part of the state [Orchard Grove]. But I mostly stuck with the place across the border. I got to know Ollie, the guy that ran the place, and you could unload most anything, especially the wicker, ornamental gates, patio furniture, car stereos, tools, tires, cheap jewelry, your run-of-the-mill antiques. I felt very comfortable with the people there, not just with Ollie but with the other [antique] dealers and auction crowd that hung there.

The good antiques I would run to Ocean City, to Scottie's son. Glassware, Tiffany lamps, old pocket watches, old iron banks, train sets. But had some local antique dealers who might buy. From before, I had a couple of people that would just buy certain things, like coins or guns.

The last five-six years I've been doing more business with Jeep, and with Lenny, Jeep's cousin. In the Orchard Grove area that is maybe a two-hour drive from Tylersville. Are Italian but not the mafia. In the local people's eye they are, but not really. But are cut from the same cloth. Is uncles, brothers, cousins, whole fucking clan like the Italians have. Own different businesses. Have their fingers into different things both shady and legit.

Is funny how this connection came about. Was a hotel in the [Orchard Grove] area I was upholstering some chairs for. Wanted to get away from the shop so I decided to deliver them myself. I am stopped at a restaurant & bar place for a sandwich. I am playing the video poker machines and this guy starts chatting with me. Small talk. Turns out he owns the place. Tells him I had delivered some chairs to this hotel but had been in the area before because a few years back I made a bar for the hotel—out of art deco, was very beautiful. Jeep is like, "Whoa, are you the guy that did that bar?" Then asks did I want to upholster the booths in his restaurant.

I went for it. Then off and on he'd send more pieces to upholster. This led to our getting acquainted 'cause he would show me around when I would do the delivery. His uncle had a big flea market. Jeep tells me I should bring some stuff up. Especially on Saturdays the crowds are good. I played it straight— "Yeah, would do that but didn't want to bring him or his uncle any headaches on account of what I'm buying in my secondhand shop you never know if it's a little shaky." Jeep didn't show any concern. See, we both was fucking on the edges, drawing the other guy out. I'm figuring he knew who I was, that I done time for the fencing and that I still had some larceny in me. Myself, by now I know from asking around that Jeep and his uncles have their fingers into different things.

In the meantime, Jeep has hooked me up with Lenny. His cousin and is about Jeep's age. Are good pals but Lenny is the main one for the fencing and I am surmising for the criminal side. Jeep is the social one, fun to be around, likes to have a good time. Lenny was more the business side. Not that he won't fuck around or have a good time. But has a good head on his shoulders. And has a rough side. We have done a fair amount of business together. Mostly, I am selling to Lenny but can go the other way that I will pick up some warm pieces from him. This has been only the last couple of years, really.

Lenny would be a helluva good spoke. A big, big spoke. If I would ever want to get into the fencing a lot bigger. No doubt, on account he can take almost anything.

Close Calls with the Law

I did get popped in Boonesboro, for receiving. Remember that? The way that went down was the second Beck boy, Jimmy, was on probation, juvenile probation. Was maybe sixteen or seventeen at the time. Him and two buddies got popped for shoplifting. I would buy from Jimmy sometimes, nickel-and-dime shit. But his two buddies, no. But I think Jimmy was unloading for all of them. So Jimmy's two buddies tell the probation officer, "Hey, we know this guy who buys stolen goods. That's where we're taking the stuff." See, they were looking for a break. Probation officer calls the police. She wanted them to charge me with corrupting youth, not just the receiving. She was a real hard-ass.

County sheriff and his deputy show up, "Goodman, we have a search warrant." There was nothing in my shop. But they still charged me with receiving. On account of my record and the two kids testifying, they thought they had a case. Eventually the charges were thrown out, insufficient evidence. But I was leery of what might go down. I didn't know if Jimmy would hold up. If he caved, then would have been three testifying against me. The oldest Beck boy, Davey, was questioned by the police. But stood up.

I had to lean on the two kids, not directly. Had Davey and a couple of his buddies work over the two kids. Not overdo it, but enough to let them know. Headache and sore nuts. The message got across, and to Jimmy, too, that I would play hardball. The one kid left town and the other one got cold feet.

It ends up I have a meeting with an assistant in the DA's office, the one you know on account he graduated from Penn State. He tells me the charges are being dropped but that I should be on notice. Given my record, I should have good reason to mind my affairs carefully, very carefully. I told him, "Blah, blah, yeah I'm sorry this happened. I do need to be more careful, check things out more carefully when I buy off the street."

The last time I got popped it was more serious. A few years ago, involved ornamental gates. The elaborate ones especially are pretty valuable. This had been going on for a couple of years, I'm driving around to the auctions, and I would spot what are antique iron gates that are on fences around people's houses. Or I might take a different route home and check out areas where you have vacation homes or cabins. Other times, it might be wicker or patio furniture, on peoples' porches or the lawn. Write down the address, where the place was at, and pass that on to one of Beck brothers or to different ones I knew who are operating. They would watch the place and take it right off the fence or lawn, then drop the pieces at a garage I rented on the edge of town. If come across a good mountain bike, then pick it up.

I'd run the gates or wicker into my shop, maybe drop it in the big vat I have to take off the finish and then spray on a different color, take it up the elevator to the next floor, let them dry. Day or two later, I'd mix them in with other stuff, mostly legit, and run it down to the auction in Bordertown, to Ollie. Dealers and private collectors would grab up the gates. Would get anywhere from fifty to four hundred, five hundred dollars, depending on how elaborate they were. Good wicker set, say, four or five pieces, would bring six hundred to a thousand dollars. This was getting to be pretty big. Lots of people lost their gates, their wicker, their patio furniture. The local paper in one of the areas even ran a couple of pieces on it. I got a kick out of that.

It covered quite an area, really. On account I had Granger and a couple of his buddies hitting places in American City. Are in-between thieves, not bad but not good either. This was risky on my part 'cause sometimes Granger would be using dope when he would go out. Mostly cocaine, said it helped keep him alert. This one time he and one of his buddies went to the address I gave them. Got the stuff off the porch, carried it to the end of the driveway and then loaded it up. Next-door neighbor saw them. Wrote down the license plate number and a description of the truck.

I always warned Granger about mixing drugs and that with burglary. Always told him, have one guy drive and then drop the other guys off. Keep the truck away from the house. Carry the gate far enough away before picking it up, put it in the ditch, come back later and pick it up. Have one guy watch, drive the truck in when see the coast is clear and pick it up. They didn't do that this time. Couple of days later, the police pick up Granger—"If that is your truck, you have a lot of explaining to do."

Granger held up. He didn't snitch on me. I did pay him a couple of visits at his parent's house, just to keep him on his toes. He ended up doing about a year in the county jail for it.

It was a fluke how I finally got caught. I am buying antiques and some jewelry from a guy named Stanley and his partner. Stanley is a pretty good burglar, pretty good thief. I am doing regular business with them. Stanley had left some pieces of jewelry at his girlfriend's apartment. The police were suspecting, more or less had a tail on him. So they search her apartment and find the jewelry. Charge her with burglary and receiving, as an accomplice, then squeezed her. Had themselves a patsy. She told them what they wanted to hear, that Stanley was selling the stuff to me, that I was leading him on. She wanted to keep him out of jail 'cause he had been convicted before for burglary.

This led to the police to suspecting me on the gates and the patio furniture. Week or two goes by, police get a call—somebody stole two gates off a lady's driveway. The police send the lady to my shop, to see if I had it. I did have her gates 'cause the Beck boys had taken the pieces. Are in my shop, on the third floor. The lady is looking at the antique gates on the first floor, which are legit. But she sees one that looks like hers. She goes back to the police, "Yeah, one of my gates is there."

I'm out of town when this is all happening. Left for the auction very early that morning. I came very close to taking those gates along, but my truck was pretty full and thought I could make a little extra if I painted them first.

Police come back to my shop with the lady and have a search warrant. They're looking around and the one cop asks if there is any other furniture in the place. One of the workers blurts out, "Yeah, there are a couple more floors." Showed him the elevator in the back of the building that was the only way to the third floor. See, the help didn't know I was dealing in warm stuff. Not really, though Donnie and a couple of them could surmise it.

Shit, then they found it. Hauled all the gates and patio furniture out of my shop, from the first floor and the third. Except for those lady's gates, everything is legit. Not a warm piece in the place. Police advertise in the paper, "If you're missing gates or patio furniture, come and identify it and pick it up." People were picking up stuff that wasn't theirs. Now the shit hits the fan 'cause my customers are getting pissed when they find out their gates and their wicker they had brought in for me to work on are gone. The police got all kinds of hell [Sam laughs hard]. Different ones thought the police were picking on me. I got a kick out of that.

It was a big surprise when I got back from the auction and learned what happened. Wanda was whacked, "You're gonna get sent back to prison." The guys in the shop were worried 'cause the shop was their livelihood. *I think that helped me—cause my going back to the penitentiary would cost them their jobs.*

In the end, I agreed to plead "no contest," guilty to a minor theft charge. I would have to pay restitution, be on probation for two years but no jail time. The detective that handled it just wanted a conviction. He didn't care if I got jail time or not. So, he wasn't pushing. The restitution was I had to make my customers happy who lost their stuff. Had to come up with replacements for the fucking stuff that the police loaded out of my shop which was legit. How is that for a punishment? It tickles me every time I think about it.

The judge, a woman judge, lectured me pretty hard. "You're getting too old for this. Next time I'll send you away for the rest of your life." Blah, blah, blah. I had on my most contrite face. Told her, "I really learned my lesson this time, that I needed to be more careful who I bought from and to keep better records. That I had Wanda and her kids to think about and the guys at the shop who were depending on me for a livelihood."

It helped this last time I had a good parole agent. Brian was a decent guy. I had very few problems with him. First on, he checked on me quite a bit. Would stop by my shop or have me come to his office. Not a hard-ass but doing his job. It turns out that he liked secondhand stuff, was into antiques. Not in a big way but just to dabble. I ran into him at an estate sale that was auctioning some antique pieces. He was interested in a roll-away desk but didn't know what he should bid. So, I gave him a range. He bid but the piece went for way more than it should of. Then a month or so later, I run across a roll-away desk and bought it for Brian. Told him I got it cheap but really I am selling it to him for less than I paid.

This softened him, you might say. After that, I didn't have a schedule to follow. Never had me come by his office. He would stop by my shop, but more to visit than to check up on me and to see what I had in the way of secondhand furniture, what pieces I was upholstering. Then, he gets divorced. Got involved with a woman he worked with. His wife threw him out, took the house and all the furniture. So, he comes to me. Could I help him out? I went with him to a couple of auctions. Another time, I'm by myself and picked up a sofa and a couple of chairs for him. When I finished upholstering them, they were nice pieces. Offered them to Brian for a cheap price. He took them and owed me the money. Was four, five years before I got paid. That was okay with me, 'cause now I'm into him too.

But really, he gave me a lot of rope right off the bat. He could have hassled me 'cause he pretty much knew I was leaving the area to run to this or that auction. Or going back to American City, even leaving the state. Down deep, Brian liked me. He enjoyed coming by my shop and talking not just with me but with the guys that was working for me. In his eyes I was a pretty decent guy. Saw I treated my help right, ran a business. Brian is a regular joe blow who treated you right if you treated him right. I didn't put on a show for him, nothing like that, but he was made to feel welcome.

Sam as a Background Operator

I am content to keep the fencing small and stay more in the background. Would *do some scouting* off and on, say, for Rocky or for Andy or the oldest Beck boy. They have a place they want to clip, ask me to take a look at. I did it for the enjoyment. And *gave tips on places to clip,* to Andy or to one of the Beck boys or to this or that one I am dealing with. The information for the tips can come about in different ways but knowing the antique people and being at this or that antique place was a main source.

This happened last spring about the time the doctor found the spot on my lung [the cancer]. I am stopped at Log Cabin's place [nicknamed after the "log cabin" building that housed his business]. A lady is asking Log Cabin about buying a hutch to put her dishware and is talking about a nice silverware set her mother gave her. Wants to know if Log Cabin can deliver it in the evening 'cause her and her husband both worked during the day. My ears opened. Then saw she signed the registry, so put her name in my memory. I am thinking I should check this out. Found out where she lived, in a neighborhood where the houses are pretty far apart. Did some scouting. Had Chubby take a package for delivery to make sure no one else was home during the day. Then had Andy and his buddy, Carl, clip the place like ten o'clock in the morning. Pulled up in a van to do some "electrical" work, broke in, open the garage door and back the van partway in. Carried out some very nice pieces that I zipped to Scottie and Corky in Oceantown. One was a set of Spanish silverware that brought a nice penny.

It wasn't so much that I was out looking to get information on places to clip but more that my mind would just click—hey, maybe I should check that out. Would do that sometimes but other times just drop it. I did not want to push the envelope too far, to take chances that I shouldn't.

Another thing, there has always been a lotta of antique fraud mixed in with my legit business. People buying what they are thinking is an antique but it is junk. I have fooled antique dealers already but you have to be careful not to jeopardize whether you are able do business with the guy down the road. Don't want him to cut you off or spread the word that you're a shyster. Is not the same as when I'm clipping an ordinary joe blow. With another dealer, you can only clip so far—enough to keep him on his toes 'cause that is only good business, but don't overdo it or beat him too badly.

You never know what kind of opportunities will come your way. Life is funny that way and with how your past affects that. A few years back a guy in Boonesboro comes to me, is beating around the bush about having his store burned down. A little clothing store, catty-corner across the street from where my shop had been. That is how we knew one another. At first he is dropping hints, then comes out with it. Store is losing money, owed the bankers a potful. Said he knew I did time and thought I might know somebody. Told him I was straight now. What was he thinking anyways? A lot of risk for him, had he thought of that? Was the insurance payoff enough to overcome that? Pumped him enough to know the possibility was there.

Next time I see Phil, I run it by him. Needed a fire big enough to damage what's in the place but not burn down the whole town. Phil is thinking he could arrange that. I should be the contact with the guy in Boonesboro, get the details and handle the payoff. So, I goes to Boonesboro and sounds the guy out. But he is too shaky for my taste, wasn't sure he would hold up. Told Phil, no, I didn't want to take the risk. He could contact the guy but leave me out of it. Was enough for Phil—"Fuck it, let it die."

Diminished Spider Web

Moving away from American City and spending those years in the penitentiary this last time, I lost a lotta contacts. A few main ones I still had, but in many ways I had to start over. I still had Scottie—really Scottie's son in Ocean City. Still had Rosen and Skip who both would handle jewelry and that. Had a couple of antique dealers and auctions I could do some business with but not as wide open as before 'cause they were more cautious. They are figuring the police will be keeping tabs on me. And I wasn't pushing as much. Eventually, yes, I did get more contacts, like with Ollie and Lenny, but nothing like before.

Even if I wanted to get back into it on a bigger scale, a lot had changed. Louie was still doing time. Then when he finally got out, he was a pretty sick man. Bad heart. Louie does get back into the fencing. Still wanted to be in the limelight. But he was nothing like he was before. Then his fucking heart more or less peters out. I didn't want to do business with Louie again anyway, didn't want to fuck with him. Louie was too well-known and after he did time I was leery, very leery, that he would snitch to save his ass if it came down to that.

Same with Angelo—too many hassles, too many risks if the cops saw us together. Not that Angelo would snitch or set you up to save his ass. But the state police and the feds wanted Angelo bad. In my eye he was a lightning rod. If I messed with him I could get jammed up easy. But I always knew I could go to Angelo on some things. That thought was always there.

Grasso was another one that dried up. From Glendale. He would handle almost anything. Eight, nine years ago I stopped by his place. Was in the area and just wanted to see what happened to him, if he was operating. No Grasso. The place had changed, was a big landscaping and garden equipment store. Turns out Grasso had a heart attack, died shortly after I went to the penitentiary.

If Grasso had still been alive, was still operating, yeah, it might have affected me. Me and Grasso had done a lotta dealing together. Back and forth. He'd buy from me what was warm, I'd buy what was warm from him. There was a trust there. We'd try to beat each other and then kid about it afterwards. He was good people. I stopped by to visit not knowing he had died, just to see how he was doing. But in the back of my mind I am saying, "Can we do business again?" In a way I am toying with kicking the fencing up a notch. Different ones like the Beck boys are clipping pretty regular and are bringing their buddies by. Grasso would have been a big help.

Fat Charlie Ciletti, the importer—big food importer in American City—was another contact that dried up. Really, he and I was good buddies. He would stop my shop a lot just to kill time 'cause there was always something interesting going on at my shop. But haven't seen him, hell, for four, five years now. Every once in a while I'd run into him if I was in American City. Especially if I stopped at Phil's 'cause that is kind of a hangout for some of the old gang. Charlie has diabetics and a bad heart. Stomach hangs over his pecker he has gotten so fat. Very short of breath. Pulled back after Louie and me was sent to the penitentiary. Maybe with Phil he'd get involved but towards me Charlie was cautious. In my eye there wasn't any play there between us for doing something shady. In a way age has caught up with him, and as fat as he is, he is running out of gas.

Phil is still doing well. Still has the used-car place and the big junkyard. He is a main one in American City, part of the local clique and has his fingers into different things. Likes to horse around, is fun to be around. Is still a bondsman but that has dropped off 'cause now the county and the city have their own bail system. The bail stuff has changed a lot. Phil always did a little fencing but he is much bigger now. Not as wide open as Louie or me once was but he handles his share. Not from the walk-in trade 'cause Phil don't deal with that. Except he will buy from the secondhand dealer who is buying from the walk-in thief. Your in-between and decent thieves, and the trucker or warehouse thief, are the main ones he will buy from. And will buy from dealers like me. Phil has the contacts and has the contacts for making the contacts if he doesn't have a place ready to unload.

My contacts with the local clique and the mafia people in Tylersville are a lot less than they were in American City. I know who the main ones are in Tylersville, but mostly to say hi. We will bump into each other. I will stop at The Lounge once in a while, is near the airport, to hear the gossip and to see who shows up. Is where some of the local clique hang out. Will usually find Bucky there. Is part of the old Terrano gang [mafia group]. Is a character, a free spirit who likes to have a good time. He has invited me to come to their poker games. But I don't want to go that route again. "Thanks Bucky, I appreciate that but will stick to the video poker. I lose enough there."

I have only seen Amato at The Lounge a couple of times. He is a main one, on the order of an Angelo or a Nicky or a Phil. Doesn't show his face around town that much, that is what I hear. The first time I met Amato, he came to my shop. I had heard of him but had never been introduced. I am showing him around my shop, then he says, "Walk me to my car." Asks me about becoming his partner in the fencing. I should do the buying, he will be the outlet. Lets it be known there are some limits but he can handle almost anything. I am guessing he has checked me out with Angelo. No doubt in my mind they were acquainted. I should think about it, we could work out a deal that was fair for both sides.

He is wanting me to be the layer in between, between him and the thief. I have the knowledge, he has the places to unload. That I needed like a hole in the head. I don't say anything, except tell Amato I'm not into the fencing anymore. Tells me, I should keep in touch. I never did, just decided to drop the subject. A few times we did bump into each other but not a peep about the fencing was said. Then one time he brought it up again. Told him the same thing, I didn't think I had it in me to go that route again. He blew some wind outta his ass about how he would like to do business with me. Was a good schemer, put it that way.

Then not a word from him for several months. I'm having breakfast at this one truck stop, in walks Amato and sits down in my booth. Small talk, then gives me a card for a place. I should check it out and check with the guy that runs the place. Let him know who sent me. Wanted to know if I ever heard of the place. I had but didn't let on I did. Had stopped there a couple of times just to see what it was but no need for Amato to know that. Big-ass place, carries a lot of small items but is known for carrying bigger items like appliances, tires, riding law mowers, all kinds of tools. New, used, damaged, throwbacks. Is busy as hell on weekends.

I never followed up on it. A couple of times, yeah, I did unload some warm items at this place but never brought up Amato's name. *I am leery about getting hooked up with him and didn't want the temptation to be pulled in deeper.* Another thing, if I bring up Amato's name, then the price I am getting will have to take into account that Amato is probably getting a cut. The more ways it has to be cut, the less there is for everybody. But mainly I was content to do my thing and didn't wanna owe somebody.

More Good Spokes Then Than Now

The really good spokes for fencing haven't been there this time. Not near as much anyways. They fell into place in American City like you wouldn't believe. The fact that I had been a thief, was a good safeman, that I had done time and never took any body down with me—this helped with the thieves, especially the better thieves, and helped with the fences. And helped to hook me up with the local clique, which itself helped a lot especially with the cops and the magistrates. Even with the local store people it helped being part of the local clique but not as much 'cause it counts more with the store people how comfortable they feel with you, how you open them and handle their leeriness.

Here's the thing, a legit businessman or a guy that drives a truck or works in a warehouse—even a thief now—can put you in touch with his buddies. But that is it. A main dealer has his own spider web, knows a lot of different ones he can put you in touch with. I can't speak about other fences but being tight with a main dealer like a Louie or a Grasso is very near a must, say, at the beginning, until you get established. Or if you get hooked up with the local clique—that is a big plus for getting the contacts and will help you in a lot of other ways.

I took a big hit from being out of circulation for four, five years and from my parole guy telling me, "Hey, no way you're heading back to American City." Still had some contacts I could still tap into but lost a lot. *For one, each area has its own clique and its crime world you might say. Is some overlap with other areas but not as much you might think. Other contacts I lost 'cause they died or packed it in. Some I lost 'cause of my record, from my going back to the penitentiary this last time. A leeriness that maybe this guy is a loser, that maybe the cops will be watching him all the time, that maybe he can be pressured to snitch if he gets jammed up on account of all the time he can get.* I do feel that some of the people in American City were backing away. Could sense that when I'd bump into them. I'd provide an opening to see if there was some play but the response wasn't there.

The spokes in the wheel this time [in Tylersville] are only half decent. Pretty half-assed. Different ones like Ollie and Rosen I can peddle to, but they really aren't spokes that could hook me up with others. This or that one like Lenny and Scottie and his son, Corky, is some help for making contacts. But there was a limit to how far they would go to bat for me.

Phil comes the closest today to being a good spoke in the wheel, as far as putting me in touch with others.

As a favor, sure, Phil would make the connection for me. We have become buddies, two guys who have known each other for a long time. We visit once in awhile, but don't do that much business together. I would be reluctant too take advantage of that, except I know I can rely on him to be a go-between or give me the scoop on somebody. But it still isn't the way it was with a Louie or a Woody.

This last time, I would not even call it a spider web. A puny one, maybe. I surely didn't have the police in my pocket. Didn't have the guy who could really recommend me, show me around. A Louie, an Angelo, a Charlie, a Woody. We were pals but we were lining each other's pockets. Ones like Amato and Silas [local racketeer in Tylersville] have made noises to bring me in but I don't personally like Silas. Amato, I am leery it would get out of hand if that door opened on account he would push too hard and I'd end up being more involved than I wanted. Maybe Lenny could be the spoke I could rely on but that has only developed the past few years. The good spokes weren't there this last time, and I am holding back from developing them. I am chipping around the edges, not letting myself go all the way.

Shifts and Oscillations in Sam's Criminal Career

Looking back, at least as far as the fencing goes, there are like three periods. I really wouldn't think of myself as a fence this last time. I did buy warm stuff and peddle it. But it never got to be big thing, never. I am mostly content to stay in the background. Not all the way, now. If something came up, then maybe take a shot at.

The *first period* is after I hit American City, you might say I am a burglar, a half-assed fence, and a small businessman. All three but more than anything I am a burglar. Jesse and me is clipping something fierce and most of my time is spent finding places to clip and scouting them. Jesse and me spent days doing that. The *second period* would be when I'm out of the penitentiary for the antique burglary, I am a fence and a businessman, with some burglaries mixed in. The fence and the businessman are about even but I was more a fence I would say. This *last period* I am a businessman and a smalltime fence. The fencing is a sideline, very much so.

It is hard to estimate, but maybe one-fourth of my money came from the fencing in the first period, one-fourth from the legit business, and one-half from the burglary. In the second period, maybe three-fifths came from the fencing, or two-thirds if you include the burglaries. The rest came from the legit business. This last period, 70 to 80 percent came from the legit side, the rest from the fencing. These are just ballpark figures now 'cause I really don't know. Were times this last period when the fencing was bringing in a good dollar but then I am laying low. I made a lot of money on fencing but my legit business always did good, too.

I can't say how much I made overall on the fencing. Can't pinpoint that. In American City, yes, I made good money. Very good. I was in it with both feet and I had the contacts. Was making it both ways: turning over the penny-ante stuff and from deals that was worth a good dollar. But if you're a small dealer, like myself this last time, you aren't making that much from the fencing. Not peanuts now, but mainly a few extra bucks here and there.

I think I made out all right with the walk-in trade but it was a lotta hassle, an awful lotta hassle, for what I made. This last period I am staying away from the walk-in trade, but still the temptation was there to buy from anyone that walked in the door. A few times I did, then later I'd be asking myself— "Goodman, why are you fucking with the penny-ante thief, with the guy selling off the street?" Bring you a lot of junk that you got no use for. Can end up with drawers of watches, bracelets, trinkets, shit like that. I'd haul it to the auctions. Sell it for a penny, just to get rid of it.

You remember the good dollar deals more than the half-assed deals. This has happened different times. Somebody comes in, are in a hurry 'cause they are ripping somebody off and are going to skip town. I am closing the place one night, this guy comes in and is peddling two rings. Ruby rings, a man and a woman's set. Very beautiful. But I didn't know that when I bought them. Car is full of other stuff, too, mostly junk—couple of clocks, TV, paintings. Guy has been drinking heavily. From what he said, I am figuring he is running out on some woman he's been shacking up with. Ran out of money, so took her stuff. Intentional now, I didn't even pay attention to what he had. Didn't even look at the rings. Said, yeah, I'll give you hundred, two hundred bucks, something like that, for all of it. Just to get rid of him. He took it. Next time, I see Rosen I showed him the rings. Said they're nice rings. I sold him the one ring for fourteen hundred dollars and gave the other one to this woman I was seeing. That was a beautiful deal. I can remember it like it was yesterday.

I would buy [stolen goods] from other dealers this last period but nothing like I did in American City. Say it is a guy who handles antiques or runs a second-hand business—who is mostly legit but will take a shot at a warm piece if he knows the thief well or thinks the coast is clear. There is very little risk. Take Emory, is a local antique dealer. Will sometimes call me: "Sam, I picked up some Tiffany lamps and some porcelain. Nice pieces but could be a little shaky." Emory is wanting to unload quick so I could chop him down a little. But even if my edge is pretty small, I will hop right on that on account of Emory is a layer in between, so my chances of getting jammed up is very small.

Altogether, I'd say my edge was better this last period but I didn't have the big hits like before. If you're buying regular from the half-decent thief, or even the walk-in trade, it will just happen that you run across a beautiful deal. The odds are the thief will now and then bring in some good pieces, like jewelry or guns, that I can get top dollar for but he doesn't have the foggiest what they are worth. But the fence has to be careful not to get too eager 'cause you can end up buying junk and more junk hoping you'll come across something really good. I would take those chances in American City but have backed away from doing that in Tylersville.

My thing this last period has been to keep the clipping small, especially the fencing. If you are a small secondhand dealer, and you cover yourself pretty well, watch your opportunities but don't get too greedy, the police won't know enough to bother you. Not that your name has never come up. Maybe this or that thief has fingered you but unless this happens more than once or twice, not much will come out of it.

[But] it was hard not to fall back into the fencing much deeper, go for it in a big way. The larceny [in the heart] is still there and I have the know-how. I still have the heart, not leery of dealing with the thieves and your other dealers. The cops are a concern, not a fear. I ain't got the contacts I once had but do believe I could have built them back up. Really, it is my record that is holding me back, that I can't stand another pop [arrest-imprisonment]. That, and just getting older—the fencing can be a lot of hassles, can be a bitch in different ways. *But the itching to get back into it, all the way now, was always there. Just knowing I could do it but couldn't let myself go would gnaw at me.*

PART III

Crime Pathways and Organization

13

Commentary

Social Organization of the Underworld:
Stratification, Continuity, and Change

Sam Goodman's career positions and experiences tell us a great deal about the social organization of the underworld. His narrative in Chapter 14 highlights the underworld code (at least in his time and experience) and also yields valuable insights into the "pecking order" or stratification of the underworld, including sexism and racism in that stratification.

In our commentary, we expand on the notion of criminal opportunity and elaborate on what Sam's career tells us about the stratification and social organization of the underworld. In particular, we discuss the distinctions Sam makes between types of thieves and criminal entrepreneurs, and his "pecking order" of the underworld. Finally, we discuss stability and change in the underworld.

Expanding the Notion of Criminal Opportunity

We return to the topic of criminal opportunity that we first brought up in Chapter 3. Criminal opportunities are arrangements or situations that offer attractive potential for criminal reward to individuals and groups vis-à-vis apparent risk of detection or penalty (Hochstetler 2001; Steffensmeier 1983). Inviting opportunities for crime are available wherever offenders believe that "the take" (reward) is acceptably promising, that no one of consequence is monitoring them, and that anyone who uncovers evidence of their crimes probably would not trigger punitive responses (Hochstetler 2000). Low-risk versus high-risk crime opportunities depend on the interplay of these three elements.

Cloward and Ohlin (1960) developed the notion that criminal opportunities, like conventional opportunities, are not evenly distributed throughout society. Opportunity structures for the learning and performance of crime are differentially available according to one's social statuses (e.g., race, gender, ethnicity, age) and the social organization of groups and networks in which one's life is embedded. Steffensmeier (1983) extended this theory of opportunity further, demonstrating that learning and performance opportunities vary by types of crime: *lucrative* vs. *petty* crime, *upperworld* vs. *underworld* crime, *organized* vs. *unorganized* crime, and, implicitly, *low-skill* vs. *high-skill* crime and *short-term, situational* vs. *long-term, sustained, self-generating* forms. In addition, criminal activities or enterprises can be placed on a continuum with respect to the modus operandi, or how victimization is accomplished (if it is not an uncoerced transaction, as in so-called victimless crimes) ranging from use of physical force or violence to use of stealth or fraud.

Learning opportunities entail access to attitudes and skills favorable for crime commission (both in general and for specialties). They involve access to *civil* knowledge (the sort of information or learning to which most everyone is exposed), to *preparatory* knowledge (the sort of knowledge or familiarity that comes from being embedded in settings where crime or vice routinely or periodically takes place), and to *technical* knowledge (the sort of knowledge or learning acquired in specialized settings or from criminal specialists). Performance concerns the "conduct" of crime itself, including access to requisite *tools or hardware* (which include physical, and perhaps mental, capabilities), to *suitable places and targets,* and to *contacts or support network* (which may include "criminal" as well as "respectable" persons).

Another important point is that *opportunity and motivation tend to have a reciprocal effect on one another, feeding into each other.* On the one hand, open, available, and attractive criminal opportunities may increase motivation for such behavior. On the other hand, criminal motivation may also lead one to seek out or create one's own opportunities. Thus, the subjective and objective availability of crime, perhaps especially lucrative organized forms of crime, are interrelated. They tend to cluster together and to reinforce one another in various ways.

Our discussion of criminal opportunity extends Cloward and Ohlin's and by extension, Sutherland's. Criminals move from one enterprise to another within the underworld according to their tastes, abilities, and opportunities. Some criminals and crime networks have more abilities and opportunities than others. Just as criminologists speak of a "cumulative disadvantage" facing some members or segments of society in pursuing legitimate work or careers, there also is a cumulative disadvantage facing many persons for pursuing criminal work or success. Some prospective offenders have wide-ranging opportunities across most levels or forms of crime (e.g., petty as well as lucrative, upperworld- as well as underworld-based), whereas most other prospective offenders clearly do not. For example, a mafioso like Angelo has a lot more opportunities than Sam, who in turn has a lot more than Rocky, who in turn has a lot more than the Beck boys.

The extent and quality of crime opportunities vary both across population subgroups (e.g., race, ethnicity, age, gender, and other locations in the social structure) and across individual offenders, and the opportunities also may ebb and flow considerably across the life course, and in the actual playing out of an individual's criminal career. So, too, some individuals (and some groups) more so than others have the resources or prerogatives to pursue either legitimate or illegitimate opportunities, depending on their wishes and what they consider acceptable.

"Occupational" Stratification of the Underworld

The underworld refers broadly to the culture, setting, or social organization associated with criminal activities and more general rule-violating behavior. It is, in Bourdieu's (1977; 1985) framing, a *field* of striving guided by mutually recognized goals and codes of conduct in which individuals and groups compete for rank, power, and (criminal) achievement. Burglary crews, auto thieves, gamblers, prostitutes, drug dealers, fences, illicit gun dealers, forgers, the syndicates, and corrupt police all have actual and potential relationships with one another that are different from those they have with people not in the underworld. These individuals and groups form a kind of *loosely coupled system*—in the sense of being linked to one another and to crime activities, while still maintaining independent identities and some evidence of physical and logical separateness. The underworld culture also both reflects and exacerbates values and identities of the blue-collar working class. Important here, for example, is the meaning of work and money. In working-class culture, one makes or earns money not so much to save or invest it toward long-term security, but more to have enough of it to spend fairly freely (e.g., to party, to have a nice pickup truck) and to be in control of one's life (which, without enough spending money, is hard to do).

The embeddedness of Sam's burglary and fencing involvement in the setting and culture of the underworld is reflected in the themes of trust, safety, reputation, toughness, and "carrying oneself right" that he uses to portray his experiences. The following key normative themes can be seen in Sam's description of the informal underworld "code." Those who follow this code garner respect from their peers in the underworld:

1. The "take" on a job or scheme is to be split equally. In practice, however, one's share of the take depends on one's status (as we discuss below) and centrality to the operation.

2. "Don't be a whiner." Carry yourself right, be a standup guy. This involves taking responsibility for one's screwups and not letting partners down.

3. Don't risk bringing extra headaches, for example, by injuring a joe blow citizen (unless one has to) or by breaking into occupied places (which also may increase the risk of injuring someone). But if you do "come upon" someone (e.g., house occupant), use force if that is necessary for escape. What Sam says is, act naturally, make up an excuse why you're there (e.g., "I got a call about a power failure"), and leave quickly. Chances are the occupants will be so surprised or frightened, they won't be able to identify you. But if you have to "use a two by four," as Sam says, do so.

4. Don't gossip or show off too much. On the one hand, status is gained by making successful jobs known to others. On the other hand, one loses respect by becoming cocky, or by bad-mouthing other underworld players.

5. "Fairness" and "understandings": within reason, criminal entrepreneurs will sometimes help each other, steer deals to each other, and try to avoid stepping on each other's toes. This is revealed in the ways Sam would steer guns to Louie, or liquor and cigarettes to Angelo, or food products to Ciletti. At the same time, all parties recognize that they are in business to make money, and fences in particular will not pass up really good deals just for the sake of an "understanding" with another fence. As Sam says, "[Fences] are too greedy and there ain't that kind of honor among fences. There's more honor among thieves—well, among your better thieves, anyway."

6. Be ready to play hardball. Since there is no authority in the underworld to enforce norms, one must engage in self-help. Sam repeatedly says that one needs the "muscle" to protect oneself and project strength.

7. Don't snitch. It is very difficult to garner trust and respect among criminal associates, or even have many criminal associates, if one becomes known as a snitch. Worse still, don't "set up" somebody to be "pinched" while actually committing a crime.

Another important dimension of the underworld is its status hierarchy, and this status hierarchy is also tightly interrelated with the code described above. Criminologists have long recognized that criminal subcultures of the underworld constitute an alternative status hierarchy for the lower and working class (Matsueda et al. 1992; Cohen 1955; Cloward and Ohlin 1960). Within the inner city, for example, there is a certain prestige to criminal occupations (e.g., numbers bookie, or pimp) that provide alternatives to low-status legitimate jobs (Anderson 1990), whereas being a truck hijacker or a safecracker is more revered among white blue-collar groups (Steffensmeier 1986). There is a pecking order or status ranking within the underworld across types of crime and criminals. Similar to conventional occupations, criminal work is stratified by prestige in such a way that seasoned thieves and illicit entrepreneurs confer prestige upon themselves and distinguish themselves and their group from other criminals, those who do not belong.

Some ethnographic studies provide a glimpse of this status hierarchy, but we do not know very much about how deviants or criminals themselves rank the prestige of criminal occupations. Sam's account indicates that the prestige of crime is an important element of the underworld.

First, high-prestige crimes seem to share many features of high-prestige legitimate jobs, such as specialized skills, long-term commitment, ambition, reliability, and strategic connections. Second, prestige flows to those who gain high monetary returns. For example, even the upper-level drug trafficker is admired (somewhat begrudgingly by Sam) because the money or profits can be so substantial. Third, high-prestige crimes seem to be those that best bridge the legitimate and illicit worlds—those that provide both a cover that reduce the chances of detection and offer respectability that lessens the (moral) marginality that often accompanies a deviant occupation.

Basis for Rankings

Both history and literature vividly describe crime as one of the most ancient human phenomena, and its manifestation as a career or lifestyle has been known for many millennia (Inciardi 1975). The *Lives* of Plutarch and the *Annals* of Tacitus register theft and prostitution as careers. Petronius's *Satyricon* portrays the craft of the pickpocket. The Old Testament recounts how Abimelech, illegitimate son of Gideon, contracted professional killers, and the recollections of Moses recognize prostitution as an occupational pursuit.[1]

The development of "professional" crime and the underworld as we know it today originated with the rise of cities and the economic changes resulting from the disintegration of the feudal order in Europe in the fifteenth and sixteenth centuries. Rogues and vagabonds, thieves and sharpers, forgers and highwaymen, swindlers and conny-catchers increasingly congregated in English towns and London specifically to practice varieties of property crime. *Conny-catching* was originally Elizabethan slang for a particular method of cheating at cards. It later served to describe any method of swindling. The *conny* (also an archaic term for "rabbit") was the victim of the swindle. *Conny-catchers* were a fraternity of thieves who lived by their wits and took pride in their work.

Already within the Elizabethan underworld, status levels among thieves were apparent. Rogues and sharpers, followed by curbers or housebreakers, were ranked the highest. Pickpockets and shoplifters were ranked somewhat lower, and extortion by prostitutes ranked at the bottom of status levels. Status levels also existed within criminal specialties. Among pickpockets, for example, the "foist" commanded greater prestige than the "nip," and city nips were considered more skilled than country nips.

By the time of the writing of Sutherland's *The Professional Thief* (1920s), a five-level status hierarchy existed across criminal specialties (Inciardi 1975): (1) big-con operators and bank burglars; (2) forgers and counterfeiters, safe burglars; (3) short-con operators, penny-weighters, house and store burglars, armed robbers ("stickup men," strong-arm thieves); (4) shakedown workers, hotel and house sneak thieves; and (5) shoplifters and pickpockets. Some thieves, however, would alter the pecking order of crime because of pride in their own criminal specialty. Furthermore, in addition to some ranking across criminal specialties, more rigidly structured indicators of stratification appear within specific categories of theft, most notably confidence men, burglars, and pickpockets. That one is a "big con operator," a "good safeman," or a "class cannon" (or very skilled pickpocket) carries special meaning.

It is important to note, however, that Sutherland dealt only with the theft subculture while ignoring racketeers and syndicate figures who—on the basis of money, power, and prestige—both then and now constitute the highest-status criminal roles. Also, as we discuss later, recent changes in the underworld, especially the expanding drug market, have contributed to some shifts in the money, power, and prestige of criminal roles.

Sam's Distinctions about the Underworld and Career Criminality

Career crime is law-violating behavior pursued (in an occupational context) to obtain a steady flow of income. Career crime begins with initiation and socialization into the world of crime, attended by a maturation process involving the acquisition of skills, knowledge, and associations appropriate for maintaining the desired specialty. Career crime is also "vocational" in the sense that participants view their law-violating or quasi-legitimate behavior as a "job" or "business." With this conceptualization of career crime in mind, we note the following six distinctions Sam makes about thieves and criminal entrepreneurs:

1. Sam makes a distinction between the "good" thief, the "decent" thief, and the "amateur" thief (somewhat analogous to professional vs. nonprofessional). The good thief has skills, contacts, and a degree of immunity that far surpasses the half-decent or amateur thief.

2. Sam makes a distinction between those who characteristically commit crime to meet immediate financial needs at sometimes great risk, and those who see crime as a business and are able to pick and choose from criminal opportunities. More elite offenders (found more among the ranks of seasoned thieves and racketeers) are more inclined to bide their time and wait for criminal opportunities, instead of jumping desperately into crimes that provide a quick dollar. The former much more so than the latter have access to social

networks and information and have less fear of being arrested and being branded as a criminal.

3. Sam makes a distinction between those who are in crime for the long term, and those whose careers are more short term (e.g., "Some guys who get into burglary or fencing just chip around the edges, maybe hit at it real hard for a few years—then pull back or pack it in. Guys jump into drug dealing today for that reason.")

4. Sam makes a distinction between those who are full-time thieves and have no legitimate job or business versus those who hold a conventional job or run a legitimate business.

5. Sam notes that the nature and strength of the immunities from sanction vary across criminal specialties and individual practitioners of crime and vice.

6. Sam makes a distinction between "thieves" and criminal entrepreneurs or racketeers, between those who "steal for a living" and "those who run an illegal business or are background operators."

The "theft" versus "rackets" distinction is an important, but not well-understood, element of underworld stratification and mobility (see endnotes 4 and 5 in Chapter 3). Theft involves a multitude of mostly nonviolent property crime and fraud by small, informally organized groups, or sometimes by individuals (Inciardi 1975:132). Some thieves obtain partial immunity from legal sanction through contacts with criminal justice officials, which enable the occasional "fixing" of cases, and through codes of ethics and self-segregation. Although their predatory behaviors are undertaken with the direct cooperation of only a limited number of individuals, sustained involvement and effective execution are facilitated by cooperative understandings and an informal system of communication and networking that is so eloquently described by Sam. The main categories of offense behavior include burglary, breaking into or theft of motor vehicles, armed robbery, pickpocketing, sneak theft, shoplifting, forgery and counterfeiting, identity theft, check and credit card fraud, extortion, and confidence operations, as well as truck hijackings and cartage theft.

Rackets tend to be market-based forms of criminality that typically involve more or less consensual exchanges between "criminals" and "clients." These include the distribution of illegal goods and services, such as gambling, drugs, firearms/guns, illicit sex (e.g., prostitution, pornography), and loan-sharking; the infiltration of legitimate businesses or running of quasi-legitimate businesses; and the plying of official malfeasance to obtain favorable government contracts or business undertakings. Both because these activities are less directly predatory than conventional forms of theft and also represent products/services desired by some legitimate sectors of society, their criminality is supported for the most part and societal reaction is mild. Varying amounts of immunity are maintained through a code of ethics and informal communication network, as well as a political power base of symbiotic relationships between criminals and members of the criminal justice system (ibid.). The lucrative nature of racketeering activities supports this power base. In addition, the understandings that exist between groups help all to profit by reducing competition and overlapping areas of activity (ibid.). Recruitment typically occurs on the basis of kinship or friendship, and advancement is dependent on ability, motivation, and length of participation.

As Sam describes it, fencing straddles the world of theft and world of rackets in that it entails elements of both. The fence as "middleman" between the thief and the purchaser of stolen goods also straddles two *business* worlds, the legitimate and illegitimate. Fences represent a group of businesspeople who operate in conjunction with thieves (defined broadly to include regular thieves, truck drivers, shipping clerks, joe blow thieves, etc.) and buyers (e.g., store customers, merchants, or other dealers) for purposes of disposing of stolen goods. The fences themselves are not necessarily thieves or former thieves, and often do not conceive of themselves as such. Rather, they are "business" people who have the opportunity and connections for the disposal of specific stolen commodities and, in some cases, almost any item in any quantity.

In Sam's view, fences or "dealers" (the term he preferred) are in a "different league" than the burglar or thief but instead are more like the racketeer. Whereas the thief tends more to be a reactive or passive offender as he goes about responding to and seeking out theft activities, racketeers and fences are more actively making and sustaining crime opportunities. Racketeers and fences are also more likely to define themselves as "businessmen," rather than criminals.

With these distinctions in mind, Sam's narrative helps clarify the stratification system of the underworld. Key distinctions exist both across and within crime specialties, and between involvement in theft versus involvement in the "rackets" or illicit businesses. *Confessions* discerns the following "pecking order" across criminal specialties in the late twentieth century (compare this to Sutherland's rankings for the early 1900s we presented earlier):

1. illicit businesses: racketeers, mafiosi, background operators, syndicate racketeers;
2. big-time fences, major bookmakers (who "bank," or control their own pool of betting money), upper-level drug dealers, black market specialists;
3. big con operators, safe burglars, truck hijackers;
4. house and commercial burglars, armed robbers, forgers and counterfeiters, cartage thieves, auto thieves;
5. short-con operators, small-time fences, bookmakers, midlevel drug dealers;

6. shoplifting and other varieties of smalltime thieves, check kiting, pimping;
7. street-level hustlers, snatch-and-grab thieves, low-level drug dealers; and
8. prostitutes and drug-addict thieves.

In addition there are generic classifications (e.g., the term "good people") that cross these boundaries. The generic term "good people" describes the thief or criminal entrepreneur who "has his act together" and often is also "respected" in the underworld. Second, how (and the conditions under which) individuals earn their living is an important source of how they are regarded by others and how they regard themselves. This is true of both the conventional world and the underworld. Thus, crimes that allow for more personal autonomy and freedom, and crimes that entail less "dirty work" seem to be particularly valued. This is evident when Sam talks about how, as a fence, he does not have to "crawl in windows," but says, "Now I have people crawl in windows for me."

At the bottom of the hierarchy are unorganized impulsive street crimes and sex crimes. At the very bottom of Sam's criminal hierarchy are what he called "dopers," "baby rapists," and "the 'fuck-ups' who will even mug old women." Although not necessarily "thieves," these categories constitute a "disreputable" reference group that thieves and racketeers use in constructing their rationales. This is certainly evident with Sam (as shown in Chapters 19 and 20). He *despised* (almost too much) the "dopers" and "baby rapists."

Crimes that better straddle the conventional world and underworld have higher status, as do crimes that offer some legitimate "cover" and greater legal immunity. These crimes seem to contribute to greater "respectability" among conventional folk. That is, it seems to be important whether the activity is "respected" or less stigmatized in the conventional world. For example, being a "doper" or dealing in drugs is often stigmatized and despised in the conventional world. Thus, mafiosi interviewed in a major study of organized crime who were known to be involved in the drug trade at high levels denied this strenuously, but were simultaneously quite willing to talk about their other racketeering activities (Pennsylvania Crime Commission 1991).

As another illustration, there is more entrepreneurship or "business" in rackets and market-based crimes than in theft. This enhances the prestige and acceptance of the rackets since "business" activity and being "a businessman" are so highly valued in American society. Furthermore, the rackets require more resourcefulness and contacts, which also enhances their underworld prestige. Finally, like Sutherland, Sam still ranks con artists and swindlers very highly. However, as we discuss at the end of this chapter, confidence games have changed a great deal since Sutherland's day, incorporating changes in technology and contemporary social life (e.g., phone and computer scams, credit card scams).

Variability in Criminal Opportunities:
Underworld Sexism and Racism

Sam's narrative suggests at least two effects of underworld stratification and power differentials on recruitment and mobility in crime. The first derives from the principle that the powerless seek power through the powerful. As in the legitimate world, persons seeking success in a criminal enterprise will be most attracted to and most in need of recognition by those with status and power. For example, a thief's career is advanced by spreading the word, either by himself or by others, that he is "solid" or that he is "good people." This is evident throughout Sam's narratives in previous chapters, and in Chapter 19. So too, criminals often seek status by making their "good scores" known to their peers. A second effect is that in the criminal world opportunities are constructed in large part by strong peer alliances and by recognition received for stand-up qualities such as having "heart" or being trustworthy. Apparently, more so than in legitimate enterprises, career success or a power base in criminal enterprise depends on peer acceptance.

The distribution of learning and performance opportunities for profitable, more organized forms of criminal activity shapes the stratification of the underworld, and the distribution of such opportunities is influenced by would-be criminal actors' race, ethnicity, and gender (as we discuss shortly). Males dominate the world of crime in general, and lucrative organized crime in particular. Through *homosocial reproduction,* or "like chooses like," and other processes, the sexism or racism of the underworld is perpetuated (Steffens-meier 1983).

Similar processes likely also account for the organization of criminal networks and syndicates along racial and ethnic lines, and along lines of kinship. Given the precarious nature of trust in the underworld, actors tend to choose those they think they can trust to form partnerships, client–patron relationships, exchange relationships, and the like. This tends to be people like themselves—those of the same ethnic group or race (Pennsylvania Crime Commission 1991).

In addition to the trust criterion, criminal entrepreneurs also choose those whom they define as having the necessary capabilities, and since success in the underworld is so dependent on peer acceptance and contact building, those who will not diminish one's reputation. Again, this will tend to be people like themselves, and of equal or higher status.

Persons seeking success in criminal enterprise, therefore, will be most attracted to and most in need of recognition by those with status and power, just as in the conventional world. As documented in *Confessions,* one outcome is the likely prospect that females, blacks, and others will benefit from being recruited or recognized by males, whites, Italians, etc., but not vice versa. This means that, just like in the corporate world studied by Kanter

(1977), *homosocial reproduction is perhaps a privilege of those with power and higher status.* Those who dominate the underworld will seek others like themselves, but those of lower status and power will not necessarily reproduce themselves.

Lemert (1951) long ago observed that any person who aspires to a role, whether it is organized around conventional or deviant behavior, will be restricted by the social definition of his pre-existing status. Rules, prejudices, and stereotypes associated with gender, race, or other social characteristics have the effect of helping or hindering a person's potential enactment of various social roles, criminal as well as noncriminal.

Institutional Sexism

Sex-segregation in the underworld is perhaps the most powerful element shaping women's experiences in the illicit economy. It inhibits their access to illicit-business work roles and in large part effectively forecloses their participation as high-level players or distributors. Women's main access to many illicit-business work roles is via boyfriends and husbands. Key elements of underworld sexism (identified by Steffensmeier 1983; 1986)—homosocial reproduction, sex-typing, and the qualities required in what is typically a physically demanding or violent task environment—are featured prominently in Sam's account.

Women are perceived (especially by men, who dominate the underworld) as less likely to have valued criminal traits or criminal capital. They are seen as unreliable, untrustworthy, unable to deploy violence and intimidation effectively, and having few worthwhile connections. Male concerns about trusting female accomplices often intertwine with male perceptions that (1) a woman's strong loyalty to her children gives law enforcement a strong club to coerce her to snitch (e.g., police can threaten her with jail and with losing her children, if she does not cooperate and provide evidence against her male partner—including one who also may be her romantic companion); and (2) a woman will turn against her romantic companion who is also a partner in crime if she suspects or learns he is cheating on her (i.e., the "fury of the scorned woman" view).

Yet, it also is clear that Sam and other offenders, while professing or preferring "not to work with" females, in fact had at one time or another and perhaps even fairly frequently. They were more likely to commit crimes with a woman in one or both of the following circumstances: (1) when a romantic relationship existed (e.g., "she's my woman") or (2) when the *usefulness* of deploying a female for committing the crime more safely or profitably was greater. The latter might involve the use of females as "cover," "sexual distraction," or "accomplice" roles—i.e., especially in circumstances where women create less suspicion, have access to helpful information, or attract a more willing or less fearful clientele (e.g., many drug users, both male but especially female, prefer to buy their drugs from female vendors, who are less likely to rob or sexually assault). Also, the reason may be situational or spur of the moment, as when the theft or hustling opportunity would be missed if not taken advantage of quickly, but male accomplices were not available.

Strong evidence of male power in the underworld and the modus operandi of partnering with women based strictly on their *utility or usefulness* for the criminal episode or enterprise is reflected in how the "score" or profits are distributed. *Female partners or accomplices typically receive far less of "the take" than their male co-offenders.* A somewhat extreme (but not necessarily atypical case) is the burglary crew of Jesse, Sam, and Bernice (Jesse's wife, who for awhile acted as dropoff driver). Jesse and Sam basically split the proceeds, whereas the "share" for Bernice was lumped with Jesse's split. One exception was, "If we grabbed loose bills or bag of coins, say, on the way out, we gave that to Bernice."

A few women do compete and carve out a niche in the "rough and tumble" underworld (including establishing partnerships with males), a setting in which a clear gender hierarchy also strongly exists. While some women may adopt fairly well a posture and rhetoric of toughness (including "being bad" and "being crazy"), women are widely perceived (by men and women alike) as less likely to have the attributes associated with serious and successful criminality, especially when it comes to "managing" clients or other offenders and in "holding one's own" in crimes involving physical strength or involving direct contact with clients or victims where intimidation is oftentimes expedient. Women generally lack the requisite "rep" for having "heart" or "muscle" (masculine qualities associated with physical prowess, toughness, and the capacity for violence) to inspire the confidence of prospective partners, clients, protectors, or other background operators.

Men's perception of women (especially street offenders) as weak, sexually available, and easily manipulated also renders them vulnerable to exploitation. Furthermore, men often have the economic resources and physical prowess to maintain control over and exploit women, and women offenders (especially on the streets) are prone to constant harassment and regular victimization (Steffensmeier 1986; Maher and Daly 1996; Miller 1998; Steffensmeier and Allan 1996). The actions of men *and* women offenders reflect an understanding of this male-dominated environment. Thus, while women's and men's motivations for crime will overlap considerably (e.g., for money, excitement, peer pressure), their ways of doing crime are often strikingly different.

Lastly, besides being less accepted in the underworld, *Confessions* suggests that female offenders (though less feared) are often less accepted in legitimate society as well. That is, they tend to have less choice or a smaller pool of prospective romantic partners (Giordano et al. 2003; Steffensmeier and Allan 1996). While many male offenders are able to hook up with "respectable" female partners, women who engage in crime apparently have greater difficulty hooking up with "conventional" males. This gendered difference in locating a romantic partner apparently becomes greater as one's criminal history becomes more extensive.

Institutional Racism

In a somewhat similar vein, there is *considerable racial segregation in the underworld*. Cumulative disadvantages or diminished opportunities for recruitment and mobility in the underworld seem to apply to blacks and other ethnic minority groups. Illicit economies, while often favoring some degree of superficial multiethnic interaction (especially at the lower reaches of the underworld), seem to reproduce the same kinds of prejudices that characterize the legal economy, but even more so (see especially the very convincing treatment of this in Ruggiero 2000).

Although Sam himself rarely professed negative views of blacks as a whole (though he was pretty harsh toward black thieves and hustlers), many of his colleagues did. They typically viewed (and strongly expressed such views) blacks as incompetent, unreliable, and violence prone, and they frequently referred to blacks by well-known racial slurs. Partnering with black accomplices was seen as legally risky and as diminishing one's status or ability to make contacts in the sense that other white offenders would frown on it. (A similar concern is often raised about male thieves who do crimes with a female accomplice.) As far as crime goes, the general "white" view was, "You do business with them if you have to but you really don't want to associate with them."

There also is the strong perception that blacks are rarely the real money-makers or influential background operators in the underworld but instead mainly operate at the street level or a notch or two above (see also Ruggiero 2000; Pennsylvania Crime Commission 1991). Although some may accumulate a goodly sum of money, they typically "end up with very little" because their criminal activities and limited network resources put them at high risk for police intervention or death or injury from one's rivals.

Change and Stability in Criminal Opportunities and the Social Organization of Crime

Both continuity and change characterize crime and the underworld over the past several decades, according to *Confessions*. Sam highlights a number of important changes in both crime and the law as he experienced or observed them. These changes mainly center around:

1. changes in illegal markets and crime opportunities brought about, first, by changing patterns of productive activity leading to more attractive opportunities for some types of fraud or theft relative to other types (check fraud or car break-ins versus commercial burglary) and, second, by the expanding illegal drug trade.

2. changes in law enforcement priorities and practices including the expanding use of informants, the growth in availability of competing or overlapping enforcement agencies and the decline of local police autonomy, and enforcement programs targeting career offenders.

Changes in Illegal Markets and Crime Opportunities

Several key changes in American society since World War II have created or expanded opportunities for the commission of varied forms of thefts and frauds that, in turn, have reduced the attractiveness of some kinds of crime like burglary or robbery and also have modified the market in stolen goods. These include:

1. changes in the production, merchandising, and marketing of consumer goods (e.g., lighter, more movable, and/or more accessible goods like cameras, laptop computers, bicycles, and all-terrain vehicles);
2. the expanding credit- and information-based economy, including society's reliance on formal credentials and identification;
3. growth in the welfare state and its programs;
4. increase in motor vehicles both in numbers and public access (e.g., cars parked at shopping malls, streets, and parking garages where they are less protected and more suitable targets for theft); and
5. emergence of cybercrime and varied forms of computer-based thefts and hustles including online selling and marketing of stolen goods.

Mass production of small and portable products, self-service marketing, and the increase in shopping malls have led to more opportunities (and incentives) for thefts like shoplifting and theft from parked automobiles, whereas the expanding credit economy has led to more credit card and check fraud or forgery, as well as the theft of credit cards, payroll checks, and the like. So, too, various programs of the welfare state also create the conditions for the commission of fraud and theft. Student loans, Social Security, Medicaid, unemployment insurance, and other government programs depend on written materials, and all involve the potential for fraudulent applications. There is also much potential for theft of government checks from mailboxes, delivery trucks, and the like. These changes are reinforced by the media's message of consumption, which encourages excessive spending and buying on credit.

The encompassing reach of the Internet during the past decade has also been accompanied by a shift in criminal opportunity structures that is potentially quite important. The Internet now presents fairly wide-open opportunities for Internet/online fencing, cybercrime/hacking, identity theft, credit card fraud, online gambling, or trafficking in illegal guns, drugs, or pornography. For many of these relatively new crime opportunities, one does not need a great deal of sophisticated computer skill, either. For example, the ability to use e-mail and navigate the Internet, plus an account with an online auction site like Ebay.com are all the computer skills and resources one would need to engage in online fencing. Similarly, search engines like Google.com and personal information-searching websites are potentially useful tools for identity thieves. These Internet-based crime opportunities may be changing the social organization of the underworld in yet-to-be-determined ways. We suspect, however, that such developments might "democratize" or broaden access to opportunities to lucrative criminal enterprise compared to the underworld that Sam knew.[2]

These changes in productive activities, in particular, have created more opportunities for fraud and dishonesty that do not require the physical prowess and dexterity of many forms of street crime, nor the learned skills of professional con artists. Instead, these crimes typically require minimal ability to read, write, and fill out forms, along with some minimum level of presentation of a respectable self (Steffensmeier 1980, 1993; Weisburd et al. 1991; Felson 1996). Moreover, while collusion may often be present, many of these crimes can be committed on one's own and may not require much in the way of contacts or criminal network.

However, the major shift in crime opportunities is the emergence of drug trafficking as the dominant criminal market. The effect of drugs on crime and underworld has at least five important dimensions. One involves the rise in drug dependency and its effects in amplifying incentives for income-generating crimes like theft and fraud. The element not only involves an abundance of drug addicts who steal for a "fix," but also involves an even larger group of "party people," who may steal, hustle for, or deal in drugs as a key feature for "keeping the party going."

A second is its effects on the "quality of thieves" and code of the underworld toward less reliable and less trustworthy co-offenders. "There are [today] a lot more 'losers' and 'assholes' out there," says Sam.

A third and related effect is the increase in criminals who use drugs as a stimulant for alertness or as a numbing agent to build courage by reducing fears or anxieties (parallels the use of alcohol among the thieves of yesteryear).

The fourth effect is that dealing or trafficking in drugs offers a more open and easier (e.g., requires less skill) crime route or way of generating income illegally than some traditional crimes like burglary.

A fifth effect is that new "syndicates" and new ethnic groups have emerged as major underworld players through their control of large-scale illicit drug-distribution systems. As shown in recent immigration and population trends, there not only are growing numbers of Hispanics and blacks (African-Americans but also Jamaicans, etc.) in urban localities today, but increasing numbers from "new" immigrant groups (e.g., Chinese, Russians, and Middle Easterners [e.g., from Pakistan, Lebanon, Israel, Syria]) who might be tempted by the profitability of the drug trade as well as, perhaps, other criminal enterprises). As a result, we now live in a more complicated world of many lesser gangs or networks, rather than simply the mafia.

Changes in Laws and Policing

Perhaps the most significant trend in law enforcement over the past several decades is the cultivation of informants as a principal police strategy, including the use of low-level informants to snitch on higher-ups. Several key changes are noteworthy. The first is the expanding use of the informant system by state and federal police to make cases against seasoned thieves, fences, drug dealers, corrupt police, and other criminal entrepreneurs. Though as old as policing itself, the practice of offering criminals relief from long sentences (i.e., reduced charges or outright freedom) by giving incriminating information about other offenders is used with particular regularity today. Snitches are used frequently to arrest street or ordinary criminals (Rosenfeld, Jacobs, and Wright 2003).

The second development is the increasing role of multiple or overlapping police agencies, both state and federal, in the internal law enforcement of many American cities and towns. In comparison with the local police, state and federal police tend to be more oriented toward making "big cases" (rather than simply making many arrests) and more capable of combating sophisticated and organized kinds of criminal enterprise—such as burglary and auto theft rings, drug networks, gambling businesses, and fencing operations. They also are not restricted to the jurisdictional boundaries of a single police agency. The more active role of outside police forces and investigative agencies has tended not only to reduce local police autonomy but also the corruption of local officials and the comprehensive protection that it perhaps provided in previous eras. Overlapping and fractured police authority prevents a single department or handful of officers from being able to issue a more or less absolute license for an illegal operator.

Third, both state and federal prosecutors have become much more sophisticated in their use of federal and state post-1970 statutes (e.g., RICO and other "Continuing Criminal Enterprise" [CCE] statutes) to bring substantial cases against mafia-type enterprises and offenders. For example, most of the existing La Cosa Nostra families, as well as many other major organized crime groups (e.g., Colombian drug groups, black crime networks, and outlaw biker gangs) were hit with massive RICO and CCE prosecutions in the 1980s and 1990s (Pennsylvania Crime Commission 1991).

Effects on Burglary and Fencing

These developments together have had some noteworthy effects on the underworld, particularly for the trade in stolen goods and for burglary in particular. As regards the market in stolen goods,

1. The abundance of cheap, popular consumer items (e.g., electronic goods, cameras, watches) has caused prices for many stolen goods to drop whether the outlets are amateur buyers or established fences. As a result, the money the fence can make from buying and reselling the already cheap consumer goods is less since the profit margin has dwindled. Simultaneously, the lower profitability of stealing popular consumer goods may have prompted some thieves to turn to crimes such as drug dealing or identity fraud/theft (e.g., forged checks or credit cards), which are more immediately rewarding than breaking and entering.

2. Meanwhile, while the exchange value of some consumer goods has declined, other goods have become popular that offer a good profit and also lead to forms of theft other than burglary. For example, bicycles and all-terrain vehicles can be stolen from playgrounds, parking lots, residential yards, storage sites, etc., and laptop computers can be stolen from unattended cars or buildings. In addition, the lucrative trade in stolen auto parts has expanded the traditional crime occupation of stealing motor vehicles.

Sam noted a big contemporary shift toward theft from parked motor vehicles as a preferred favorable crime opportunity. Jewelry, guns, CDs, and other property items as well as cash, checkbooks, and credit cards can be stolen this way. Although it often involves "breaking in," stealing items from parked motor vehicles (or theft of the vehicle itself) is defined as a theft (rather than burglary) in legal statute and in police reporting programs. Also, because it generally requires less in the way of criminal skill or capital than does burglary, breaking into motor vehicles is a more attractive option for less experienced offenders. For example, Sam encouraged the Beck boys (who were not highly skilled or experienced thieves) to break into cars more than he encouraged them to break into houses or businesses. Similarly, Sam encouraged thieves to steal from constructions sites, storage lots, or other "open areas."

3. Growth in flea markets and other outlets for consumer goods has expanded the amateur trade in stolen goods, including the trade in stolen antiques and collectibles. Established fences now must contend with pickers

and dealers (and some ordinary citizens) who scour flea markets and estate auctions to buy antiques and collectibles "no questions asked."

4. Drug dealers accepting stolen goods as payment for drugs has become more widespread, especially in minority neighborhoods characterized by heavy drug dependency.

5. It may be harder or more formidable today to be a "wheelin' and dealin' " fence (i.e., wide-open, large-scale dealer like Sam was in American City) because of greater competition from the amateur trade in stolen goods (including eBay and both more part-time and drug-dealer fences) and because of diminished immunity brought about by developments in policing such as overlapping enforcement agencies, the expanded informant system, and more proactive targeting of fences.

All these developments also appear to have contributed to recent declines in burglary and in at least some forms of professional crime (especially crimes like pickpocketing, "big con" swindles, and expert safecracking, which already were in a half-century decline). Notably, there are fewer burglars, fewer "good burglars," and fewer "safemen" in particular. Changes in crime opportunities and perhaps improvements in policing and preventive security (e.g., better lighting, better commercial safes, better alarm systems) have lessened the attractiveness of burglary as a crime option and have eroded the subcultural elements and recruitment processes for establishment of burglary networks and careers. Would-be recruits into this type of traditional crime are drawn instead into drug trafficking, varieties of fraud and forgery, or other forms of theft. Furthermore, improvements in law enforcement record-keeping and tracking of career criminals may have reduced the number of active professional burglars who can commit many burglaries, and who also recruit younger thieves for burglary involvement.

Last, there are a number of other overlapping changes suggested by Sam in *Confessions:* the underworld appears to be younger, more amateurish, and less professional today. There is the ascendancy of the drug market with a simultaneous decline in the theft subculture as components of the underworld (including the decline in "good burglary, as well as old-style pickpockets, card hustlers, and con men). There is more snitching and less allegiance to the underworld or thieves' *code*. Finally, there are more "hustler types" and smash-and-grab thieves, and fewer specialist thieves today. In addition, there has been some decline in La Cosa Nostra's strength and influence (as one kind of mafia organized crime) but no clear-cut decline in Italian organized crime as a whole (see Chapter 15).

In the next chapter, we present Sam's account of broader features of the underworld having to do with its code, stratification system, and recent changes. In Chapters 15 and 16, we then take this focus on the social organization and stratification of the underworld further by examining those at the top of Sam's ranking: racketeers and syndicated organized crime figures.

Notes

1. This historical treatment comes largely from Inciardi (1975).
2. Senator Ted Kennedy recently remarked about shifting crime opportunities: "In those days, break-ins required a physical presence, burglar's tools, lookouts and get-away cars. Today, theft may only require a computer and the skills to use it and the will to break in" (*Centre Daily Times,* 22 October 2003, p. A10).

14

Sam's Narrative

Social Organization of Theft and Criminal Enterprise

At one time or another I dealt with almost every kind of thief you could think of—the ordinary joe blow thief to the good burglar. If not dealt with them, then come across them. In the penitentiary, in the fencing, in just living this long and being involved in different things. Could've done without the assholes and hustlers. Do anything to make a buck. But what's done is done.

Underworld Pecking Order

There are different classes of thieves and the better thief don't want to be around or be associated with the asshole thief. Take my shop in American City: first on it was a stopping place for the better thieves. Like Bowie and Whitey. I was handling some of their stuff but mostly they'd stop by to talk, bump into other decent thieves. Then, more and more, I am buying from the ordinary thief and they are hanging around. This drove away the better thief. Not all the way, but would stop by in the morning, especially Sunday morning. Whereas the ordinary thief would be stopping by later in the afternoon. In Jesse's eye, even the in-between burglar like Rocky or Mickey was the wrong crowd. Even more so were the dopers and the walk-in thief. Guys like Jesse will just stay away if that crowd is there.

Selling dope and pimping are at the bottom more or less. Watusi, the main black pimp in American City, thought he was big stuff. But he was only blowing wind outta his ass. We would take his money. Played cards with the local clique. He could attend but we really didn't accept him. Wanted his money. Worst gambler I ever saw. Wanted to be a big shot. Spend his money, go out and get more money from his girls, then come back in and blow that too.

Your ordinary hanger-on is at the bottom, too. Are more or less asshole thieves and hustlers. Too lazy to work, too dumb to be good at stealing. Hang around different places in towns, like the video machine places or the secondhand shops, looking for something to do. The ones that hung at my shop were bad enough, but the other secondhand places had even worse assholes hanging around. In a way I got a kick out of their antics and bullshitting but a nuisance, too. This last period I would only tolerate them so much. If this or that one started coming around too often, I would let him know he wasn't welcome.

Lackeys are a notch above the hanger-on. Don't know how to work and don't wanna steal unless you guide them. More or less they are bums. Hanging around to pick up a penny, free meal, or just to be part of something. They are more a nuisance than anything. Take Chubby—he's a lackey. All these years has hung at my store. A fucking lamp fixture, but in many ways I got a kick out of him.

Being a fence, even more so being in the rackets, is in a whole different league from being even a good burglar or a good con man. You are running in a different crowd. On account of the contacts, the spokes in the wheel it takes. And 'cause you have a legit business, for cover, and in the public's eye you are a businessman. Not just a crook but a businessman, too.

In my eye, the guy in the rackets is at the top, is the most looked up to. Guys like Nicky and Angelo, and Angelo's old man when he was alive. Stay in background where there is less risk and you are making a good dollar and a safe dollar. See this in the penitentiary. Last time at Midstate was a mafia guy there for a year or so, then got transferred. Had the run of the place. Other inmates catered to him. Not just the white guys, but the black guys too.

A lot depends on who you associate yourself with. If you hook up with a couple of good burglars, are part of that crew, then others will say, "Hey, he must be pretty decent 'cause he is working with them." My getting hooked up with Jesse was a big help that way. Same as with the local clique. Being associated with them added to my being a somebody as far as the local criminal element. And goes the other way. If you hang with the bottom barrel thief, then you will be seen as bottom barrel.

Guys will brag a lot, that they know so and so, have pulled some crimes with this or that guy—like, "hey I am doing business with this guy who's in the mafia." Are puffing themselves up and many times are only blowing wind outta their ass. But that is understandable 'cause I would want it known that I was teamed up with Jesse or that I hooked up with the local clique. That is only human nature and opens up a lot of doors.

The fence is up there pretty high. Not the nickel and dime guy who runs a pawn shop or a secondhand place, but a dealer like Louie was or I was, or what Phil is now. I don't know where you'd put Rosen, the jeweler fence, or the foundry guy that Jesse and me peddled to. 'Cause they are on the edge of the criminal element. The good thieves and the guys in the rackets would know them, but not your ordinary thief.

The fence who stays all the way in the background would be higher than a regular fence. Like Angelo eventually got to be. Or a Louie Sica [mob guy, see

Chapter 16]. Mostly are a referral, don't deal direct with the thief but will make the connection for the thief to unload. Are keeping layers in-between that are taking away the risk. That is very much looked up to but are very few fences who strictly operate that way. But even the nickel-and-dime dealer that runs a secondhand shop, or whatever, is way above the ordinary thief.

I think the guy doing robberies has dropped as far as being looked up to. Sure, if it's a good bank robbery outfit or rob a Wells Fargo truck, that is ranked pretty high. There are so few good stickup men today. Years ago, like in the penitentiary, a stickup man if he was half decent was looked up to. Held his own. But today, robbery is more associated with being on dope and with mugging old ladies or a convenience store where their picture is taken. How dumb can you get? Even robbing banks today isn't looked up to like it once was. Are too many risks with the cameras watching and the score can be puny 'cause the bank girl will just hand you a bag that is mostly little bills. Are marked to boot. Dopers and losers are the main ones robbing banks today.

Is iffy about the guy pulling hold-ups or mugging people. In a way shows he has heart. He is not one to be messed with. That is respected. But does he have anything upstairs or does he have rocks in his head? Mugging people is something kids do. If that keeps being your main thing [as thief gets older], then he'll be shied away from as being on the crazy side, as bringing heat from the cops and as someone to avoid.

Being a good conman or good card player—guy who can deal off the bottom and get over on the other players—is looked up to. Being a good safeman is ranked right up there. A good burglar, too, but a good safeman, even more.

In my eye pimping is pretty far down. Is dirt. But younger guys today, like the one Beck boy, will have his girlfriend peddle her ass if they are short of money. This is funny in a way—most white guys will look down on someone who is a pimp. But black guys don't. And most of your bigger pimps are black guys. Why, I don't know. But that is a fact. A young black guy, you ask him, he would want to be a pimp over almost anything else. Same with other kinds of hustling, the ordinary white thief looks down on that whereas the black thief doesn't.

With dope, it depends on the involvement. The higher-ups, the guys in the background, yeh, that is high status. 'Cause the money is so good. Myself—in a way this is hard for me to say 'cause I hate the dope—but if I was younger and the good opportunity was there, it would be hard to walk away from it. Guys like Angelo and them are involved in dope, are the money bag, and have the contacts with the cops and that for bringing the stuff in. As long as you stay away from the street dealing and you are involved in other things, too, then they are looked up to. Not always now 'cause you will find different ones like Phil or Jesse who look down on those who are into dope, no matter how much you are staying in the background.

I don't know where you'd put the corrupt cop. In a way they are hated. But in other ways, if not respected, are accepted. Depends on how they come across: if they are crooked and then still bust your ass, will be hated. Duggan was a helluva corrupt cop but he played fair. A hard-ass with the run-of-the mill thief and with the losers, the ones mugging old ladies and the baby rapists. But with the local clique and ones like Jesse, he would look the other way. Have his hand out but not fuck you over. If a cop is honest that way, then if he is on the take that is okay. Why not? He has his scam, you have yours.

As far as cops go, my thinking was—he has his job to do, I have mine to do. If you got me you got me. But don't blow it out of proportion, don't show me up. Don't lie on the stand and make up the evidence. A cop who is a fucking hypocrite is the bottom of the barrel, only a notch above the baby rapist.

This last time I was in the penitentiary Duggan sends me this letter. More or less buttering me up 'cause he knew I was under pressure to snitch on Angelo and on him, too. State police especially wanted to nail Duggan, was a helluva thorn. I showed you that letter, remember? "Dear Sam, I hope you're making out okay. I am sorry you got involved in crime again. I know you are basically a good person but got mixed up in some things you are sorry about." Blah, blah, blah—words to that effect. "If I can do anything to help you turn your life around when you get out—find a job or open your business again—we should keep in touch." Duggan is offering to help but is really protecting his ass, to keep me on his good side. Is thinking, hey, this guy is solid but you never know for sure if somebody will turn. Knew I could bury him.

I'd say your better thieves and the higher-ups will be more aware of the rankings but even your ordinary thief will many times know. Especially if he has done time in the penitentiary. Will want to hang with the better thieves and will puff themselves up. Badmouth the losers and the run-of-the-mill thief— "Hey, that guy is a fucking amateur." The line can be thin across the layers, but there is a helluva pecking order—who is the penny-ante thief, who is the in-between thief, who is the decent thief, who is the guy in the background who doesn't get his hands dirty?

I don't know where you'd place the biker guys. I have known quite a few. In the penitentiary and with the fencing. Are respected but some are regular fuck-ups.

The good con man is still near the top. I don't mean the street hustling but more what are swindles or where you got a scam going that is a regular thing and there is good dollar. Can be almost anything. Get some guy to invest his money with you or some widow lady to spend money on house repairs she doesn't need. Doesn't have to be a widow lady, can be anybody 'cause the public is very gullible.

In a way I was known as a con man. That's what Jesse will tell you. On account I would get over on people—say to buy what they thought was an antique but maybe was junk. Fooled antique dealers already. Even when I was heavy into the burglary and then later when the fencing was my main thing, was always some conning mixed in.

I would have to say that this last time in penitentiary, the thieves and the other cons looked up to me. Saw me as a good burglar, as a dealer too, but more as a confidence man. That my main thing was playing on the greed of this or that one who is wanting a handout or wants to earn an easy dollar. Really, the fencing is a lot of conning, even more so if you are dealing in antiques. Is a fine line for what is an antique and what isn't, what is worth a decent dollar and what is junk. Can egg people on and pull the wool over their eyes, all the time they think they are hustling you.

Someone like Angelo is a con man. Is mafia but he is also a swindler. Would run the bingo, the raffles, the gambling games at some of the churches, at some of the community clubs. Take his percentage and also chisel off the top, but in their eye Angelo is doing them a favor.

Don't find that many con men in the penitentiary, I guess because today they are mostly businesspeople or they are preachers, so their records are pretty clean. Won't have to do time. But the confidence man is still looked up to.

The Code

There is a code, a helluva code for some things like not being a snitch and what are more like understandings for other things. Say, when Jesse was messing with Doug's girlfriend, when Doug was our dropoff. I don't care if she had the rocks for Jesse, was dumb on Jesse's part. You don't want that tension if Doug were to find out. And what if we got popped, you don't want to add to the chance that Doug would snitch to get back at Jesse.

Can call that a rule, an understanding really, for doing what is right and for avoiding trouble when you're doing business together. But it is not a rule to the same level as there is for keeping your mouth shut and not ratting on somebody. The threat is much greater for that. Does not mean there isn't any snitching, not by a long shot. But the thief will know, that the snitching comes with a price. You will lean on him, or spread the word not to do business with him.

Another rule is everybody on a job gets the same, that the score is split equally. But it don't always happen that way. The main guys in a crew will split it evenly amongst themselves but will chisel the other ones. Take Jesse and me, we would fill our pockets before we came out of a place. Or, if we had to unload the stuff, we would chisel the other guy by telling him the price was lower than it actually was. But had to be careful 'cause it may come out in the paper how much was taken.

Normally, you want to get along with one another. But there are exceptions. Bowie and Gordon [two good burglars] don't really get along, personally.

They would both bitch to me about the other one. That is unusual. In my eye, they were both whiners and got on one another's nerves. Most burglary partners like each other, are comfortable with one another. Me and Jesse was.

Do What You Have to Do, Including "Putting Someone to Sleep"

My putting the motherfucker to sleep in American City, that is accepted. I am helping him out, while he is robbing this bookie. But things didn't turn out as planned. Bookie is carrying a gun and fires shots at this guy when he was running back to where I am parked. Bleeding bad, very bad. There was no hesitation on my part.

Wasn't really a decision on my part. He was hurt bad. Needed to go to the hospital, get sewed up. But then questions would be asked. It would come out what happened and I'm back doing time, a lot of time. That the bookie was connected [with the local mafia] was another consideration, no need to be on their bad side. Knew what I had to do. I did it with my hands. Choked him.

I don't feel bad about it. Not good either. Know what I mean? Snuffing somebody out like that is accepted. Not by the cops and the ordinary joe blow. But among thieves and them, yes. Or, say, you were in the military—you are going to plug the other guy before he gets you plugged. You have to do what you have to do, same as the other guy is going to do what he has to do.

There is murder and there is murder. Not all murders are the same. If your wife is causing you grief, that is no reason to snuff her out. Know what I mean? You should get big time. That one life is done with. It ain't like you replace one television with another one. I'm not saying the death penalty, not necessarily. For a baby rapist, yes. He deserves the chair. I'd pull the switch myself. I am a strong believer in the death penalty for that.

It is different if a guy is ratting or the chance is there he will rat. Then you're protecting your own life. If he is putting me away for years and years, by doing the motherfucker in, that is eliminated. Let's just suppose Jesse and me is in a place and somebody comes in on us and we could get hurt. I'm going to take care of him. I wouldn't feel guilty about it at all. That is accepted.

Even more so in this type of situation where you are helping this guy rob somebody and the guy is someone you hardly know. If it had been Jesse, yes, I would look at it differently on account we had been partners for so long and had been through so much. But otherwise, no.

Don't Be a Whiner, Carry Yourself Right, Be a Stand-Up Guy

I don't think I ever made anybody do something he himself didn't want to do. Know what I mean? Same as nobody made me do something I didn't want to do. You hear this bullshit, so and so came from a broken family, he was raised poor, he got in with the wrong crowd. Blah, blah, blah. That is blowing wind out your ass.

I could point to this or that which made me a burglar or a fence. Blame it on my mother, on my stepdad 'cause he was a real asshole. Or that I didn't get a fair shake from the judge who sent me to the juvenile reformatory. That Angelo and the local clique were pushing on me to do the fencing. You see this in prison. Guys whining, crying it wasn't their fault. They are blowing wind out of their asses. What I did, I did because I wanted to. Nobody got me to steal, nobody made me be a fence. All the rank shit I pulled—I, Sam Goodman, did it.

How you carry yourself means a whole lot. Is the man an asshole or not. Is the man honest or not? Will he hold up his end of the deal? Does he know what is going down and can he take care of it?

Even if I wasn't sure of myself, I would always let the thieves and them think I was, that I was on top of things. I would not show a weakness that way.

Don't Break into Occupied Places

The rule is, don't break into a place if you know or surmise somebody is there. Unless the person in the place is drunk or is on his deathbed, most burglars will not touch a place that is occupied. The risks are too great. What if the fucker has a gun and is so fucking scared he just starts firing. He is a witness, too, has seen your face. Don't forget that. And what if you have to hurt him or snuff him out. Then, there will be heat on the police to solve it and you're facing big time.

Now, if it turns out there is somebody in the place and they surprise you, you have to be ready to get rough. Be able to hit someone across the side of his head. To do what needs to be done, but that is a last resort.

Don't Gossip or Show Off

Hard to be a thief and not want to blow yourself up to your buddies and to your lady friends. Your girlfriend or whatever. Guys will wear jewelry they've stolen or keep a good antique in their house, just to show off to their buddies or to get some pussy. Then run out of money and have to peddle the stuff anyway.

Not letting it go to your head, not become a big shot and come across as better than you are. I was always very careful that way, not to act cocky and not to badmouth one thief to another thief, behind his back. You got to figure, too, the guy is thinking, "Hey, if he talks about this guy this way, what the hell does he say to others about me." I was always very careful not to run somebody down that way.

Racket Values about "Fairness" and "Understandings" with Other Dealers

Not that I didn't try to outdo Louie or some of the smaller secondhand dealers. There was some of that. But you also help each other, work together in some ways. There can be understandings, where fences won't buck each other. You handle this and I'll handle that. I'm talking about your bigger fences, now. For a long time, Louie was the main one for guns in American City. If guns came my way, I sent the business to Louie. Same with liquor and cigarettes—that business mostly went to Angelo, to the mafia. You didn't want to buck that. It worked the other way, too, Louie and Angelo were sending antiques my way.

You're doing it as a courtesy and to avoid hassles. But not all the way now. Even on the guns, I am bypassing Louie as my operation got rolling. Run the guns down south or to Oceantown. There was tension between Louie and me when I started doing that. With the liquor and cigarettes, no, once I was peddling that to Angelo, I stayed with him. There's a helluva grapevine and I didn't want to take that risk. Not that I feared Angelo but didn't want to be on his bad side either.

Another thing, the thief don't want to risk harming that relationship, what each side is doing for the other. Buying from Rocky over the years, he would feel he owes it to me to give me first shot at any good antiques he runs across.

Are courtesies among burglars, too. Say, you read the newspaper and see that a fire company is having a carnival. Then go to scout it but see another van checking out the place. Well, if you are pretty sure that is another burglary crew, then back off 'cause they have gotten there first. It works the same way if you're inside a place and another crew is aiming to clip it, too. This happened to Jesse and me once. Doug has dropped us off, told him to meet us at a spot in one hour and forty-five minutes 'cause we knew it would take us a while to open the safe. If we're not there, come back every half hour. I am going back and forth, watching and then helping Jesse peel the safe. It was a bitch. Shit, we hear a noise and two guys come into the place—are carrying tools and that for breaking into a safe. So, shone my light—just to let them know, hey fellas, we got here first. They were like, sorry, we'll be on our way.

Be Ready to Play Hardball

The thief has to know you can play hardball. I was always a firm believer of that. Can lean on the guy if you need to. Say the cops have a thief who is fingering you, are making him promises. I am going to lean on the guy or have someone else lean on him. Do whatever needs to be done. It was well-known I was a nice guy in most ways but could be nasty. There was a threat there that was well-known.

Leaning on somebody doesn't mean there is revenge. You do that to keep the guy from snitching or from testifying if it has gone that far. Take Bobby Hoyle. He snitched on me but then backed down, wouldn't testify. After the case was settled, no, I didn't go after him. Thought about it but figured what is done is done. Unless you want to send a message all the way down the line that you're not to be fucked with, but normally no—whacking him or working him over would bring me hassles. Just don't do business with him again and spread the word he is no damn good.

Same way when my shop in American City was set on fire. This is a year or so after I got out of jail for the antique burglary. Have my business going again, am pretty much back to where I was when I got popped. Fire damaged most of what was inside. No insurance, so I lost a good dollar—seventy, eighty thousand for sure. My suspicion first on was that Louie did it 'cause I was cutting into his territory on account more and more of the half-decent thieves are coming to me. But could've been one of the secondhand dealers 'cause my legit business was hurting some of them. Nosed around but no proof. So just let it go.

But not let it slow me down. Whoever did it, would not give them that satisfaction. Rented a bigger place a block away, had been a furniture store. Just what I needed. Paid a visit to Angelo and Charlie [for cash]. Boom, boom— I'm back in business, buying and selling like you wouldn't believe.

Can't be a pussy but doesn't mean you go off half-cocked and blow people away. Say you're shopping for a partner. May want someone who can hold his own, will get rough if he has to. But you don't want someone with his hand on the trigger. Will bring you nothing but headaches. Comes down to it you start blowing people away, you will get blown away. More than anything you want a guy that is solid, which can mean different things. Does he have heart? Can you depend on him to do what needs to be done? Can he keep his mouth shut? That is the biggest thing. Ask Jesse, he will tell you—if you like the guy and you trust him, that is more important than anything.

Snitching

Myself, I never snitched. The police in American City did try to open me up but never really pushed on me, "Just tell us if we're on the right track." Couple of times in Tylersville this one detective would come in my shop, had an envelope with a bunch of mug shots: "Have you seen these guys, have they come in here?" In my eye I would have a hard time looking at myself in the mirror if I did that. Worst thing in the world is snitching, except setting somebody up. That is worst than the snitching.

Another thing, the thieves and them saw me as "solid." I didn't want to undermine that. The snitching will hurt you in the long run, especially with the better thief. You also got to figure, once the snitching starts and the police got their foot in the door, they can squeeze you in different ways. The police can play dirty, too. That doesn't mean I have never thought about snitching. If you're dealing with dopers and asshole thieves, the temptation is there.

There is a lot of snitching and gossiping in any walk of life. Anytime you can squeeze somebody, the snitching is going to be there. But still the rule is there and you will know that you can pay a price if you do the snitching. As far as trust and not worrying about the snitching, I would rather trust a good thief or somebody like Phil or Angelo than I would your ordinary businessman or your ordinary joe blow. Isn't that much honor among your ordinary businessmen. I would be leery they would not hold up if the cops are squeezing them. Even your ordinary thief in many ways won't snitch as quickly as the businessman on account the thief knows the ropes and is looking ahead that he can get a headache or have his nuts kicked and that others will shy away from doing business with you. The doper is the worst for the snitching and the asshole hustler is the next worst. Some of your fences, yeah, you could lay your faith in them—but others, no, I would only trust them so far. Would trust a good thief a helluva lot more than most of your fences.

Would not call this a rule but is an understanding that you go to bat for someone or show a helping hand if a partner or a buddy gets popped or is sent to the penitentiary. Maybe help out with the bail money or recommending a lawyer. Pay a visit if he's in the penitentiary or send cigarettes, a card at Christmas time. This last time at Midstate, Jesse came to visit a number of times and different ones like Charlie would send a card or a package. Jesse and Phil would stop at my shop in American City, to see how Becky was doing with running my shop. This meant a lot to me but was nothing Jesse could do to keep the place from going under. Not a peep now out of Angelo. In a way showed me his true colors.

Women, Race, and Crime: Sexism and Racism in Underworld

I can't say if women are committing more crime today, but dope would be the main reason if they are. Saw that with Lisa. She was a helluva person to be around when she was off the dope. But then she'd fall back into the dope and running with her doper friends, she was a real fuck-up.

Most women who are into crime and are doing it fairly regular, are doing it on account of some asshole they are hooked up with. Whether they are doing it for love or just a feeling of closeness, or because they don't have anything else to hang onto in life. Or they are on dope, or they are doing it for their kids—at least that is what they are telling themselves. Myself, if a woman said she was stealing for her kids I would find that believable, at least I will entertain that. But a guy tells me that, I am thinking he is only blowing wind outta his ass.

What I remember most about female crime is your asking me about it. What crimes are women committing? Have you ever done crimes with women? Are women committing more crimes today? I told you, "Hey, I will tell you what I know but it ain't that much 'cause I didn't involve myself with women that way." It turns out, there was more involvement than I thought. Then keeping my eyes open to help you out, I'm more aware of that side of crime on account of your interest.

The time I was on the run, a fugitive, I did use a woman to help pass some checks. Payroll checks. Stole them from the place where I was working and talked this woman I am seeing to help me pass them. Figuring there would be less suspicion 'cause she could pose as an ordinary housewife who worked at the place as a secretary. She was leery but then decided she'd do it. Were like eight, ten checks. Passed three of them at a couple of grocery stores and at a hardware store. Went smoothly except was some nervousness on her part that got worse by the time she cashed the third check. So, I pulled back. Had an inkling she would unglue. Next morning I am gone 'cause I am thinking it is about time to get out of town anyways.

Later on, I found out check guys use women to pass checks. Give them so much per check or will hire them for the day. But she has to be careful they don't chisel her, on account they are figuring what can she do about it. Except run to the cops, so will want to keep her happy that way.

But real crime, no. The burglaries and that I pulled were with guys. With Ronnie and then with the guys at the paper mill. Same with Jesse, for a long time anyways. Then we needed a dropoff 'cause Jesse's brother who was doing the dropoff at that time was losing his courage. We got a tip on a place to hit and Jesse says, "Bernice [Jesse's wife] will drop us off." Was leery but had faith in Jesse that it was okay. She was very dependable and we trusted her to do the dropoff. As far as snitching or taking off if something came up, you could lay your faith in her. But to take her inside or have her be a lookout, no. Would be leery she would get shook up. She did it for Jesse 'cause he would tell her he felt more comfortable if she was doing the driving. Was a bond there, a closeness. Some excitement for her, too, but that was wearing off. And she liked the money 'cause she wasn't working at the time.

This is another thing about Bernice which you couldn't beat—she didn't get a cut. Her share was with Jesse. Whatever he wanted to give her from his cut, that was his problem. Me and Jesse each got our split, but the loose bills and that, like silver dollars, fill our pockets and give that to Bernice. She got a kick out of that.

Normally you wouldn't trust a woman that way. Women ain't known to be trusted. Not that you can trust that many guys but there are very few women in the world people trust. As far as looking out for their kids, their family, that is different. But as far as crime and where there is some risk, you would worry about whether they would hold up.

It isn't that women don't have any heart or won't take the risk. Not saying that. Women can have a lotta heart in some ways. Doing things for their kids. Or even doing things for some asshole they are associated with. Bernice had a lotta heart on account she was doing it for Jesse. Same as Barbara, on account she was doing it for her daughter, to provide a living for her [see below]. Especially for their kids, what a women will put herself through. But if you're talking just about the criminal element, I don't think a woman's mind is into it the way a man's is.

If a guy and a woman do crimes together, chances are he will get a bigger cut. Usually a much bigger cut. With Jesse, Bernice was part of his cut. It is the same with other guys I know. Now, with dope or forgeries, the women may get a percentage or a flat rate. Pay you fifty or hundred dollars for this or that job or so much per check or drug deal. Other times, the lady may think she is getting a better split, even a fifty-fifty split, but she is being chiseled by the guys she is with. Maybe are some women who can hold their own that way but would be very few. Are better off to clip by themselves as far as the cut they are getting or for keeping what they are bringing in.

Later on I did run across other burglars that used women as the dropoff driver. This isn't often now. Most times it was a woman where there was a strong bond, where the trust is built up. A wife, a girlfriend, maybe a guy's sister. But it would never dawn on me or Jesse, or other burglars really, to take a woman inside. Inside a house, inside a building—that's a different world when you go in there than the outside. When you're opening a safe or searching out a place, you don't want to worry about anything else, that someone might sneak up on you. You want someone who won't panic but can take care of whatever needs to be done. A woman would be too emotional in there. Are very few women who can swing a two by four or whatever, hit somebody on the head. *You don't have to be all muscle, now, but strong enough to swing something hard, and have the heart to do it. That, and I would not want to have to worry about her.*

I have never heard of a female *safe* burglar. I have never heard of a woman who is known as a *good* burglar. I do know of women who break into apartments or houses during the day when people are working. But even that is rare. Maybe go with another woman or with a couple of guys. Knock on doors until they find a place that is empty and even find the door unlocked. Or maybe break a window and crawl in. But women don't do much in the way of "breaking in" where you gotta deal with the alarm system or even where you have to break some windows. Not on their own anyway but may help out if a guy is along. A few times I bought warm stuff from women who cleaned out a house where their ex-husband or ex-boyfriend lived. Whether they really broke in or had the key I can't say. Can call that a burglary but it was still a one-time thing.

We did get some tips from women. That is fairly common. One was Barbara, worked at Casey's pub as a waitress and a bartender. Very attractive. Was divorced. Had a little girl. She knew who I was, what I was into. We kidded around a lot. I am having a sandwich at Casey's and I overhears a guy blabbering about the jewelry he has bought his wife over the years. That when he moved out, took it with him. Running off his mouth to Barbara. I am egging her to find out who he is, what he has, and where it is kept. Teased her about her cut, she could take a trip or whatever. She went for it. Jesse and me hit the place, was a nice haul. It just mushroomed from there. It even got to where she hustled a couple of guys, would go back to their places. Find out more details. Not have sex with them, at least that is what she said. But lead them on. Would call to check on her daughter, then say she had to leave because her daughter wasn't feeling well. Sorry. Pass on the information to me, let it sit a while, then clip the place.

Barbara was good people. Takes a lot of heart to do what she did. Respected her for that. If I was to use a woman as a partner, I'd take Barbara. Even more so than Bernice. Had more toughness and just the way she carried herself, gave you more confidence that she would hold up.

Here's another thing. Just suppose your daughter wanted to be safe burglar or a fence or somebody in the rackets. She will have a hard time getting the connections. Being able to associate with the right kinds of people like the right lawyer, the right fence, the right partner, the right person for giving information. Really, just all the way up the line. *It is mostly guys who are the main ones and they generally prefer to do business with other guys and have a leeriness when it comes to involving women.*

The women I came across who were into the hustling and clipping, if doing it over a long haul, had pretty rough lives. Into things when they were pretty young [teenagers]—dope, peddling their ass, shoplifting. Hooked up with some asshole. Have a kid or whatever. If they got involved in burglary or breaking into cars or even selling dope, came from going along with some guy. If he gets put away [incarcerated] or they break up, then maybe go on her own. She won't just be into burglary or breaking into cars but will be hustling a buck in other ways, too. Shoplifting, selling dope, conning guys. Is really a thief and a hustler, with maybe a little burglary mixed in.

The closest I've seen to a woman who was a decent burglar was the Greene girl, Cindy. A little on the stocky side but not bad looking. Was part of a family that was into burglary and stripping cars. Her dad, his brother, and the one son. Were pretty good at cracking safes and breaking into places. They operated quite a while. If they needed a fourth person, then Cindy would be the dropoff. I bought antiques from them. Dealt mainly with the old man. Then he gets popped. The daughter and the son kept on clipping. From what I could tell, she was going inside with him. She was very gutsy, had a tough side to her, could pull her own weight. She was the go-getter, more so than her brother.

Then didn't see a peep of them for two or three years, except Jesse heard they petered out. The old man got big time and the son was chicken without him. A guy Jesse knows contacted the son to go along on a safe job but couldn't get any play. Then, shit, who walks into my shop? It is Cindy. "Hey, Sam—long time, no see." Tells me she is married and there is a baby on the way. Has a job at this little beautician shop on 12th Street cutting women's hair. After that, off and on I got tips from her. She'd call or stop by the shop. Would show off her little boy. If the information checked out, I might follow up on it. Otherwise, no, I let it die. She was solid but as far as really trusting her, I was leery. With the baby and that, she had gotten soft. If the cops were to pump her, I am thinking she would give me up.

Another thing, if a woman is involved and she's an okay looker, then what if the other guy hits on her or she gets interested in him. There can be a tension. I have seen that happened. It is best to avoid that before it starts.

Generally a guy would have a hard time putting his confidence in a woman, as far as committing crimes together. Not that there are that many men you can lay your faith in.

In my eye, if a woman got popped and she has kids, the cops will squeeze her: "If you won't tell us we're gonna take your kids." *Her children are more important to her than I am. I'd have to go. That is my biggest fear.* A guy doesn't have strong ties to his kids, not like a woman. A man going to jail still has his wife out there taking care of his kids.

The cops will hammer away or let her know, "Hey, you will be sitting in jail and who's gonna take care of your kids?" Can squeeze her about having to report this to the welfare people, that she is an accessory. I have seen it happen—charge her as an accessory, let her sit in jail for a week. Then get her to thinking the guy she is with is running around on her, is chasing pussy while she is rotting in jail and may lose her kids. The cops can play dirty, "Why are you doing this for him?"

Depends on the woman, what is your relationship with her. If she's got the rocks for a guy, love or whatever, then you could trust her. I trusted Bernice 'cause she was doing it for Jesse and also could see she had done it before. Handled herself very well. But still I think most guys will have some uneasiness, even if they are together and she is his woman. I would make sure she didn't know any more than she has to, like drop you off and pick you up, but nothing more. Like I am saying, if she has kids and the police threaten her with that, the guy is gonna lose out.

That's what happened to Andy about a year or so after I started buying from him. Police were suspecting him of breaking into places. Did a search of his girlfriend's apartment and are telling her the jewelry they found was stolen. Whether they planted it or it was jewelry Andy gave to her, I don't know. Just that they dangled to her, about her going to jail and who would take care of her little girl. She held up but Andy was shitting in his pants that she would rat him out.

You have to trust somebody. You can't work by yourself. It is hard to work alone pulling off a burglary. Even if you can handle that, if you want inside information or whatever, you will have to trust somebody else. Your druthers are to work with a guy you trust and can depend on, but it don't always work out that way. What if a good opportunity comes up and this is all you have to work with? You will have to decide whether to pass up the opening or clip but involve somebody that doesn't have your confidence as much.

This happened on one of my trips to an auction. Becky is with me and we stop at a hunting lodge to eat, a hillbilly place that is having a barbecue, a fund-raiser. Is a Saturday night. I just know there is a cracker box safe there. I am thinking, hit the auction, and then come back early Sunday morning to clip the place. I beat around the bush, then raised it with Becky—she could drop me off, then circle back every fifteen minutes. At first, she wanted no part of it but then agreed. We're leaving the auction, I raise it again, but I can tell she is getting cold feet, that I am pushing her buttons too far. So, said fuck it, let that opportunity pass by.

Now, I have known a couple of husband-wife teams. These are older guys who want to stay out of the limelight, just pull a few jobs a year. Plan out what they will do. Involve their wife as a dropoff or maybe even take her inside to watch, be a lookout. Bucky and Jeannie worked that way. But you very seldom see that.

It depends, too, on how much the woman has been around, does she have any world-wiseness. The ordinary guy has been around the block in different ways, is more streetwise. Is more exposed to the cops and different kinds of people. That is why I would trust a prostitute a lot more than an ordinary woman 'cause she has had to deal with the police and has probably been to jail. Will know what it means if she snitches, that she can get rapped up aside of the head. The ordinary guy has learned from experience that it pays to keep your mouth shut.

Same thing today with some of the women who are involved in dealing dope. Are more likely to be streetwise and know how to handle herself. Will have more of the criminal element. As long she isn't a doper herself, you will have more faith in her. If a doper, then forget it. A woman on dope is the worst, as far as trust and that.

The physical part is important, not that you have to be a muscle man. Lots of crime is hard work, physically hard work. That is a big reason why guys work with other guys and women are less into crime. It's not just committing the crime, but down the line. What if somebody burns you or comes up short on the money? You will have to rap him on the side of the head, lean on him if it comes down to that. Others have to know that if they fuck with you, you can fuck them back. Know what I mean?

A gun can help, but it's more than that. Most of the time, a gun ain't of much use. I never carried a gun when I was into burglary. With the fencing, yes, off and on. It is more how you carry yourself, can you take care of matters in this situation right here. Either do it yourself or have some backing. There are some pretty tough women out there but this is a very serious matter for women. They more or less need some backing or be known as so and so's woman.

In my eye, the younger thieves and the dopers and the asshole thieves are more likely to do crimes with women. The higher-up you go, the less you will see women involved. If it happens, then there will be a close connection or there is a layer in between. The better burglars, the better crews, that is all guys. The only exception was Cindy, the Greene girl—after her dad got popped. Then her and her brother continued and she was the main organizer. As far as selling the stuff to me, she was the one in charge.

Buying Stolen Goods from Female Thieves

I was more leery of buying from the female thief. But if it is something legit or just a little on the shady side, I will buy from women all the way. They have always been a big part of my legit business, both for the buying and the selling. Preferred dealing with them in many ways 'cause a lot of guys think they are sharp bargainers. So they hassle you. My thing was to treat the women who came into my shop with respect, don't talk down to them. Maybe ask how their kids are doing or comment on how good they are looking. Puff them up in other ways. Just have to be patient 'cause some women can take a lot of your time. Can't make up their minds and some are talkers, can make your ears ache.

Couple of the dealers I bought from would buy from female thieves. Still, male thieves were their main source for the warm stuff. Like Slim, has a second-hand shop on 4th Street. We visit back and forth. Maybe have coffee or break-fast. Not an ounce of fat on him. Handles clothes but his main thing is small items. Some of the stuff is new, some is used. The better jewelry Slim would sometimes pass on to me. 'Cause I had the contacts to unload whereas he is mostly selling the stuff out of his store. The past couple of years Slim is hooked up with Amato.

Myself, I didn't handle clothes, which is what female shoplifters are gonna bring in. Steal mostly little things, not worth a decent dollar. Pick up Barbie dolls, shit like that. Their main thing is shoplifting but also might go into somebody's apartment or steal from where they work. I would take it slow, see how it worked out, whether they are bringing decent stuff, whether they were on dope, whether they stealing for some asshole. Still the tendency on my part was to pull back, to turn them away or not get back in touch with them if there was a message. Just a leeriness, that it didn't feel comfortable. If kept doing business with them, then often I would have Chubby be a go-between. He would give a ballpark of what I might pay. If the stuff brought more, I would make up the difference. Pay a little now, settle up the rest later. They were happy with that. What it comes down to, though, this was a small part, very small part, of the fencing side of my business.

A main one I have dealt with has been Holly. Holly Giddens. Wiry, little redhead. Is now in her thirties. Very likable. Can be pretty tough when she has to. Into and out of dope. That is her big problem. Has a daughter who is now a teenager. Got married when she was young but I don't think the kid is from her husband. Holly and her husband were into partying, into dope. She went along with him and another guy on burglaries. Would have her knock on doors of houses, check if the door is unlocked. Or maybe go around back, and check the back doors. The guys would come back later and hit the place. Husband gets jammed up for selling dope. Him and Holly split, but then Holly hooks up with a guy who is a supervisor of maintenance for apartments. Another loser, is into using and selling dope. Has Holly break into this or that apartment when the people are out. Gives her the key and tells her what to look for. Make it look like a break-in. This is more like an ordinary theft but in the cops eye, would be a burglary. This can be pretty safe, just as long as you don't do it too often and don't take too much. Turns out he likes to hit women, and worked Holly over pretty good. Wanted her to take him back but that was it.

Now Holly is going out on her own. Takes another lady with her. Drive around and watch a place. Not expensive houses, but your ordinary homes and even trailers. Knock on the front door. Check the back doors, maybe is a sliding glass door. Look if there are any alarms, a security system. If somebody answers, then pretend you're selling something or are looking for somebody— "Oops, are sorry, must have the wrong house." If not there, go right on in. Or come back later. Grabs what she can—mostly cash and jewelry. But will pick up food and horseshit stuff, too. Would peddle to people she knows and look for little dealers like me.

Bought from her a few times but was getting more and more leery. She was falling back into dope and different kinds of dope. Told her she needed to get her fucking act together, get a different life for herself and her daughter. If you're going to steal, then steal for yourself, not to fuck it away on the fucking dope. I find out later she is peddling stuff to Slim [local secondhand dealer].

But Holly will still stop by my auction booth. We have always stayed on friendly terms. Is a roller coaster whether she is strung out, eyes have that dopey look. Or whether it will be "Hey, Sam, I'm doing good now." Will tell me she is in a [drug] program and how many days she has been clean. Her and her daughter are back together. I would build her up, that she could turn her life around and should do it for her daughter. She has had a hard life but the will is still there. Wants to pull her own weight and not be a lackey. Now has the fucking losers ["asshole guys"] out of her life, if she could only beat the dope.

But that is very rare that a woman would be involved in burglary and be involved by herself or with another woman. Normally, women are more in the background if you're talking about burglary or robbery. The women burglars I knew of were hitting houses or apartments in the daytime. Not sure I ever heard of a woman breaking into a place at night or breaking into a business like a hardware store or an American Legion club. Or hijacking a truck. Same way if we're talking about safes or breaking into places where you have a good alarm system or with getting good tips on a place, it would be hard to find a woman who is involved that way.

If she isn't working with a guy now, then got her start that way—like a boyfriend or maybe her brother. Gets a taste for it, sees how it can be done. Realize that you don't have to be a muscle man. Just stay within yourself, go after the jobs you know you can pull. Break into houses, trailers, apartments. In some ways it is harder today for women because of more alarms, more motion sensors, and because there are more safes. But is easier, too, on account have fewer people at home 'cause both the man and the woman are working today, kids are in school. So clip in the daytime when the house is empty and fewer people to see you.

Women in Rackets and/or Fencing

In the rackets, whew, it would be hard to find a woman. A couple of bookies were women. That involvement came from their husbands or was their dad's operation. But never knew a really big bookie who was a woman. But you do see women working for the bookies, run the lines or whatever. Help with the paperwork and that. Will be a family operation, where the wife or a sister pitches in. Are mostly staying in the background. Not a single woman in the local clique in American City. Same way in Tylersville, the local clique was all guys. The women I knew who were into the higher-up crimes, like the fencing or the gambling, nearly all of them got into it 'cause of their husband or their dad or maybe their brother.

There are some fences who are women. But mostly are men, especially the bigger ones. The main lady dealer I dealt with was Dorothy, was one of the biggest antique dealers in the area [American City] as far as the legit side. Handled the same kinds of things I did but had more expensive stuff, too. I did a lot of business with her over the years. Some warm but mostly legit. Dorothy did a little fencing, not the walk-in trade but people she would know. I don't think Albert [husband] ever knew Dorothy was involved that way. Was a helluva nice guy. Hardworking but a little slow mentally. Every other word is a cuss word. Dorothy would peddle some of the stuff at the auctions but many times she was selling the warm stuff to me. That's how she set me up, tipped off the state cops, when she got jammed up herself from buying from her cousins. I should have never trusted her the way I did.

The first time I went to see Dorothy after I got out of Midstate, you were along. I wanted you to meet her and for me to bury the hatchet with Dorothy. Albert is there and says he will go get Dorothy. Then he comes back and says she must of left 'cause she's not around. In my eye she is too embarrassed to see me face to face and is fearful, too, that I am holding a grudge. It is maybe six months later, we stop again and this time Dorothy comes out of the house to greet us. Our stopping before and talking to Albert assured her. She snitched but what is done is done. Had no one to blame but myself, being that dumb to trust her that way. I didn't want to keep a grudge that way and then have her avoid me, say, if we ran into each other at the auctions. I couldn't do business again with her if it involved the warm stuff but I didn't have a score to settle with her.

It is known, though, that women can sell dope. Outta their house or apartment, or maybe even on the street. Lotta women and even guys that use dope are more leery of buying from a guy, that he will rip them off. So, will prefer to buy from a woman. Is less worry about coming up short or getting hustled out of your money, or getting beat up or having to give a blow job. But most people selling dope are guys and the higher-ups even more so. Will use the women to transport the drug or sell the dope outta her house, as a cover and to keep a layer in between.

It is hard for women to go it alone on the streets, whether it is peddling dope or peddling ass. So will have to hook up with this or that guy. Otherwise what is to keep some asshole from ripping her off or hitting on her. Take any woman who is a half decent looker—if she is into crime, maybe is using dope or has other hustles, guys will try to get into her pants or take advantage of her in other ways. Take Lisa, when I first met her, she was using dope and dealing a little in dope. In a way I am thinking, if she is doing that, then she is probably into other things. Is more of a free spirit or whatever. Is an easy lay is what it boils down to. I feel a little shitty to admit that, but that is the way guys are thinking.

The crimes women are into are mostly shoplifting, selling dope, and prostitution. Next would be checks and credit cards. In my eye I would say that prostitution and peddling her ass in one way or another is still the main thing for women who are into crime—if they are doing it regular and are making a decent dollar at it. Will oftentimes mix in all three—selling dope, with a little shoplifting and prostitution mixed in. Or, mostly will do prostitution but mix in selling dope and shoplifting and other hustling games.

Take Timmy, the youngest Beck boy, and his girlfriend, Laurie. She is a knockout, fifteen, sixteen years old. He has dropped out of school, works off and on, and does some stealing, like breaking into cars or shoplifting. They are into partying. Into dope but not real dopers [addicts]. If the money he is bringing in comes up short, then she peddles her ass. He is streetwise and knows where she can peddle without getting hassles from the cops or from the prostitutes who are doing it regular. Other times, Laurie might be a lookout for Timmy and his buddies when they are breaking into cars. This is pretty common among the kids today. The guy will do more of the stealing, but their girlfriend will peddle her ass or maybe sell dope. Maybe peddle her ass to the guy selling the dope, or do a blow job on him to get the dope cheaper and share it with her boyfriend. Myself, I could not do that—have the woman you are with peddle her ass that way. But, you'd be surprised at how many guys will do that and more so today than in the past.

A guy that has sometimes helped me out on Saturdays, Kenny, his daughter is a hell-raiser. Acts very tough. Into dope and shoplifting. Then she gets popped for robbing a gas station attendant. Her and a couple of other girls. Got started when they are driving around and smoking pot, then stop for gas. Pay the attendant but are claiming he has shortchanged them. Were trying to hustle him, is what it boiled down to. Attendant is an older guy, on the small side, but he isn't backing down. So strong arm him and take all the cash he has. Then are getting more cocky. Pulled the same thing at couple of other gas stations but now are pointing a gun at the attendant and wanting money out the cash register. Ends up he gets the license plate number. Kenny comes to me, wanting to know what he could do about getting a lawyer and that. I did that for him but am thinking, whew, a little jail time might do her some good. Has a nasty attitude, a very big chip. Dare her to do something, she would probably do it. Could use a knocking down.

Wanda showed me this in the paper a few days ago. This black woman robbed a convenience store where Wanda's cousin once worked. Ten o'clock at night. Chubby woman, early twenties. Buys a bag of chips, leaves, then comes back. Has her hand in her pocket, is pointing like she has a gun. Tells the clerk to give her fifty dollars out of the drawer. Takes the money and runs. Are still looking for her. In my eye she is on dope or is a mom with a kid she is feeding. Maybe there is more of that today but that is a pretty horseshit robbery.

I'm not saying that women are so much more goody-goody as compared to guys. When it comes to stealing and hustling, like the shoplifting and stealing from where they work and using their ass to get what they want, you'd be surprised how many will do that. *But as far as the criminal element, they are less involved and will shy away from it. Especially, over the long haul. Whereas myself, Jesse, Angie, Louie, and different ones have been at crime our whole life more or less. It is hard to find a woman who has done that.*

The ordinary joe blow woman? Yes, there are quite a few who will clip if the good opening is there but will keep it small. If go shopping, then pick up this or that without paying. If into the party scene, then maybe sell a little dope. Steal from where they work, this is pretty common—are as bad or worse than the guys. That is what the guys in business tell me. Are a lot of women who have some larceny in their heart and will clip in little ways, whereas guys if they clip, the amount will be bigger.

Someone like Dorothy Ford has as much larceny in heart as me or anybody else for that matter. Maybe has the know-how. But she doesn't have the heart and the contacts. Can't get the connections to really do well at the fencing. Like with the local clique, there was no way they'd do business with her except maybe if the edge is big in their favor and the coast is clear. But on a regular basis, no way.

Another thing, say it is a woman you are hooked up with, sleeping with or whatever. You know sooner or later the woman is gonna nag you to quit. Like with Bernice, she went along with it and enjoyed the benefits, you might say. But then she would drop little hints, that Jesse should quit. Same with Rocky, when he and Melanie were dating, she was all for it. Was a thrill for her and she enjoyed the partying. Then, they get married and she is changing her tune. After he got popped [arrested], Melanie skidooed.

Take myself—with Becky and with Connie before that, and with Wanda now. They all wanted me to quit, more so Wanda 'cause she is very honest. Whereas Becky liked the extra benefits. Was afraid of what might happen to me and to herself, but looked the other way on account she and her kids now have a decent life. Even Lisa, as fucked up as she was, would worry about me getting jammed up.

They would all cover for me in some ways, would lie a little at least. But you would not want to push that very far. Now, as far as coming to the penitentiary to see you if you got sent away or as far as taking care of the kids, you could count on Becky and Wanda to do that.

No way Wanda would do crimes with me. Becky maybe but only if I pushed her hard enough. Lisa, no doubt—if I had wanted to use her that way, it would be scary what she would do. Just to hang onto something, she would have gone all the way. As far as women and crime, this is a side that is hard to understand—what they will do for some asshole, what they will put themselves through.

But you could never trust Lisa to hold up. A little, yes, as long as she had the rocks for me. But say I was to dump her, she would not hesitate to do me in. That is why I was very careful that she not have any real knowledge of what I was into. Whereas Wanda or Becky would not be as bitter that way.

In my eye the kids and the young thieves today are more likely to have women involved in their crimes. Maybe I'm just an old head talking. Could be it is dope—there is more dope around and your ordinary thief is less careful today. Do anything and do not think things through or even worry about what might happen.

If women are more into crime today [theft, fraud], it's because they are more having to fend for themselves. Isn't a free ride like maybe it used to be.

Are more and more the ones who are taking care of their kids. But the dope is the main thing. Not only 'cause dope itself is a push for having to steal or hustle your ass to pay for the dope. But the dope will hook them up with the assholes, guys who are real losers. Who take advantage of them, really. Then, once they get involved, see they can do it themselves and don't need this asshole who is just mooching off them. Become more a part of the criminal element. Not that the women aren't to blame. I hope I'm not blowing wind outta my ass for thinking this: in my eye dope is a big reason for guys getting into crime but more so that is the case for women on account guys are more part of the criminal element to begin with.

Looking back I did more stuff with women than I had surmised. Same as most guys I would guess. Would not want to broadcast it or even think that we had pulled crimes with women. Same thing as a white guy clipping with a black guy, you would not want to be known for doing that.

Racism in the Underworld

I do think black guys use women for committing crimes more than do white guys. Are more likely to live off a woman, is what it comes down to. But still, most black guys don't like to do crimes with women. From what I've seen, black guys who are breaking into cars, who are robbing convenience stores, who are selling dope are mainly doing it with other black guys. Same thing with Hispanics, it is mostly guys who are doing those kinds of crimes and they are doing it with other Hispanic guys, not Hispanic women. I don't care if it's burglary, if it's fencing, even dealing dope. That's the way it is.

It's only natural that white guys will have partners who are white, and black guys with black guys. The trust, the feeling comfortable, to know what the other is thinking. It is harder to have that with another race. Same way as it is harder for a guy to have that with a woman than with another guy. Even if she's his woman and there is a closeness there, women think differently.

There's more mixing of the races at the street level. Then move to higher levels, the mixing is less and less. Except may find the black thief peddling to a white fence 'cause your bigger dealers are mostly white. Another thing, a black thief is gonna trust a white fence as much or more than he'd trust a black fence, and will know the white fence is gonna have the cash to pay. But a white thief won't sell as easily to a black fence. The trust and feeling comfortable won't be there.

If a black guy and a white guy work together, maybe the trust comes from being in jail together or from being recommended by someone they both know. Depends, too, on what they're into. If a white is into robbery, then having a partner who is black can be a help 'cause a white person being robbed has more fear of a black guy—is thinking, "Take it, don't shoot me." Same way, if a black guy is robbing or clipping people in the white part of town, it helps to have a partner who is white on account of suspicion—a black guy in a white crowd will raise some eyebrows. Same with peddling the warm stuff, a black thief is better off with a white partner 'cause most of your better fences are white.

I did know of a couple of burglary outfits where you had a black and a white working together. This is at the in-between level, never knew of a really good burglary outfit that had that. As far as the fencing, I have bought from some blacks who were pretty decent thieves. But really good, no.

But, whether it was a decent thief or an asshole thief, I was more likely to turn the black thief away, and the Hispanic thief, too. Was always more leery that your black thief was a doper, into drugs. I didn't like that.

To my thinking, black thieves don't believe in trust like a lot of white thieves do. Not just for snitching but are cutthroat in other ways, even with their buddies and the people they are doing business with. Is a line there for carrying the hustling too far and playing too dirty. And will take whatever they can grab, so are bringing you more junk that anything. Then hassle you, whine and whine about what you are willing to pay. Give you a lotta hustle bullshit. I don't go for that.

Another reason I shied away from the black thief—they are more likely to be into mugging and robbing people. That is a crime that gets the attention of the police, so why bring yourself extra heat? A few years ago I was buying from Stubbie, short black guy I met in the penitentiary. Was bringing me jewelry and small antique pieces, pretty good stuff. Then, the police come by and show me mug shots of him and two women—a white woman and a black woman. Did I know them? Had they ever stopped by? Turns out they are hitting apartments where your older people and senior citizens live. The women would knock on the door and see if anybody was home. Would wear wigs and that. Would break in, or if someone answered then ask to use the phone or whatever. If it was an older person living there, they might rob the person. I couldn't do any business with Stubbie after that. In the cop's eye and the public's eye, robbing old people is as bad, maybe worse, than selling dope to kids. You don't want to be associated with those kinds of people.

I am leery, too, that if black thieves are coming too regular into my shop, this would be a red flag. This is in Tylersville now. On account my shop is away from downtown, isn't that close to the black areas. Off and on a black person would stop by my shop, legit now, but not that many. Not like in American City where they were a decent part of my store business. This time I would run into more black people at my auction booth. Still, if it is a young black guy and he is dressed like the ghetto, will be some suspicions. Why is he making the rounds at the flea market? Why is he in your shop? That is the way the cops and even the ordinary joe blow will think.

The black thieves more went to Louie and the other secondhand places. They'd peddle to Louie, even though he'd snitch on them to get slack with the cops, on account Louie always had the cash and he was more willing to buy junk than I was. Same way with the other secondhand places, not that they had the cash, but they'd buy the penny-ante stuff more than I would. But the secondhand places and even Louie were more leery of buying from the black thieves.

I don't think I am prejudiced against blacks, like a lotta white thieves and many of your dealers are. 'Cause in my legit business, I always did a lotta business with blacks, and with Hispanics too. In American City they were a main part of my business. Gave them credit and everything. They were better at paying in many ways than most whites. But pulling a burglary or buying what's warm, where there's some risk involved, I was less likely to take a shot at it if the thief was black. In my eye I just felt safer dealing with your white thief.

Guys likely Rocky and Mickey, just listening to them talk, you can feel the hate there. Myself, I don't feel that way. I pretty much always got along with blacks, even in prison. I treated them okay and they respected me. Not let them intimidate you but don't put them down. Hey, we're in this fucking place together, let's not bring any hassles for each other. I didn't fear blacks like some white guys in prison do. It was more I didn't want to put up with their music and their ways of doing things. Especially at Midstate this last time, were a number of blacks who were decent cons. This or that one I have bought from since they got out, and they have recommended some other thieves to me.

It was known that I treated people fair—black, white, brown, or green. It is not in my nature to hold something against somebody on account of their background. Is a soft spot in me, too, for kids and that who've had hard upbringings. Black person comes into my shop, got the same treatment as a white person. Same way if I met a black person or a white person on the street, hold the door for one the same as hold the door for the other. At my shop or at the auction, give credit to the one same as give credit to the other. Hustle the one, same as hustle the other. Black or white or green, if you are whining and giving me hassles, then we can't do business anymore.

Maybe there are some blacks who are making good money [at crime], like with the dope peddling that is much bigger today. I can't say but do not think that is the case. They mostly are the front people and are taking the risks. Are not the ones in background who are earning the good dollar. Same thing with the Puerto Ricans, are the front people.

Take Angelo in American City. He was hooked up with different blacks as far as dealing dope and even the prostitution. Angelo was the money behind it and he had the contacts for bringing in the dope. Angelo thought he couldn't be touched and was getting too greedy. Phil would complain to me about that,

that Angelo was getting deeper into the dope peddling and was getting more and more involved with black guys. Phil would not touch the dope and he was very leery of doing business with blacks. So was a tension there with Angelo. Not that Angelo would admit that he was dealing dope or was operating with blacks, 'cause he would not want Phil or the local clique to know much about that.

Even in the dope business, I don't think there are many blacks who are getting rich at it. As far as Tylersville, it is mostly white guys and Dominicans who are taking in the good dollar. Are working together. Why, I don't really know. But guys like Angelo and Amato have a lot of dealings with Dominicans, at least as far as the dope goes. Aren't that many in the area but are known for not using the dope, for the trust and for knowing they can handle their end of things. Dominicans aren't dopers, which is different than a lotta blacks and Puerto Ricans. Don't use the dope themselves but have the connections for getting the dope, say, with other Dominicans in Oceantown. Don't blow money and don't blow themselves up the way the blacks do—like wearing the gold earrings and looking like the ghetto. Don't bring attention to themselves. Are safer to deal with all the way around.

As far as being part of the local clique, no, aren't any black guys really part of that. Not in American City, not in Tylersville. You will sometimes bump into Willie, Willie Smokes, at Airport Lounge. Is the main pimp in town. Will have a drink, shoot the breeze with different guys that come by. They are friendly with Willie and may do some business with him. Willie is a good operator, will give him that. On the order of Watusi [main pimp in American City], only bigger and into more things. Has some association with this or that one in the clique but you will not find him at the private clubs. Even more so, not at the Columbus House [Italian Club]. He would not be welcome.

In both places (American City, Tylersville) the main pimps were all black guys, same as other places I've known about. Is that a coincidence or not? Maybe they have a lock on that, the way the Italians have a lock on the gambling. This is for the street-level hooking, 'cause get further away I don't think you will find many blacks involved. Your strip joints and massage places are mostly run by white guys. Take the Airport Lounge, local clique may have card games there and bring in girls—sometimes ones from Willie, but other times more high class than that.

I don't know much about the gang stuff. I guess they are worse today. That's what the cops and the papers say. In this area they mostly are Hispanic, Puerto Rican. Never paid much attention to it. I did have Puerto Rican kids in my shop off and on or they might hang out in the parking lot a couple of blocks from my shop. White kids would drop by my shop sometimes, too, mostly on account of the Beck boys who would stop by with their friends and that. But I didn't buy from kids and mostly it is kids who are in the gangs. If one was ever in my shop, I wouldn't know it.

Looking back, yes, I did do crimes with blacks. But still nothing like the business I did with blacks on the legit side. That was a whole lot more.

Change and Stability in the Underworld

The world has changed, so there is change in the fencing and in being a thief, too. Not altogether different 'cause some things are pretty much the same. But still is not what it used to be. See this in the penitentiary too. Are fewer good thieves and the code is weaker.

The big change today is dope, is a lot more dope today. That is number one. Has become a bigger pathway for getting into crime and for staying in crime. Not only because this or that one is stealing on account they need a fix, but on account of the money they can make from peddling dope or because the crowd they run with is using dope.

Number two, I'd say, is there are a lot more assholes out there today who will do anything to make a buck. The all-around thief is bigger today. When me and Jesse was operating, you had guys who more stuck to doing one thing. If it was shoplifting, that's what you did. If it was burglary, if it was checks, if it was sticking people up—you stayed with that. Most guys would do some switching if the good opportunity was there but wouldn't do any damn thing just to make a buck.

Are more greenies today. Guys wet behind the ears. Too dumb to know what they don't know. Pull anything and with anybody. Don't do the planning and scouting like they should. Not that I didn't pull dumb shit when I was young, but do think the younger thief today has less know-how and takes chances when he shouldn't.

Not sure what I'd call myself when I was clipping with my buddies from the paper mill. In a way we was snatch-and-grab—break into a car or take the tires off, then next time break into a hunting cabin or a gas station. But still we weren't shoplifting or robbing people but stuck to things we knew something about and were comfortable with.

Is less of a code today. Used to be a helluva code. Even in prison the code is a lot less. Is less honor among thieves. The snitching is a lot worse today. Why? The quality of thief is less today, are more assholes, and the dope adds to it. But the main reason is, the cops rely on the snitching today. Tell me this or rat this guy out, you will get a break—less time or even go free. Cops have always tried to get guys to snitch but nothing like today. Is the biggest change over the years with the DA and the cops. Use the snitching to bust a guy's balls and make themselves look good. This is a much bigger worry today—is this guy gonna dime me out? Is he on the cops' payroll? Are they pushing him to set me up? Get this guy or that woman to snitch, then make your quota and have the chief [chief of police] pat you on the back.

Another change is you got to worry more about the feds today and not just the local cops. There are more cops now and at different levels—you got a task force on drugs and maybe another one on gambling or burglary, and you got the FBI and the U.S. Attorneys. The state police are a bigger worry today. It is still pretty safe to cross state lines to sell the warm stuff, but even here the cops work together a lot more than they used to.

When Jesse and me was operating, we had little worry from the local cops. Our big worry was the state police. We more or less had the local cops in our pocket, either through our lawyer or from paying them off. Local cops didn't have their act together to really go after guys like Jesse and me anyway, and didn't want to bothered. Going after the ordinary thief was more in their league. Weren't any task force people and the feds pretty much kept to themselves. They are much more active now.

I never gave it much thought. But for people like Angelo and Amato, a worry is the drug laws and what is called the "racketeering" law. Can put you away for a long time and hammer you with a bullshit stack of crimes. This is how they nailed Angelo, said he was a kingpin—a drug kingpin but into other things too. Feds got enough people to be snitches and put on a good show for the jury. Even with Angelo's money and contacts, he couldn't slide out of it. Feds put Angelo away for so long I don't think he'll see the light of day again.

These laws came up this last time I was popped for the gates and the wicker, mainly on account the one cop who was pretty cocky. This is right after they first brought me to the station, asshole cop is giving me the third degree—to send me the message that I should come clean. Confession or whatever, otherwise they could run up the charges—that I was heading a *criminal organization, was doing the fencing for a ring of thieves.* Or something to that effect. I just kept my mouth shut, then later asked my lawyer what the fuck this asshole cop was talking about. He explained it had to do with the racketeering laws—can charge a guy with running an organization that's into crime, that I am pulling the strings to have other people do the crimes but am staying in the background. Said it would be a stretch to go after me that way on account the cops didn't have the evidence and 'cause they usually go after bigger fish. It never came up again in any conversations with the police, so I'm guessing the asshole cop was throwing words around to put some fear into me and to get me thinking they had a case when they didn't.

How these laws work, I really do not know. Leave a bad taste in one's mouth, I do know that. Just encourages the snitching. Be a snitch and walk away. Makes it easier for the cops, gives them a free ride, but end up being patsies for the snitches and assholes.

Don't get me wrong. There is still a code and still a helluva pecking order—more amongst your higher-ups but even your street hustlers will have some of the code. There is still respect for the guy that keeps his mouth shut and carries himself like he isn't an asshole. The pecking order and the code is not the same but they go together.

I don't know if you'd call this a big change in law enforcement—the rope is shorter for what you can get away with. Are busting people today for the tiniest bullshit. Smoke a little pot, knock down a mailbox, bloody somebody's nose. If they catch you, it is bang, bang. The cops are tougher today. Are hard-asses. Bigger pricks. I'm not saying they shouldn't bust me for dealing in warm stuff 'cause I would have it coming. But to throw the book at somebody for a little shoplifting or for a little dope dealing, or for kicking a guy in the nuts 'cause he's an asshole and was hitting on your girlfriend. There's no need to hammer someone for that. Or to bust a guy's balls for calling a cop a motherfucker, or getting in his face 'cause he's pushed you to the wall. The cop should walk away from it, not bang you with an assault charge.

I would not want to be a kid today, a young person who is out for a good time and maybe some devilment. It is easier to be done in by the cops on account of all the snitching that is going on and 'cause the cops are bigger hard-asses. See this in the penitentiary today, how many kids are there and there for penny-ante bullshit.

Changes in Burglary

The paths into burglary ain't the same. The old heads, the guys with experience aren't breaking in the younger guys. Don't take them under their wings like they used to. In my day, more younger guys messed with burglary, not only to make a buck but also for devilment and for horsing around with their buddies. The chances were better to hook up with a decent burglar and give it a shot. Find out what you were made of. Or you'd meet guys in the penitentiary who were into burglary, learn from them, and have those contacts when you got out.

Are fewer good burglars today. Used to be you'd have four, five, half-dozen good burglar crews working in an area. Guys who were pretty decent. But just in general there is less breaking into houses or business places today, especially where there is a good dollar involved. What burglary there is, is mainly horseshit burglaries. Break in, grab something, and run. Is less in the way of breaking into safes as part of the hit. Carry the safe out and worry later about getting it open. Is a still a lot of that. But seldom hear today that so and so is a good safeman. Are some decent burglars today but not like it used to be.

If you're shopping for a partner today, your choices aren't as good. Same way if you need a bigger crew to pull off a job, it is harder to put all the pieces together. If you talk to Bowie or Steelbeams and even Rocky, they will tell you—aren't that many young guys whose main thing is burglary, especially ones who are half decent at it. Right now Steelbeams is teamed up with Ricky Porter, is like twenty-two, twenty-three years old. Seems to be pretty decent. Is solid but hasn't really been tested.

There is more breaking into cars and vans, into trucks. More breaking into delivery trucks. Is more stealing bicycles, stealing wicker off somebody's porch, stealing riding lawn mowers, clipping at a construction site. Somebody has a nice boat and has parked it for the winter, steal the motor and peddle it. Stealing cars and selling the parts and that, is a lot bigger today. These are changes that have taken a cut out of burglary. In a way it is a form of burglary—cause it involves the breaking in, the searching, the knowing what to do afterwards. But still it is different. Is more snatch-and-grab. Falls in between a regular burglary and something like a purse snatching or smashing a store window, grabbing what you can, and then running like hell. Is more suited for the ordinary thief.

As far as there being less burglary today on account the cops are cracking down or because there's more alarm systems, is some of that. The business places are harder to break into on account of the alarms and the cameras, and the safes are better. But your houses and that, no. They are not that hard to break into and the safes are mostly little cracker boxes. Your business places will spend to get a decent safe but the ordinary house owner won't—buy a cheap safe, foreign made or whatever, that are easy to open or can be carried out.

In my eye, it is more the dope that has changed things. The dope is everywhere and is an easy way to make a buck by peddling it. You are seeing your buddies selling dope, see there is decent money in it, and the path is open. I'm not saying it doesn't take heart and that to sell dope but does not take as much knowledge. You don't have to learn the ropes or have the contacts like you do with burglary. At least for dealing dope to your buddies and the circle you run with. So, for the younger guy out to make a buck or needs a extra dollar to party, why not deal in dope.

Your better burglar is also figuring the snitching goes with the dope. Just knowing the younger guys are using it or are hanging with a crowd that's into dope, will make the better thief leery. So will shy away from working with the younger guy or to break them in. It's not that the better thief will never use dope—quite a few do, say, a little pot or some cocaine as a pastime or to relax. But don't overdo it. Even someone like Gordie, who is a very good burglar, may do a little coke before he clips—tells me it makes him more alert and so he won't tire out. Is that bullshit or not, I can't say.

This is funny. Myself, I never used dope. Except tried it in the penitentiary this last time. I am working in the laundry shop doing repair work, putting in shelves, shit like that. One of the guys is having pot, marijuana, brought in. So I smoked it, maybe half-a-dozen times. But it wasn't for me. Other kinds of dope like coke or heroin—the opportunity has been there to try the stuff, but no way. If I'm going to tie one on, just stay with Jack Daniels.

Changes in the Stolen Goods Market

When me and Louie were put away for the fencing, from what the cops and the DA were saying you would think that stealing in American City was going to dry up—on account now the thieves wouldn't have any place to peddle the stuff. This is blowing wind outta your ass. Has always been a lotta hot stuff that doesn't go through dealers like me and Louie. Are a lotta ways for peddling what is hot. Flea markets, even your little garage sales, are places to unload. Peddle the stuff at this or that bar, this or that truck stop or restaurant. At the video arcade places. Peddle the stuff to your buddies, to somebody you know, or to the people you work with. Little secondhand dealers will many times buy. Are private collectors who will buy from the better thief.

Now, if you're stealing regular, then the chances are you will have to unload with regular dealers. The shoplifter, the guy who breaks into cars, the doper thief—if they're clipping regular, it is hard to peddle all that to people you know or peddle it at a flea market or with a guy that runs a tavern or whatever. Sure as hell can't peddle that much on the street. There is a helluva lot of risk if you have to shop around that much and you can end up making pennies.

But still, in my eye more of the warm stuff today is peddled to people who aren't regular fences. Guy runs a restaurant or bar, has a little shop, or a gas station. Maybe the places becomes a hangout for thieves or your hustler types. Will buy warm stuff off and on, and sell it to his customers or to people he knows. Is a lot of that going on.

I don't think you have as many wide-open dealers today, like I was or Louie was in American City. You do have some big operators but the license to steal is not as open as it once was. Are too many snitches and you're dealing with more than just the local cops. With the feds and the state police, you are more likely to have cops who won't look the other way and more have the know-how to go after the bigger fence. I'm not saying there aren't guys who can handle truckloads but there is less of that today.

Smaller dealers, like I am now, are still around. Are pretty plentiful. Guys who run a pawn shop or secondhand place, a coin shop, or have a junkyard or an auto parts place. Maybe guy has a booth at a auction house or he runs a flea market. These are still places that are good covers for handling the warm stuff and the opportunities will be there 'cause your thieves will check them out. Another one is guys that run a check cashing business on account they will have the connections for handling warm stuff and are dealing with a pretty shady crowd. But even these places have a harder time now on account of the snitches and the state police.

Here is another thing that has changed: there ain't the markup on a lotta items today. I'm talking about your ordinary household items and entertainment pieces, what your ordinary thief is likely to steal if he's breaking into houses or shoplifting. TVs, cameras, binoculars, watches, stereos, microwaves, tools. You can go to a K-Mart or a Wal-Mart and buy those items dirt cheap and they are *new*. Hard to turn those items into a decent dollar. Twenty years ago, a regular TV cost four, five hundred dollars. I could pay the thief a hundred dollars, then sell it for two hundred dollars to someone shopping in my store or even ship it out to a legit place that sells TVs. There was a decent dollar in it for everybody.

As far as fencing clothes or furs and that, I can't say, 'cause that is something I never handled. Never wanted to mess with it and what the hell do I know about clothing. But it would be the same as what has happened with your ordinary household items—you can buy clothing today dirt cheap at your K-Marts and discount places. So, if you are fencing clothes, the turnover will have to be big for you to make a decent dollar. Sure, if you are handling expensive clothes, say, good fur coats, the profit margin is better. But for the ordinary secondhand guy who is catering to the ordinary joe blow who shops at the secondhand places, there isn't a market for the expensive stuff. Will have to ship that out if he wants a decent price but he is unlikely to have the good contacts for doing that.

Jewelry is good today, is maybe better than ever. Is a big profit margin and is hard for the thief to know what he has. As long as you have the outlets, say, with a Rosen or a Skip. But they will deal only with the better thief or will deal with fence like myself to keep that layer in between. Have to know the thief or he will have to be recommended by someone who they can trust.

The better thief can still get the outlets and can make a decent dollar. But, no, your penny-ante thief and even the in-between thief will have a harder time making it. What they many times are stealing isn't worth what it once was and they don't have the good outlets if they come across good jewelry or a good antique piece. If you're stealing the little laptop computers instead of TVs or cameras, those [laptop computers] have a bigger value but are harder to peddle. Bicycles are good today and not hard to peddle. Same with guns, has always been a good item and are still good today.

More fences today are dealing in dope. Combine the two. Will pay the thief in dope instead of cash. To me, they many times are hustlers more than anything. For some, they are mainly peddling dope but mix in a little fencing, or other times the main thing is fencing and mix in some dope peddling. I'm talking about small-time operators really who are more or less operating on the street where there isn't a layer in between. Especially in your black areas this is a main thing. Maybe are involved in a mix of things—shylock loans, asshole con games, peddling girls.

Are taking extra risks on account of the fact that there is dope involved—the police will have more snitches and the fencing will be getting more attention.

Shifts in Market for Antiques and Collectibles

Is still a market for antiques but it's not what it once was on account people know much more about whether this or that is an antique, and does it have a decent value. It is harder to buy cheap and sell for a good profit if you are in the antique business. Used to be you could go to an estate auction or even to a flea market and pick up good antique pieces for a cheap dollar. Is less of that today. The ordinary joe blow has more knowledge of antiques but also you have dealers and buyers today who will buy anything in sight. Are figuring there will be some good pieces in the pile that will bring a decent dollar and that they can break even on the junk. Or an antique dealer will have pickers who do the buying—go to an estate auction, say, buy anything that looks like it can have value as an antique.

Your better antiques are more likely to be marked, to be registered. So is more risk today on some items. Will be harder to unload them because other dealers maybe won't touch them. That has helped a dealer like me on account the ordinary secondhand guy won't have the contacts to unload what is registered, whereas I still might have the contacts to handle that, say, with Scottie.

Breaking into Cars, Stealing Credit Cards, etc.

In American City my main trade in warm stuff came from guys who were into burglary—breaking into houses, into businesses, into warehouses. This time [in Tylersville] my main trade is from guys breaking into cars and vans and trucks. Next from guys stealing from lots and front yards, like patio furniture or ATVs or your mountain bikes. I'm still getting stuff from guys breaking into places but that has dropped off.

If you are a thief today, breaking into cars is the way to go. Or maybe stealing the cars if you have the connection with a good outlet who can strip them and peddle the pieces. In many ways breaking into a car is easier than pulling off a burglary. Easier to get into a car, easier to find whatever is there 'cause are only a few places to look, and the getaway is easier. Maybe the score will be bigger in a burglary but you'd be surprised at how well you can do knocking off cars. Not just radios and stereos. But will come across jewelry, guns, small antique pieces, laptop computers, tools. You name it, items that can be worth a decent dollar. Can be on the seat, under the seat, in the glove compartment, in the trunk, in a briefcase.

And will come across cash. Be surprised at how often people leave money in their car or truck. Or leave their purse or wallet. Same with checkbooks and credit cards. That is a big attraction for breaking into cars but then you have to peddle the checks and the credit cards to somebody who is into that. Or maybe pass them yourself or get a lady friend to do it. But then you are adding in more risk.

In my day you more shied away from stealing checks and credit cards. Have more guys today who will break into a house or hotel room or a business place and look as much for checks and credit cards as for cash. Same with a lot of car break-ins. But there are a lot other ways to steal checks and credit cards. At somebody's party, go through the lady's purses, or grab a purse at a shopping mall.

Some of the thieves I dealt with would use credit cards and buy merchandise, say at a department store, and then peddle the merchandise to me. This mostly involved thieves, like the Beck boys, who as part of a burglary or breaking into cars would pick up credit cards they came across. Many times the cards are unsigned, so it is easy to use them. Drive to another town and go from store to store, sign a phony name. Maybe even have a stolen driving license and use that name. The one Beck boy, Bobby, did this a lot. May have his girlfriend or another floozy sign her "Jane Doe."

There is more of this today. Are more credit cards out there. Can buy almost anything on credit today, so this opportunity has gone swoosh. Really, these are crimes you see more women doing today. Not just passing the credit cards but stealing a lady's purse at a party or going into a hotel room or somebody's house to steal the cards. I do believe that women are better at passing the credit cards, is less suspicion, or whatever. It is the same thing with cashing checks.

Bobby Beck would steal checks and credit cards. Was his main thing for awhile. If came across a bunch of credit cards, only take one or two—that way the person won't notice, won't do anything about it until he is notified that someone is using his card. Bobby would sometimes hit hotel rooms, the better hotels where the guy making a good dollar will stay. Will be a higher limit on how much you can run up. Another thing, a guy staying in a hotel finds out his card is missing will think he just left it at home. Will give the thief a longer lead time for using the card. Or steal a purse or wallet from people at a nightclub or a bar. Maybe even hook up with the bartender to encourage a guy who is drinking to be careless. Or, hook up with a desk clerk or somebody that works at a hotel. Get a key to the rooms. Just have to be cautious not to clip too often. Lay low for awhile, maybe switch to breaking into cars or get a part-time job. Bobby knew the ropes, was a decent credit card thief.

There are lots of ways to come across credit cards or a checkbook. I bought a few times from a guy who had a hookup with somebody that worked in the postal office. Would stick on a new address if he saw a letter that looked like it held a credit card and have it sent to a different address. But this can be risky 'cause that will bring in the feds.

Some guys will steal cards or checks but won't pass them. Sell to a forger or check passer, which is what your experienced thieves will do. Have the other guy take the risk of being identified through a signature or a photograph. But still have to be careful on account the one you sell to may snitch if he gets popped.

In many ways it is easier than ever to pass a credit card. On account of it is so automated. Run it through the machine, don't check the signature or anything. Bing, bing. Just need to make sure you buy merchandise that is easy to peddle.

This is another thing that is happening, guys going into the computer [Internet] for getting peoples' names and their social security numbers, say, for getting credit cards; or they are using the computer in other ways to chisel someone. Donnie and Benny have pushed me to get a computer to keep our books. I can barely turn it on, so do not know how you can clip this way—except do know it is happening from listening to the Beck boys and different ones. You wouldn't think they have enough upstairs for using the computer that way, but can surprise you how the smarts are there to know what they want to know.

Has been a lotta change in my lifetime. Hard to believe all that has happened—with the dope, with the penitentiaries, with the burglary and the fencing, with the snitching. But the main threads are still there—is still a helluva pecking order, still have the decent thief and the asshole thief, still have the local clique, and still have the shady businessman and the crooked cop. A lot of the old ways to chisel are still here but are newer ways, too. Had my druthers, yes, I would take the old days—on account of the dope and the snitching. But you have to roll the dice you are given, work with what is there and take the good opportunities that come your way. Not whine about it.

15

Commentary

Organized Crime and Racketeering

Sam Goodman's experiences as a "good thief" and especially as a business fence brought him into repeated contact and dealings with individuals and operations connected to syndicated, mafia-style organized crime. More specifically, Sam had frequent business and social dealings (via the "local clique" or gambling club) with criminal entrepreneurs connected to cosa nostra elements, the American mafia, which had a substantial presence both in American City and in Tylersville. Throughout our discussion, we refer interchangeably to cosa nostra or mafia to indicate traditional Italian-American organized crime elements having historic or current ties to "La Cosa Nostra" syndicates. Considerable ambiguity exists in many U.S. localities (including American City and Tylersville) in sorting out (1) the "reality" of the mafia versus its "reputation," (2) the "tie" between a particular entrepreneur and a mafia group, and (3) the current strength of a Mafia network as distinct from the group's historical stature.

Sam, of course, was not a "made" member of the local mafia network (his non-Italian ethnicity prevented membership even if he had wanted it), but he looked at them with a mixture of wariness, respect, and sometimes envy. This chapter examines what we can learn about organized crime from Sam's experience.

Organized crime is a complex, multifaceted phenomenon that is difficult to define and analyze. It refers very broadly to the general organization of the underworld, more narrowly to the groups within its economy that plan and execute elaborate, sustained criminal activities. We use the narrower meaning here. Relative to other kinds of crime groups (e.g., a burglary crew), law enforcement practitioners and social scientists typically define an organized-crime group as (1) having some manner of formalized structure whose primary objective is to obtain money through illegal activities; and (2) tending to dominate specific crime markets or enterprises in particular locations and to maintain its position through use of actual or threatened violence, corruption, and extortion.

Competing Views of Italian-American Organized Crime

Two views of Italian-American organized crime emerged during the 1960s and 1970s. The first view is identified with sociologist Donald Cressey, the second with sociologist Joseph Albini and anthropologist Francis Ianni. In recent years the enterprise model of organized crime has been proposed as an alternative to both the Cressey and Ianni views. But, as we discuss below, it is better seen as a complementary rather than a competing framework.

La Cosa Nostra: A Hierarchically Structured View of Organized Crime

The view that organized crime (including Italian-American organized crime) is synonymous with the mafia or La Cosa Nostra stemmed partly from the latter's strength and influence when compared to other crime groups. It also is shaped by the picture of organized crime that emerged in the 1950s and 1960s—especially the disclosures of the Kefauver and McClellan Senate Committees' investigations that first directed national attention toward organized crime. Public fascination with the mafia also has been strong. Books, movies, and television series have represented the "Mob" as something akin to what is depicted in "The Godfather." In the everyday language of the police, the press, and popular opinion, organized crime referred to a tightly knit group of Italian men who ran a business whose structure was reminiscent of feudal relationships. This perception mandated law enforcement's focus on that group. Indeed, legislation used to counter organized crime, notably the Racketeer Influenced Corrupt Organizations (RICO) Act, was designed with cosa nostra in mind.

Donald Cressey (1967) agreed with the traditional view of cosa nostra as a nationwide criminal network and the most powerful of organized crime groups in America that had, to some extent, taken the form of a corporation. However, Cressey rejected the alien conspiracy view that the mafia is an international organization that controls organized crime, particularly in the United States. The American mafia "is not merely the Sicilian Mafia transplanted," Cressey wrote, but "the similarities between the two organizations are direct and too great to be ignored" (ibid.:8). Cosa nostra is said to be characterized by four key features:

1. "family" structure with graded ranks of authority from boss to soldiers;
2. bosses who oversee the activities of family members and associates;
3. families (and their spin-off mafia networks) that are linked through understandings, obligations, and shared membership in or identification with cosa nostra; and
4. a "commission" of bosses that handles interfamily relations and disputes.

A Kinship/Patron–Client View

A very different rendition of Italian-American organized crime was offered by anthropologist Francis Ianni, based on his observations of one specific crime "family" in Brooklyn (around 1970). Ianni (1975) concluded that Italian-American organized crime does exist, but cosa nostra or mafia does not. Moreover, rather than a hierarchical structure, Italian organized crime consists of more or less organized local criminal groups held together by cultural attitudes and kinship webs peculiar to the Italian scene.

Sociologist Joseph Albini (1971) complements Ianni's view, arguing that patron–client relationships are the key to understanding Italian-American organized crime in the United States. The patron–client relationship is based on an unbalanced exchange of favors, involving differences in power and obligation. The "patron" (or mafioso) is able to perform favors on behalf of a "client" such as providing economic aid, vital information, protection from the police, contacts, or ensuring that other criminals will not jeopardize his operations. He (the patron) acts as a power broker between the client and the wider society, both legitimate and illegitimate. The client, in return, rewards the patron with money, a "piece of the action," loyalty, or other forms of support—thus making the relationship reciprocal.(We see aspects of this patron–client partnering, for example, in Sam's dealings with mafia figures.)

In sharp contrast to Cressey, the Ianni/Albini approach does not acknowledge the existence of clear-cut roles and relationships coordinated by higher positions and a "shadow government" that includes a "commission," nor does it acknowledge a national network of crime families. Instead, Italian-American organized crime (and organized crime more generally) is characterized as a series of informal, flexible, and overlapping patron–client relationships. A criminal syndicate does not exist that has a structure independent of its activities and current personnel.

Organized crime is also often described, alternatively, as an "enterprise," that is, as a business activity that represents a deviant variation on legitimate activity. The enterprise framework is useful, and it is not at all at odds, as some commentators suggest, with hierarchical or patron–client models of organized crime. All organized crime is entrepreneurial and is shaped by market forces (Steffensmeier and Martens 2002). One key difference is that the enterprise approach focuses more on how crime *activities* are organized (e.g., a drug smuggling operation, a bookmaking business, an auto theft/resale operation), whereas the hierarchical and patron–client network approaches focus more on how crime *groups* are organized.

Cressey and Ianni both erred in viewing Italian organized crime as a *unitary phenomenon*. Cressey incorrectly equated Italian organized crime with cosa nostra, while Ianni mistakenly denied the existence of cosa nostra, and failed to recognize the hierarchical structure and "shadow government" of some Italian crime groups (including the one he studied). Ianni's kinship or patron–client treatment is significant because it offers a modified view of cosa nostra and points to a form of Italian organized crime that is distinct from cosa nostra groups. The patron–client framework is important for another reason, as we discuss later, in that it provides a useful way of characterizing crime partnerships and network alliances in criminal enterprise more generally.

Though analytically distinct, the two forms of Italian organized crime often overlap, thrive side by side, and cooperate and compete in many localities (in American City and Orchard Grove, for example, but less so in Tylersville where traditional cosa nostra elements dominate). The non-cosa nostra Italian groups often draw upon mafia reputation and contacts. In practice, it often is difficult to distinguish mafia-affiliated activities from those generated by non-mafia but Italian racketeering groups. This is even more the case today as traditional cosa nostra elements (but not necessarily Italian crime networks) have weakened. Citizens, law enforcement, and criminals tend to ascribe "mafia" status to Italian racketeers whether affiliated with cosa nostra or not. In this sense, the term "mafioso" or "mafia guy" aptly refers not only to members and associates of a formal criminal association, but also to individuals who are part of Italian-based crime networks held together by traditional bonds of honor, kinship, and instrumental friendships

Today, perhaps a *third recognizable group* falls in between these two depictions of Italian-American organized crime. This possibility is strongly suggested by Sam's narrative. There are persons or networks having a historic association with cosa nostra, but not necessarily current ties with them, such as the Gucci network in American City. That is, *there may be a continuum of ties to cosa nostra among Italian-American crime networks: strong cosa nostra ties on the one end and few, if any, cosa nostra ties on the other end, with other Italian crime networks falling somewhere in between.*

The Place of the Mafioso in the Underworld

Confessions suggests a number of conclusions about the relationships between organized crime and other illicit entrepreneurs, professional criminals, corrupt or complicitous officials, and the larger underworld (see also Abadinsky 1994). First, a single member of an organized crime network (1) is likely to have an extensive criminal portfolio as well as (2) an extensive network of informants and connections, and is likely to be (3) the center of, and act as a catalyst or broker for, a large amount of criminal activity (examples in *Confessions* are Angelo, Louie, Phil, Lenny, and Amato). These features may sometimes characterize other illicit entrepreneurs (e.g., to a lesser degree, Sam), many of whom will have at least some ties to the local "mob" but operate mostly independently.

A mafioso controls certain resources or has contacts with people who do. More than anything else, he is able to put a client "in touch with the right people"; in doing so he acts as a broker or layer in between. In this way, too, a mafioso (and his family or network) may dominate a particular geographic area or enterprise. As described by organized crime expert Howard Abadinsky, an important mafioso will have available

> a network of informants and connections, for example, with the police and other officials, as well as specialized criminal operatives such as papermen (persons who convert stolen "paper," for example, stocks, bonds, checks, into cash), torches (professional arsonists), muscle-men or leg-breakers, and enforcers. He is in a position to fence large amounts of stolen goods or to lend out various amounts of money at usurious interest—loansharking. He will act as a center for information (providing targets for professional burglars, for example), "license" criminal activities (for example, allow a high-stakes dice game to operate), and use his position to assist criminals in linking up for specialized operations (for example, finding a driver for a robbery or hijack team). (ibid.:27)

Indeed, a major operational difference between a cosa nostra mafioso and other illicit entrepreneurs (including non-mafia Italian racketeers) is his greater connections and more extensive network. Rather than being confined to the local area or to specific criminal enterprises, mafia members or associates are more likely to have connections extending considerably beyond local boundaries and covering a broader range of criminal activities.

Second, professional criminals and illicit entrepreneurs who are independent operatives may pay financial tribute to, or do "favors" for, an organized crime member (or associate) or group, indicating appreciation or "respect" (ibid.). Rooted partly in fear but more in quid pro quo, this show of respect both protects criminal operatives from violence from a mafioso and enables them to secure vital information and other assistance, such as contact referral or intervention if arrested.

Third, to be successful, each member of a local syndicate or organized crime network (from boss down to a soldier to an associate) must display an interest in and talent for cultivating relationships with strategic persons, keeping well informed, providing services, and enhancing power and income. Since doing these deeds requires considerable time and energy, organized crime criminals usually steer clear of conventional schedules but remain free to "hang around" to pick up and disseminate important information. Somewhat like the family physician or bondsman, they are "on call." Moreover, because building and preserving a crime network or reputation is an ongoing and inherently fragile process, ineptness or inactivity (e.g., imprisonment, semiretirement) can quickly weaken or wreck the network.

Fourth, whether the structure of the group is hierarchical or patron–client, syndicate members can be characterized as *entrepreneurs on the prowl* who more or less make money any way they can (although some activities like drug distribution may be off limits, depending on the views of the member or group). They stitch together partnerships and small, fluid networks for specific criminal endeavors or "enterprises." These may be rather amorphous in structure and characterized by considerable opportunism. This fluidity, however, does not negate the overall permanence of the network ties and involvement of key entrepreneurs that often prevails across criminal ventures or ongoing criminal enterprises.

Fifth, most members or elements of a syndicate group or "local clique"—whether a mafioso, professional criminal, or illicit entrepreneur—identify with each other as a subculture and develop a long-standing careerist attitude toward a criminal lifestyle. Mutual economic interests, evasion of the law, and often the prison experience bind them together. They may combine business interests with their racketeering or criminal activity, but they tend to be full-time career criminals who would rarely be considered community leaders (even though they may be "respected"). On the other hand, some organized criminals are businessmen first, who dabble heavily in illegal activities and then plow their illicit gains back into their legitimate businesses. These "racketeer-businessmen" may be seen as respected community leaders. *Indeed, one mafioso described by Sam was selected for an "Outstanding Community Leader" award.* Still others may fall somewhere along the continuum depending on circumstance and stage of the life cycle—for example, tending to become more "businessman" than "criminal" as they age.

Application to American City, Tylersville, and Orchard Grove

In *Confessions,* examples depict the presence of varied forms of Italian organized crime, the considerable variability in organized crime from one locality to another, the dynamic nature of organized crime, and the significance of a particular mafioso or criminal entrepreneur as a hub of criminal activity. Important specifics include the following.

First, organized crime in American City in the 1950s was dominated by Jewish and Italian elements. The Italian element consisted of at least two mafia families, one headquartered in Franklintown and the other in Oceantown, and involved a number of mostly independent Italian operators or networks as well (e.g., the Gucci group). Today, the Jewish influence has tapered off considerably, although several Jewish racketeers—with ties going back to the "old Jewish mob"—continue to be important players in the local rackets.

By the early-1960s, Italian organized crime elements (already major players in the 1950s) increasingly dominated the rackets in American City. Their influence remained strong well into the 1990s. Key Italian racketeers (e.g., Angelo, Louie, Phil, Nicky) had strong ties with cosa nostra groups (e.g., in Oceantown) but also operated independently in many endeavors. Other Italian racketeers operated largely independent of cosa nostra but dealt with them on a guarded quid pro quo basis—and these types of racketeers became more predominant into the 1990s.

The decline in cosa nostra influence reflects, among other factors, the death or aging of key members and close associates (e.g., Mario, Angelo's father) and the aggressive enforcement against mafia elements not only in American City but also in major localities like Oceantown. That enforcement weakened cosa nostra elements and obstructed efforts to dominate or gain reentry into the local rackets. There is an interesting historical twist here. Whereas in the past the police often stymied competition and protected mafia interests by raiding "outlaw" operations, the aggressive police action aimed at cosa nostra today is opening up racketeering opportunities for other groups (although this may be changing with the switch of many FBI and other law enforcement agents to combating terrorism). Finally, because the two main forms of Italian organized crime overlap so much (and are now at times morphing into an unsettled *in-between* form), it is difficult to currently assess the balance of influence between mafia and Italian but non-mafia elements in American City, as well as to assess the independence of mafiosi and racketeers with historic ties to cosa nostra elements.

Second, by comparison, Tylersville was a one-mob town from the 1950s to the mid-1980s, dominated by two Italian racketeers—at least one of whom, Sammy Terrano, was a "made man." There were some independent racketeers and gambling operatives in Tylersville, but they frequently paid "tribute" to the Terrano group (e.g., by entering into business partnerships with him) or steered their involvement toward illicit activities unrelated to the Terrano organization. Following Terrano's death in the early 1980s, a number of his key lieutenants of Italian descent (e.g., Freddie Amato, Bucky Travis) and a key Middle Eastern associate, Ben Silas, carved up his territory. Although they benefit from a "mafia" reputation and maintain strong linkages with cosa nostra elements (e.g., in Oceantown and Franklintown), these mostly Italian racketeers apparently do not have allegiance to a particular cosa nostra group. In this sense, again, the traditional influence of cosa nostra has been weakened, but the overall influence of Italian organized crime remains considerable.

Ben Silas has longstanding ties to the old Terrano network. His involvement reflects the growing Lebanese (or Middle Eastern) presence in Tylersville and the increasing number of Middle Eastern entrepreneurs involved in a range of local businesses, legitimate as well as quasi-legitimate. There also is evidence of some other groups (Russians, Sicilians, Dominicans) becoming more active in criminal enterprises in Tylersville. There are at least a few "nonethnics" who have been involved for a long time but they are a clear minority.

Third, Italian, non-mafia racketeers have been major players in the rackets of American City and in other localities familiar to Sam both recently and in the past. Their presence and strength depend on the unique history of the specific area, the influence and reach of cosa nostra, and the contacts, resources, size, and reputation of the non-cosa nostra group—particularly its capacity to co-opt the law and corrupt public officials. Italian racketeers who achieve leeway from the law have little to fear from competing crime groups, even cosa nostra. Thus, a key point is that present and future assessments of the American mafia must take into account: (1) not only cosa nostra as traditionally defined, but also the longstanding presence of non-mafia networks dominated by Italian involvement and influence, along with (2) the recent expansion of these non-cosa nostra but mafia-like networks, which may become the dominant form of Italian organized crime in the U.S., if it has not already done so.

Important examples are the Caparella clan in the Orchard Grove area and the Gucci group in American City. Both are Italian kin networks that act independently and operate more or less alongside traditional mafia elements. The Caparella group for decades has been involved in gambling, loansharking, extortion, and fencing stolen goods, as well as a whole range of businesses (e.g., restaurants, nightclubs, vending machines, car dealerships, flea markets) and entrepreneurial activities. The Caparellas also sometimes form criminal partnerships with cosa nostra elements or with other local criminal entrepreneurs. Their relationship to the former has been based on "mutual respect"—occasional joint ventures and reciprocal exchanges of favors, but mostly steering clear of each other. The Caparellas' reputation, influence with law enforcement, and large family size all contribute to their considerable influence and staying power in the Orchard Grove region.

The Gucci family of American City has been involved in gambling, burglary, fencing, bootlegging, and drug trafficking in that city for at least the past several decades. The family includes several brothers, and their sons and relatives. The brothers have been closely associated with Angelo and less closely with other cosa nostra elements. Like the Caparellas, the Gucci brothers operate jointly owned businesses (e.g., vending machine operations, auto repair shops, building supplies), which typically entail partnerships between various family members and their associates. The Gucci group differs from the Caparella clan in catering to cosa nostra operatives and shying away from direct competition with them.

Fourth, *Angelo and Louie reveal similar yet contrasting examples of Italian racketeers.* Both have extensive criminal portfolios, both own or operate several quasi-legitimate businesses, both are brokers or hubs for a great deal of criminal activity, and both have extensive ties with mafia elements and considerable influence with local law enforcement. However, they differ in some key respects. Angelo had stronger ties with local racketeers and cosa nostra elements, locally as well as nationally. Angelo's father, Mario, was a major mafia figure in the region and a close friend of ranking mafiosi in other localities. His father's affiliation provided Angelo with strong cosa nostra ties, but Angelo also had considerable autonomy and essentially ran independent operations. Other relatives of Angelo's have also been involved in organized crime, including both of his sons and several first cousins (e.g., Phil, Joey Page).

In contrast, Louie was a maverick and more independent, even though he had important connections with cosa nostra elements (mainly through his uncle). Louie also was not part of a kin network extensively involved in organized crime, a circumstance that contributed to the "ending" of Louie's crime network following his imprisonment in the 1970s. In contrast, Angelo's operations remain ongoing despite his recent incarceration. While Angelo has been in prison, his sons and cousins have sustained most of his criminal enterprises. With the death of Mario and the weakening of cosa nostra, Angelo and his network have become increasingly independent from cosa nostra in recent years. So, perhaps, Angelo's network is better characterized today as an Italian but non-cosa nostra organized crime network.

Fifth, both American City and Tylersville have been dominated by a local clique whose "members" form coalitions of partners and associates for carrying on moneymaking schemes with each other and with other criminal or quasi-legitimate entrepreneurs. Each clique member or coalition has its own spider web and sponsors its own mixture of ventures, legal and illegal, while also sometimes working together or investing money with other clique members in joint ventures. These varied business activities (legal as well as illegal) are often an important part of the normal economic life of their local areas. Which member or alliance within the clique holds greater sway in each city depends on strategic contacts, particularly those most influential with city or criminal justice officials. Although the coalitions frequently include mafia involvement, members of the clique and their business associates also engage in independent legal and illegal business enterprises.

Sixth, independent but accommodative relationships existed between professional criminals (e.g., "good thieves") and organized crime elements. Many professional criminals had friendship or associational ties with members of the local clique, with whom they sometimes formed partnerships for specific illegal ventures. However, the professional criminals in large part operated independently. When Sam and Jesse's burglary partnership was in full bloom, for example, they stole and sold the merchandise without interference from, or participation with, the mafia or local syndicate. Nevertheless, they occasionally received "tips" (inside information about the burglary target) from local mafiosi, fenced stolen goods through them, and so forth. After Sam became a large-scale dealer in stolen goods, he "massaged" local mafiosi and some clique members by being a "big spender" at gambling events, offering them stolen merchandise at breakeven prices, and so forth. These can be construed loosely as "tribute," but in another sense they are a quid pro quo for the contacts and other services that Sam derived from his association with the clique.

Seven, American City contrasts with Oceantown, where cosa nostra power and influence remains strong. For example, Sam noted that the mafia still dominated Oceantown's shipping docks and airports. This contrast may represent a difference between the large urban centers that are the central location or "headquarters" for the mafia families and the more distant cities, where overseeing and controlling "mafia" members or associates is difficult, and has evaporated or become more tenuous over time.

Finally, from Sam's description, there seems to be a loose network of Italian and non-Italian racketeers and quasi-legitimate entrepreneurs in American City, Orchard Grove, and Tylersville who make up a kind of *umwelt,* or life-world. (See Adler 1993 for discussion of "unwelt.") This network seems to form an underbelly to the organized crime world. These men are involved either part-time or full-time in illicit activities. Sam could name two hundred or more people, many of whom were on the fringes of the local clique, who fairly regularly were involved in crime, vice, or illicit business activities and scams. Many of these men were Italian. Some were small businessmen (e.g., owners of stores, restaurants, motels, bars, nightclubs, private clubs, notary office, check cashing, food services, cleaning business, secondhand shops, laundries, plumbing business, auto shops, trucking, real estate). Some worked at conventional regular jobs, some freelanced at a variety of jobs. Others were employed mainly as providers or facilitators of illegal goods and services, such as the sex trade, drug distribution, or gambling. Notably, this umwelt also included some corrupt police and public officials. These individuals would "show up" and "hang around" at Sam's shop, at Phil's used-car place, at card or dice games, or at certain nightspots. In such places, they would cross paths with others who are part of this loose organized crime underbelly or umwelt.

Reasons for Mafia Success and Durability

Confessions suggests why some crime networks or locally based syndicates succeed and survive for a lengthy period of time. The success and durability of the Italians or cosa nostra elements is based on no single factor, but on a blend of features.

Superior Financial Resources

Significant upfront or quickly acquired financial capital is often needed to start up and bankroll criminal ventures or a significant criminal enterprise. Cosa nostra or Italian organized-crime figures themselves tend to be investment-oriented businessmen who run financially solvent operations. Italian-

American and cosa nostra criminal networks enjoy economies of scale that come from the typically greater size of their enterprises and from the multiple social networks in which they are embedded. For example, they can share legal services, financial and tax advice, credit, office space, communication facilities, and rank-and-file staffing. Also, reduced overhead costs also may derive from a more disciplined workforce and enhanced quality control that inhere in a mafia organization or network (see below).

Recruitment and Leadership Succession

Cosa nostra and other Italian syndicate members have extensive access to social networks for recruiting both rank-and-file operatives and leadership personnel. These networks involve extensive contacts with the larger community as well as access to their own kin networks (which typically supply core, inner-circle operatives). These networks provide a large pool of people for staffing, partnering, and leadership succession. Network members also have the financial capital or money to buy human capital—not only rank-and-file operatives but also support persons like accountants, lawyers, and financial advisors.

Enforceable Trust and Quality Control

Running a criminal enterprise, especially a good-sized one, relies on trust and accountability. The basis of the trust may not necessarily entail faith in the integrity and rectitude of others, but may rest as much or more on the conviction that others would not dare to violate understandings for very practical reasons, such as loss of reputation or retaliation (i.e., "enforceable" trust). As Albert Cohen (1966:5) observed long ago, successful business enterprise—whether legal or illegal—depends on effective organization and cooperation, which, in turn, depend on trust and accountability.

Mafiosi, since they benefit from the *mafia* reputation for violence and organizational power (and also kinship obligations), also benefit from a milieu of enforceable trust. This trust contributes to *quality control* by curtailing cheating or snitching by associates, by enforcing norms for fair dealings among the involved parties, and by discouraging rival operations. These together reduce costs for the enterprise, while also fostering and sustaining a reputation as "someone good to do business with." It is more difficult for individual independent criminal entrepreneurs to do this.

Also, *intimidation* or the threat of strong-arm methods as a key element of enforced trust better enables mafia-associated enterprises to fend off competition in the sense that (1) competitors shy away from expanding into a territory where mob-connected operations exist, and (2) rival operations already established in a territory are less likely to contest when a mob-connected operation expands into another's territory.

However, while it remains an important mafia resource, intimidation is largely implicit and its significance easily exaggerated. On balance, mafia resiliency seems to have more to do with organizational and business skill and resource-rich networks than intimidation. Moreover, Chubb's (1989) description of mafia organizations as "vendors of trust" is applicable here in the sense that the underworld seems to need institutions of enforceable trust to uphold conventions and standard practices, in a manner at least somewhat like the upperworld of business. Mafia groups seem to provide such enforceable trust.

Cultural Equipment and Know-How

Criminal entrepreneurs of Italian heritage operate within a set of subcultural traditions and cultural capital that advantage them as providers of illegal goods and services. Although Italians may have been one in a succession of immigrant groups to become involved in organized crime in the United States, Italian-American organized crime (of which Cosa Nostra is the archetype) has achieved broader dominance over a wider range of criminal activities than that of any other ethnic group, and for a longer period of time (see Schatzberg and Kelley 1996). Organized crime groups of Italian or Sicilian heritage have centuries of cultural traditions, knowledge, and organizational templates, and cognitive schema to draw on for organizing and running criminal enterprises. This cultural body of knowledge runs from the centuries-old Mafia, Camorra, and N'drangeta groups in Italy and Sicily, through pre-cosa nostra groups such as the Black Hand in the 19th Century US, up to the present day cosa nostra.

In other words, Italian criminal entrepreneurs tend to have the know-how for organizing and sustaining illegal enterprise, an ability to make contacts and form patron-client relationships, favorable attitudes toward "bending the law," and a greater tolerance for vices such as gambling. All this likely enables Italian mafia and non-mafia criminal entrepreneurs to more ably exploit criminal and quasi-legitimate opportunities than groups lacking such a cultural toolkit. For example, a mafia associate interviewed by Steffensmeier describes the cultural affinity for gambling enterprises: "The Italians will always have the gambling. They have so damn many to step in if one retires or is sent away [imprisoned]. They grow up with it. It's second nature; like wine or pasta. They have all the pieces in place. It's like their birthright."

Durability Begets Durability

Finally, we note that durability and longevity themselves foster more of the same. Organized crime groups that have been around a long time become a fixture, an institution in the underworld. As Sam observes, cosa nostra and mafia-like groups have been around so long and have dominated the criminal enterprise field for so long, that it is hard for anyone else to break in and challenge them.

Implications for Understanding Mafia-Style Crime Networks

The nature of organized crime and its forms have been topics of considerable debate within law enforcement and among scholars. At one end of the spectrum, organized crime is described in terms of large hierarchical organizations structured rather like traditional corporations. The prototype of this model of organized crime is the Italian mafia or La Cosa Nostra—a national network that, according to some writers, is the foundation of organized crime in this country. At the other end, organized crime is described in terms of small, fluid networks that are rather amorphous in structure and characterized by considerable opportunism.

These tend to be erroneous dichotomies, however. First, combined with other recent evidence, we have learned from *Confessions* that organized crime exists but has forms other than the mafia or cosa nostra. Second, cosa nostra may be less structured and organized than it is often portrayed. Third, cosa nostra is a key part but not the sum or total of Italian-based organized crime. In fact, Italian but non-mafia groups may likely become the dominant face of Italian organized crime in America, if they have not done so already. Fourth, perhaps the most significant dimension of organized crime is local racketeering syndicates—long-standing collusion involving a local clique or network of illicit entrepreneurs, professional criminals, and corrupt officials to dominate or monopolize the local rackets. Cosa nostra or Italian gangsters are frequently key players in these local syndicates, but individuals from other ethnic backgrounds also participate. Fifth, the three main models of organized crime— hierarchical, syndicated patron–client network, and enterprise models—are better seen as complementing one another.

Three additional implications derive from our discussion of organized crime and the underworld both here and in Chapter 13. The first is a call for a new perspective on criminal enterprise that articulates the significance of *a group's cultural equipment* in carrying out ongoing criminal enterprises, including the role of ethnicity in criminal enterprise. Ethnic culture seems to matter, and in ways that go beyond limited opportunities for social mobility in the legitimate arena. Sociocultural characteristics of ethnic subgroups define the manner in which they respond to consumer demand, with some groups better endowed for syndicated illegal enterprise than other groups. Illegal industries like gambling, upper-level drug distribution, large-scale fencing, and racketeering require resources, and those with more resources are more likely to succeed in organized crime. As with legitimate entrepreneurship, different ethnic groups have different cultural schemas, organizing templates, and stocks of knowledge that may advantage or disadvantage them in different illegal industries.

The second implication is the usefulness of the patron–client framework (which has gained prominence in discussions of mafia-style organized crime) for characterizing *collaboration among offenders* in other illegal-business settings or long-term criminal ventures. First, in a fashion similar to mafiosi, criminal entrepreneurs like Sam often act as patrons or "catalysts" for other crime participants for both short-term and long-term criminal ventures. Second, operators like Sam can be a patron to crime participants in some ventures, and be a client in other transactions. In this sense, the patron–client framework is a useful conceptual tool for understanding not only networking among offenders and but also how one may shift roles—from being a patron or a client, an organizer or an accomplice, etc., from one circumstance to another.

Last, a fully developed perspective on illegal enterprise will also need to distinguish between lesser and more organized forms of illegality, and the amounts and types of criminal and conventional social capital needed for each. For example, it appears plausible that criminals pursuing less organized or street-level forms of illegal enterprise will need less business-oriented social capital, but more criminal capital (e.g., conning ability, "larceny sense," ingenuity, violence). On the other hand, entrepreneurs involved in illegalities that entail greater organization and longevity will have to rely more heavily on more conventional business-oriented cultural and social capital.

Also, it may be that a lack of resources and legitimate employment opportunities are among the causes leading to involvement in organized crime (defined loosely) only at the low levels of its stratification. However, a similar etiology may not explain criminal entrepreneurs at or near the top of the organized-crime status system [see Ruggiero (2000) for a similar conclusion]. Their involvement and activities may instead be explained through the availability of resources, access to markets, and entrepreneurial wherewithal. Sociocultural characteristics, then, may affect the manner in which provider groups respond to lucrative business opportunities whether the industry is legal or illegal, but perhaps even more so in the illegal realm.

We turn now to Sam's account of mafia-style organized crime as he experienced it in the varied settings where his criminal career unfolded.

16

Sam's Narrative

Racketeering, Organized Crime, and the Mafia

It ain't like you see in the movies or read in the papers. There ain't one boss or one family or one guy telling the others what to do. Different ones each have different pieces. They more work together, do each other favors, and have understandings about who is doing what. But try to outdo each other, too. If there is an opening, the one guy or the one clique might try to move in on the other. Can be hard feelings but mostly they get along.

In the public's eye, yes—they will think the mafia is involved. In the cops'eye, many times too. No doubt they [mafia] do have their fingers in a lot of things, but many times it is very hard to sort out, who is doing what, who are the main ones. A lot of the main ones were Italian, at least the ones I knew of. But there also were some Jewish guys and Polish or German or Greek or whatever. Guys more or less like me. But still the Italians would be longest list.[1]

The Italians are connected to one another and also to people like myself. Have a spider web with each other and then have other spider webs with ones like me. Whether the Italians are the same as the mafia, I can't say. It is more they have ties going back to ones who were mafia. Guys like Phil and Amato and the Guccis still have the connections but they're not as tight as before, as when Mario and Nicky were the main ones. It is more that the spider webs are still in place and the name is still there.

Not sure I ever heard someone say, hey, that guy is "made" or he's a "wiseguy." Think I heard that from you. Just hear people say he's "in" or he's "really in"; or will hear, "He is connected all the way," or "He is connected but not all the way." If he is connected and high up, then may hear, "He's a main one," or "He's a top guy."

Mafia in and Around American City

When I first got to American City, the gambling, the prostitution, the boot-legging, the fencing, the paying off of the cops, the different scams where there's a kickback—was more or less split between the Italians and a couple of Jewish guys. Not the little shit but the bigger stuff. What you call the rackets.

The Italians were pushing on the main Jewish guy. But he was holding his own. Stayed on top on account he had the cops, the mayor, the city council—all in his pocket. Get in his way or cut into his territory, the cops would bust you. Was himself connected to the mafia in Oceantown. That was his muscle. Is paying them a piece. Like any big card game, the mafia gets a cut. Was an accommodation 'cause some of the local Italians are also connected to the mafia in Oceantown, which is playing both sides

Then the Jewish guy gets popped for the bootlegging and the prostitution. By the feds. Did a short bit in the penitentiary and with the feds watching, he was losing his grip. Was a rumor he had a heart attack, is in bad health. This was an opening for the Italians who already were knocking on the door. Italians pretty much took over, especially the gambling—the big poker games, the bookmaking. Not all the way 'cause it ain't that this person or that group takes over everything.

A couple of Jewish bookies have stayed big—like the Feldmans, who are related to the main Jewish guy. Held on to part of his operation. But the Feldmans don't buck the Italians, don't overstep their bounds. Really, they work together 'cause the Feldmans have the knowledge as far as the bookmaking and are known to pay [those who win on bets waged]. Have a lotta contacts with the police and different judges, too.

In a way there is still a "Jewish mafia," if you wanna call it that. Will find them in the gambling and the fencing, and will find different Jewish businessmen and lawyers who stay in the background but still pull a lotta strings. Work with the Italians but know the Italians can get rough. Push comes to shove or the Italians want a piece of the action, the Jewish guys will cave in.

The main Italians [when I first got to American City] were Nicky Moretti and Mario, Angelo's old man. Gus was big. Owned several restaurants and nightspots in the area, but had a piece of other businesses that were involved in construction and that. Was an operator as far as land deals and getting local contracts from the city or the government. Stayed more behind the scenes, so to the ordinary joe blow he was mostly legit. You could usually find Mario at this little sandwich and ice cream shop, right off the main drag in American City. Was attached to a toy store. If want to say "hello" or have business with Mario, then meet him there. Down the road I had dealings with all of them but more with Mario on account of my connection with Angelo.

Nicky and Mario and Gus were tied up. I can't say if they were "made" as you use that term, but they were thought of as the mafia. Mario was with the mafia in Franklintown, was very tight with the top guy. Nicky and Gus were connected more to Oceantown. See, you can be connected to, do business with, more than one mafia outfit. Both the mafia from Oceantown and the mafia from Franklintown were involved in American City. Would go back and forth as to which one had a bigger pull according to who had the cops, who had the DA, who had the better spider web. Some people in American City were more tied to Oceantown, some more to Franklintown. Do business with both, but cater toward one more than the other.

There are lots of Italians, too, who are into crime but who are not tied to the mafia. May know each other but is no real mafia connection. Except the Italians work together, will scratch each other's back. Are many times related to each other. So and so from this group is married to so and so in that group. It is hard to sort out who is *mafia,* who isn't. Who is crooked and who is just a businessman. Many times they are both, a crook and a businessman.

Take the Presti family. Old man Presti is dead now. English was very broken. This is a very big family. Own a lotta property, lotta businesses in the area. Like Laundromats and pizza places, couple of motels. Are legit but they have their hand in some shady stuff, too. One of the Presti girls is married to Jerry Gucci's son, which is a cousin to Angelo. So, is some connection but not really that much.

This or that one from the Presti group were part of the local clique but not at the center. More on the margins. Are very big politically, like on the school board. So have their hand in who gets a job in the schools or in the county. That's how Jesse got hired by the county to do maintenance 'cause he knew Jimmy, one of the Presti brothers. Called him "Jimmy Low." He was a source of tips for Jesse. Even after Jesse is saying he quit, I'm surmising Jimmy Low is still giving tips to Jesse. You will have to ask Jesse about that.

The Guccis are four brothers and each has sons and son-in-laws involved. Were getting to be good-sized operators when I first hit American City and are still going strong. Are about my age, a little younger. I had a lot of dealings with them. With Jerry and Vinnie mostly, the oldest brothers. Even now I have some dealings but it is very off and on. They have their fingers into different things. Some legit businesses that bring in a decent dollar and are a good cover, too. Have a good-sized lumberyard, home supply place. Have opened a nightclub on the edge of town that is pretty swanky that will cater to the yuppie crowd. Still have the vending machines. Jerry has been messing with the marijuana for a long time. Has been a main one for bringing in the marijuana. Now his one son, Tommy, is involved. Off and on will bring in cocaine but mostly stick with marijuana. Vinnie and Jerry are connected in some ways but aren't really mafia in the same way as Angelo and Phil and Amato are.

"Understandings" and Turf

My first dealings with the Guccis was on cigarettes. I had guys come to me who were clipping trucks for cigarettes. I contacted Jerry. Yeah, he could handle it. Was good money in cigarettes at that time 'cause taxes had shot up. Just have to get around the state tax. Had the vending business with cigarette machines in different places, so could unload them. Whether they had other outlets, I don't know. I dealt with Jerry a few times, then I could tell he was pulling back. I brought it out in the open, "Hey, what the fuck is going on? Do you want the stuff or don't you?" Comes out that Angelo has gotten into the cigarette business and Jerry is leery to buck him. More or less is telling me I should give Angelo the first crack.

Angelo was into vending machines, too, and with his connections to other mafia, he had the outlets to peddle the cigarettes all the way. Had his own operation but was part of a bigger operation, too. How it was done I don't know, but involved having the cigarettes stamped to show the tax was paid and then could sell them to a lot of legit places. Whereas Jerry could only handle so much, Angelo had the spider web to handle whatever cigarettes came his way and his back was covered better. Had an advantage from being connected [to the mafia]. As soon as the cigarette tax shot up—bing, bing, Angelo and the other mafia guys are running an operation that is making an easy dollar. Once Angelo got involved, was an understanding that Jerry would back off. If Jerry stayed at it, then he would keep it small.

Same thing with the liquor. First on, I was taking that to Jerry. Then, when I got in thicker with Angie, I was running the liquor through Angelo. I didn't want to cut Jerry off, but Angie was opening a lot of doors and had the connection with the DA. Jerry understood that. No hard feelings. We stayed tight.

Jerry and Vinnie had a lotta dealings with Angie. In some areas they might compete, like with the vending business, but mostly they each did their own thing or worked together—say, on some of the dope that was being brought in. Jerry and Vinnie would cater somewhat to Angelo, wouldn't buck him or try to take over what Angie had. But Angelo wouldn't push that too far.

No, I didn't talk to Nicky or Mario about the *mafia*. No way. You would not want to get in their face that way. You are just blowing wind up your ass to do something like that. But with Angelo, not that there was much conversation, but different things would come out. I heard a lot from Louie 'cause we palled around, and from Phil. Louie had a loose mouth, liked to puff himself up. Was connected but he wasn't "in" the same way as Nicky or Mario, or Angelo. Now to the ordinary joe blow, Louie was the *"mafia"* maybe even more than Nicky or Angelo. Louie played on that. Wanted to be in the limelight. But if push came to shove, Louie was not that big. Not that he didn't have a lotta connections, 'cause he did—with different ones and in different places. But Louie was not as high up, not as respected.

Phil was a cousin of Angelo. I have stayed in touch with Phil all these years. We will run into each other, at a restaurant or auction. Then, too, I will stop by his auto shop. Even more so than Louie, Phil always knew what was happening in American City. On account of his relatives being involved and because people trusted him, and on account of his own involvement. I would say today Phil is very near the top. Right up there. Very big in the fencing and becoming bigger in the gambling. Him and his sons, Joey and Phil Junior, have picked up the slack from Louie going down and now Angelo being sent away.

This is funny—I would razz Phil about getting himself a bodyguard, now that Angelo is out of the picture and Phil is a main one. See, the top mafia guys pretty much all had a bodyguard. Would come to the card games, bring along a bodyguard. When I first met Angelo, he didn't have a bodyguard. Then he starts showing up with one. Is moving up you might say and his Dad [Mario] is staying more in the background. It got to where you would seldom see Angelo he didn't have a bodyguard. Many times he had two. We just referred to them as "Angelo's boys." Were more than just bodyguards now. Were a go-between for Angelo for different things. Like the fencing—I would contact Angelo, he would have one of his boys meet me to take care of what needed to be done. Were Angelo's muscle, too, if somebody needed to be leaned on. Were toughies. You would not want to mess with them. Contact Angelo and he would have his boys handle it.

Mafia in Tylersville

What I know about the mafia and the local clique in Tylersville is from the past ten years or so, after I moved here. I would hear tidbits when I was in American City but not enough to amount to anything. Same thing in Boonesboro, this or that name would come up but didn't pay much attention. The top guy died about a year after I opened my shop here in Tylersville—Sammy Terrano. Never did meet him. Was high up in the mafia, on the order of Louie Sica [see below]. Had a pretty tight grip on things, especially the gambling and the shylock loans. Didn't hassle the little guys but the bigger stuff, he would want a piece of. After Sammy dies, their operations are split up among different ones that were part of his clique. Amato, Ben Silas, Bucky Travis, Frankie Biviano—those were the main ones. Sammy Terrano was the old school, ran a tight ship. After he was gone, it has become a lot looser. Amato, Bucky, and them work together but more are doing their own thing.

That is the main difference between the two places, in American City you had different ones who were main operators whereas in Tylersville it was mainly the Terrano group. What is happening now, is Tylersville is getting to be more like what American City was when I operated there. You have Italians and some non-Italians, too, who at one time were connected to the mafia but the tie is weaker now. The spider webs are still there, but is harder to tell if it is *mafia*. Have a local clique in Tylersville, same as you do in American City, that each has its fingers into different things. This or that one in the clique in

Tylersville is acquainted with guys in the clique in American City, and have connections with mafia guys in other places.

Is no doubt that Amato and Angelo were acquainted and did business together. Same with Amato and Lenny [see below]. Phil would not let on but it would come out in little ways that, yeah, he had gotten together with this or that one in Tylersville. Each will push to get the edge on the other but are more doing each other favors and have understandings about who is doing what and that each should stay in his own territory. So you will not see Amato or Bucky edging in on American City, same as Phil or Nicky would not be edging in on Tylersville. Would be hard to do anyways on account the local cops in each place is gonna hammer the clique from the other town if there was much butting in.

It has always been looser in American City than in Tylersville. The mafia, the Italians, have a tighter grip in Tylersville. An operator like me, or someone like Puddy who does the bookmaking, it is harder to have a free rein in Tylersville. Not that they are telling you what to do but you have to be more leery of stepping on toes. Are more understandings, of, "Hey, to do that you will need to work with us."

Take the fencing, the local clique was a big help in American City. No doubt. But the clique only helped so much. It is pushing but I am making my own openings to become a main dealer you might say. I don't know how to say it but you would have to be "in" more with the local clique in Tylersville. Couldn't make it on your own as easy, to get the contacts with the police and with the magistrates or to get the local businessmen as an outlet for unloading the warm stuff. In Tylersville, it would be harder to get the really good spider web.

The connections you have in one place can be a help but that don't mean you will have connections in the other place. There is a grapevine but it don't necessarily travel that far. Myself, the connections I had in American City helped a little but did not carry over that much to Tylersville.

Italian but Non-Mafia Racketeers

I don't know what you'd call Jeep and Lenny, are Italian but aren't mafia. Are part of the Caparella crowd. Is a whole bunch of them, cousins, nephews, this or that in-law. Are all related. Go way back, thirty, forty years, even longer. The younger ones like Lenny and Jeep are more taking over but it is their dads and uncles who for many years were the main ones. Different ones are involved in different businesses but they more or less work together. Some businesses are shady, some are mostly legit. If somebody gets busted or can't pull his weight, there is another one to take his place.

The one you hear about the most is Ralph, Jeep's uncle. Is now in his seventies but is still kicking. Has a helluva temper. Is not someone you want to cross. The restaurant that Jeep runs is really owned by Ralph and Jeep's dad. Jeep is a free spirit, likes to gamble and chase women. Does not have a good eye for business. Will buy the dumbest junk at the auctions, thinking it might be an antique or whatever. Then dip into the bar monies to cover his expenses. Then has to deal with Ralph when they go over the books. His uncle would rake him over, which Jeep will complain to me about. Jeep takes it in stride, is easygoing, and knows inside he deserves an earful.

They [Caparellas] are big in the gambling—at one time in slot machines whereas today it is the video poker machines. Lot of shady business stuff. Into real estate, have a trucking outfit, have a couple of junkyards for cars, shit like that. Couple of flea markets and auction places. Own different bars and pinball places. Have the main vending machine and amusement business in the area. If a bar or another place in the area has a poker machine or pool table, it has come from one of their businesses. It was well-known that they would play hardball to make sure of that. Handled a lot of shylock loans, a whole lot, which many times will go with the gambling. As far as fencing [stolen goods], yes, they are pretty big in the fencing, especially Lenny. He has been the main one I have dealt with.

Not mafia, now. But cut from the same cloth. Are some mafia in the area, but stay on good terms. More or less tolerate each other, keep out of each other's way. Will work together too, do favors back and forth. I have been at Jeep's restaurant and a guy will come in for a sandwich or play the poker machines, and he is chatting with Jeep. Jeep might introduce the guy. Then later Jeep tells me, hey, that is so-and-so—"He is real mafia, not me." Jeep would get a kick out of telling me that.

Durability of Italians

In my eye the Italians do have an advantage. They stick together better. The family thing and even just being Italian. The trust is there. That you should patronize one another, help each other out in little ways. One hand is feeding the other. Just have a knack for moving back and forth between the legit and illegit. Look the other way if another Italian guy is a little shady. Big thing is, who is part of the family, who are the relations. Is a trust that comes from that, that you can depend on somebody else to fill in, to help you find a contact or get a job done. This cousin, this in-law, can pull some strings. Is a helluva spider web.

Going to jail doesn't hurt the Italians the same way. Will have different ones to fill the shoes. Will keep things going and keep other ones from horning in. If somebody does horn in, chances are good it will be another Italian. Can see this with the main Jewish guy, how doing time can hurt you. Helped to push him out. Can lose a lotta connections unless you got things in place before you go to the penitentiary, unless you have different ones who will keep the operation going. The Italians were already pushing, now the door is open all the way when he went to jail. Jews more work alone. Have a son or whatever, but not cousins and uncles who can be brought in.

Take myself when I went to the penitentiary [1970s], I had to turn my business over to a couple of friends. It didn't take long, they had fucked it up. Lost everything. If I had been an Angelo or a Jeep or a Jerry Gucci, a cousin or relative could have run my shop, and other ones would have chipped in to make sure it didn't go under. The shop would be there for me when I got out.

The Italians and the mafia will shy toward the background. Say you are a bookie, they will be the layoff and the shylock loan, and back you in other ways. Take Puddie who is about my closest buddy as far as Tylersville goes. Little Italian guy, a bookie pretty much his whole life. We have known each other eight, ten years. Is an early bird like me. Will be driving by my shop, sometimes 5:30 or 6:00 in the morning. If sees my truck, will come in for coffee or will see if I want to go for breakfast. Can talk business or whatever and know it will stay between us.

Puddy isn't mafia, nothing like that, but is connected with Amato and the old Terrano group. Is like a partnership where Puddy runs his own operation but where he gives a percentage to the Terrano people, and they in turn are doing things for him. Say you wanna bet on a football game, go to Puddy. He has a lot of regulars. Puddy does the collecting and the settling up. Does what needs to be done. His wife and family help out, with keeping the books and that. Is bringing his sons into the business. The younger one has a knack for the business but the oldest one is nothing but a fuck-up, which Puddy's eyes are too shut for seeing. If somebody owes money or something comes up, Puddy can go to Amato or the Terrano group to take care of it. Same way, if somebody needs a shylock loan, pass that on to Amato.

Can be almost anyone who will want a shylock loan, but is mostly people who more or less are operating on the shady side. Come up short on cash and don't want the whole world to know what they are into. Like myself when I was into the fencing in big way—it was very unpredictable when the buying would go crazy, then have to go to Angelo or Charlie for a quick dollar. Or say a guy is dealing dope, is a lot of money at stake, and is many times working on credit. Same with guys that gamble heavy, roll the dice when they shouldn't. Then fall too far behind and are betting on the house's money. Or they owe their bookie. That is why at the big card games, there were always mafia guys there in case somebody's money ran low. This or that business guy who is in a pinch, is another group. Especially a guy who runs a tavern or nightspot 'cause that is a business with a shady angle and the guy running the place will know who the shylock guys are. Are maybe into the tavern guy already. There is good money in the shylocking. The ones I've known were all pretty much Italian. If not Italian, then connected to them.

Main thing they have, is the contacts and can be a go-between. And just from doing it so long, from having their operations in place, it is hard to break in if you are somebody new. Have so many people to step in. There is a lot of trust within a family and the relations, to go to bat and do favors for one another. And have the know-how for mixing the legit with the illegit, skate between the two. In many ways are more legit than illegit, can go either ways.

More than anything they have the name. That is why you hear some guys puff themselves up, try to let you think they are in the mafia or that they know somebody in the mafia or they are doing business together. That way people will think you have some backing, that you are someone they can do business with, or that you are someone not to be fucked with. Louie liked to have people think that, wanted it to be known that he was "mafia." As a threat, to scare them. Myself, I wanted to get along with them but still do my thing. Don't step on toes but don't back down either. Is a fine line there. Who is using who? It is more I am helping them, and they are helping me.

You will hear people say, yeah, "He's a top guy" or "He's the main one. But that term is used very loosely, just means he is high up and his word carries a lot of weight. In my eye someone like Sica, Louie Sica, is what is meant by saying so-and-so is a "top guy." No doubt he was high up, a notch or two above a Mario or a Nicky. Came off and on to the Sunday night poker games. Two bodyguards. Was from outside the area. People respected him. Was shrewd like Angelo but had more toughness about him. Just the way he carried himself. If he showed up, he was noticed—put it that way. Was someone Angelo or Phil would go to if they needed a contact. Just have to cut Sica a slice of what was going down or owe him a favor down the road.

Same thing if there was disagreement, Sica has been known to step in and settle it. Was a blow-up between the Guccis and Angelo over the video poker machines. The Guccis got into it first, before Angelo. Have their machines in different places. But Angelo is pushing his way in, is even hitting some of the same tavern people where the Guccis have their machines. Angelo is offering the places a better cut. The Guccis weren't backing down this time. Is getting nasty. Sica stepped in and vouched for the Guccis, that Angelo shouldn't horn in that way—is plenty to go around, so each one should take the other into account. This pisses Angelo and he is running to Phil to complain. But Angelo knows he can't buck Sica on account of Sica's standing and just the understanding, hey, the matter was taken to Sica and this is what he decided.

How it works is, the poker machines come from someone like Angelo or the Guccis. Or from someone like Amato in Tylersville. They own the vending companies. So go to this tavern, this nightspot, this club—"Hey, you can use a couple of poker machines." Then every week a van comes by and empties the machines. So much goes to the tavern guy, so much to the company that owns the machines. Then maybe chisel the tavern guy besides but keep the chiseling small to avoid hard feelings.

The video poker is very big—in Tylersville, in American City, in Boonesboro. Is big in just about any town you go into. It is easy to blow a good dollar, which a lot of guys do. For the ordinary Joe Blow who runs a tavern, having the poker machines in your place can be a big help. Will be extra dollars you are taking in from the machines but also you are bringing in people like me who want to play the machines. Then will have a drink, eat a sandwich, spend money in other ways. I wish I had back just a little of what I've put into those goddamn machines. Is a very good racket.

Sam's Relations with Mafia a "Love-Hate Thing"

I'd say for a lot of operators like myself, it is love-hate thing with the Italians. They don't really hold you back or get in your way but you wanna get along with them. May need a contact or may need a favor done for you. Just looking back, it would hard to remember the different times I went to Louie or Angelo or Phil for a contact. It was always in the back of my mind, say, I didn't have an outlet for stolen property that came my way, I could go to Angelo. Chances are good he would have a contact and you would have confidence in him to handle his end of it.

This [confidence] comes from my doing business with Angelo but in a way, too, because he is known to be *mafia*. Same thing if I wanted to light [burn down] my shop to get the insurance or I wanted somebody leaned on. You would be more likely to go to someone like Angelo. You are figuring they can handle it or will put you touch with someone who can. Even if they say no, you know they will not be snitching to the police.

They [the mafia, the Italians] *respected me and I respected them. I wouldn't buck them but wouldn't back down either. It was mostly one hand helping the other.* I did favors for them and they did favors for me. Helped me out, like for unloading the stolen stuff or with the magistrates. I catered to them in other ways.

Take the gambling. Angelo and Nicky would use my store sometimes. Clear off the second floor, for the big crap or poker games. Would be on a Friday or a Sunday night. Big money. I was to get a 5 percent cut but I really didn't collect. Angie and Nicky both got a cut, and then a cut went to mafia people in Oceantown. This is a favor I done for them. Now they owe me a favor or will give me freer rein to operate.

See, at that time in American City, Angelo is more and more becoming the main one, especially once his man became the district attorney. So now, different ones in the local clique and ones like me will cater more to Angelo. Not all the way but it will tip in that direction. I still did some business with different ones like the Guccis. But I would cater to Angelo. Not take orders now, nothing like that. But more an accommodation. That is why any liquor or cigarettes I would run through Angelo. I wanted to keep that "in" with him, know what I mean?

If push comes to shove, sure, Angelo could probably do me in. But he would think twice before trying. But that is not a consideration. I would not get in Angelo's face. No need to. I wanted to get along with him and different ones, but I wasn't kissing their asses. I wasn't trying to outdo Angelo like I was with Louie. That would be dumb. I would not want to get on the wrong side of Angelo. With Louie, that was not a worry. I could hurt him as much as he could hurt me. Maybe more.

I once had to put a gun to Louie's head. This was way back when Jesse and me were doing the burglaries. We had a small load of copper and instead of running to the foundry guy in Franklintown, we let Louie handle it. Said he could get rid of it and pay us a better price. It is now more than a couple of weeks and Louie is jerking us around, that the copper didn't bring the amount he thought it would. Is wanting to pay us less. Jesse said, "Let's just forget it, not do business with him again." See, Jesse didn't want to deal with Louie in the first place. Didn't like Louie. I told Jesse, fuck that bullshit. I went by Louie's place and put a gun to his fucking head—not literally, but showed it to him and let him know I would use it if I had to. He should get the money to us and the amount we agreed on. Blah, blah. Couple of days later, Louie drops by my shop and drops off the money in an envelope. Just "Hi," and "Good-bye." Then he didn't speak to me for almost a year. Then, I'm at an auction, Louie bought me a cup of coffee and sat down and we chatted. After that, we became pretty tight.

Same with Joey Page, Angelo's cousin. I did not like the man. Thought he was more than he was on account of that connection. Was a bail bondsman at that time but also did some burglaries, truck hijackings, different scams. Mostly horseshit. A little fencing. Would snitch to save his ass if he got jammed up. We'd run into each other on account of we knew a lot of the same people. One day he comes into my shop. I'm in the back working. "Sam," he says, "we should go into business together." Blah, blah, blah. "We should pool what we got." I gave it to him straight, that he can take his fucking ass and get the fuck outta my shop. I could not stand the man—thought he was more than he was, and was leery of him, that he could be a snitch.

Joey is still operating in American City, with his sons who are taking over. Have their fingers in different things. Have gotten pretty heavy into dealing in dope. The backing for that came from Angelo. But the man is an asshole. Now, down the road, we was friendly to each other, but I did not want to be involved with him.

How much ones like Angelo or the Guccis are into the dope peddling, I can't say. Is not something I (ever) messed with and is not something that ones like Angelo would want to discuss. As far as the gambling and the fencing, yeah, you could rap about that. *But you would not want to bring up the dope dealing.* Yet it is very known that the Guccis have been involved with the dope for many years and that Angelo had become a main operator. Not directly but more in the background. Phil would not touch the dope. Was upset with Angelo. Was a tension between them.

Jeep and Lenny, and the Caparella outfit, are involved in the dope business. But more on the edges. Don't really want to be associated with it and don't want it to be known if they are, but is hard to walk away from the money. Are involved with some of the bikers, that I am sure of.

Future of Mafia

If you trace it back, sure, the main ones who are operating has changed some—but a lot of the names are the same. This goes all the way back to when I first hit American City. Even more so, if you just go back to when I left, whew, that is twenty, twenty-two years. If not involved themselves, then their sons or their relatives. Just go down the list. Mario is dead but Angelo was the main one until he got popped a couple of years ago. His one son is pushing to make a name for himself but doesn't have enough heart. Are other relatives who are stepping in. One of Angelo's nephews is operating—has a travel agency, a notary business, does money transfers. Angelo was the money behind that. Now his nephew has it. Phil, whew, he has been at it even longer than me. Has taken over some of Angelo's slack. Phil's two sons are involved. The Feldmans—is the biggest Jewish bookie in American City—their old man was involved going way back to the main Jewish guy. A couple of the cops that I dealt with are still around. Nicky, jeez, he is in his eighties. Stays in the background. But is still the money behind a lot of things. His word still goes a long ways. The Guccis have a bigger slice of the vending business and are bigger in the fencing. The big card games and the big dice games have gone to Nicky and to Phil. Jimmy Low is getting bigger, becoming more open. There is a lotta jockeying going on.

In some ways, there is less of the mafia now. But I don't think the Italian part is less. What I have seen is, one Italian is replaced by another Italian. They still play on that little threat, that little fear—"Yeah, I'm *mafia.*" In Oceantown, yes, the mafia is still going strong. But in places like Tylersville and American City, a lot of the old connections are still there, but it is mostly a local clique that will have quite a few Italians in it.

It is hard to know who is legit and who is really shady. The main operators in Tylersville and American City are legit businessmen, as much as they are illegit. *Go where they can make the most money.* Ones like Charlie would be legit almost all the way, whereas ones like Angelo would fall more toward the illegit side, and then there ones who are in between like Phil. In some areas they might compete, but they mostly do their own thing or work together.

Really, that is the way I operated. *Is the way the underworld and the shady business stuff works. Not one big boss telling others what to do. That is bullshit. But scratching each other's back, doing favors back and forth. Whoever has the most connections can do the most favors. The more favors you can do, the more people you will have in your pocket. The more you will be on top.*

Different ones in the clique had a lotta connections. Will depend on the area and whether it is the gambling, the fencing, the nightspots, the local deals on the shady side, or whatever. Can be a main guy or two, but more so it is spread among different operators, different factions of the clique. And will be changing, not all the way, but back and forth. Who is on a roll, who is pushing the hardest.

But it is hard for a newcomer to break in, hard to get accepted. Until you have a few spokes in the wheel, say, with the local clique, the opportunities won't be there. New guy can break in but will he last? Five years down the road, is he still operating?

Note

1. Sam used the term "mafia" freely and loosely when referring to individuals who had some sort of present or historic ties to cosa nostra groups. He used the term reluctantly in other cases, for example, when assessing current mafia influence or when the term might suggest a "big" or very powerful organization. He also often used the terms "mafia" and "Italian" interchangeably, whereas at other times he clearly distinguished between an individual or group who is "mafia" as compared to others who are "Italian but *not* mafia."

17

Commentary

Ebbs and Flows of Criminal Careers

In previous chapters, we examined the trajectory of Sam Goodman's criminal career in burglary and fencing. In particular, Chapters 11 and 12 centered around the theme of Sam's later, "moonlighting" phase of his criminal career, and discussed the notion of desistance. Sam's offending declined in scale during this later phase, but we described a mix of rewards, investments, and stakes in fencing that, together, help explain why he never desisted completely.

Sam's narrative in Chapter 18 addresses pathways into and out of crime, as well as specialization vs. versatility in criminal offending and careers. Sam's narrative also suggests a pattern of early desistance for "ordinary" property criminals but persistence, with shifts in the type and scale of offending, for a relatively smaller subset of criminal entrepreneurs.

Current treatments of criminal careers have made many useful contributions to our understanding of criminality over the life course. These include improved understanding of types of career trajectories for some kinds of offenders (Blumstein et al. 1986; D'Unger et al. 1998), recognition of both stable criminal propensity and changes in criminality across the life course, better understanding of the careers of street offenders and "bottom-barrel" thieves and hustlers (Jacobs 1999), and to a lesser degree, the careers of mid-level offenders (Shover 1996). But life in general and the world of crime in particular are far more complex and have more "gray areas" than is often recognized in the contemporary literature on criminal careers.

In this commentary, we offer a continuum of ideal types of specialist vs. generalist offenders. Then, we briefly address the rationality of Sam's criminal activity. After that, we further discuss how Sam's experience suggests support for themes from labeling theory, as he describes the effects of labeling and doing time on his opportunity structures, sense of self, attitudes, and behavior. We next address themes of continuity and change in crime across the life course, and detail some lessons Sam's experience and social world teach us about criminal careers and social worlds. We then engage in a critical reading of theories emphasizing developmental damage as the major cause of persistent offending, especially Moffitt's two-path theory of adolescent limited vs. life-course-persistent offenders. We end our commentary with a listing of what we believe are key empirical and conceptual distinctions to be made between money-oriented crimes and criminals.

Generalization vs. Specialization in Offending

Insights from differential association, as well as social learning theory as expanded by Akers, help us to understand dimensions of Sam's narrative that have to do with versatility and specialization in offending. Both versatility and specialization are congruent with, and in fact predicted by, contemporary differential association/social learning theory (which incorporates notions of opportunity). The key factors in producing either versatility or specialization are (1) differential access to messages and opportunities that encourage or discourage either one or (2) differential payoffs across available criminal opportunities. Switching from crime A to crime B tells us less about the kinds of individual offenders that exist (e.g., "amoral," "low self control" or "unstable temperament") than about messages, opportunities, and offender identities (Tremblay and Morselli 2000). Below, we describe some factors that may contribute to offender versatility on one hand, and specialization on the other.

Versatility in crime is often described as evidence for stable individual traits of offenders, such as low self control, developmental deficits, or unstable temperament. However, we can think of four main explanations for criminal versatility besides such individual traits:

1. Some criminal subcultural lifestyles may be conducive to involvement in a variety of offenses, at least for some offenders.
2. Transference of skills and contacts—from one kind of crime or setting to another, especially to related kinds of criminal activities.
3. "Larceny in the heart"—since deviance is defined by conventional standards of behavior, some overlap is expected between general deviance or crime and any particular kind of deviance.
4. Subcultural norms may exist both for and against criminal specialization.

First, the lifestyles of criminal subculture as whole (Jacobs 1999), and specific types of crime in particular, involve access to settings and people involved in other kinds of deviant activities. A kind of contagion effect may occur in which involvement in one type of crime feeds into involvement in another.

This contributes to versatility, or involvement in multiple forms of crime or antisocial behavior. Street criminals in particular are often part of the "partying scene" (Hagan 1991; Jacobs 1999) and come in contact with persons on society's fringe much more than the average person. However, this factor may not be as important a force for versatility among seasoned, skilled offenders like Sam or Jesse. Sam and his ilk tend to be older, to "run with a different crowd," and to be far less involved in the party scene than younger, "ordinary thieves."

Second, some criminal skills and contacts may be transferable from one type of crime to another, which makes a variety of crimes objectively possible, and which encourages versatility. For example, skills and contacts necessary for successful burglary may also be helpful (as they were for Sam) for success in fencing, and the skills and contacts necessary for success in fencing might easily transfer to other kinds of criminal enterprise, such as drug dealing or racketeering.

The subjective acceptability or willingness to offend may also be transferable. For example, "larceny in the heart," or willingness to violate conventional standards in one area (e.g., burglary), sometimes indicates willingness to violate standards in another area (e.g., fencing, rackets). Having the heart for one kind of crime will contribute to the heart for another type of crime, leading to some versatility. Conversely, one can have the heart for one type of crime but lose it, or not have it to begin with for another type of crime, thus leading to specialization. One's rationalizations and neutralizations may also foster specialization. Some may try to maintain their respectability by pointing to even less respectable behaviors, crimes in which they do not engage. Sam repeatedly did this (see Chapter 20), as did Jesse and many of the merchants to whom Sam sold stolen goods.

In addition, people can come to define themselves in terms of specific criminal identities, which is in turn a source of personal commitment to those specific identities. That is, individuals may define themselves in terms of a particular niche in the criminal world, and define themselves in a favorable light in terms of a particular criminal role. For example, one might take pride in being a burglar as opposed, for example, to being (just) a shoplifter. Sam's associates Jesse and Rocky are examples of such specialized identification.

Norms and status evaluations in some underworld subcultures encourage specialization, while in other parts of the underworld they do not. For example, an all-around hustler or jack-of-all-trades offender is an admired status in some underworld circles, as is a member or associate of cosa nostra who is known as and sees himself as an entrepreneur on the prowl to make money any way he can. On the other hand, a specialized skill or role can also yield high status and value in some criminal subcultures. For example, there is the *background operator* (which Sam became to some extent in his later career), who may support or direct a variety of criminal activities. This underworld role is played especially by older offenders who "mature" into the position, at which time being a background operator becomes their specialty.

Mafioso-type criminal entrepreneurs, like Sam's associates Angelo and Louie, fit both the generalist and specialist distinctions to some extent. They may be better characterized as specialists, in order to distinguish them from the jack-of-all-trades or "snatch-and-grab anything" offender that typifies many street and ordinary criminals. That is, Mafioso-types often specialize as background operators in the context of being entrepreneurs on the prowl, to more or less make money any way they can.

Finally, skills and contacts cannot be infinitely stretched, and while a "good thief" or criminal entrepreneur may be involved in a variety of criminal activities, one can probably only be *really good* at one or a few types of crime. Similarly, criminal opportunities are constrained by existing contacts and reputations, and these may channel offenders into one or a few types of offending. These factors can produce specialization.

A central point we draw from *Confessions* is that current discussions often confuse rather than clarify the specialization versus versatility issue, particularly as it was conceptualized by Edwin Sutherland. Sutherland argues that offenders have a line (or main type of crime) for a given period of their careers. He did not argue that this line never changes, that offenders never switch to other kinds of crimes. In view of Sam's narratives, it appears that criminals tend to move from one line or niche to another within the underworld, according to their *tastes, abilities,* and *opportunities.*

Furthermore, many studies and reviews of this issue exist, but they repeatedly rely on only a handful of datasets as the basis for documentation. The issue of versatility vs. specialization is usually examined using arrest statistics, other official statistics, or self-report surveys of criminal activity. Such data are typically limited to juveniles or young adults.

This presents several problems for examining the issue of specialization/versatility, and these problems would create a bias toward finding more versatility than probably exists. First, younger and less experienced offenders are less likely to specialize, as Sutherland clearly recognized. Second, given the lifestyles of many offenders and their elevated risks of detection (e.g., they are under parole surveillance, on police suspect lists), one would expect some crime mixing in the arrest or conviction records of these offenders. This does not mean, however, that such offenders do not have a main kind of crime that is their bread and butter. For example, if a burglar like Sam's associate Bowie were arrested and convicted for an assault or for using cocaine (and perhaps *not* arrested for burglary), *arrest records would indicate that Bowie did not specialize in burglary at all, when in fact it was his main criminal activity.*

Further, one recent analysis concludes that specialization is more common than many criminologists recognize, even among juvenile offenders (Ryan 1998:86–87). Ryan (1998) argues that his and other research finds that offending patterns of youth are more likely to be patterned and specialized than random and versatile. That is, juveniles tend to engage in *primarily* one set of related offenses. For example some specialized in "violent and robbery offenses," others specialized in "burglary and other property offenses," and still others specialized in status offenses (ibid. pp. 86–87).

Examination of criminal careers up close raises several questions. How do offenders mainly make their livelihood or at least earn a decent income from crime, and is their income from one line of crimes or from a variety? If the bulk of one's offending is for a specific crime, or one closely related to it, but one occasionally commits another type of offense, does this indicate specialization or versatility? Jesse committed burglary almost exclusively over his entire lengthy career, but he still might occasionally buy or sell stolen goods, or cheat on his income tax. Was he therefore not a criminal specialist? What about Sam, was he a specialist or a generalist? He was certainly more of a generalist than Jesse or Bowie. But even Sam essentially had two or three closely related lines of criminal activity: burglary, fencing, and occasionally conning and antique fraud.

Further, is versatility in offending defined in terms of a very specific offense, or is it defined more broadly to include nearly specific or closely aligned offenses (e.g., burglary, truck hijackings, maybe even auto theft and breaking into motor vehicles)? In addition, besides patterns of actual offending, specialization also involves self-identification as a burglar, a car thief, a cocaine dealer, etc. This self-identification with a specific criminal role should be treated as much more central to the debate about criminal specialization vs. versatility than it currently is.

Sutherland himself depicts professional thieves as developing a preferred *line of crime* over a period of time. By specialization, Sutherland did not mean that the offender only commits one type of crime over the entire life course, and neither do we.

Below, we propose a continuum of specialization and versatility:

1. *The Complete Specialist:* These offenders specialize in only one line of criminal involvement for a lengthy period of time. The main example from Sam's narratives would be Jesse.

2. *The Medium Specialist:* These offenders have a main line of crime, a type of crime that is their "main thing," though they will engage in other kinds of crime occasionally. Examples include Sam during the peak of his burglary career, or Rocky, who was primarily a burglar but interspersed burglary with drug dealing as a mid-level importer. The older Beck boys also are examples of medium specialists.

3. *The Medium Generalist:* These offenders engage in a variety of crimes as opportunity presents, but consider some crimes "off limits." Examples include the youngest of the Beck boys, and Mickey.

4. *The Complete Generalist:* These offenders engage in virtually any kind of criminal activity. The key example here would be Lemont Dozier.

Complete specialists and complete generalists are probably rare, with most offenders being medium specialists or medium generalists. Such offenders would engage in some variety of crime as opportunity presented itself, but have clear-cut preferences and identities for committing some crimes more than others. In addition, there are "background operators," some of whom specialize and some who do not. For example, Angelo would be a generalist background operator, while Sam was a specialist background operator in the later stages of his career.

This continuum is consistent with Sutherland's earlier statements. Differential association and social learning theories predict both specialization and versatility in crime, along with variations within and between offender groups. Furthermore, we propose that the degree of criminal specialization is strongly correlated with:

1. *Age,* with older offenders tending to specialize more than juveniles or young adults.

2. *Underworld niche or status,* with more professional offenders as well as moonlighters tending to specialize more than the kind of "disorganized" offenders described by John Irwin (1970).

3. *Category of crime,* with more specialization among those who commit money-oriented crimes than for other types of crime. Many offenders are willing to commit almost any kind of money-oriented crime, but other crimes (e.g., sex offenses, etc.) might be off limits.

4. *Race and ethnicity.* For example, white thieves seem to specialize more than black thieves.

In addition, we note that some offenders specialize as being background operators. These background operators, in turn, may be generalists, operating behind the scenes of many different kinds of criminal enterprises, or specialists who focus on only one or a few related kinds of criminal enterprise.

The Rationality of Sam's Offending

We agree with Akers (1998) that rational choice and social exchange theories are consistent with and actually are a component of the more general theory of differential association/social learning. Criminal behavior is committed in expectation of results anticipated and valued by offenders (excitement, money, possessions, power, admiration of peers, the defense of interests). Sam's offending certainly exhibits this kind of instrumental rationality throughout his career. In fact, some kinds of criminal decision-making, like that of Sam Goodman, resemble the kind of rational "strategic analysis" described by Cusson's (1983) discussion of decision-making.

As we argue in the Chapters 11 and 19, offenders like Sam likely continue in crime (even as moonlighters later in life) because they judge it to be rational. In fact, an individual's assessment of his/her structural and personal commitments presupposes at least a basic rationality in decision-making (though not necessarily instrumental rationality). As with most realms of human behavior, this kind of rationality is bounded (March and Simon 1958) by limitations such as lack of information, errors in judgment, and availability of attainable options *as well as* nonrational factors such as personal preferences and moral limitations (e.g., there were activities that Sam refused to engage in, like drug dealing, because of his moral qualms about them, no matter how profitable they were or how available the opportunities were).

For Sam, the opportunities were plentiful, the risks were manageable, the rewards were attractive (e.g., money, excitement, pride in his skill), and the criminal behavior was a part of his sense of self. At the height of his career, Sam (and many of his co-offenders) believed he would gain an attractive income from crime, would not get caught, would not serve much prison time if he got caught (e.g., because his business employs workers who provide economic support to their families), and he was not afraid to serve time because life in prison, while unpleasant, was not threatening to him.

We also reiterate our previous arguments that opportunity is often key for understanding criminal careers and desistance—many offenders may be "driven out" of crime by a lack of attractive opportunities. Alternatively, lack of opportunities for one kind of crime may drive offenders out of that crime into another kind, where pastures look greener. After all, it is hardly remarkable that criminals—like conventional workers—might reach a point in their lives when they seek less arduous careers, choose to move on to less demanding activities, and seek opportunities in related fields (e.g., switching from burglary to fencing, like Sam Goodman did).

Effects of "Doing Time" and Labeling

It is something of a moot point whether "labeling" and the imputation of self-characteristics (e.g., "I'm a thief") initiates or causes criminal acts or the furtherance of a criminal career. Our focus is more on the effects of labeling and official sanctioning on self-definitions, attitudes, and participation in conventional society, and less on the issue of whether labeling in itself causes crime or chronic offending (see Lemert 1972:81).

On the one hand, prison was far from a pleasant experience for Sam, and it was not one he really wanted to repeat. The prospect of returning to prison caused Sam significant concern in his later years in at least three ways. First, prison or "doing time" is part of how the criminal justice system "wears down" offenders, as Shover (1983) aptly describes. Sam simply grew tired of the hassles and hardships that another long stint in prison would bring. Relatedly, well into middle age, Sam did not want his remaining physical capabilities (crime-related and otherwise) to be wasted as he languished in prison. Third, repeatedly getting caught and sent to prison can lead to a "loser" reputation in the underworld, to a loss of prospective partners or accomplices, and to an overall rejection by the criminal community—especially its better elements. One would then have restricted opportunities for pursuing safe and profitable criminal activities as a result.

In several ways, Sam's prison experiences fostered increased sources of commitment to crime (especially structural and personal), for example, by increasing his criminal capital. First, Sam described prison as a "school for crime." Sam's narrative in Chapter 4 and elsewhere described the many skills he learned from "good thieves" while in prison, such as safecracking, planning jobs, avoiding detection, and how to treat crime as a business. He also developed less tangible skills from his interactions in prison, such as a sharpened larceny sense, and how to read and "size up" others involved in crime. Second and equally important were the criminal contacts Sam made in prison, which led to snowballing criminal network contacts once he got out. As Sam said, "the name carries," and his reputation preceded him to American City and, later, Tylersville. Sam's extensive network of criminal ties would probably not have developed, at least not as easily and elaborately, without his prison reputation and experience.

Third, Sam's prison experiences (and his learning of the inmate code) reinforced norms operative in both street and thief subcultures. For example, prison reinforced to Sam several lessons. These included that one must take care of oneself and stand up for oneself, one must grab whatever one can, however one can, and one must settle differences with others without recourse to outside authorities. Prison also reinforced and expanded upon Sam's understanding of the underworld and its pecking order.

Fourth, it is well known that punitive social reactions to crime can erode offenders' stakes in conformity (Lemert 1951; Braithwaite 1989). Going to prison has negative effects on later conventional employment opportunities and other conventional roles, and these negative effects can add up to a significant cumulative disadvantage in the conventional world (Sampson and Laub 1997). As Sam says at one point, "I did my time but I'm still paying." Furthermore, after one has been sent to prison once, the concerns about the disapproval of family and friends are diminished. Having "done time" damages one's conventional reputation and status. Once this damage is done, there is less to fret about in terms of additional stigma.

Fifth, once people have already done serious prison time, they tend to no longer fear prison the way a first-timer would [see Jones and Schmid's (2000) very fine study of the social, psychological, and emotional changes that follow from a period of imprisonment]. This is clearly evident from Sam. Sam did not like prison, and did not want to return, but he knew that he could manage it both physically and psychologically. In other words, after several bouts of juvenile and adult imprisonment, Sam had learned, in his words, "how to do easy time." In fact, the correctional literature tells us that some not only learn *not* to fear prison but find their "niche" in prison and are more comfortable there than on the outside.

Finally, repeated, negative social reaction to deviance tends to be accompanied by a change in view of society and of legal authorities (see Lemert 1972; Sherman 1993; Ulmer 1994), and this certainly was true of Sam. Sam's experience in and out of prison taught him to see most police as corrupt, and most people as willing to take an edge ("Most people have larceny in their heart"). Sam developed a thorough sense of cynicism toward the criminal justice system and what he perceived as its injustice, unfairness, and inconsistency. Relatedly, even though Sam took pride in his skill and status as a criminal, he was also quite aware of his marginality and his estrangement from the larger society. For example, Sam only truly felt comfortable with other ex-cons, often felt quite lonely, and was only really close to a handful of people in his life.

Clearly, a variety of opportunity structures and social learning processes, as well as personality factors, produced Sam's criminality. However, it is equally clear that, in Sam's case, there are several ways in which formal and informal social reaction to his offending entrenched his commitments to crime, his interpersonal involvements with other criminals, and thus his criminal capital.

Lessons for Understanding Criminal
Offending Across the Life Course

We sketch here some cautious implications of *Confessions* for evaluating current developments in the study of criminal careers and crime across the life course in hopes of encouraging more research and discussion on the topic. We want to emphasize strongly that our commentary here focuses on and mainly applies to careers and life course variation in property crimes and crimes of economic gain. Careers and life course variation in violence, aggression, or other antisocial behaviors are likely different from crimes of economic gain, but prior literature often entangles them together in a way that we feel is unwarranted (e.g., Delisi 2003; Wilson and Herrnstein 1985; Gottfredson and Hirshi 1990; Moffitt 1997). The lessons we draw below from *Confessions* about criminal careers and the life course may or may not apply to violence or antisocial behavior not oriented toward material gain.

We find that much in *Confessions* supports some prior ethnographic research, such as Shover's (1996) studies of the ebbs and flows of property criminals' careers, or Irwin's (1970) discussion of "disorganized" and "organized" offender types. However, we find that lessons from *Confessions* clash with other depictions of criminal careers, such as those of Moffitt, who emphasize individual maladjustment and neuropsychological deficits as responsible for crime and its variation across the life course.

Stability and Change in Criminality over the Life Course

The common element among life course models is to explain similarities, differences, and changes in criminal behavior at different ages, stages of development, or periods of life. We agree with Akers and Sellers's (2004:285) assessment that life course criminology is not a new perspective. That is, it has not introduced any new explanatory variables, nor has it produced a new general theory of crime. Rather, it represents ways of pulling in concepts and ideas from existing theories at different ages or stages of life. In the sense noted above, Sutherland's differential association theory is a life course perspective, especially when combined with Akers's social learning theory.

Stability in criminal propensity and change in criminality over the life course are both empirically possible (Akers 1998). On one hand, delinquent behavior developed in early childhood may persist throughout life (Sutherland 1947:7). In other words, exposure to criminal influences in early life can have a long-lasting influence on behavior. Also, exposure to criminal influences over prolonged periods of time has a greater effect on behavior than exposure over more limited periods. Both of these patterns, especially the latter, can be seen in the life of Sam Goodman.

On the other hand, criminal careers empirically exhibit both consistency and change, as well as key turning points. As abundant literature shows (see the review in Ulmer and Spencer 1999), many pathways exist into and out of crime across the life course, and criminal propensity is not inherently stable over time. Some of the themes from Sam's narrative suggest that much change in criminal careers stems from variations over time in differential association processes and in access to attractive criminal opportunities and networks. Furthermore, labeling processes can heavily influence deviant career trajectories, as can luck, and situational and other factors. In addition, the original causes of behavior may not be the same as the later causes that sustain or entrench criminal behavior. There is considerable ebb and flow in (most) criminal careers as offenders adjust to shifts in *tastes, abilities,* and *opportunities.* Furthermore, these shifts are often age-related.

Broadening the Focus of Criminal Careers Research

Sam's narratives suggest a broadening of the focus of criminal careers research. Sophisticated quantitative studies of variations in criminal career trajectories like that by D'Unger et al. (1998), well-done and informative ethnographies like Jacobs' work (1999), and overviews of the literature like that by Benson (2002) are valuable, but tend to focus on lower-level or lower status street offenders (Shover's [1996; 1983] work is something of an exception to this tendency). This focus ignores empirical material on offenders like Sam, including chronic and serious offenders, whose careers, networks, opportunities, and commitment to crime as a way of life are probably quite different than those of the ordinary, "bottom of the barrel" street offenders that are the focus of most criminology.

In addition to *The Fence,* studies by Adler and Adler (1983, 1993), Bryant (1974), Letkemann (1973), Prus and Sharper (1977), Klockars (1974), Miller (1978), Ulmer (1994), and Conklin (1994) depart from the usual focus on bottom-level street offenders. In addition, the 1990 Pennsylvania Crime Commission Decade Report on Organized Crime essentially identified and provided mini-case studies of a very sizable number of racketeers, illicit entrepreneurs, professional criminals, moonlighting specialists, and background operators involved in gambling, loansharking, drug-dealing, the sex trade, theft, fencing stolen goods, political corruption, and other illicit scams and hustles. Most had lengthy criminal careers going to back to adolescence or early adulthood, but did not necessarily have much in the way of an official criminal record. Most were between their midforties and midsixties, but some continued to be criminally active and practiced their criminal trades well into their seventies. Similar findings are reported in some analyses of chronic or systematic involvement in lucrative kinds of white-collar criminality (Clinard 1952; Shapiro 1984).

Most criminologists working in the life course tradition ignore almost completely a substantial portion of chronic, serious offenders. These chronic offenders, as reflected in the material from Sam, include white-collar offenders and business merchants, secondhand dealers, professional thieves, racketeers, and corrupt public officials (as well as a variety of "former" thieves and "ordinary joe blow types" who moonlight at crime). By contrast, Sampson and Laub's (1993) reanalysis of Glueck's data is sophisticated and valuable, but limited in scope. The Glueck's data came from very disadvantaged and "cruelly" abused boys who also were mostly "bottom-barrel" street offenders.[1] No matter how sophisticated Sampson and Laub's analysis, it cannot overcome this limitation in skewed sampling, and the resulting problems for generalizability to other kinds of offenders. What is remarkable about their results is the high percentage of these deprived, abused boys who eventually desisted, apparently because of adult social bonds such as marriage and good jobs. However, an alternative explanation is that these men may have been so lacking in criminal skills and sophistication ("losers"), that they owe their desistance to the lack of opportunity to do otherwise (i.e., they were lacking in opportunity for profitable crime or access to networks of reliable or skillful co-offenders).

In any case, the key question we want to raise is whether, or to what extent, findings from contemporary studies of criminal career offending can be generalized to the full population of chronic offenders like Sam Goodman (and a sizable number of his colleagues or co-offenders). To that end, we present some key points from *Confessions* about criminal careers.

Views of Criminals as Developmentally Damaged

According to many prevailing views, criminal careers begin in early childhood, and have distinct beginnings and endings, and that chronic offending (why one begins and persists) is a function of some personal trait or deficit, such as low IQ, impulsive personality, low self-control, or low self-esteem. Criminal careers researchers differ about how much social experiences, events, and life circumstances influence the onset, unfolding, and ending of a criminal career. A chronic offender or career criminal is often said to be characterized by the following:

1. social rejection by (conventional) peers;
2. academic failure;
3. severe neurological deficits (latent individual traits) such as low intelligence, hyperactivity, impulsive personality, and emotional disturbance; and
4. early onset of offending (stealing, physical aggression, lying) beginning at a very early age (e.g., as early as age two and almost always by age eight). In effect, these theories predict that persistent adult offenders seem to nearly always possess early childhood risk factors.

We focus on what has become perhaps the most popular of these developmental views of criminal careers today, the work of Moffitt. We also suggest this perspective's major tenets and their implications may not be fully understood by many criminologists who apparently espouse it. We invite readers to consider the tenets of this developmental theory, and consider whether they agree with those tenets in light of the information we have presented in *Confessions*.

Moffitt's Two-Path Theory

Moffitt's theory draws from concepts in neuropsychology and developmental psychology, as well as from a long history in theoretical criminology (dating back as far as the nineteenth century) that attributes persistent criminality to biological inferiority and inherited deficiencies. Moffitt's theory proposes a taxonomy distinguishing between two types of criminal offenders that represent two distinct causal paths for crime: adolescent-limited and life-course-persistent offenders. Adolescent-limited offenders engage in antisocial or delinquent behavior in their teenage years, desist in their late teens or early adulthood, and probably display no more neuropsychological problems than the overall population. Adolescent-limited offenders are the most numerous type, and most of their misbehavior is due to a "maturity gap" between their adolescent status and desired adult roles and rewards. In addition, adolescent limited offenders may imitate the rebellious or antisocial behavior of life-course-persistent offenders in order to obtain adult rewards (e.g., money, sex, drugs, autonomy) and appear mature in the eyes of peers.

Life-course-persistent offenders represent a relatively small portion of any given birth cohort, but are said to account for a large proportion of antisocial behavior and crime. They display early onset of antisocial behavior due to *neuropsychological deficits* such as low intelligence, negative emotionality, hyperactivity, and/or impulsive personality. That is, life-course-persistent offenders are marked by behavioral problems as children and begin delinquent involvement at an early age because of neuropsychological problems. In interaction with environmental factors, these deficits result in social maladjustment. For example, low intelligence or weak self control causes difficulties in school, which in turn interfere with the development of conventional human and social capital, which in turn produces disadvantage later in life.

In particular, these neurological deficits can combine with family dysfunction to entrench antisocial behavior patterns, including crime. Peer influence for the life-course-persistent offenders is said to be slight, though it may be strong among adolescent-limited offenders. Community-level factors such as poverty and disorder are said to have little direct effect on their behavior.

The notion of adolescent-limited offending is not distinctive to Moffitt's theory. The belief that most delinquents do not continue offending into adulthood has been around as long as criminology itself, and is known as the "maturation effect," or "aging out of crime." Often, the paths to adolescent "misbehavior" involve prodding by or imitation of delinquent peers, or else conflict with parents or school. They do not become career offenders in adulthood. This viewpoint has been around almost as long as criminology itself (see Lemert 1951).

What is distinctive about the theory are these tenets about life-course-persistent, career offenders:

1. Persistent or career offenders "suffer from" neuropsychological deficits, i.e., are *biologically inferior.* That is, something already present at or before birth fundamentally preprograms a developmental sequence toward becoming a life-course persistent offender.

2. Life-course-persistent, career offenders are universally early-onset offenders and manifest multiple behavioral problems as children and later as adults.

3. This and similar stable criminal propensity theories imply a distinctive image of human nature and of criminals. That is, "problem" children are bad, they are bad in many ways, they have always been bad, and they always will be bad.[2] We will return to this point more forcefully in Chapter 19.

This adolescent-limited vs. life-course-persistent distinction is Moffitt's answer to the widely accepted finding that most antisocial children and/or adolescent delinquents do not become antisocial adults or adult criminals. If Moffitt and others who espouse similar stable-criminal-propensity theories are correct, then the most chronic or persistent offenders should manifest the lowest self-control and the greatest neuropsychological deficits.

We note two things in connection with this prediction. First, the evidence for biological and early childhood effects on criminal behavior later in life is relatively weak (see Akers and Sellers 2004:284). According to the broader focus of the life course perspective, it makes sense that this would be the case, as Benson argues:

> Theoretically the assumption that adult behavior can be predicted in early childhood flows against the central premises of the life course approach. The life course approach is based on premises that development is an ongoing process that unfolds over the entire lifespan, and development involves interactions between the individual and the environment. . . . Predicting the life course of an individual based only on factors present at an early age ignores all of the causal factors that come into play later. (2002:14)

Furthermore, careful reviews of the empirical literature question whether childhood "risk factors" explain much variation in either antisocial behavior or crime later in life. Lipsey and Derzen's (1998) review and meta-analysis of thirty-four longitudinal studies of the development of antisocial behavior covering the childhood-adolescent period is especially instructive. The list of risk factors that they found to be *relatively poor predictors* of serious delinquency (all of which are emphasized by developmental damage views in criminology) include: prior problem behavior (other than offending and substance use), development history, medical problems, psychological condition or deficit (including high activity level, impulsiveness, psychopathology), family characteristics (including abusive parents, broken home, parent-child relations in childhood, and family management strategies), and peer rejection.

Instead, the best predictors turn out to be (Lipsey and Derzen 1998; Farrington 2003): prior criminal offending (general offense, substance use); peer influence and parental criminality; structural position or background factors like gender, poverty or low family economic status, and minority status; lifestyle (including substance use); and prosocial values and socialization (i.e., messages unfavorable to violation of law). All theories of crime, of course, posit the significance of prior behavior or criminal history as a fairly strong predictor of future criminality. What is important for our discussion here is that the "good predictors" of criminality listed above are strongly consistent with differential association/social learning and the learning-opportunity-commitment framework that we have outlined in previous chapters.

Second, as we stated earlier, according to the logic of Moffitt's developmental theory, the most chronic, persistent offenders should most manifest neuropsychological deficits and early onset. The material in *Confessions* is incompatible with this prediction. We do not have neurological data on any of the research subjects in this book, but our impressions are that the biographies, behaviors, and social relationships of Sam, Jesse, Rocky, Steelbeams, Bowie, Angelo, and others do not seem to show evidence of neuropsychological deficits or early-onset maladjustment.[3] We find little suggestion of obvious neuropsychological deficits (including "developmental damage") among even the "run of the mill" or mid-level offenders like the Beck brothers, Lemont Dozier, Mickey, Danny Turner, or Andy. And it is glaringly apparent that the most persistent offenders in *Confessions,* like Sam, Jesse, Angelo, Phil, Rocky, Steelbeams, Bowie, Puddy, Woody and others are the least likely to manifest low self-control, neuropsychological deficits, or other maladies like early problems in school or peer rejection.

Our point is not that developmental or other stable criminal propensity theories are completely inaccurate, but that they may be much more limited in scope than they imply. We have no doubt that *some* persistent, long-term offenders accurately fit the picture painted by these theories in terms of neuropsychological deficit, early onset, or low self-control. However, *Confessions* suggests that these perspectives are seriously limited in that they may not apply to a substantial and important set of life-course-persistent offenders.

The Need for A Broader View of the Criminal Landscape

In conclusion, we want to suggest some key empirical and conceptual distinctions between crimes and criminals that will help criminology to better sort through the confusion that surrounds debates about specialization versus versatility in crime, the skill level and loyalty or lack thereof of criminal offenders, and persistence or desistance in crime. These distinctions can serve as guides for theory and analysis aimed at bringing about a fuller understanding of the patterns and dynamics of criminal careers and illegal enterprise. All of these distinctions are found throughout Sam's narratives—they are distinctions he himself made, and they ordered his perception of the many different types of offenders he encountered.

Our focus is on money-oriented crimes, although its application may be relevant for crime more generally. In the real world, of course, gradations and mixtures across our distinctions will often exist. Most real offenders, like real people more generally, just do not fall neatly into uniform patterns. We offer the following six distinctions.

1. Juvenile and adult offending and offenders are quite different. Sam made this distinction repeatedly whenever he talked about thieves, crime, or the underworld. This distinction is an obvious one, but it is often ignored in criminological discussions of versatility versus specialization in offending, skill levels of offenders, degree of planning of offenses, criminal rewards, scope of criminal opportunities, and commitments to crime and/or conventionality.

2. Key differences exist between strictly predatory or more market-oriented or entrepreneurial types of crime. Predatory offenses (e.g., simple robberies) are much less business-like (if they are business-like at all) than market oriented crimes. Also, predatory crimes do not require an offender to build an ongoing network or working environment in which an efficient use of contacts enhances monetary outcomes. Predatory crimes are more likely to be event-based and may often also require the temporary but close, co-present involvement of co-participants.

Market-oriented or enterprise-type crimes are more consistent with business-like environments in that they often are designed around transactional settings and support networks, where co-offenders may participate in ongoing criminal activities or enterprises either directly or indirectly at a distance. These kinds of crimes require some level of interpersonal and business skills (especially on part of central individuals or group leaders).

3. Relatedly, there is a tendency today for criminologists to focus only on the discrete criminal event, rather than recognizing that the event is often part of a sustained involvement or a chain of decisions and circumstances. This discrete event-based focus, however, contains a bias in favor of assessing an offender's actions as being relatively unskilled, impulsive, and as providing only short-term benefits. Instead, we suggest that criminologists more fully locate the criminal event in its trans-situational context, and in its interactional history. A crime may look impulsive, present-oriented, and requiring of little skill when viewed as a discrete event. However, that same crime might sometimes be part of a larger chain of events where "one thing led to another," and it might be part of an ongoing relationship with criminal associates, and the offender might possess other criminal skills that the present event did not require.

4. Market-oriented crime styles of ghetto blacks and whites appear to differ. Sam's narratives suggest that black ghetto hustling is more "dog eat dog" or "anything goes" compared to white market-oriented crime or hustling. While the exploitation of others is a central feature of much criminal entrepreneurship and hustling more generally, the black ghetto hustler role seems

to involve a more significant lack of reciprocity with other hustlers, and less "playing by the rules" than characterizes the white hustler role (and perhaps of some other race-ethnic groups like Hispanics). Such a distinction is important for understanding, for example, the degree of offender specialization (i.e., ghetto hustlers will tend to have less specialization) or loyalty to an underworld code (ghetto hustlers will tend to show less adherence to such a code).

Other literature also argues that black hustlers or thieves appear to be less tied in their hustling activities to an ideology of loyalty and group norms than to financial incentives and other forms of self-interest (see Malcolm X 1965; Liebow 1967; Anderson 1990; Jacobs 1999). Relevant here is Anderson's (1990) characterization of ghetto crime and social interaction as often involving a constant struggle for respect in which individuals try to gain symbolic status advantages by attacking or challenging or exploiting others. Similarly, Jacobs (1999) describes ghetto hustlers and drug dealers as clever men (and a few women) with few norms and rules. Trust is rare and there is little in the way of collective obligations.

5. As we described at length in Chapters 5 and 13, it is important to distinguish between offenders on the basis of their status in the underworld. The careers, skills, opportunity structures, and commitment portfolios of "doper thieves," "asshole thieves," or "roughhouse thieves," will be quite different from other offenders, such as mid-level to high-level thieves, as well as criminal entrepreneurs.

6. As we mentioned in connection with offender specialization versus generality, it is important to distinguish between upfront offenders versus background operators.

7. As we discussed in Chapter 11, it is important to distinguish between full-time career offenders versus moonlighting career offenders. Moonlighters can be further distinguished on the basis of frequency of involvement and the degree of planning and risk involved. For some, moonlighting at crime is fairly constant and is done on a careful, planned basis. For others it is more sporadic, but still planned and done carefully. For still others it is sporadic and relatively unplanned and risky. Moonlighting can also fluctuate between periods of inactivity and high activity.

Finally, we draw on the material in *Confessions* to suggest the following points for broadening our understanding of criminal careers and the criminal landscape, and as a corrective against the overgeneralization of stable criminal propensity theories like Moffitt's developmental perspective.

Stability in deviant behavior over the life-course is more likely produced by *cumulative commitment processes* stemming from stable social relationships and social contexts than by individual predispositions. Furthermore, we are attracted to Lewontin's (2000) argument that all human behavior is produced by a very large number of weakly determining biological and environmental forces. If this is true, then criminal careers are also a product of multiple influences, none of which are strongly deterministic, and can ebb and flow with the complex interaction of those influences.

Confessions points to different *pathways* and *trajectories* of offending careers (i.e., short- or long-term offending, intermittent or sporadic offending, high- vs. low-rate offending, early vs. later starters). Furthermore, each stage in the life course (childhood, adolescence, young adulthood, middle-age) presents factors that are conducive to or inhibit criminal behavior. Conducive factors include (1) cumulative economic and social disadvantage; (2) the learning of skills and attitudes favorable to crime in general or specific kinds of crime; (3) situational pressures and circumstances due to changes in one's financial situation or social relationships (as Sam says: "When people get in a financial pinch, you'd be surprised at how much larceny they have in their heart"); (4) criminal opportunities, which in turn may shrink, expand, or change across the life course; and (5) finding crime rewarding because it provides money, status, excitement, a sense of accomplishment, and self-satisfaction with one's abilities (including, perhaps, the satisfaction of avoiding detection and punishment).

Factors that inhibit crime or foster desistance include the development of commitments to conventional life, such as marriage, family, children, employment, conventional hobbies, shrinking criminal opportunities, and tiring of the physical, social, and psychological wear and tear of a criminal lifestyle. However, criminal behavior itself, as well as incarceration, can have negative effects on factors that foster desistance, like conventional employment and marriage, and positive effects on factors that encourage persistent offending, like criminal skills, attitudes, and opportunities.

We suspect that desistance owes as much to diminished access to crime networks and lessening attractiveness of crime opportunities as it does to access to legitimate work or family roles. This is a point that seems to be often ignored in discussions of persistence and desistance. Perhaps many offenders who were chronic at one life course stage desist from crime later because they lack decent opportunities for doing otherwise. Furthermore, Sam's narrative suggests that chance or "luck" plays a role in the ebb and flow of crime across the life course. Finally, Sam's material suggests that a lot of vacillation back and forth may occur in criminal careers. Sam's (and others', like Jesse's) offending waxed and waned over the course of decades. Thus, we suspect that, contrary to the picture painted by most of the quantitative criminal careers literature, criminal careers often do not have a clear-cut, definitive beginning or ending (except death). We also suspect that the quantity and normalcy of who qualifies as a "persistent" or "career" offender would be far greater if our knowledge-base better encompassed the criminal landscape.

Each of the factors listed above that are conducive to or unfavorable to crime or desistence from crime, in turn, implicate sources of structural and personal commitment to crime or conformity. Our learning-opportunity-commitment framework, described in Chapters 2, 8, 10 and elsewhere, provides an integrated and more complete way of understanding mechanisms that underlie criminal offending and criminal careers, coupled with a theory of illegal enterprise. Together, the elements of this learning-opportunity-commitment framework recognize the complexity and scope of the criminal landscape and its embeddedness in the fabric of the larger society, including its criminal justice system.

Notes

1. See Jerome Miller's (1991) analysis of the Lyman School during the 1940s and 1950s, the time period when the Glueck subjects were incarcerated as young teenagers. Miller's depiction of extreme physical punishment, psychological intimidation, sadistic discipline, and verbal humiliation experienced by Glueck's subjects is both heart-wrenching and difficult to comprehend. Indeed, the resiliency of many of the subjects (as evidenced by their fairly high rate of eventually exiting from crime/delinquency) in the face of such treatment is somewhat remarkable.
2. By extension, the Moffitt framework implies that persons *without* neuropsychological deficits are basically "good," so that, while some straying from the norms may occur (especially during adolescence), they are more or less destined to avoid chronic antisocial behavior to any serious degree. That is, they are virtually immune from becoming life-course persistent offenders ***regardless*** *of their life history or circumstances.*
3. For Moffitt, the *life course persister* (e.g., a Sam, a Jesse, a Louie, a Rocky) ought to have distinct traits such as cognitive deficits and personality disorder. These offenders have low intelligence, do poorly in school, have fragile mental health, have inadequate social skills, and have inadequate self-control.

18

Sam's Narrative

Pathways Into and Out of Crime

Lying in that hospital bed many times I thought about it, "What happened that I became involved the way I did?" You would ask me that, too. Not just about me, but what about so and so. What has happened to the different people I did business with—not just the thieves but the local clique and the different dealers, and the business people, too. I would keep my eyes open 'cause you wanted to know that.[1]

Criminal Backgrounds and Criminal Lifestyles

In a way I had it rough as a kid but not any rougher than a lot of others, and not near as rough as some. Mainly 'cause my stepfather was an asshole. Buy his own kids a toy or bicycle, but not one for me. I had to get mine hustling or do without. But my grandparents took care of me. Were stingy the way the old Germans were. But what I needed was there for me. Made me toe the line. Get your school work done, do your chores, then go play. If going to a friends' house or ride my bike to the gas station, let them know.

That is different than the Beck boys. Mom and Dad can hardly take care themselves, much less the boys. Just come and go as they please, looking for a place to hang out or get somebody's attention. The dad is a down-on-your-luck guy. Not a bad egg but doesn't have much going for him. Would do odd jobs or isn't working. Their mom worked in a greasy spoon restaurant. I can't say if the Beck boys would go hungry, not so much that, but they had to do without things that kids would normally have. Would hang at my shop to have something to do and to make a buck for doing little chores. Were a nuisance but then I am feeling sorry for them. Could see they had a rough life. If I was at an auction, I would pick up clothes, shoes, pocket knives—"Here, help yourselves but first you have to mop floors." Would always give them a job to do, so they didn't learn to get something for nothing.

I had to go without for some things, but in other ways I was taken care of pretty good. Paper and eraser when I went to school, and a roof over my head. I wasn't free to come and go, and people sort of knew where you're at or what you're up to. After grade school, yeah, then I'm more on my own. Am working and now staying mostly at my mom's house. But just to hang my hat. As far as crime—my first crimes, really, were the gas station break-ins when I'm about sixteen. Did some hustling and pulled kid stuff, but I wasn't stealing from kids at school or going into stores to shoplift. The Beck boys are doing that by the time they were ten or eleven. Whether they ever stole from me I can't say. I would be watchful but was careful not to undo the trust, their feeling that I have faith in them.

Is probably a good thing I wasn't around my stepdad that long. Am seven when my mom married him. No problem until his own kids came along, by the time I am ten or so—an age where you're old enough to remember. Then more and more he is an asshole. But even then I'm staying at my grandparents house a lot more than I'm over at my mom's. Then, after I finished eighth grade, I went to work and hardly ever saw my stepdad. Not that it would matter that much 'cause by now I am full grown and could handle myself pretty well, so he'd be leery of pushing my buttons.

In the public's eye the Beck boys would be the typical criminal. Were raised poor and their parents are fucked up. Then maybe get to hanging with the wrong crowd. With other ones who are into devilment, out for a good time. For quite a few, yes, that is a background for getting into crime. Especially for the walk-in thief and the street criminals. Being poor, having to do without and seeing what other kids have, can leave a bad taste in one's mouth. More likely to be a resentment and will be push to have some larceny in the heart. Then have buddies who will egg each other on.

Same with a lot of the black kids and the Puerto Rican kids. Are poor, so come to learn you have to do what you have to do to get what others have or what you think you need. Have to have your eyes shut not to see that. But it's more than that. See people outside their house selling dope. See their parents using dope. See the doper on the corner. Have an older brother who is mugging people or breaking into cars. Have a sister who is hustling her ass. Are thinking what's to stop me from doing that. See their buddies go to jail and see they got through it, so what the fuck does jail mean? No fear on their part. Then, if get to using dope themselves, is a new ball game as far as getting into crime and becoming a fuck-up is concerned.

Don't know if you'd call it a ghetto but the kids raised in the black areas—what they have been through, what they've been exposed to. Is hard to ignore the hard row they have to hoe. Some of the ones that came in my shop in American City or from seeing them when I'd stop at Mookie's shop in Tylersville, makes you appreciate what you have.

But a lot of criminals don't have that as a background. There's all different upbringings, different paths, not just this thing or that thing. I wouldn't say that most thieves and criminals were bad kids or that it started in childhood. Some did have hard going, like the Beck boys. But other ones, no.

Off and on I have dealt with bikers, guys in the Pagans or whatever. Some are fucked up and come from fucked-up families. But others are ordinary joe blows. One is Diesel. Met him when I bought motorcycles from the Pagans, way back. I'm talking twenty-five years ago. Stole the motorcycles from the another biker group. The main biker I am dealing with brought Diesel along. Wild looking. Tough guy. Was in his twenties back then, so I have known Diesel a long time.

Diesel just fell in with the Pagans. His dad and mom had a hardware store and were wanting Diesel to work there. He should go to a technology college or whatever, to get more training and to take over the business some day. But Diesel is itching to get away. Gets out of high school, goes to work for his uncle, who runs a bar that caters to the working man. Biker guys would drop in, have a sandwich, kill time. Diesel starts messing with them. Would invite Diesel to party with them, let him drive one of their Harleys. Diesel got to liking the excitement, the high that comes from being noticed, all the pussy he was getting. That people fear you, think you're a little crazy. Young guys can get into that and if the good opportunity is there, is hard to walk away. Then later on, Diesel got to liking the money that came from peddling dope. With their branches and all the members the bikers have, is a helluva spider web for peddling dope.

My connection with Diesel came from buying those motorcycles that time, then afterwards I'd buy when he and his buddies would break into a place or maybe hijack a truck. But the state cops were watching the bikers very closely, so I hooked them up with Grasso. But Diesel and me always stayed in touch. He would stop at my shop or I'd bump into him at a auction. Is fun to talk to. Will tell you that he has good parents, that they have always stuck with him. Is a closeness there. Knows he has been an aggravation for them, that they have been through a lot. But is his life. Has to live it his way.

Has more or less packed it in. Is running the hardware store with his dad and is his if he wants it. The dope, the fights, the women Diesel has messed with. His body is a fucking mess. One big tattoo, really—his back, his arms, his legs. Covered with tattoos. Has been in the penitentiary for dealing meth and then for fucking up on parole. Is tired of the hassles, that his body can't keep up with it anymore, but misses the excitement and the money. He would like to be back in it but not all the way. So still does a little clipping on the edges.

This you know from talking to Jesse many times. Is a fluke how he got started with the burglary, after he gets out of the military. Jesse is done with the military, the army, and is loafing. Looking for a job but mostly is killing time. Meets some guys who were into burglary from hanging at the same nightspots. Turns out they are looking for a guy to do the dropoff, so asked Jesse if he would do that. Jesse went along with it and was the dropoff a few times. Meanwhile, Jesse gets to messing around with a woman in this one bar, which is pissing the guy she is with. Is a squabble and Jesse decks the guy. The people that saw can't say for sure, but are saying the guy's head hits the table when he's going down. Head is bloody but seems okay. Then, shit, the guy dies a month later from a concussion. Jesse did only about three years 'cause he had a clean record and in a way it was self-defense. Still, somebody died so he had to do some time.

That's when he meets Whitey, a very good burglar, very good safeman. Big man, very powerful. Very respected. Took Jesse under his wings in the penitentiary 'cause Jesse was a greenie. Then after they get out, teamed up. Whitey taught Jesse how to open safes, taught him the ropes you might say. But Whitey was getting older and slowing down. In his (late) forties, so some jobs he didn't want to do. And Whitey had a long record, was well-known. Was bringing too much attention from the police, who were figuring he was behind many of the safe jobs that were being pulled. Jesse was leery of that, so decided to go his own way. But he and Whitey always stayed close. Drove a delivery truck later on and was a main source of tips for Jesse and me. Whitey was very good people.

Are a bunch of them I've come across who were more or less like a Jesse. Not that they were in the military but, yes, some of them were. Steelbeams for one. And Kevin Foley, the one who broke Rocky in. Come home, are pissing around at nightspots or at a neighborhood bar like Caseys, where some of your better thieves would hang out. Get to know each other and see that someone like Jesse or Steelbeams is solid and maybe has some heart. So, need a dropoff or a lookout, "Hey, you can do this and is a good dollar in it for you, too." For Jesse, no moral qualms on account of all the stealing and rank shit he came across in the military.

I'm not saying the military turns guys into becoming criminals. But guys get out, are at loose ends. Have seen a lot in the military, maybe have been through a lot. Is a code for being solid and that, and is more likely to have the heart for clipping than the ordinary joe blow. So if a crew is shopping for a partner, hey, why not try somebody like Jesse.

This is funny but some of the guys in the after-work burglary went into the military [when Sam was in his early twenties]. See, at that time, if you got busted—as long as it wasn't something like murder or very serious—you could walk by going into the military. Charges would be dropped or pleaded down. From what I hear, these guys did not fall back into burglary or clipping when they got out. Just settled down, became ordinary joe blows. So the military can be a boost or a hindrance as far as crime goes.

Rocky and Kevin were neighbors. Knew each other growing up, except Kevin is five, six years older. Is a smooth talker, a ladies' man. Good head on his shoulders. Outta high school, goes into the military. Ends up being sent to Vietnam. Left a bitter taste in Kevin's mouth that he still gripes about. Comes back and is into partying, smoking pot, having a good time. Then is breaking into places with some guys he is palling with. Is peddling the stuff to Louie and then to me. When I met Kevin he was half-assed but a quick learner. Is peddling drugs back and forth with the crowd he is hanging with, but mostly is sticking to burglary. Kevin would bump into Rocky at a party or nightspot, or see Rocky on the street where they both lived. It was natural for it to come out that Kevin would come to Rocky if he needed a dropoff or an extra man.

Angelo and Louie and Phil grew up with it, you might say. From the time they were teenagers to now, have been involved. Were part of a group of young guys, called themselves the Park Owls. Gucci brothers were in it, too. Lotta break-ins, rough housing, even some holdups, stealing cars, hijacking trucks. Were into the gambling already back then—the small stuff, at the lower end. Were more hands on, more out front when they were young. Then more and more stayed in the background.

Well, Phil was a little different. Wasn't part of the Park Owls but was connected to the mafia through his dad and his uncles. But Phil went his own way. Was older when he got involved. Got married out of high school, to Mary and then worked for her dad. She is a very classy lady. They are still together. Then Phil has a falling out with Mary's dad, says the hell with it. Goes to work for Phil's uncle, who runs a big junk yard and is in the bail bond business. Eventually, Phil took it over. But wasn't doing shady stuff before that. At least not in a big way.

Ones like Kevin and Rocky, and Angelo and Phil, didn't come from backgrounds where you had to fend for yourself. But still, lot of ordinary thieves and a quite a few of your burglars have come from hard backgrounds. Other ones maybe got into dope or partying and running with the wrong crowd. Some don't wanna work or the jobs they can get are horseshit jobs. In their eye, the job is beneath them. Some are just plain assholes—too dumb to work and too dumb to be good at stealing.

Lot of thieves, especially the kids, steal for party money. See things they wanna buy. Steal when they run out of money. Main thing, is how much money is in their pocket. Live day-to-day, don't know where the next paycheck or the next dollar is coming from. Take the younger Beck boys, are partying and using dope, then one thing leads to another. Run out of money but want to keep on partying. Maybe are being pumped up by other ones they're partying with, especially if there is dope or pussy involved. Want to impress their buddies, the women they are with. More or less are going with the flow. So, go out and clip a place or break into a car. Not a helluva lot of thought involved, put it that way.

Getting "high" or "doped up" is a big thing today, especially for the younger thief. But is a lot of drinking, too. In my day, it was mainly just alcohol. More of your thieves and hustlers today are into partying. Paying for that is a big part of their thieving. That, and wanting to puff themselves up with the ladies. If can't get nookie from a regular woman, then hook up with a has-been. A lot of the women the thieves hang with are into partying, too. Are on the edge, peddling dope outta their apartment or peddling their ass—if not this way, then that way. Are easy lays but know how to string the guy on for dope and get him to empty his pockets for them.

Lot of thieves have never gotten used to working at a regular job, where you have to be on time and where you have to listen to some asshole tell you what to do. Even if they work, the jobs they can get won't cover their expenses. May not even cover their living expenses and sure as hell not their partying. And the partying gets in the way of working. So is hard for them to hold a job.

Take Rocky, he isn't lazy. Is a good worker if it is something he wants to do. But doesn't like to punch a clock or take orders. Another thing, if you are clipping a lot, it is hard to be working and punching the clock. Take Jesse and myself, whew, we were hitting something fierce. Spend hours and hours looking for spots to clip and checking out the place. Could not have done that if Jesse worked or I held a regular job. With my shop, I could come and go— have Chubbie or somebody watch the shop for me.

But generally it is better to have a regular job. That way you have money coming in and won't be under the gun to get cash quickly. Is a cover, too, 'cause the cops will be less suspicious. Really, all the way down the line you're more likely to get a break. That is why I always told Rocky, the Beck boys, and different ones—get a job, even a part-time job. Then you'll have some bread and will keep the parole people happy, too. *That, and having a woman. Will think you're settling down and have somebody to get on your case.*

Funny thing is, a lotta thieves look down on guys that work and puff themselves up with their buddies by not having a regular job. Unless they can make good bucks, they won't work and will put down those that do work. Guys will say, hey, pay me twenty-five, fifty dollars an hour and I'll work a regular job. But they is only blowing wind outta their ass 'cause who in the hell will pay them that?

Now if you listen to some of these guys talk, they are bitching—"Who will hire an ex-con?" Is a lot of gray here. More of them can find a legit job then you are led to believe. But still isn't a cakewalk. Take Rocky, when he first got out of the penitentiary, he kept getting turned down. Check the classified for the job ads, but no go. Takes a job as a janitor but the pay is horseshit. Barely enough to live on, sure as hell not enough if you want to party and chase pussy. And was beneath Rocky. In a way he was embarrassed to tell his buddies what he was doing. Would tell them, "Yeah, I have this horseshit job on account it keeps my parole guy off my back."

Are only some jobs an ex-con has a decent shot at. Driving truck or working in a warehouse, jobs like that. Has always been that way but is worse today. *That a person has done time, has a record, is kept better track of today. Are fewer places that will hire an ex-con.* But still there are jobs out there. If not pay enough to cover your expenses, then you are still ahead to take the job and clip on the side. The job can be a cover to give you some leeway and is a backup, another source of bread so you don't have to be clipping when the decent opportunities aren't there. Not that the younger thief will think that way but as guys get older, this is more their mind-set.

Guys get older, then even a loser job is better than not working. Will settle for what they can get and make the best of it. Are tired of the partying and will take the money whichever way it comes. If a legit job brings in more money than the clipping, then pack in the clipping or at least slow it down. Whereas the younger guy is more likely to quit working, stay with the clipping. *Get older, you're past the excitement thing and the palling with your buddies. Have been there, done that. Your mind-set is more on making money, not to get rich but enough to live on and do your own thing.* Maybe clip once in a while but keep it small and wait for the good opportunities.

Depends a lot, an awful lot, on the kind of thief he is. A lotta thieves aren't doing that well, aren't making that much. Have a so-so eye for the clipping and don't have the contacts. They should grab the first decent (legit) job that comes their way. Whereas the better thief can take it or leave it. Will many times have a legit job but keep on clipping when the good opportunity is there. If he is getting too old, say, it is burglary—then pack in doing that but do something else. Like Whitey, he ended up driving a delivery truck, but would still give tips and may even be a dropoff. Or someone like Angelo who more and more operates in the background. Or myself, stop crawling in windows, but more and more just stay with the fencing.

Specialization versus Versatility

If a guy has an eye for clipping for one kind of crime, you have to figure the eye can be there for other crimes. The know-how and being able to spot the openings for doing this or that crime will be a help for doing other crimes. Same as the contacts for doing one crime may help with the other. If you are into burglary, chances are you will know people who are involved in shoplifting or checks or dope or whatever. Will depend on the crime whether your paths will cross.

It is only common sense that if somebody has larceny in the heart for one kind of crime, then the larceny for another crime is more likely to be there.

Break the law one way, more likely to break it another way. Money is money, no matter how you make it.

If the *excitement* is there for doing one kind of crime, have to figure it may be there for doing another crime. Devilment is devilment, especially for the younger guy. Need a little kick once in a while. The burglary did that for me and the fencing, too, 'cause life can be dull as hell sometimes. It'd be the same with *heart*. If you have the heart to clip one way, then more likely to have the heart to clip in other ways, say, compared to the average joe blow. Not all the way now. *Can have the heart for one crime but are chicken for doing other crimes.* Same as you can lose the heart for crime like burglary but can pull other crimes like writing checks or selling dope out of your house.

But that doesn't mean the thief will do any goddamn thing. May break into houses but won't rob old ladies. Same as the store guy who is buying stolen goods from me or cheating Uncle Sam. He is comfortable with that. But couldn't look at himself in the mirror if he was on the other end, the one who is selling the warm stuff or the one doing the breaking into places. Would upset him if you said, "Hey, you're a thief, you're a fence."

Take Woody, he mixed in some fencing with his auction business. But he didn't break into places or rob people or shoplift. Would not want himself or others to think of him that way. Same with someone like Puddy. Has been my good buddy for eight, ten years now. Is a bookie, been doing it a long time. That is what he does, how he sees himself. Comes by my shop pretty near every morning, is there by six or so 'cause he is an early bird like me. If sees my truck parked, will stop in for coffee. Even if I was to ask him, I don't think he would peddle stolen goods and sure as hell wouldn't break into houses or sell dope.

The opportunity has been there, many times now, for me to get into peddling dope. Not on the street, but to be a layer in between for the guys bringing the stuff in. Could not look at myself in the mirror if I was peddling dope, especially if it ends up with kids. I always hated the dope and the dopers. Is a fact that a doper can't be trusted. Will do anything to get the dope, really lower themselves.

There are different sides to whether a thief will specialize or not. Many will want to avoid that 'cause they will know if you are doing anything to make a buck, you will more likely end up in jail. Will depend, can the guy can get the contacts, can he hook up with other guys who are decent, which will limit what kinds of clipping he is doing. Then, are you good at it and how comfortable do you feel. If that falls into place, then this will become your main thing.

Same way if you're a carpenter, you will know something about plumbing and wiring. Will come across guys doing one or the other. Good with your hands in one area, then chances are will be good in another area that it's related to. *Have a mind for one thing, this can be extended into other areas.* The burglary helped me with the fencing and the fencing helped me with the conning. *Is overlap in the legit as in the illegit.*

Take myself. Just messing around on my grandpap's farm, just doing different things. Like fixing up old bicycles or old cars, driving the tractor and different machinery. I had an edge as far as working at a gas station or driving a tractor trailer or, later on, even working with wood and antiques. I think this [farm experiences] gave me an edge even as far as learning about burglary. Of course, you still have to have the nerve for that. Is not something you can learn.

Some thieves are all-around thieves. Will steal in almost any way imaginable. Other thieves will stick to this or that type of theft such as shoplifting or burglary or passing credit cards. In my eye, guys who are into burglary are more likely to specialize than other thieves. Will see themselves as burglars, in a way set themselves off from other thieves. If don't just stick with burglary, then clip in ways that are related like breaking in cars or hijacking trucks or maybe even stealing cars

Some of your students are dealing in drugs, right? Say it is pot for their friends and other students. Will have some of the know-how for dealing in other drugs. Maybe the contacts, too. Are gonna be part of the partying crowd, so can get into other kinds of devilment. But do they have the heart to move into dealing dope all the way? Can they get the contacts? Can they look at themselves in the mirror?

Maybe yes, maybe no. Sure, more so than someone who is naive or the guy who's a nerd—'cause a nerd is a nerd, no matter how you cut it. But many will stop with dealing dope at that level 'cause that is what they know and are comfortable with, and 'cause the opportunity is handed to them and is so easy to do. But very few would have the heart and the contacts to go all the way. Even more so, they would be in a different league if we're talking about getting into burglary, stealing cars, or the fencing. Wouldn't have the know-how and your decent thieves wouldn't clip with them.

I did do a robbery one time (see Chapter 19). With Jesse. Had a tip on this place where a guy lived alone, was stashing his money in a safe. Scouted and scouted but he never left. His sister would bring him groceries and that. So, we put on masks and robbed him. But wanted no part of that again. Stick to breaking into places. If somebody is home, then forget about it.

Myself, I have never shoplifted. I'd be scared or whatever. Just wouldn't be me. Know what I mean? Don't get me wrong, there are some good shoplifters and that, and who are respected. But not the same way as a decent burglar. In a way is a sissy thing, maybe on account so many women are doing it. Really, they have a lock on the shoplifting, are better at it than men. A lotta guys—a Rocky, a Steelbeams, a Bowie, a Jesse—would see it as lowering themselves, as not being what they really are. You might be willing to pass checks or clip in some other ways, but not be willing to sell dope or steal from old ladies. There's a line there the guy won't cross.

The burglars I knew, most of them, would shy away from shoplifting 'cause the chances of being seen and getting caught is higher. Is the same with checks or credit cards, you are seen and your handwriting is right there. With robbery, some burglars will do that if the good opportunity is there, but more shy away from it 'cause you have a witness and 'cause you don't want to hurt someone to get money. And don't want to carry a gun. Is a way to get big time in the penitentiary, too.

It is hard to answer that. *If you mean by "specialize" that someone does the same crime his whole life or even for years and years, then the answer is "no."* Jesse comes close. And Steelbeams and Bowie. *It is more that this becomes your main thing, maybe your only thing. And may involve doing other things that are similar.* Bowie mainly broke into places, is known for safes, but has hijacked a number of trucks along the way—which in a way is like a burglary. Like a load of whiskey one time, that Bowie ran by me and I ran through Angelo.

Doesn't mean you never clip in other ways. Chances are you will have done at least some other crimes, especially if different avenues open up. Theft is theft and hustling is hustling, and one can lead to the other. But is usually a limit there. Jesse was into burglary, that was his thing. But he would not hesitate to cheat Uncle Sam [on taxes] or buy stolen goods if the good opportunity was there. But he wouldn't sell dope or rob people with a gun, or steal from old ladies, or be a baby rapist.

As far as this or that crew, yes, I would say they do stick to a main thing. Say you are all-around thief like a Danny Turner, then are contacted by Rocky and his buddies on account they are short a man or need a backup. Danny would be doing a burglary with them 'cause if those guys are working together, that is what they do. Same way if a couple of guys are passing checks together and brought in Danny for that. Or say it was for bringing in dope. If this or that crew or outfit is involved, they will stick with a particular crime. That would usually be case.

It is natural that you will more and more specialize if you stay in crime. It's like anything else, any kind of a job—legit or illegit. The more you do it, the better at it you get, the more comfortable you feel. Guys will even see themselves that way, as "Hey, I'm a safeman." Or will say, "My thing is breaking into places." You have the contacts, you have an eye for that kind of clipping, so the risks are less. *The more crime becomes a business, the more you won't do every damn thing that comes along.*

Will depend on one's situation. Can happen the opportunity isn't there any longer on account of your contacts have dried up or you're getting too old to pull those kinds of jobs. Or maybe you're getting too known for that kind of clipping on account there is a lot of heat from the police. Then switch to something else or pack it in. *It is more that guys do mainly this type of crime for that part of their life or that they do some types, but not other types.*

Guys like Angelo or Lenny, or Silas the Lebanese guy, are involved in different things but stay in the background. Are bringing the drugs in you might say but aren't peddling to the doper or the street thief, not direct anyway. Mafia guys, or the guys in local clique in American City, have their fingers in lots of things. Have the contacts and the money to go into different things, go where the money is—whether it's legit, strictly shady, or in between. Have limits but are out to make money anyway they can. Same as the street hustler, but each is in a different league and the local clique guy would not stoop as low.

Remember Stu. I get a kick every time I think of this. How you were looking for a motel in American City but there weren't any vacancies on account of the centennial celebration? So, you stopped at this seedy place that Stu runs. He wanted to know how long you wanted the room and you tells him you'd be leaving in the morning or at least by the following day. Then he says, "what— that long?" Turns out Stu's motel is for guys wanting a quick nookie, say, at noontime or whatever—not to stay overnight or for a couple of days. Or, could be a hooker who takes the guy to Stu's place—pays him a rate for an hour or two. This sort of thing is fairly common. Are a lotta guys like Stu who dabble at crime. Maybe have been doing so their whole life. Keep it small and stick to a couple of things you know and are comfortable with.

The ones who will do anything are more the fuck-ups. Are misfits all the way around—not just into crime but are losers in other ways. Not sure I'd even call them criminals. *Give criminals a bad name is what it boils down to* [Sam laughs].

In my eye, a jack of all trades is a master of none. Are putting yourself at greater risk. But some guys are proud of being an all-around thief, like Tommy Grier. You name it, he has done it. Selling dope, burglary, stealing cars, breaking into cars, checks, credit cards, shoplifting. Has done a lotta time. A jailhouse lawyer in the penitentiary. Very smart guy. As far as know-how, is decent at what he does. But he doesn't have the good contacts, like for burglary, and takes chances he shouldn't.

The ordinary thief is nickel and dime, if the opportunity is there, will take it. The younger guys and especially your kids [juveniles] are the worst for doing any goddamn thing. Sell dope, break into cars, grab somebody's purse, even peddle their girlfriend's ass on the street if they run low on money to party. Are hustlers as much as they are thieves. But if stay in crime, like the older Beck boys and Andy, most will prefer doing this crime over other crimes.

The better thief is going to specialize more than the ordinary thief and sure as hell more than the asshole thief or the doper. The better thief will have the know-how and will have the contacts where he won't have to pull anything to make a buck. Can stick to this or that thing, and make a go of it. But doesn't mean they have never done other crimes or wouldn't if the good opportunity is there. But will stick to kinds of clipping where there is overlap. If into burglary, might break into a van or might steal a car if he has a ready outlet for it. Or hijack a truck, that is fairly common. Not exactly the same as burglary but there is a lotta similarity, say, compared to shoplifting or passing the checks. Will feel more comfortable just doing burglary or just doing shoplifting. Then get to be known by their buddies or even the cops for being a "burglar" and may take pride in being that. Will look down on the all-around thief. Take Rocky, saw himself as a burglar, wanted to be seen that way. Would be upset if you said he was an all-around thief.

Jesse might handle jewelry and coins for some decent burglars he knew. They would contact Jesse to help them unload 'cause Jesse had the contacts. But this was very seldom 'cause Jesse wasn't comfortable doing it. Didn't like taking the risk and didn't want the guys bitching back at him if the price wasn't right. It is pretty much the same with Steelbeams, with Rocky, with Bowie, with Teddy. Now with Andy. With other ones, too. Their thing has been burglary and hijacking trucks. Anything else was a sideline.

Bobby Porter was into shoplifting. Very good at it. He did pull a few burglaries. But shoplifting was his thing. Now, if you look at Bobby's *record,* you will see some other offenses—like assault and carrying a weapon, some disorderly conducts, and using some dope. But those aren't crimes the same way. He didn't do those to make money, know what I mean. *Crimes like those in many ways are part of being in the criminal world, the places you hang out, the people you associate with, and from being watched by the cops and the parole people.*

Same with some of the cops who will line their pockets. May take handouts from me or Louie. Maybe even give tips on a burglary. But won't sell dope or take money from dope dealers. Even Duggan, who was a pretty corrupt cop, it never came out he was peddling dope or taking money from dope dealers. There probably is this or that cop who will do almost any goddamn thing but is usually a limit as to how far a corrupt cop will go.

I'm not sure what you'd call someone like Chubby. Is a lackey but a decent joe. Have to like him. If you look at his record, it is pretty clean. Some DUIs and a couple of checks that bounced. Chubby likes to be part of something. Is more a bum than a thief. Does enough to get by, to have food on his plate and a place to hang his hat. Into stealing and hustling the whole time I've known him. Little pissy stuff. If you're at an auction, Chubby has clipped something from another booth, then wants to sell it at my booth or at my shop. I would go along with it. Bounce a check here, bounce another one there. Then pay them off to have the charges dropped. Hustle older women and has-beens for money, and a place to sleep. Then they get tired of his bullshit and throw him out. Chubby keeps the hustling and the stealing small so they won't go to the police. Has even clipped some places for me that had some good antique pieces. Would have to guide him, but he was dependable that way.

Is a lotta gray when you ask about specializing. Is iffy, put it that way. Kids don't specialize, as a rule that is the case. But are some who will stick to this or that main thing. May pull some other devilment but that is more part of being a kid, from hanging with other kids and each is egging the other one on. One thing will lead to another. Then, if they are into partying, are drinking and using dope, there is a pretty wide range of bullshit crimes that can come about. Guys get older, if they stay in crime and don't pack it in, then more of them will have a specialty or will clip in ways where there is overlap. I'm talking about guys in the twenties and even more if they're in their thirties or forties. They will feel more comfortable clipping this way but not that way. Will more recognize they have the knowledge for this but not for that. And will have the better contacts for this but not for that. Even more so are the guys who mainly got involved in crime when they were older, like Jesse or Woody. Don't see them jumping around from one crime to another.

Now if the guy is into dope or is an alkie, will be a different story. On account he more will do anything for a fix and more so will be an all around fuck-up. But even your doper or the alkie, as he gets older will many times limit himself to this or that theft or hustle. I'm talking about the doper who can handle his habit, knows when he needs a fix and knows what he has to do to cope with that. If at one time robbing people, breaking into somebody's house, shoplifting, peddling dope, and hustling anyway he can—now just stays with the shoplifting and the breaking into cars or stay with little con games and credit cards. Doper still has to feed their habit, but can manage it now to where they stick with a couple of things. Maybe even get a part-time job. This kind of doper thief I would buy from. But you still have to worry in case he runs out of dope and needs a fix, will he fall back into the old ways.

You have the same thing on the legit side, there are ones who are nothing but fuck-ups and losers. Difference is, just have more assholes on the criminal side. Quite a few will end up in prison or get blown away. If don't get blown away, then blow themselves away. Or do themselves in with the dope. Other losers fall into becoming alkies or live like bums, with their hand out.

See this in the penitentiary. Guys there with a criminal record—not just for burglary or different kinds of stealing but for baby rape or mugging old ladies or blowing someone away when there was no need to. Real fuck-ups. But you seldom find that among older thieves, guys in their thirties and forties who are still clipping, will not be involved in being assholes that way. Turns out, you will find that quite a few of those in the penitentiary for the baby rape or for putting a woman to sleep or for blowing the whole family away on account she is getting on his case, *they don't have that much in the way of record for crime. Weren't really a thief at all. Just an asshole.*

Depends, too, on whether we are talking about the white thief or the black thief. The black thief is more likely to do anything to make a buck, more likely to take pride in being an all-around thief. Now even the black thief as he gets older is more likely than the younger black guy to settle into a main hustle or a couple of main hustles. But the races are different here. The black thief is more strictly a hustler, is looking out for himself in a way that you're leery of doing business with him. In his eye, if the opportunity is there to hustle or steal, don't pass it up. The black thief is more cutthroat. Out to get what he can, even if you're his buddy.

The white guy who is into hustling, is more of a limit there. Will not go as far to do anything to make a buck. Is some loyalty on their part, that you can trust them to do right by you. Is a different code. You at least can have a little faith in them.

Dope has a lot to do with thieves doing anything to make a buck. So many thieves today are on dope. That is a big change and more so for robbery than burglary. If you go back to when me and Jesse were clipping, were more guys into robbery who were decent at it and weren't on dope. The good stickup guy stuck to robbery. Today, it is even hard to find a good stickup guy or a good stickup crew. Is more a thing of the past. What you have today is mostly kids doing the muggings and holdups—see it as a quick dollar and are being egged on by their buddies. But take the guy in his twenties and he is still doing the holdups, whew, he is on dope and has a fucked-up life. Are very few who are really decent at it.

Myself, yes, I pulled a lot of rank shit in my life. Burglary, fencing, and a lotta scams where I conned people. Some fights, even an arrest for an assault, but these [fights] were when I was younger, when I am running with a rougher crowd and hanging at rougher places. Except I did have to lean on somebody a few times—that comes from the territory, from being in crime you might say. You sure as hell can't call the police if somebody is fucking you over or is about to. People have to know you can dish it out if that's what it comes down to. If know somebody is going to snitch, have to let him know the price he will pay.

Was always some conning mixed in with the burglary and the fencing. Not the street hustling but more conning people about antiques or a business scam. Say, if there was a big storm, flooding, or hail, or whatever, I might jump at that. One time there was a big hailstorm, size of golf balls, in the Eagleton area about sixty miles from American City. Lotta, lotta damage. Insurance companies couldn't keep up with it. Painted up a couple of my trucks: "Roofing and Siding: Family Business for 33 Years." Took Cletus from my shop, a neighbor guy, and a couple of burglars who knew about roofing. I am in business. Knocked on people's houses. Charged a good penny but was putting on cheap shingles and siding, a fair amount of which I am buying warm. Banged it on, got the hell out of there. So, I'm combining the fencing and the conning.

Guys who have crime as a sideline (what you call moonlighting), they pretty much will stick to a main thing or two. Steal from where they work or break into a place off and on. Or peddle dope to people they know. Or do a little fencing. Maybe mix in some stealing with a little fencing. If branch out, are still careful not to spread themselves too thin. This is good common sense, too.

In a way that is what I am doing this last time. Stay away from breaking into places, not just because that is something I am getting too old for, but also because it is something the cops are concerned about and you can get hammered for. This last time I am skating between being legit and being a crook. I am doing several main things to make a buck but staying within what I know and feel comfortable with. On the shady side, it has mostly been the fencing but has always been some antique fraud and a few burglaries mixed in, and then quite a bit in the way of giving tips and vouching for people to make the connections. Am more behind the scenes. Does that make me all-around thief? Not in my eye, that is more or less my specialty.

Guys who operate behind the scenes, who more stay in the background and have their fingers into different things, that is their specialty. Like Nicky and Phil today. Sure as hell aren't the jack-of-all-trade thief.

Effects of Doing Time

I really believe this. Once you do time, you're never the same as the guy who didn't do time. Ask Jesse or Rocky or anybody about that. You're different. The only time you really feel relaxed is when you're alone or maybe with another guy that's done time. Like my being with Jesse. Probably me and him understand more, are more relaxed than any two people I know of. We can communicate even without saying anything.

Don't get me wrong, I like being around people but down deep I am a loner. At times I don't want to be bothered with anybody. I mean nobody. Just leave me fucking alone. It's a funny feeling that you can't explain. Now I'm at ease with Wanda but I'm not totally at ease.

See, *no one knows what loneliness is until you enter the goddamn penitentiary,* looking out the window at two o'clock in the morning, rainy or whatever it may be and nowhere to go. That is lonely. *When you lose your freedom you lose something else with it.*

Except for someone like Jesse or Steelbeams, everybody forgets you in prison. Take Angelo. When I got out, remember what he said? [Steffensmeier was with Sam on several occasions when they bumped into Angelo in American City]. "What do you need, Sam? Do you need anything?" Fuck it. "Why didn't you send me something when I was in the penitentiary?" You got me? You hear what I am saying?

Except maybe your woman or if you have kids. Then maybe they will keep in touch. Becky was pretty good that way this last time. But still, the longer you are there, the more the chances are the woman will be pulling back. Not saying a guy should bitch about that 'cause it comes down to it, if it was the other way around—if it was the woman who was doing time—not many guys would stand by her. So long baby and move onto another piece of nookie. Guys are a lot bigger assholes that way.

I sat down and thought about it a lot of times. *Prison takes something out of you. I can't explain it. You come out a different person. I don't know if it makes you bitter, hard, or whatever. You learn to trust only yourself in life.*

I don't mean you're mad at the cops on account you got caught. That pisses you off but that is the end of it. The only time I ever hated a cop was when they put you down, treat you like dirt, or if the sonofabitch lies on the stand. To me, when I was operating, it was a job. They had their job, I had my job. If we got busted it was our stupid ass, or they were lucky. That was it.

When you're in jail a lot of things go through your mind. You say, man, this is it. Ain't worth it. When you get out, it's a different ballgame altogether. When I left the prison, got my papers to go, I did tell myself, Sam, pack it in. Get yourself a little shop, stay legit. Really, I think I was even trying to lie to myself. In the back of my mind, now, I am knowing that if eight, nine grand came up fast, I'd grab it.

I am a firm believer that prisons don't rehabilitate. When somebody gets tired of crawling in windows, then he'll stop. Even with all the psychologists and counselors in the penitentiary, prisons don't rehabilitate. When I got to the Midstate Penitentiary this last time, it was a shocker how the penitentiaries have changed. This time, holy fuck, you got the counselors, the teachers, the psychologists, the psychiatrist. You got programs for this and that, you got furloughs for good behavior, you got hearing boards for misconduct shit. A lot more kids, a lot of dopers and penny-ante thieves in prison now. A lot more assholes. Guys come in with radios and TVs. I'm thinking, holy fuck, is this really a penitentiary? The older prisons were tougher, a lot tougher in terms of doing without. Just the bare essentials was all you got.

But doing time is harder now 'cause today you got all this psychological bullshit, all the assholes who are in prison, and the code is weaker. There used to be a helluva code in prison. That is weaker now. Myself, as far as doing time, I just skated by. Go by the rules on the outside, play along with the counseling bullshit, get along with everybody but don't kiss anybody's ass. There's a borderline there.

Don't forget this, there are a lot of guys that can't make it out there. I don't know if you can understand that. A whole lot of guys become something in jail, and out of jail they're shit. Can't make it on the street. They'll do something to get caught so they can go back to jail to be somebody. Believe me. Not that going back to the penitentiary is going to do that person any goddamn good.

Is more of this today on account there are more losers who can't make it on the outside and 'cause the penitentiaries are softer. In jail they at least will have a roof over their head and a couple of meals a day. So, it is no big deal if you are sent back to the penitentiary, say, if you are the ordinary street thief. Except if you are a doper or an alkie, then maybe will fear going back to the penitentiary on account will have to face the grief from doing without the dope.

You hang with your own kind in prison. You got cliques. I wouldn't be messing around with the baby rapist and the dopers. Different society, know what I mean? Your safecrackers and good thieves would hang together. Your stickup men would hang together. You'd rap about what you were into and that stuff. Same as you. You're a professor, right? You aren't gonna hang with the hippies and losers.

This has changed some since I did the big time in the fifties. This last time at Midstate, you are still hanging with your own kind. But are fewer decent thieves in prison. So now hang more with the lifers on account there are more of them in the penitentiary today. Big thing in the penitentiary today, is you have a lotta assholes and dopers. A lotta kids, really, who shouldn't even be in prison. *That is a main reason it is harder to do time today, are so many assholes and kids.*

I did get involved with some of the counseling this last time in Midstate. On account the one program dealt with juveniles, with kids that were getting in trouble. Was asked by the superintendent if myself and couple of other cons would meet with them, let them know what prison was like, what they were headed for if they got in more trouble. Wanted us to scare them, is what it boiled down to. Some of them I shook up pretty good—"Yeah, would like to see you come to the penitentiary, you have a nice ass, soft face—not as good as real pussy but can't be choosy in here." Other ones blew you off. But still I'm thinking I am making a dent, am helping them even if they're thinking, "This guy is only blowing wind up his ass."

For me doing time was more a nuisance than anything. I sure as hell didn't want to be in the penitentiary but I could block out the outside world and skate by the rules on the inside. Is a fine line there for getting along with the guards or the other staff people and not being an asshole *inmate* that is kissing up to the officials and is probably a snitch too. [Sam uses inmate as a derogatory term for a convict who goes out his way to please the officials.]

This last time especially, the other cons looked up to me and the guards too. It was known in prison that I was a pretty decent guy but could get nasty if I had to. And the name carries from having done time before and from different ones knowing what I was like on the outside.

Is a lotta tension, lotta bad feelings, between the races in the penitentiary but you can skate your way around that. A lotta white guys hate the blacks. Is that way before they do time, but is worse after they come to the penitentiary. Goes the other way, too, where the chip on their shoulder a lot of black guys have toward the white guy is worse after they've been in the penitentiary. I got along with just about everybody. Even with the blacks.

I learned a lot in the penitentiary. How to get over on people. Be a hustler but not an asshole hustler. Am learning this from being a merchant and from having to hold my own with other cons. Will test you in a lot of ways, will find out what you're made of. If I had a store [barter site for scarce goods] I was careful to not overdo the getting over on someone but still let it be known, yeah, any debts have to be paid. And stayed away from the loansharking.[2] *Learned how to read people,* especially where different kinds of thieves and hustlers are coming from. Who's a bullshitter and who isn't? *Learned who to hang with, that there is a helluva pecking order.* Hang with the assholes, then will think you're an asshole too. Can hang with this or that black con if he's accepted and isn't a snitch. But otherwise, no, the white guys and the better thief won't associate with you.

Is the same with larceny in the heart. In a way you're telling yourself, when I get out I'm going go straight, pack it in. But, really, what you are seeing and the conversations you are hearing you are becoming more jaded. All you are hearing is about this scam or this way to hustle—but even more so, how the system is fucked up. Sure, it is guys whining, but it is sinking in, too, that this or that cop is on the take. That, hey, the ordinary business guy is more than just a little shady. *Put it this way, the penitentiary didn't knock any larceny outta me.* In a way gave me more confidence that if I did fall back into crime, there is a better way to go about it.

Main thing I learned is, crime is a business. That was the biggest change for me. If you're going to stay in crime, then do it for the money and treat it as a business. Get past doing it for bullshit reasons—for the devilment, for the kick, for being part of something or being noticed by your buddies. Is a realization that how you were doing crime before—whew, how little thought there was, just do it. May have thought you were decent at it at the time but now know you were only blowing wind outta your ass.

I would say this is a big thing for most of your thieves, even the ordinary thief. Especially for the thief who is in his twenties and if he does a good bit in the penitentiary. May start before that if the guy has done short bits in jail or the juvenile reformatory, *but that first good bit in the penitentiary is a wake-up to the fact that crime is a business.* I have heard so many guys say that. Take Rocky, before going to the penitentiary, I would get on his case. He would listen but only so far. After coming out of the penitentiary, was a different awareness on Rocky's part. Same with the older Beck boy. May still clip for the excitement and to go along with the crowd but is a whole lot more of the business side to their clipping than before.

Having done time in the penitentiary, yes, you will worry about getting popped and doing time again. But less than you are thinking. The main change is between your ears, in the mental side, to where you are thinking ahead more and doing more of the little things so you don't get caught. More preparation, be more careful about who you work with and about who knows your business. Be ready to accept it [going back to the penitentiary] but that thought is more on the back burner.

Doesn't mean you will keep doing crime. If all that comes your way are bullshit crimes, the penny-ante stuff and where there is a lot of risk, might as well pack it in. Do something else. Same thing, if a good legit job comes along or fall into decent money, then pack it in or at least slow down. Go where the money is, that is now more and more your mind-set.

I'd rank next [*right after learning that crime is a business*] *that I met a lot of people from the penitentiary, that a lot of contacts came my way from doing time.* Not that you intentionally keep in touch or send fucking Christmas cards but more that you bump into guys you knew from the penitentiary. Maybe because you stop at the same places or end up getting the same kind of legit jobs. Even more it's because the name carries—from this guy knowing that guy who knows that guy, "Yeah, I knew him in the penitentiary, you can do business with him." I'm not sure what you'd call it, a sixth sense or whatever the ex-con has, but knowing without even asking that this or that guy did time. Will know, too, that if this guy has done time, he knows the ropes and will not be blabbing to the police. If he's not interested in clipping, will still help you out in little ways—like, "Hey, what can you tell me about so and so?" Is a helluva a grapevine that comes from doing time, especially if you're a decent con.

The worst time for me was the seven, eight months I spent in the halfway house after I was released from Midstate. Place was a zoo. Fucking kids and the staff just drawing their paycheck. I had to let everybody know I wasn't to be fucked with. This you know 'cause the guy in charge was there when it happened and told you about it. Is a refrigerator in the place so guys can buy food and make sandwiches and that to take with you to work or eat a snack when you get back from working. I am buying myself lunchmeat and orange juice, right? But this is happening pretty regular—I go the refrigerator and the lunchmeat is gone. Same with the orange juice. It is a Thursday evening and everybody is pretty much there, mostly watching television. I gets back from work and go to the refrigerator. Is one slice of lunchmeat left and a few drops of orange juice. I am hot. I yanked the plug out of the fucking television. Stood right next to it, pulled out my dick and pissed in the orange juice container. Then rubbed the lunchmeat on my dick. Put the lunchmeat and the juice back in the refrigerator. Walked out. No more needed to be said.

The first months, the first year out of the penitentiary is the hardest. Especially if you've been in the penitentiary a while. Can be pretty edgy when you
get out. Want to make up for lost time. Maybe have a chip on your shoulder,
are thin-skinned about how you fit in. Can be a bitterness there that will slant
how you see things. Will have the parole people watching your ass to see if you
slip up. This pisses a lot of guys. Their old buddies are pushing on them, and
some loser women too. Big thing for most guys is to get money in their pocket
'cause have been doing without for so long. Can be easy to fall back into the
clipping and the kind of clipping that can take you back to the penitentiary.

Get through the first year, then there is a settling down. Will have a better
outlook on how to handle things, to walk away from the bullshit. If go back to
clipping, then know more what you're doing. Accept the risk of getting
popped and maybe doing time again. Not that this is dwelled on but is more an
inkling, yeah, it could happen. If you wanna stay legit, find a job that you're
content with.

Persistence, Desistance, or Something in Between

Lying in that goddamn hospital bed, many times I would go back over you
what you would ask: Why do some guys pack it in and other guys like me stay
at crime so long? Even more so, why do some guys pack it in when they're
younger, say, in their twenties or thirties? Pretty much everybody packs it in
eventually—same as any legit job. Get too old or can't hack it physically or
just lose interest on account you been doing it so long or on account guys your
age have packed it in and you don't want to put up with the kids and the assholes. Sure as hell don't wanna spend your last years in the penitentiary. But it
is more than that. Get older, you have been there, you have done that. You are
more content with what you have. More mellow, I guess.

*It ain't cut-and-dried. Many guys pull back but don't quit all the way. May
eventually quit but it drags out.* Then for other guys, they get busted or have a
close call, maybe get shot at, or somebody leans on them—so have had enough.
For them it is bang, bang, just pack it in.

One group is your ordinary thief that gets involved when he is kid, a juvenile.
Does horseshit stuff—breaking into cars, into homes, or whatever. Maybe sells
dope. Most are doing it for devilment, raise hell, be a big shot with their buddies, and for money to party with. If they are clipping pretty regular, will get
popped or have a close call. This will get their attention. Even if they don't get
popped or do time, quite a few will pack it in. Not necessarily all the way, but
will stop the horseshit stuff—more or less by the time they hit nineteen, twenty,
twenty-five. On account of the hassles 'cause, not that they would admit it, but
most of them will lack the know-how and the contacts to make a decent dollar
and to stay out of jail. Have a girlfriend or get a job, it is time to move on.

Here's the thing. When you're a kid you will steal for pennies 'cause it is still spending money and for the devilment. But, you will outgrow that. The satisfaction is gone in stealing pennies. If you can't do better than that, then will pull back or clip in other ways. Same as a kid who is working at a McDonald's and they are paying him shit. That is still money and maybe is more than other kids his age have in their pocket. Now he is older and out of (high) school, chances are good he won't be happy if all he is making from crime is pennies. So, will look to do something else.

Another group is guys like Lemont, a half-assed thief. Are into their twenties and are still clipping. Probably have done some time, maybe even a quite bit of time. Some are real losers, others are pretty decent thieves. But crime is more a business for them, is what they more or less do. Ones like Lemont will keep doing crime even though they keep getting hammered by the cops. Don't want to work or can't hold a job. Need the money to live the way they want. Pull jobs 'cause they are short of cash. Maybe is a little thrill in doing it and hanging with other guys who are living the same way. Feed on each other, "Hey, there's a place to clip. Let's go for it." But if they stay half-assed, the hassles and that will take away their wind. If they can get a job, even a horseshit job, or get some woman to support them, just as well pack it in. If they stay at the clipping and are doing it pretty regular, the penitentiary is waiting.

This you will see, guys packing it in when they are hitting their late twenties or thirties. If don't quit, then slow down. Know the chances are good they will get popped if they are clipping on a regular basis. The hassles of doing time and that do them in. But not all the way. If the coast is clear, they will clip off and on. Chisel at the place they work, maybe peddle some stolen goods, give tips to other burglars. *They are reformed but not reformed, know what I mean.*

Take Kevin Foley, he was a decent burglar, one of my regulars in American City. In his late twenties when I got popped for the fencing in American City. This shook him, so he packed in the burglary. Opened up a motorcycle shop and is doing very good. When he's in the area, will stop by my shop in Tylersville. Off and on he will deal dope or does some shady stuff with his business. That is fairly common.

A lot will depend on what the opportunities for clipping are, how big is the temptation. Remember Randy? Did some clipping with the oldest Beck boy. Is now in his thirties. Did time for stealing cars and breaking into cars. That was his main thing. Is now working for cleaning business that is a chain, drives one of trucks that runs supplies from one town to another. Turns out that a couple of the other drivers and some of the workers are peddling dope. The cleaning business is a good cover and can transport the dope from one place to another. Is pretty safe, so Randy is going along with it but is leery too. Tells me, yeah, he should go straight but is finding it hard to walk away. Not making big money from the dope but, with the legit pay, he is doing okay. The other guys involved are just ordinary joe blows. Is extra income. In my eye there is a lot of that.

You'd be surprised at this or that ordinary joe blow who has a regular job or has a business and wasn't really involved in crime when he was younger, then ends up getting involved in dealing dope. This happens more than the public thinks. Especially if they are hanging with the party crowd. The Yuppie people is one part—this or that lawyer, this business guy, different ones that have good jobs. But also are ordinary *joe blows* who like to party. Not just guys but party women. Live on the edge, at least a little. Manage to find one another. Is more of this today, the partying and using dope. Will be an opportunity for this or that one to peddle dope but stay within that circle. The risks will not be that great. Just don't get greedy.

But can be hard to keep it small on account dealing in one circle can open up the contacts to deal in other circles, and the temptation will be there for the bigger dollar. Maybe a guy has a garage or a place to warehouse the dope or say he drives truck or knows how to fly a plane, he will be useful to people who are higher up in the dope peddling. But if he gets involved too heavy, then too many people will know and he will be taking more chances the police are knowing too.

This happened to Fuzzy's son, the one we call Elvis on account of his sideburns. Real name is Todd. Have a good-sized garden and nursery place on the edge of Tylersville. Is a partnership except Fuzzy is the one who keeps it going. Todd likes to party. Is in his late thirties, a free spirit. Fun to be around. A ladies' man. Not a doper or alkie but is into drinking and using dope. Comes five o'clock, Todd is done working and out the door. Is ready to party. Whatever money he makes, he is ready to spend. He will end up short of cash. May borrow from his dad or other times he will sell a little dope to people he is partying with. But this is pulling him in deeper. The guy Todd is buying from wants a layer in between. Turns out the police are eying this guy and the people he is seen with. Are squeezing this or that one, and the snitching starts. Bing, bing. A whole bunch are popped for dealing pot and cocaine and different kinds of pills. Was blown up in the paper like you wouldn't believe. Todd was one of them, had his name on the front page.

Fuzzy came to me, to advise him on what to do. Gave him the name of my lawyer and another lawyer who I knew was okay. But not much a lawyer could do 'cause by now everybody is snitching on everybody. Was a circus. Different ones are saying Todd was a main dealer. Except for a DUI [driving under the influence], Todd had a clean record. Takes a guilty plea and gets a short jail sentence like for six months but had to be on parole for a couple of years. Does his six months but then fucks up on parole. Now the judge has it in for Todd and sends him to the state penitentiary to do the time for the rest of his sentence.

Was a helluva wake-up for Todd. Didn't do well in the penitentiary. Was a greenie with a pretty face and not enough roughness in him. The other cons took advantage of that. This time when Todd got out, you could see the change in him. Even in his eyes, is a sadness and some bitterness. The fun side is missing. To hear Fuzzy talk, Todd is way more serious about taking over the business now but his spark is gone.

Even more so, you will find guys who peddled dope when they were younger but now are in their forties or whatever—need the money or just miss the excitement, and then are dealing dope again. Know they have the know-how and maybe want to see if they can still do it. Doesn't have to be dope now, maybe they were into other kinds of clipping. Can be a helluva temptation on account they've been there, still have the larceny in the heart, and the extra dollars are a pull. Maybe have kept in touch or just bump into guys you palled with before and it comes out this or that one is still operating. *Especially if you're in a pinch* [financially], *it is easy to fall back into it—not all the way like you once were but on a smaller scale. Lotta guys don't retire, don't quit all the way.* Just slow down or shift to other areas. Maybe stay more in the background, more part-time. If the opening is there and it is safe, they won't walk away. But they really aren't thieves anymore, at least not like they once was.

Getting Older and Other Turning Points

I don't know how to explain it. When you get older you get tired of the hassles, all the bullshit you have to put up with. When you're young, you don't think about prison—doesn't really concern you. When you're older, it's not that you fear prison but that you don't want to waste your time there. *There's more to lose when you get older.* This last time I lost my shirt—my business, just about everything. Look at what I would lose now. The shop I have built up. Being there for my grandkids. Not just myself, but Wanda and the guys in my shop would be fucked too. When I did time in my twenties, I didn't lose shit.

Most thieves are penny-ante. They're not getting rich off of stealing. No way. So with all the hassles and bullshit, why not pack it in. The higher-ups, like Phil and Nicky, are making good money and there are fewer hassles. If they are careful, stay in the background, don't get too greedy, there is very little risk for them. May have to pay a horseshit fine once in a while, for gambling and that, but that's about it. With one foot in the grave, they will still have their fingers in it.

Same with Steelbeams and Bowie and Gordie—they are still clipping and very regular. Steelbeams is in his forties. Bowie and Gordie are close to fifty, maybe older. They work on tips, pull inside jobs. I would like to make what they are making. The last couple of times I saw Gordie, he was hobbling like an old man. Arthritis will flare up and then you would think he was a cripple. Bowie more and more is bitching about the physical side. That he is getting to old to crawl into places, should come to work for me in my shop. I told him he was blowing wind out of his ass. But you know the time will come to pack it in. Can bring in some younger guys to help out with the heavy part but you can only guide them so far.

The law of averages is against you, if you are clipping a lot. But if you are careful and limit the jobs you do, it is hard to catch a burglar or a guy who is stealing cars. Even when the cops are figuring you are the ones pulling the jobs. If there is no snitching, no blabbering to one's buddies or girlfriend, it is hard to get the evidence to make an arrest and put someone away. Jesse and I were never caught for safes, never caught for stealing the nickel and copper. Only time we got nailed was for the antique job. All the jobs we pulled, only got nailed that one time.

Take Rocky. Has been twenty years since he did time for burglary. Was okay at it but not what you would call "good." First years out of the penitentiary, he was pretty reckless. Would do the scouting and planning okay, but then would sometimes be drinking or using dope on the job. Was hooked up with a couple of decent burglars but would also pull jobs with some assholes. This led to Rocky getting jammed up but the cops couldn't pin it on. But they weren't going to let him walk. So played dirty—got him on a parole violation, for having a gun in his possession. See, it was the start of hunting season and the police were watching 'cause they knew Rocky loved to hunt. He comes out of the timber, is heading for his truck—bang, bang, did you clear it with your parole officer to have a gun?

Rocky ended up doing about a year in the county jail. This time he gets out, you could see the change in him. Not to get out of crime, but for getting his act together. Was more caution in him, more careful who he worked with. Look for the good jobs. Don't fuck with the penny-ante stuff. Not that he still couldn't do dumb shit. Rocky's main problem is he is hard-headed. Has the smarts, the know-how, and can keep his mouth shut. But cement in his head. I would chew him. Find a decent partner and stick with him. Otherwise hook up with one of the decent crews if they are looking for another guy to pull this or that job. Keep on the good side of your parole officer. Not let little shit get in your craw if he comes down hard on you. Get yourself a job so he thinks you're legit. Even get yourself a girlfriend, so it will look like you're settling down.

Rocky wanted no part of a regular [legit] job or having a girlfriend. Liked to chase pussy but didn't want somebody nagging at him. Would work odd jobs off and on, but for many years never held a regular job. Didn't wanna be tied down and some jobs he could get, he wanted no part of. Got his first regular job like five, six years ago, working for a vending company. Drives their van filling and emptying vending machines, like for cigarettes and picks up the cash. Has a route he's responsible for. So can work out his own hours. This in a way has changed Rocky. Likes driving the truck, likes meeting the people on his route. If they call, he is right there. It is funny to hear Rocky talk—wishes he had gotten a job like this sooner. Beats doing the burglary on account he doesn't have to be looking over his shoulder if the cops are on to something or if somebody is gonna snitch. Would like the pay to be better but is enough to live on. At least knows the money is coming in 'cause for someone like Rocky there would be dry spells between the stealing. He is very near to packing it in and maybe has done so already.

Is the job changing Rocky or is it because he is getting older? Or, are they working together to change him? A lot of thieves don't work and don't wanna work. Especially the younger ones. Are too lazy to work or because it interferes with their partying. Or because they don't wanna take the jobs they can get. The better thieves aren't lazy, it is more they don't wanna be tied down. Jesse didn't work when him and me were clipping. Jesse never really worked until he took the maintenance job after we got popped for the antique job. Bowie and Gordie have never had regular jobs. Still don't.

But most of your thieves as they get older will end up at regular [legit] jobs. Especially the better thieves will have a job or maybe a little business. Is a cover and are bringing in bread you can fall back on it if you run short of cash. For the ordinary thief, the big thing from having a job is you don't have to steal to keep the money coming in, to take chances when you shouldn't. That is what I would tell them. Not that they listened to me but some did.

This is something that makes me feel good, lining up a job at Fuzzy's for a friend of Donnie's [foreman in Sam's shop] that has turned him around. I'm talking about Wayne, the one who you sometimes see at my shop. Did time for breaking in cars, which he fell back into after he got out of the penitentiary. Got him a job with Fuzzy [runs a garden and lawn business] doing deliveries and helping out in other ways. Has gotten to liking it. In my eye Wayne would've gone straight when he first got out of the penitentiary if that job had been there. Being in prison shook him. Was ready to go another direction. That he couldn't find a job and is finding out in other ways that people hold it against you if you're an ex-con, soured Wayne. Do the time, but you are still paying. I'm not saying Wayne was pushed back into crime, but you wonder if it coulda been otherwise.

Are a lot losers and a lot of dopers who will fall back into crime anyways. *But a legit job is the biggest avenue for packing it in.* Especially if the guys are little older and can cut back on the partying and chasing pussy, or can pull back from showing off to their buddies. Just listening to guys talk, will many times find they are making more from a legit job than from clipping. Or the difference ain't that great and are doing without the hassles.

A good woman can help but in my eye that is many times blowing wind outta your ass. Some guys, yes, and if they have kids, may help too. A lot of guys hook up with women who are little shady and maybe are losers themselves. Not that the women are pushing them to stay in crime but won't be on their case to quit either. Lot of other guys won't stay with a woman if she is nagging them and getting in their way. Will want to come and go as they please. Older thieves especially, will live with a woman but are ready to pack their bag if she gives him much hassle. Not that they have never been married. At one time probably were married. But now can take it or leave it whether there is a woman in their life. Rocky's mother would nag Rocky, he should find a good girl—as if that would turn Rocky around. Is after nookie once in a while, but is no way that will happen.

Rocky has taken up fishing the past few years. Very serious about it. Spends a lot of time at this hunting and fishing club. Is palling with some of the guys there. *Is a niche for him, a satisfaction.* He would rather do that than party or spend money. Has done for him what his mom has been hoping a girlfriend would do. I kid him about that. Is a factor in why he is pulling back from the burglary, no doubt about that.

Off and on I will bump into Mickey at the auctions. Goes as a pastime. An all-around thief, was decent at it and solid. I bought a lot of stuff from Mickey. Has packed it in all the way. Doesn't miss it and his wife would dump him if he got involved again. She keeps an eye on him. They both work, so the money is okay and don't have to worry about the cops being on your ass. That is what Mickey told me. I would egg him, give him a hard time about being henpecked and wearing a skirt. But there wasn't any play. Not that I wanted to pull him back in [into stealing] but more to hassle him.

Myself, I preferred to have a woman in my life. As long as I could come and go as I pleased. Don't ask me too many questions. Then my bags are packed. I was with Becky about five years before I got popped for the fencing and ended up at Midstate. Was a close relationship and with her kids, too. Same with Wanda and her kids. Was a close relationship. Even more so I am closer to Wanda. She is a good woman.

Lisa is another story. She is more like the woman a lot of thieves and ex-cons hook up with. Was on dope, into partying. A good lay but as far as pulling me away from crime, no way. That I am still clipping and might fall back into crime all the way, isn't on the radar screen for Lisa. She would not want me to get caught 'cause then the money and a roof over her head would be gone. But as long as what I am doing is a benefit for her, didn't interfere with her partying, then no big deal. Not that she was a bad person, not saying that, but she was living a pretty fucked-up life. Maybe down the road she would straighten herself out, then would probably get on my ass to reform or at least pull back. But while we was together, she wasn't into reforming me. Not that it would've made any difference.

A main reason guys pack it in or pull back is because they lose the heart for clipping. Or find out they never had it. Happens more as guys get older, lose some of the edge they once had. Become more leery of who they can trust and just don't want the hassles or the worries of clipping when others are involved. But it is hard to work alone on account four eyes or six eyes are better than two. Even more so, very few can clip alone. It isn't in them to go out at night and break into a place, by their lonesome. Most guys will want somebody along. Their nerves are better.

In a way some guys stay at crime because that is what they are good at. Are making a living and is a satisfaction in earning a good dollar. What they know is how to clip a place. Someone like Bowie, at his age what kind of a legit job could he get? Can maybe drive a truck or work in a warehouse, but where is the satisfaction? And can he handle the physical side of working at a warehouse, the lifting and that? Main thing is, what else is out there? It is hard to give up what you have. You don't want to go backwards.

Here's another thing. Once you pull back or, say, you do a long stint in the penitentiary, you are out of practice and have lost some of the edge. Say, I beat the cancer and get my legs back, I'd have a harder time doing burglaries today. Don't think I could think quick witted as well as I should. Mostly because I am out of practice. Maybe don't have the nerve I had before. Wouldn't be as intense. Now, if I had a couple of jobs under my belt, I would get that back. It would be the same thing if you stopped teaching. Would lose that edge but is something that would come back to you. I would have a harder time until I pulled a couple of jobs, then be right back to where I was— except couldn't run as fast, that is for sure. But couldn't go out tonight and be at ease.

A lot of the same ones who were clipping in American City when I was operating, are clipping today—if not this way, then another way. Pretty much all of the little dealers, the secondhand and pawnshop guys are still at it. If not them, then their sons or a cousin has taken over. More of them have moved from the downtown 'cause the downtown ain't what you used to be. But other ones have stayed put. A lot of the same bookies are still operating. A lot of the same ones are running the taverns and the night spots where you will find the shady mixed in with the legit. Some of the businesspeople who I was dealing with are now hooked up with Phil or the Gucci brothers. Different cops who were shady back then are mostly retired but some are still hanging on. Don't know who broke them in but are some new cop faces that are just as shady as the ones I operated with.

Even ones that are doing half-assed, if they are pretty well covered, they are still at it. Like Joey Page, cousin of Angelo. Always wanted to be a hotshot, wanted to be a big fence but couldn't get the trust of people—especially from the better thief and from the business guy for unloading. How Joey lasted all these years without the cops busting his balls or somebody doing him in, is a mystery. Is a real asshole. But Joey is still hustling, still clipping one way or another. Some fencing, some dope dealing, shyster loans. Now one of his sons is involved.

Most of the big ones in American City, like the ones in the local clique, are still at it or they are dead or have one foot in grave. Someone like "Fat Charlie" Ciletti—stomach hangs over his belly, walks two steps is out of breath. Sold his business, ain't doing nothing. Takes care of his grandchildren and that's all. Gambles a little. Some shyster loans if he knows the person well but that is about it. His heart is bad. He had to pull back.

Guys like Charlie, if his heart hadn't petered out, have more on the ball than the ordinary thief and got the better connections. *They're in a situation where they can make money, where they don't really have to take the chances. So why pack it in?* But say you are a penny-ante thief or horseshit burglar like Stevie Walljasper. I will give Stevie credit, could see the handwriting on the wall and had enough sense to pull back. Is mostly clean now but still may hit a place or pick up something. And sells a little dope, to his friends and to their friends. *So, he is reformed but not all the way. Are quite a few like that.*

Moonlighting versus Regular Clipping

Is a big difference between regular clipping and moonlighting,[3] in how each is approached. When Jesse and me was clipping regular, that was our focus. Was almost a day-in and day-out thing. Jesse even more so 'cause I am running my upholstery and secondhand shop. But the clipping is what we was about—the planning, the scouting, the thinking ahead about what we will do after we clip the place, a lotta conversations between ourselves. Same with Rocky when he was clipping regular—is breaking into places with his buddies nearly every week, sometimes two, three times a week. That is what they talked about, is what they did. Outside of loafing and some partying, they are eating and sleeping the clipping.

Moonlighting is more laid back, take things as they come. Someone like Jesse is spending a whole lot less time on the burglary now than he was before. His main thing now is his job and taking out his boat. Most days the burglary is not even on the table, except that he is keeping his eyes open. Is an awareness but hardly a conscious thing. Is on the lookout for a good opportunity, yes—in a way all the time but in another way hardly at all. Will keep in touch with the lawyer and that for tips. Check them out. If Jesse likes what he sees, then the scouting and the planning becomes a main focus. But otherwise the burglary is very much a sideline.

Same with Rocky these last years. He mostly is at work or is putzing around with one of his buddies or is out fishing by himself. Has places he will stop at for lunch or to kill time, like at the one hunting and fishing club. Keeps in touch with some guys who are into burglary. Are pretty much like Rocky, have slowed down from what they were once doing. Or will bump into one another from dropping in at the same places. This or that opportunity may come up in conversation. Maybe this guy will check it out. May egg each other a little but usually in no rush. Have a different mind-set—the burglary may still be an important side of you, but have a life that is more than that and you are weighing the risks better. *The eye for clipping is still there but is more restful, which is different from the guy who is regularly clipping.*

To do what Jesse has been doing is a good way to go. *Has everybody thinking he has packed it in, even me. Then find out later he is still clipping places but is working alone.* Does a job or two a year, from tips he is getting. Jesse has worked himself up to supervisor of maintenance in the county, is his own boss, and the pay is good. He would not want to jeopardize that. Would not want the ones he works with and different people he knows to find out he is a thief. Is very leery about Bernice finding out, would not want to put Bernice through the worries anymore.

The big change in Jesse is after we got popped for the antique burglary, but he already is pulling back from safes. We were getting too known in Jesse's eye. But Jesse is getting older, too, can see the writing on the wall. He is thinking it is better to have a legit job, only clip when the really good opportunity is there. The burglary is now a very sideline thing for Jesse, when before it was his main thing. *In a way that is what it means to be a good thief, that he knows when to pull back or move to a different racket.*

But say Jesse doesn't like the job, doesn't wanna take the bullshit that comes with it—In my eye Jesse would have gone back to clipping. Him and me would've lasted a lot longer as partners. Eventually, yes, Jesse would have slowed down—you pretty much have to at some point. Same way as in a legit job where you are getting tired of the hassles and can't take the physical side.

Even myself, not sure I could do what Jesse does. Very few can clip alone. It isn't in them to go out at night and break into a place, by their lonesome. Most guys will want somebody along. Their nerves are better. I don't think I'm that much of a pussy that I wouldn't break into a place myself [Sam in fact has]. I don't scare easy. For me, it is just a feeling of being more comfortable or whatever if there is an extra pair of eyes. Maybe 'cause I am more trusting than Jesse. In a way, too, I like to be part of something, which is different than Jesse.

Life's Twists and Turns: Linkage of Biography and Circumstance

Are a lot of twists and turns in anybody's life, sure as hell in mine. A push here, a push there, but then is a linkage for one thing leading to another thing.

My doing time in the juvenile reformatory itself was a big push. Not so much for learning but you hear guys talk. Are puffing themselves up about the shit they've pulled. Are making it sound easier and better than it is. You know they are mostly blowing wind outta their asses but still you are taking it in. Very little penitence on their part. Main thing I learned was I could do the time. I don't know how to say it, when I first got popped there was a fear there—'cause you hear stories about the shit that goes on in jail and that. I didn't like jail but found out it wasn't so bad. For some guys, yes, but quite a few other ones could handle it.

This paved the way, at least a little, for the after-work burglary. I'm twenty, twenty-one, when this got started. Guys just horsing around after work, the night shift. Went on for a couple of years. Steal tires, break into places. A couple of the guys hadn't done time like me but did some clipping when they were kids [juveniles]. Was quite a bit of devilment on their part. For myself, having done the burglary with Ronnie and then doing the time in the juvenile reformatory, there was very little second-guessing on my part. Should we do this, should we do that? "Yeah, let's go."

Take yourself, say, you didn't pull much when you were a kid. Some devilment but not really into the clipping. Now you're twenty, twenty-five, the opportunity is there to clip and maybe are some guys who are egging you. Say you go along with it, once or a few times. The chances are you will be looking over your shoulder, there is a fear there and maybe you can't look at yourself in the mirror. So, you are holding back. Whereas myself, I have been there— will have some knowledge, very little fear on my part, no problem looking at myself in the mirror. Not that I really know what I'm doing but I'm thinking I do. Am comfortable with myself and can enjoy it—not just at getting away with something but palling with the guys and making a buck, whereas you are too shaky to do that.

Same way, if you are an angel as a kid, if there is very little devilment in you. Even more so if you are a nerd, not a free spirit in you. You will be less likely to get into crime down the road. Just won't feel comfortable doing it. You're not gonna touch the clipping even if the good opportunity is there. Unless maybe, you really hit hard times. You'd be surprised at how much larceny is in people if they are in a pinch. But otherwise, no, you won't be able to look at yourself in the mirror. Even more, you won't have the heart or the knowledge. It just wouldn't be you.

When you're young you want to be part of something, do what others are doing. Is an enjoyment in jerking the adults' chains, of getting away with something. Get older, will outgrow some of that but most people will still have some larceny in them, will want some excitement in their lives. But can be a point there where you can get to liking the clipping and are feeling comfortable with it. Is now more than just devilment. This will pave the way down the road 'cause in a way you have some knowledge and the fear isn't there, and can look at yourself in the mirror. And will be more likely to hang with a crowd that sees things the same way, are on the take at least in little ways, so will be more openings for clipping.

But a bigger push for me was the escape from jail. Whew, only a couple of months from my release date, then a fucking queer hits on me and I end up busting his balls. Bang, bang, I am given more time. Being on the run changed things, which ended up with me doing the big time. I don't know if there's a new me when I leave the penitentiary that time, but the old me is not the same. I have been through a lot, learned a lot, saw a lot. I have a better eye for clipping and more larceny in the heart. In a way there is an acceptance on my part to combine the clipping with the legit. Go after the dollar both ways. Whichever way brings in the better dollar, then do that.

Here's the thing. Same as any ex-con, I am knowing the good jobs won't be coming my way. Guys will bullshit in prison about having a good job lined up or wanna go into business. But deep down you know, it doesn't work that way. My thing has always been to have a legit job, to knock on doors until you get one. Even a horseshit one like the one at the furniture place when I first landed in American City. It turns out this helped to get a little business going in upholstery and antiques. Now I had a new thing, being a businessman you might say. Then the fencing takes off.

If that hadn't happened, would I have stayed with the burglary longer, say, like a Jesse or a Bowie? No need to answer that. You have to do what you have to do, to put bread on the table but more so to where you don't owe anybody. I am big believer in that—you live your life, not somebody else's. As far as this last period: if my legit business wasn't doing so good, yes, then notch up the fencing. At least a little anyways.

Notes

1. Sam adds, "It is surprising how many I would bump into. Would ask how they're doing? Is their nose clean? Hey, who is operating? What about so-and-so? Some of them were no longer clipping, weren't active any more. But they were curious to find out what was happening and gossip about what they know, and to reminisce about the old days."
2. Penitentiary "loan sharks" loan cigarettes (a main medium of exchange in prisons) to inmates who want to get in a card game. The going rate in Sam's time period was a carton of cigarettes for one and a half cartons back. If you lose in the card game, the loan shark is owed fifteen packs. The loan shark is often seen as a dicey, exploitative role because the "pull of gambling" and "poor gambling skills" can easily lead to high debt.
3. This is Steffensmeier's term that Sam eventually adopted to describe the shift between regular versus part-time or sideline clipping.

PART IV

Sam Takes Stock: Dealing with Dying

19

Commentary

Rewards and Rationales of Crime, and Images of Criminals

Sam's final narrative is drawn mostly from the final weekend of interviews before his death. Sam's comments really "zero in" on appraising his life, his points of pride and regrets, his moral apologia, his sources of emotional pain, and his imminent death.

In Chapters 3, 11 and elsewhere, we have discussed structural, personal, and moral commitment to crime. In this commentary, we describe Sam's rewards, preferences, identities, and positive attitudes connected to crime, and how they built strong personal commitments to stealing, fencing, and hustling. Then, we discuss Sam's moral apologia for his actions, some elements of which invoke moral commitment to crime while others implicate sources of personal commitment.

Sam deploys well-developed accounts and neutralizations (Sykes and Matza 1957) to rationalize his crime. While some might see this apologia as a set of convenient excuses, it does show that Sam had a conscience. Sam does have a "moral code," he does want respectability, and he does respond to the *powerful pressures for conformity that inhere in the larger society.* As a result of his criminality, though, he experiences a kind of marginality.

Sam's guilt depends on the moral field of reference. Like people more generally, Sam's morality and "conscience" vary relative to differing *moral spheres* in which he is embedded, or the different *fields* in which one is seeking economic and social achievement and recognition. For example, Sam's theft and hustling activities are defined as illegal and dysfunctional by the larger society. To the entrepreneur of crime and vice, however, his normative reference group is not the larger society but is (mainly) the blue-collar, working-class community and his own network in crime, and so his criminal activities are positively defined.

Rewards of Sam's Criminal Career:
The Power of Personal Commitment to Crime

Sam Goodman enjoyed several different kinds of rewards from burglary and, later, fencing. These rewards continued to entice him until he was too sick to work. Sam felt the "seductions of crime" (Katz 1988) strongly. In Chapters 3 and 11, we discussed three types of commitment to crime and conformity—structural, personal, and moral. Crime brought Sam rewards, positive emotions and attitudes, preferences, and valued identities, which in turn built for him a strong *personal commitment* to his criminal activities. *In fact, one cannot understand the continuity and longevity of Sam's criminal career without understanding the degree to which Sam was personally invested in the social world of criminal enterprise, and found it personally rewarding.* While Sam also enjoyed the rewards of his legitimate work and was personally invested in it, Sam's life and identity were strongly molded around fencing, and his financial and social well-being were heavily dependent on it. Sam's attachment to fencing was built up by favorable definitions of the experience that he acquired from others (as many of the previous chapters show), and from the action itself.

Thus, we see in Sam what is a more generic process. One becomes personally committed to lines of action to the extent that: (1) one has received rewards (material, cognitive, or emotional) from the activity itself in the past, (2) one has previously enjoyed associating with the others with whom one participates in the activity, and/or (3) one received self-validation from the identities or roles one enacts in the activity. In this way, a person develops preferences for repeated involvement in lines of activity.

Positive Attitudes toward Criminal Activities

Most of Sam's personal commitment to crime came from positive attitudes toward *his criminal activities themselves.* Some of these positive attitudes take the form of Sam's moral apologia for crime, which we discuss below. However, the first and foremost attraction of theft and criminal enterprise for Sam was the money—both having it and the fun of making it. One could say that money was perhaps the central preoccupation of Sam's life. Until he got sick, most of his time and energy was spent making, and spending, money. When asked why he did what he did, he always quickly answered something like, "What do you mean, why did I do it? Because it was good money!" Whether it was about burglary or fencing, he could talk at great length about the business end of the activity—angles and techniques for maximizing his profit. Sam enjoyed making even trivial amounts of money, as Steelbeams once related:

> This is hard to believe, but some Sunday mornings Sam would drive around town, hit all the Hope Rescue Mission boxes. Check to see what people threw away.

Like an old radio, TV and that. He'd fiddle with it and get it working, sell it for $5, $10 in his store . . . What the fuck would he make from this? No, it was just the idea of making a buck, pulling something. He got a bang out of it.

Sam also loved "getting over on somebody." Jesse described this tendency when he said, "Sam's gotta always think he's pulling something. I think that's the only way he's happy in life. That he's doing somebody in" (cited in *The Fence*:227). This view was shared by other associates of Sam, some of whom would add "but couldn't get mad at him cause he was a good guy in other ways."

These aspects of Sam's "working personality" were partly carryovers from his childhood and adolescence, when he had to hustle for himself (or do without), and his quick realization that he was pretty good at this. In effect, Sam never lost that early reinforcement and satisfaction (partly survival) of "hustling to make a buck."

Sam also loved spending money. Sam's associates like Rocky, Steelbeams, and Jesse talked often about Sam's appetite for relatively expensive fun, such as "womanizing" and gambling, for buying things he didn't need, and being a "good joe" or "good sport" who spent money on others and paid his help well. Sam's friend Jesse once said, "Sam don't think nothing about a buck. I mean Sam can go through money, geez, like Sherman going through Georgia" (cited in *The Fence*:221). Even at his death, one thing he regretted was that he didn't make *and save* more money, that as he got older and mellowed, he passed up some opportunities to score really big.

On the surface, it might seem that Sam was similar to lower-prestige property criminals and drug dealers described in the research literature (e.g., Shover 1996; Tunnell 2000; Jacobs 1999), who adopt a "life is a big party" attitude, and crime fulfills the need for money to keep the party going. Sam was different, though, from these lower-prestige property offenders in some key respects. Sam was quite skilled at what he did, capable of very hard work, self-discipline, and delayed gratification, and possessed of "people skills." These were crucial sources of his prosperity. Sam might have liked to have a good time, but he also was capable of putting his nose to the grindstone.

Second, Sam's skills as a burglar and fence were also a source of rewards. Typically, one enjoys what one is good at. Sam was successful at both burglary and fencing, but he especially enjoyed the latter. Sam enjoyed the rough and tumble of illicit business as a kind of competitive play as he matched wits with others, such as thieves, buyers, and police. At the height of his career, he was quite a successful illegal entrepreneur, and in even his later "moonlighting" phase, he enjoyed being an "old head" and often expressed the wish that he could pass on all his criminal skill and knowledge to a solid, promising younger man.

Third, Sam was drawn to the excitement and action of *making money* from crime. The wheeling and dealing of fencing, the risk of getting caught, the possibility of a really big deal, were all sources of stress and tension, but also excitement. As Sam said in *The Fence,* "In different ways, there's a challenge in fencing that in truth I could say I liked" (p. 225). At times in Sam's narrative of his later life, one of the things he seemed to miss was this very excitement, that "little kick you need once in awhile." The desire for excitement seemed to be one thing, along with the money, of course, that could draw him back into crime in his moonlighting phase.

Fourth, not only is fencing interesting and challenging, it also allows a lot of liberty to make decisions about one's own and others' working conditions and activities. Sam could set his own and others' agendas, in both his store and his later business. Sam enjoyed both the autonomy and the responsibility of running a fencing operation. He liked being his own boss and not having to work within the structure and boredom of ordinary employment.

Positive Attitudes toward Criminal Others

Personal commitment to crime for Sam also came from associations with and mutually positive attitudes toward others in the underworld. Sam enjoyed having a reputation as a player, a "big shot," especially at the height of his career. He enjoyed congenial relationships with employees, other legitimate and illicit businesspeople, hangers-on and wanna-bes, and active and retired thieves who hung out with him at bars, the gambling club, and his businesses. He also found great satisfaction in the feelings of camaraderie and shared interests with other dealers in stolen goods, like Louie, Woody, or Angelo. He especially loved and was proud of being included in the gambling club, and rubbing shoulders with local organized-crime players, as described in a previous chapter. These local organized-crime elites were also role models for Sam, and he aspired to be more like them, at least in some ways. In particular, he admired their money, prestige, and power.

Sam's involvement in fencing was not only the medium for the formation and ranking of his social relationships in general, but served as the source of the majority of the satisfying relationships that he had. Sam willingly embedded himself in the satisfying relationships and mutual obligations to thieves, buyers, dealers, and organized-crime elites, and these were a major source of the continuity and longevity of his criminal career.

One important point we emphasize is that this nature of Sam's social world and its relationship to his criminality does not fit the picture of social ties between criminals painted by theorists like Travis Hirschi (1969; Gottfredson and Hirschi 1990), Ruth Kornhauser (1978), and their followers. These scholars argue that criminals lack self- and/or social control, and therefore are unlikely to form relationships of significant durability and strength, and this is especially said to be true of relationships between criminals. Control theorists (whether they emphasize self- or social control) tend to see relationships between criminals as "cold and brittle" (Hirschi 1969). Sam's significant criminal ties were neither cold nor brittle, and they provided an important set of rewards and a source of his personal commitment to crime.

Self-Concept Tied to Criminal Identity

Finally, a key source of personal commitment to crime for Sam was that his self-concept was wrapped up in his criminal identity. It is true that Sam's self-definition presents some contradictions and ambivalence (something that is probably true of many people). On one hand, Sam was aware of the marginality and labeling effects of being an ex-con. In the last years before his death he preferred to think of himself as a mostly legitimate businessman (which, by that time, was true). At the end of his life, he noted that he did not want the ordinary citizen to see him as a "crook" or at least as "not just a crook." Of course, the kind of "crook" mattered quite a bit. Sam didn't mind being called a "good burglar," a "wheeler-dealer," or a "con man" in relation to his fencing activities. Sam thought of himself as a good thief and, later, a successful fence, and enjoyed being a wheeler-dealer and an underworld player. Over the whole course of his life, these were Sam's most salient identities by which he defined and evaluated himself.

Overall, *Sam was a man remarkably comfortable in his own skin.* He looked at himself, and felt that he was pretty much what he had worked at being, though he sometimes wished he had been an even bigger or more successful criminal entrepreneur. "If I had to start life all over, I would be a fence. 'Cause it was really beautiful," he said in *The Fence* (p. 233). He reiterated this at the end of his life when he said, "If I was to live life over, I would want to be a fence. Only get into it sooner. Or be a guy in the rackets, like an Angelo." A good part of the reason for his comfort with his criminal identity was that he really did not consider himself a morally bad person, or at least no worse than anyone else, and in fact better than some.

Of course, Sam's personal commitment to crime waxed and waned throughout the course of his life. The height of his personal commitment to crime was during the second phase of his career when he was a "big," "wide-open" fence. His attitudes toward crime and other practitioners of crime and vice remained favorable in the third, "moonlighting" phase of his career, but he also moved toward more positive attitudes toward legitimate people and associations (for example, his employees, legitimate antique dealers, and other business people). Furthermore, the moonlighting phase of his career also saw some changes in Sam's self-definition (e.g., "I'm not just a crook") in his later years, as the narratives in Chapter 12 and the next chapter show. That is, Sam came to see himself mostly as a legitimate businessman who dabbled in crime.

How can a person like Sam, who spent most of his life committing serious property crimes, maintain that he is really a decent fellow after all? Below, we explore Sam's moral duality.

Sam's Apologia: Neutralizations and Accounts

In *The Fence* (pp. 237–256), Steffensmeier explained Sam Goodman's *apologia pro vita sua,* or his moral rationales for his burglary and fencing career. At the time of the research conducted for *The Fence,* Sam did not spend a lot of time on a day-to-day basis reflecting on the morality or lack thereof of his criminal actions. Even so, when Steffensmeier probed Sam on the subject, Sam was able to articulate many offense-specific excuses, justifications, and rationalizations for why he "wasn't that bad."

At the end of his life, Sam had more time and motivation to further develop and elaborate his apologia, as his final narrative shows. Many of the elements of Sam's moral universe serve as sources of personal commitment to crime, functioning as action-specific attitudes or definitions of situations that defined his criminality in a favorable rather than a negative light. In other words, Sam's moral themes and neutralizations, which we describe below, are actually a subset of attitudes favorable to lines of action, a major source of Sam's personal commitment to crime.

Sociologically, these justifications, etc., are known as "vocabularies of motive" (Mills 1940). Vocabularies of motive are rhetoric that one uses to rationalize or justify one's violations of social norms to others and, equally importantly, to oneself. In the context of Sam's narratives here and in *The Fence,* his use of these vocabularies of motive served as accounts (Scott and Lyman 1968) more than as neutralizations (Sykes and Matza 1957). The difference between neutralizations and accounts is that neutralizations are deployed before norm violations occur, while accounts are articulated after violations occur (which is the case with Sam's narratives here). However, the forms of the justifying rhetoric, or "techniques" as Sykes and Matza (1957) refer to them, are similar in both cases. Also in both cases, people use these to justify the behavior in an attempt to ward off moral censure from others and guilt from within oneself (with varying degrees of success). Importantly, Sam's apologia indicates that he did in fact have a conscience—one must care about moral norms, at least at some level, for accounts to be necessary in the first place. *If one does not care about the morality of one's actions, then one does not need to justify them.*

Key Themes in Sam's Moral System

Below, we have listed seven key themes of Sam's moral system or apologia. Sam especially emphasized the first four:

1. "The business world don't care how you make a buck, just as long as you make it." Sam had a kind of social-Darwinist worldview in which he saw life as characterized by competitiveness, illegal behavior, and corruption, all of which were tolerated and often encouraged. Such behavior can be found especially in the "business" and "political" sectors of society. Offenders like Sam are seeking to achieve their success in a manner not unlike these "other people."

2. Relatedly, there is a fine line between the legitimate and illegitimate. Sam also believed strongly that most people have "larceny in the heart," and said things like, "Who isn't on the take at least a little? Even 'the do-gooders' will chisel if they are in a pinch."

3. Sam and associates like Jesse strongly believed in the *inevitability of theft*. As Jesse put it: "Holy Christ, you have people that have property or money, and you have people that wanna take it. I don't care what kind of jail they put up, you're gonna have so many thieves. Same as there's always plumbers, electricians, carpenters, and teachers like yourself. It's been that way since time began and that is going to be until time ends. You are always gonna have thieves." Sam nodded his approval as Jesse said this. Since "you are always gonna have thieves," the thief role is acceptable because it reflects the natural order of things. Jesse and Sam displayed a disbelief that any intelligent person could see it otherwise.

To reinforce his conclusion, Jesse (if prodded further) would note the universal existence of related phenomena like prostitution and war: that society has always had and hence always will have prostitutes and johns, or those who plunder and those trying to keep from being plundered.

4. As we elaborate later, "life as a ledger" is a central theme in Sam's assessment (especially as the curtain winds down on his life). Sam believed that people's behavior is a mix of good and bad. As Sam sees it, the good he did outweighed the bad. "Yes, I have done some rank shit, but have done a lot of good too." So, Sam sees himself on balance as a "morally okay" guy.

5. Sam had an abiding belief in a conception of manhood in which "you do what you have to do get by, to do okay." In this conception of masculinity, being a man meant not having to depend on others, to keep up with or do better than others in life's competitions, and "to live your life, not somebody else's."

6. Sam recognized the ideal nature of public morality, and its inapplicability when applied to concrete situations and "real people" (we expand on this later). That is, society's standards for merit and respectabilities are seen as exceeding the capabilities of many of its members (see also Suttles 1968).

7. On the other hand, there is also in Sam a recognition (and even some admiration) for people who are highly *un*likely to break the law because they see the law or rule as a moral obligation. This is seen in the next chapter in his evaluations of his domestic partner Wanda, as well as of Norm, his antique dealer friend.[1]

Neutralizations and Accounts

We also can group Sam's accounts according to several of the forms of neutralizations (rhetoric used to excuse a deviant act prior to its commission) and accounts (rhetoric to excuse a deviant act after its commission) as described by Sykes and Matza (1957), Scott and Lyman (1968), and Klockars (1974): denial of injury, denial of the victim, condemning the condemners, denial of responsibility, and the "metaphor of the ledger." These neutralizations and accounts are nourished by subterranean values of the larger society (especially the blue-collar working class) and also are institutionalized features of the underworld.[2]

Sam's apologia is complex, however, and many of these themes interweave and mutually support each other. His apologia also reminds us of Mordechai Nisan's point that "people do not aspire to be saints" but allow themselves leeway "to deviate from the right course" in making moral choices (Nisan and Horenczyk 1990:29; see also Nisan 1991). In deciding whether to violate a specific rule or law, individuals balance moral considerations against non-moral considerations such as financial pressures, personal crises, or unusual opportunities. Nisan's emphasis parallels that of the conception of neutralization and accounts. That is, law violators are not necessarily improperly socialized, nor do they necessarily have a predisposition for rule breaking. Nor do people break the law necessarily because of a lack of moral knowledge or a distorted view of right or wrong, or because of an inability to resist temptation.

Denial of injury and denial of the victim are evident in a variety of Sam's accounts both here and in *The Fence*. Sam explains that fencing stolen goods really did not harm people directly—rather, his fencing role occurred after the victims (who had their property stolen) had already been harmed. The fence is simply putting a bad situation to good use. It is the thief who is doing the actually victimizing. He also notes that there are much worse crimes than fencing, such as robbery, drug dealing, rape, and child abuse.

Furthermore, in Sam's view, fencing is not a very serious crime because it causes little injury to the victims. He supposes that they are usually individuals or businesses that can afford the loss, and will simply recover losses from insurance or tax write-offs. "I don't feel I hurt any little people 'cause most of the stuff did come out of business places and big places, which were insurance write-offs and which they will many times mark it double what it was," Sam explained in *The Fence* (p. 241). In that case, Sam saw himself as really stealing from insurance companies or the government, whom Sam saw as deserving victims since they cheated others anyway.

This latter theme shades into denial of the victim—that is, Sam believes the victims probably engage in dishonest activity themselves. Sam also denies the victim when he often describes how "dumb" people are, how they do foolish things that make them easy targets for theft or being conned. Such "suckers" are fair game to Sam.

Sam did admit that not all victim losses were insignificant, and that some victims might not be deserving. He explains this by observing that, in some instances, he arranged for the stolen property to be returned. Sam described a situation like this in the current narrative, where he anonymously returned a stolen gun of sentimental value.

Denial of responsibility is an evident theme in Sam's rhetoric, and is related to denial of injury. Sam reasons that theft and fencing take place regardless of whether Sam participates or not, so he might as well profit from it. If he did not buy a thief's stolen goods, someone else would. In *The Fence,* Sam turned the old saying, "If there were no fences, then there would be no thieves," on its head. He always maintained that fences do not cause goods to be stolen. As a former burglar himself who saw the issue from the other side, he found the notion that fences are responsible for theft preposterous. He knows that thieves steal regardless of what fences want or do not want, and that most fences offer little direction or support for thieves. To Sam, the fence–thief relationship is not a conspiracy, but simply a transaction. As Sam says in *The Fence,* "Tell me this: why did I do all that time in the penitentiary for the burglary? I didn't hear no judge say, 'Sammy, you can go free 'cause your fence made you do it'" (p. 255).

Condemning the condemners is also a recognizable but complex theme in Sam's apologia. Sam's justifications here and in *The Fence* are full of themes like "Everyone does it," "Honesty is relative," and "Everyone has some larceny in them." In effect, Sam offers a claim of "normality." Sam emphasizes the contradictions between the world as it is and the world as it should be, and observes that others in society fail to live up to society's ideals. Sam favorably compares himself with others, whom he sees as dishonest and deviant as himself, if not more so. In *The Fence* and here, he especially singles out those otherwise law-abiding citizens and businesspeople who knowingly buy stolen goods from him. "They are as guilty as the ones who steal," he says. He also has little good to say about police, many of whom he views as crooked and corrupt. As he says, "The cops I have known in my life were always looking for a handout. There are some very crooked cops who have pulled a lotta rank shit."

It is hardly surprising, therefore, that Sam sees as lopsided the old observation: "If there were no Receivers there would be no Thieves—Deprive a Thief of his sale and ready market for his goods and he is undone" (Colquhon 1800:289). Sam instead believes (somewhat tongue in cheek) that if there were no thieves, no bargain-hunting private citizens, no dishonest businesspeople, and no corrupt police, there would be no fences.

He also deflects moral censure and perhaps guilt by taking note of others in society who lie, cheat, con, and chisel, such as "TV preachers" and significantly, the tobacco companies who push and peddle the addictive cigarettes that got him hooked and led to his cancer. "They are the ones that ought to be locked up," he says. Sam claims that his actions are relatively acceptable compared to others, as in, "There are others worse than me."

Finally, Sam frequently deploys the *metaphor of the ledger* (Klockars 1974). The ledger refers to the balance sheet of good and bad acts. If one's bad acts are balanced by good ones, then one is not so deserving of condemnation. He points out, "I done a lot of wrong, but I done a lot of good, too." Sam could go on and on about good deals he gave people, charities he donated to, friends and acquaintances he helped out in some way or another. He also took pride in the fact that his store and later his furniture/antiques shop employed many people, giving them chances to prosper that they would not have had were it not for Sam. Most importantly, Sam often pointed to his generosity and kindness to children as proof that he was really "not that bad a guy." Sam (and also those who knew him) pointed out that he often gave kids free toys from his store, especially poor kids and he would take neighborhood kids out for ice cream or to baseball games. "I was always tops with kids," he said.

Sam's moral code is a *practical* morality rather than an abstract, *ideal* one. The moral dilemmas of theft, conning, and illicit business activities were not abstractions whose morality was to be debated. Instead, they were realities of life, a significant aspect of Sam's social world. One copes with everyday life in terms of the concrete rather than the abstract or hypothetical. Sam does not so much approve of theft and hustling in the abstract, but he is easily able to discover reasons for them as a way of responding to the context of one's everyday life. Thus, he sees theft and criminal enterprise as acceptable ways to meet subsistence needs, or else to have a standard of living comparable to what most people in the community enjoy.

Moral Commitment in Sam's Criminal Activity

Moral commitment is a difficult, and to some extent counterintuitive, concept to apply to crime (Ulmer 2000:324–325). Johnson (1991) originally used moral commitment in the context of relationships, where, for example, one stays in an unhappy marriage out of a sense of general or specific moral obligation. Nonetheless, we believe the concept has some usefulness for examining continuity in criminal behavior, and that more research and theorizing is needed on the notion of moral commitment to crime.

Recall from Chapter 11 that moral commitment involves *internal constraint,* and has three sources. First, it flows from action-specific norms that discourage the termination of a line of action once involved in it. This source does *not* refer to individuals' attitudes or beliefs about the moral rightness or wrongness per se of a given line of action. Such attitudes or beliefs function to define actions in a positive way, and are thus a source of personal commitment (as we describe above with Sam's apologia). Rather, this source of moral commitment refers to norms that impose constraints against quitting a specific activity after becoming involved in it. The second source of moral commitment is the extent to which people see themselves as having moral obligations to specific others with whom they are involved in lines of action. The final source of moral commitment involves the extent to which one generally values consistency in one's own action.

As we have seen in Sam's discussions of the underworld code, embeddedness in some kinds of criminal networks can entail learning action-specific norms, such as those emphasizing dependability, trustworthiness, loyalty, and a sense of moral obligation to other members. Such codes of conduct and informal rules of obligation are especially important in coordinating and safeguarding activities among networks of higher status and perhaps even mid-level thieves and criminal entrepreneurs. Furthermore, as Sam says in dozens of ways throughout this book, a reputation for dependability and for not letting others down, for recognizing obligations to associates by keeping one's mouth shut when one gets in trouble, and an ability to keep one's word are all prized attributes in criminal enterprise. Sam captures the importance of this kind of dependability and trustworthiness, which can be seen as involving moral commitment to crime through action-specific norms and perceived obligations to others:

> Thieves have to have confidence in each other. That's where heart comes in, too. That's when you're going to have to depend on a person. Not have a guy that's going to get all shitty and run out, and he gets away and you get popped. That's part of being trustworthy, too. Being dependable. You got to know the man's on your back all the time.

In addition, general consistency values figured into Sam's moral commitment to crime. Sam believed that one should finish what one starts, and that a person should not quit an endeavor just because the going gets tough or the work gets hard. For Sam, to some extent these beliefs applied to theft and criminal enterprise. He spoke with pride about how hard he worked at his criminal activities and adversities he overcame, and he took pride in his "being solid" when the going got tough. He had disdain for those in the criminal world who did not show such persistence in the face of hard work or adversity.

Recall our discussion and Sam's narratives about the underworld code in Chapters 13 and 14, as well the discussions of trust and character in Chapters 9 and 10. Believing in and living up to consistency norms and interpersonal obligations was a big part of what Sam meant by "being solid," and part of what he meant by having "heart." By implication, this means that *moral commitment to crime is a form of criminal social capital* that encompasses such attributes as heart, solidness, trustworthiness, and character. Furthermore, this implies that a significant portion of the underworld code concerns sources of moral commitment to crime, even though the extent to which underworld participants learn and follow this code varies (see Chapters 13 and 17). Further research should explore the notion that sources of moral commitment are forms of criminal social capital that increase the potential longevity and success of criminal enterprise.

Images of Crime and Criminals

Our knowledge of criminal careers and chronic offending, and of patterns of criminal behavior and organization, is at best incomplete. *Confessions* is, to be sure, not entirely an unimpeachable source as well. It relies largely on the assessments of a veteran criminal entrepreneur and, interconnectedly, on the researchers' first- and secondhand knowledge of a network of associated criminal entrepreneurs, some with short but others with long criminal careers. This is both a strength and a weakness. That said, it is still useful to extract all the insights we can from this material about the nature of crime and criminals, and how this squares with scholarly and popular depictions of them.

Imagery matters. The cultural and intellectual imagery we have about a phenomenon or a category of people structures and delimits the ways we can think about that phenomenon or those people. Overall, what we see is that conceptual and moral distinctions between crime, criminals, and conventionality are muddier and messier than current discussions often acknowledge.

Sam Goodman is an exemplar of the duality of human nature. On one hand, he engaged in a lifelong career of stealing, fencing, and racketeering. As he repeatedly pointed out, property crime was his business, and he derived considerable material, social, and psychological rewards from making money from crime. On the other hand, Sam's life very much challenges the notion that "career criminals" are morally corrupt, they have been corrupt all their lives, they will always be corrupt, and they are corrupt in all areas of their life. This is a picture of career criminality that is widely held by the public, and it is implicitly or explicitly espoused by some types of criminological theories.

We do not for a moment romanticize Sam's activities. Sam did indeed "pull a lot of rank shit," as he says. However, people are not one-dimensional. Sam was both immoral and moral, and the morality of his conduct did concern him. Sam was deviant in his choice of livelihood, but he was conventional in a variety of other ways. Put differently, Sam "crawled through windows" to burglarize businesses and homes, and he sold stolen antiques, televisions, or furniture, but he also paid his employees well and you could also trust him to watch your children.

As is true of most case studies of criminal offenders, one can find in Sam's life evidence supporting almost any framework or theory of crime causation. Depending on one's lens (and one's moral or political stance), one observer might see one factor as decisively causal, while another observer might see a different one. For example, one could see "faulty parenting" (a single mother, an unfair stepfather) in Sam's biography as the cause of his lifelong behavior, in support of self-control theory (and to some extent social learning theory). To do so, in our view, would be a gross oversimplification of Sam's criminal career.

We find that some criminological perspectives view criminals either through narrow lenses or moralistic lenses, or both. Some perspectives heavily emphasize socioeconomic disadvantage as the key cause of crime, and focus almost exclusively on street crimes of the urban underclass. Other perspectives view criminality through the lens of individual pathology or deficit. In fact, some observers seem as interested in morally condemning and stigmatizing criminal offenders as in explaining their behavior (e.g., Wilson and Herrnstein 1985; Delisi 2003). The underlying moral stance is itself an allegiance to an idea of criminality that separates saints from sinners, and places a clear boundary between criminals and the rest of us (see Weisburd and Waring 2001:153). This view of criminality has been reinforced by scholars who have tried to identify what manifestly distinguishes criminals from others. Intentionally or otherwise, this view strongly tends to divorce crime from the fabric of society in which it is embedded.

Gottfredson and Hirschi (1990) emphasize lifelong, stable self-control deficits as the major cause of crime—deficits caused by poor parenting and inadequate socialization. Moffitt (1997) emphasizes early onset maladjustment propelled by biological or cognitive deficits. Both of these approaches depict a particular image of the criminal landscape: criminals are bad or "antisocial" from childhood onward (or even already in the womb), they are bad in nearly every way, they are bad most of the time, and they will always be bad. We disagree with this as a general characterization of criminality. This image of human nature reflects more of a moral stance than a social scientific viewpoint with a sound empirical basis.

In our view, criminological perspectives that focus on individual deficit or maladjustment have a narrow view of the criminal landscape that ignores or fails to recognize that criminals are a heterogeneous lot. We would like to see more recognition of and research on the apparently great variation in the nature and task environments of crime, and the variation in the individual characteristics of practitioners of crime and vice. We do not doubt that some kinds of persistent, serious criminals fit the picture painted by Hirschi and Gottfredson's self control theory or by Moffitt's developmental perspective. These are the ones that Sam calls *"losers," "misfits," and "fuck-ups" who "give criminals a bad name."* We argue that there are many offenders—like Sam and his associates, as well as mafiosi, corrupt police, cartage thieves, ordinary joe blow citizens moonlighting at theft or hustling, semilegitimate business-people, and perhaps white-collar criminals—who probably do not fit this imagery. Most of these kinds of offenders are very understudied in criminology. Our point is that self-control theory and Moffitt's developmental perspective provide very oversimplified imagery of crime and criminals, and thus should not be reified or overgeneralized.

Among the indicators or elements of low self control enumerated by Gottfredson and Hirschi (1990) are risk-taking and impulsivity, insensitivity, being physical rather than mental, being nonverbal, and lacking capacity for deferred gratification and diligence. It strikes us that this list of characteristics is not social class neutral. That is, the markers of self control deficits are also markers of lower- or blue-collar working-class culture. According to Miller (1958), lower-class culture fosters distinct focal concerns, such as trouble, toughness, (street) smartness, excitement, fate, and autonomy, that are conducive to criminal and delinquent behavior. In particular, Miller's description of the focal concerns trouble, toughness, and excitement closely map the description of low self control markers like impulsivity, physicality, and lack of deferred gratification.

Moreover, descriptors like *physicality* both beg the question and ignore the *work environment* of criminal enterprise and lifestyle—where, more so than typifies conventional economic endeavors, physical characteristics such as strength and "muscle" (capacity for force or violence) have special usefulness. That crime activities and sustained criminal enterprise are often *intrinsically* physical (also risk-taking, etc.) is noted by Steffensmeier, as follows:

> Strength, prowess, and muscle are useful for the successful commission of crimes, for protection, for enforcing contracts, and for recruiting and managing reliable associates. Physical strength and speed are obviously useful for committing crimes such as robbery, burglary, and many kinds of cartage theft. Less obviously, they are important in hustling and theft activities in which the *potential* of violence or need for quick getaway are omnipresent. Muscle has specific utility for the protection of property and enforcement of contracts. . . . The criminal has to rely on his own, or that of his or her organization's ability to protect, retaliate, or inspire respect among criminal associates (and perhaps others as well, such as victims or law enforcement). (1983:1014)

In other words, physicality and risk-taking are instrumental to a lot of money oriented crime, and are often intrinsic part of the criminal working environment, lifestyle, or field. Criminological theorizing should avoid committing the *imploding tautology* of using attributes or characteristics that are intrinsic to the crime itself as markers for stable, enduring individual dispositions toward crime (e.g., low self control, neuropsychological deficits, or antisocial personality).

Relatedly, Hagan (1991) links risk-taking, the search for excitement and thrills, and conspicuous consumption of entertainment and "partying" to deeply rooted "subterranean values" of American society, particularly among masculine working-class and youth subcultures (see also Matza 1964). He also follows Veblen (1934) in observing that risk-taking and thrill-seeking are often seen as valued character traits. Thus, orientations said to be indicators of impulsivity and thus a lack of self-control appear to be quite correlated with working-class, masculine culture and lifestyles. We also note that crime as a pursuit or lifestyle almost by definition requires a sort of risk-taking stance, especially in responding to and building crime opportunities—in Sam's words, "You either do it now or you don't do it, otherwise the opportunity may be gone."

Gottfredson and Hirschi might argue that similar causes (lack of self control) lie behind socioeconomic status attainment and criminality, and that at least one of the causes of low self control (inadequate parenting) is correlated with social class. Still, it may instead be that socialization into lower- or working-class cultural lifestyles and focal concerns fosters some of the above markers of low self control. If this causal sequence is correct, then differential association/social learning theory would seem to provide a better explanation of both low self control and class-linked criminality (for a related argument, see Jensen and Akers 2003).

Furthermore, risk-taking or being adventuresome or a "free spirit" and impulsivity are not the same things, and they carry very different social class and value connotations, depending on the status of the individual who exhibits them. These two concepts are often conflated, both by Hirschi and Gottfredson and others who advocate their general theory of crime. Instead, we see a need to conceptually and empirically distinguish between risk-taking and impulsivity. What are needed are conceptual and empirical ways of measuring impulsivity (i.e., present orientation, lack of planning) and distinguishing it from "risk-taking capacity" or tastes for risks, which need not entail impulsivity and its components. As Greenberg and colleagues point out: "Gottfredson and Hirschi do not carefully distinguish inability to control oneself from simple failure to do so on the part of those who *could* control themselves *if they wished*" (Greenberg, Tamarelli, and Kelly 2002:82, emphasis added).

Our culture admires and celebrates risk-taking among legitimate entrepreneurs, military leaders, adventurers, and others. We denigrate it among criminals, however. Among criminals, risk-taking becomes linked with impulsivity and a symptom of low self control.

We also argue that theoretical pictures of rationality and planning are sometimes unrealistic [something March and Simon (1958) also argued long ago]. Some depictions of crime point to a lack of long-range planning and deferred gratification among criminals and argue that most criminals are therefore impulsive, irrational, and lacking in self control. However, such models require as a litmus test of rationality a level of long-term planning and deferred gratification that typically does not characterize the lives of most people (especially those from the blue-collar working class—whose culture forms the underpinnings of, and are embellished in, underworld culture).

As Lemert notes, most of us live life on mostly a *day-to-day* basis. That is, most of us seldom plan anything much more than six months or so ahead (except perhaps in vague terms), often our plans are not even that far-sighted, and our plans are always subject to situational negotiation (Strauss 1993). As Lemert stated:

> While some fortunate individuals by insightful endowment or by virtue of the stabilized nature of their situations can foresee more distant social consequences of their actions and behave accordingly, not so most people. Much human behavior is situationally oriented and geared to meeting the many and shifting claims which others make upon them. The loose structuring and swiftly changing facade and content of modern social situations make it difficult to decide which means will insure ends sought. Often choice is a compromise between what is sought and what can be sought. (1972:79–80, emphasis added)

In sum, our position is that the Gottfredson and Hirschi conceptualization of low self control belongs in criminological theory as *one potential cause* of criminal behavior. However, we argue that (1) self control has been conceptualized in a narrow and perhaps class-biased manner and (2) that self control probably cannot be the basis for a "general theory of crime." Self control may be important, but so are a variety of social controls, complex opportunity structures, learning processes, and motivational factors.

The Role of Situational Factors

We also recommend a renewed focus in criminology on the role of foreground factors, or proximal, situational factors in offender decision making. Symbolic interactionists observe that the most proximal, direct cause of behavior is actors' definitions of the situations in which they act (Maines 2001). Applying this conception to criminology suggests that more research should focus on processes of how criminals or would-be criminals define situations, develop motivations, and weigh situational alternatives as they consider and choose to engage in crimes, as well as how these processes are shaped by larger social contexts (see Lemert 1951; Lofland 1969; Athens 1997; McCarthy and Hagan 1992; Wright and Decker 1994). Such factors are typically relegated to secondary positions compared to background factors or individual traits (e.g., family structure, social bonds, poverty, self-control, impulsivity, neuropsychological deficit) in contemporary criminological research. A situational focus, however, fosters a different type of imagery of crime and criminals.

On one hand, the notion of "situational crime" refers to crime committed by ordinarily law-abiding adult citizens with a relatively well-integrated set of roles and with little in the way of observable neuropsychological deficits or pathology. External stresses and strains may temporarily disrupt one's moral code or fear of the law in ways leading to criminal behavior.

Relatedly, Lofland (1969) and Wright and Decker (1994) focus on "encapsulation," where offenders' lifestyles, associations, and socioeconomic characteristics combine to push them toward offending. An offender who comes across a promising crime opportunity, has a pressing need for cash, and has associates at hand with whom to engage in the crime is more likely to commit the crime. This situational encapsulation process is not irreversible or deterministic. Instead, it is a process involving chains of decisions made in the face of desires and constraints, a process that over time becomes a constraint itself (see Becker 1960; Lemert 1951).

This picture of situational crime and/or encapsulation probably accounts for a lot of offending, especially by younger and less-skilled offenders; and also may contribute to "first-time" offending or intermittent offending by older persons. This situational focus directs our attention to the offense and its situational context to a greater extent by isolating potential criminal and noncriminal options and how participants define them. Thus, a situational focus is hard to square conceptually with the imagery of individual offender pathology.

Other Negative Imagery of Crime and Criminals

A related image of crime and criminals is presented by the stubborn folk idea that persons leading lives persistently departing from society's approved rules and regulations *must be* unhappy, demoralized, and emotionally maladjusted. The notion is almost foreign that crime can be "fun" (but see Katz 1988) and that one can be doing crime regularly while also being relatively self-contented, like Sam Goodman. We agree with Lemert (1951, 1972) that neither adjustment or maladjustment, nor feeling happy or unhappy, nor having low or high self-esteem are *inevitable* consequences of chronic criminal offending.

Most proponents of stable criminal trait or propensity theories make a great effort to counter the view that loyalty and trust are key elements of the underworld code and that criminals are capable of loyalty, interpersonal commitment, and trust. Criminals, they point out, have too many character defects to be loyal or trustworthy. Thus, they point out that criminals frequently "snitch" on one another as evidence of this lack of loyalty, trust, and interpersonal commitment among criminals. This implies that law-abiding people, in similar circumstances, would be more loyal or "solid" and thus less likely to snitch. But Sam Goodman often noted that he would trust "a decent thief to hold up and not snitch much more than I would your businessman, or your ordinary 'joe blow citizen.'"

As we implied above about unrealistic conceptions of rationality and planning, the same logic applies to notions like deferred gratification. The fact that criminals often do not engage in long-range planning, live their lives in the present or near term, tend to spend money in an "easy come, easy go" fashion is taken as evidence of impulsiveness, lack of self control, and inability to defer gratification. Yet, our observation is that many conventional, law-abiding people, especially among the blue-collar working class, behave similarly, at least at times. For example, the news is full of stories of "ordinary folks" hitting the lottery or coming into "easy money," and blowing the money in a short-sighted manner. Thus, an "easy come, easy go" attitude toward money and planning on the part of many criminals also reflects the lifestyle and norms of their network circles and reference groups.

In effect, scholars, journalists, and the conventional public sometimes create negative imagery of criminals by highlighting their shortcomings, and suggesting that they really are incapable of, and do not manifest, any valued traits. Perhaps Sam's narratives exaggerate the "solidness," or the degree of trust, loyalty, and commitment to associates in at least some parts of the underworld. However, we suspect that writers like Gottfredson and Hirschi or James Q. Wilson (see also Delisi 2003) exaggerate the lack of these behaviors among criminals, and overgeneralize the image of the impulsive, dissolute criminal.

Finally, focusing on self-control, neuropsychological deficit, or other stable individual criminal propensity notions overlooks or denies the nexus between the legitimate and the illegitimate that is a key theme of both *The Fence* and *Confessions*. Some criminologists and their theories want us to believe (and perhaps want to convince themselves) that illegal enterprise—and the underworld in a general sense—are separate and detached entities from the rest of society. Furthermore, criminals, thieves, swindlers, illicit businessmen, etc. are depicted as distinct "kinds of people" who are very different from law-abiding folk.

However, as Thorstein Veblen (1934), Edwin Sutherland (1947), Alfred Lindesmith (1941), Walter Miller (1958), David Matza (1964), and John Hagan (1991) have all observed, many subterranean values in the legitimate world overlap with the norms and codes of the illegitimate world. These scholars would argue that it is a mistake to regard the underworld, illegitimate entrepreneurship, or theft and fencing as activities separate or detached from the larger culture and social structure. To quote Alfred Lindesmith: Crime "is rather an integral part of our total culture. . . . It is in this sense that we have the criminals we deserve" (1941:120).

These links and porous boundaries between the criminal and conventional worlds can be illustrated by many examples. First, members of the lower and working classes often sympathize with the cynicism (and disillusionment) of the underworld. Second, an individualistic, predatory philosophy of success is reflected in both the conventional business world and in the business of crime. Third, the underworld meets the demand for goods and services that are defined as illegitimate, but for which there is nevertheless a strong demand from respectable people (cheap goods and liquor, illicit drugs, sex, gambling, etc.). Fourth, the underworld offers an informal economy that supports many people for whom only marginal low-paying conventional jobs are available. Last, respectable folk like and admire illegal entrepreneurs like Sam.

Differential Social Organization and the Underworld as Field

To us, a more useful perspective and set of images of crime and criminals comes from combining Sutherland's notion of normative (or moral message) conflict and differential social organization with Pierre Bourdieu's (1977; 1985) concept of "fields" and "habitus," and Anselm Strauss's (1993) similar conception of social worlds. Bourdieu's fields are arenas for rule-guided striving in which one competes or cooperates with others for rewards, upward status mobility, and well-being. Within fields, people acquire, employ, and exchange different kinds of economic, social, cultural, and symbolic capital in their goal-oriented striving. Furthermore, the rules guiding activities in a field are not unbreakable constraints. As Sam's narratives often show, conformity or nonconformity with field rules are strategic choices with different advantages, and these advantages vary according to different situations and one's position in the field.

Different social worlds or fields present different bodies of knowledge, definitions of situations, moral systems, and cognitive schemes—that is, in Bourdieu's term, *habitus*. Habitus guides people's activity in a field by organizing their perceptions, and habitus also depends on one's position in the field. By implication, different fields also present participants with different goals, strategies for achievement, and identities. Furthermore, norms and values are not general aspects of culture, but are field-specific, and navigating between fields is a complex task.

Thus, an extension of Sutherland's concept of normative conflict and differential social organization is to see the conventional world and underworld as distinctive but overlapping fields. Within these fields, people acquire the habitus of cognitive schemes, skills, and knowledge appropriate to given conventional or criminal fields, through differential association and other social learning processes. *All individuals are located in a number of fields, each with its own morality, practices, and available identities.* Some of these fields are primarily classified as conventional by the dominant cultural and political order, and some are classified as criminal. Thus, Sam Goodman is an employer and businessman, a family man, a donor to charity, and a criminal.

Thus, in terms of imagery, differential association/social learning theory, as well as viewing the underworld and conventional world as overlapping fields, removes some of the stigma from criminals. Criminals are no longer intrinsically evil people; they are products of the same generic sociological processes that characterize every person throughout life. This also presents a more optimistic view of human nature. If crime is learned in the context of differentially organized fields, then if the criminal socialization is not too entrenched and the individual is not too embedded in criminal networks and relationships, crime can be replaced with more useful learning in the context of more conventional fields.

At the same time, as we noted above, there also are countervailing cultural pressures and contradictory messages even within dominant cultures. Just as there are powerful pressures for conformity in society (which Sam clearly felt), there are also messages and opportunities that encourage the opposite. Subcultural values and identities, and subterranean traditions and beliefs in the general culture condone or encourage "dishonesty." For example, mainstream American culture values honesty and trustworthiness, but also makes folk heroes (real and fictitious) out of Jesse James, Al Capone, and Don Corleone. Indeed, many readers of *The Fence* found Sam Goodman to be a sort of admirable rogue. Furthermore, even most deviants are conforming in most aspects of their lives most of the time, and people are often deviant in some but not in most aspects of their life and activities.

That is how Sam Goodman was. He was a thief, fence, and racketeer. He punched and robbed an old man one Halloween, and he strangled a wounded co-offender to death to save his own skin. He was also friendly, hard working, generous, loyal to friends, and loved children. He hated drugs, sex offenders, crimes against children, and those who victimized the elderly. Sam shows that the reality of crime is not a television morality play, and that criminal nature, like human nature, does not come in one-dimensional packages.

Notes

1. As Talcott Parsons noted in his classic work, *The Structure of Social Action,* the calculation of the costs of crime varies by one's morality. Among those for whom "a rule is a moral obligation, the attitude of calculation is lacking" (1937:403).
2. To expand on the notion of the timing of their use, the types of neutralizations and/or accounts could be used as motives (1) *before* contemplating an illegal act, releasing the actor to be morally free to choose the act, (2) *while* contemplating an illegal act, to seek self-conscious approval that it is acceptable to go ahead, or (3) *after* an illegal act, to seek to reduce blame and culpability.

20

Final Confessions

Sam Takes Stock

Attitude Toward Life

When I was growing up if someone said I'm gonna cut your motherfucking throat, I would have said, "Get it on." That was my attitude through life—let's get it on. I never cared that much. If you can hurt me, so can I hurt you. We have to get our shit together or hurt each other. That was always my philosophy of life. Maybe that is why I lived so long—that I would try to work things out but if not, I could take the first shot.

I think I am very brazen. I don't scare easy. Even now I don't. It takes a lotta "heart" to be a fence or even a good burglar. You can't scare easy, fall apart on a close call like when the police call you in for questioning or there's a search warrant on your shop. The thieves and even the other dealers can pull some pretty rank shit. Same with the snitching, you can't stop it all the way but you can make them think twice. It was known I was pretty easygoing, a nice guy, but that I could be very nasty. You can't be a pushover. There are a lot of assholes out there.

I think I always had a little larceny in me, too. Looking for the buck. To this day it is hard for me to walk away from making a dollar, even a little one. Maybe this is more so in me than the ordinary joe blow on account from little on I had to hustle to get a bicycle or glove or do without it. I knew early that you have to look out for yourself. This came early from my grandpap, was tight-fisted with money and would let you know, hey, there's no handouts. Maybe for the "higher-ups," but not for the "little guy." Doing time and having to fend for myself just added to that. My attitude was I could pull my own weight.

I've always had that ability to understand people and figure them out. Whether I did it for bad or for good, I always had that ability—to read people. That's why I can get over so easily. It is only human nature to do that, to try to outdo the other. Beat the guy, at least a little.

Remember Amos? Kooky guy who bought a lot of antiques from me. Very educated man, very brilliant. Believed in devils, was very strange. One time I got two old chairs, paid like ten bucks a piece. I scratched the name of someone who was a governor one time. Then I put "Death Chair" on one and "Life Chair" on the other, and stained over it. I tells Amos this long story about the legend behind the chairs, how the governor kept them in his bedroom. He fell for it. Two junky chairs and I got like $600 apiece for them.

In my shop or if I peddled at the auction, I didn't come right out and say, "Hey, my prices are cheap 'cause I'm selling hot stuff." But I would give them an opening, play on the larceny that is them. Create a trust so they will feel it is safe, that they can get away with it. Play on the greed that is there. Ninety-nine of a hundred will go for it.

Most people would steal if they had the nerve to do it. Will take the extra dollar if they can get away with it. In my eye I really believe they would. If you knew where twenty grand was and you thought you had a half-decent chance to get it, you'd take a shot at it. It's hard to let twenty grand just sit there. Ninety-nine of a hundred have larceny in them, at least some larceny in their heart. Everybody, if they don't steal in a big way, they steal in a penny. Which is just the same goddamn thing.

You go to an auction, right? You're going to buy something. How are you going to know where it came from? Say it's a yard sale. Even if they think it is hot, if they think it's a bargain, they will buy. I don't know of anyone, very few in fact, that ever would walk away from something hot if it was cheap. If you go to the bank and there is an extra twenty dollars in there that don't belong, your ordinary joe blow will snap it up and just leave. Very few would not do that. I did it on a bigger scale, that I will admit. But what is the difference?

Am I rationalizing? Am I really a "bad" person? Should I feel sorry for what I've done? The ladies would pray with me and then the thought would cross my mind. All the shit I've pulled, some really rank shit, yet I don't feel bad about it. *Don't see myself as a bad person. That is the way I feel.*

I am not saying I would recommend the life I had for somebody else. A life in crime is hell in many ways. That is what I told your students. I would not wish them to go through what I went through. I think they appreciated that.

Some Mellowing

I think I have changed. Some. Not all the way. I think I am less aggressive now, more concerned about the feelings of others. I don't think I could go back to the mold I was in fifteen years ago. I don't think I'd fit. Why, I don't really know. I know I was changing down the line. I was getting mellower. I am still aggressive but not near what I used to be. Now, I can walk away if someone gets under my skin.

Talking to your class, coming up there, I think made some difference. The students would ask me if I felt bad about what I done, was I sorry for what I had done. "No, I'm not sorry. No, I don't feel bad." I drove back a couple of times, thinking: "Am I helping them or is this fucking class helping me? Or was we helping each other?" It seems to me we was both getting something out of the class. I could be wrong like a son of a bitch but that is what I think.

Going to class, but more so talking to you, made me look at myself more. On account of you would ask me. Head-on. And in different ways. "Did you do that? Why did you do that?" That would linger on in my mind even afterwards. Why the fuck did I do that?

Ten years ago I would use a Bobby Beck that would hang around my shop. Not only would I buy what he would steal but I was many times encouraging him. But then I was working with him, too, to turn himself around, to get a job. "Hey, you got a life to lead, don't fuck it away. If you're gonna steal, then get your act together doing that." I do believe that in the last few years I helped turn Bobby Beck around and that makes me feel good.

Same with Donnie—my foreman you might say. He was on his way to being a delinquent when he showed up at my shop. Has really turned himself around. I saw he had a knack for working with wood and converted that into something good. Donnie called just before you came. He may stop by later. Have a new guy in the shop, Pete. Hired him from another upholstery place and thinks he has some knowledge but is blowing out of his ass. Cuts corners to get the job done. I get on Donnie's ass to make sure Pete uses the hand tools 'cause it does a better job. That's why I bought those tools. Don't use the table saw. Those big scissors do a better job. Make sure now. If he tries to use that table saw, put it up his fucking ass.

The shop means a whole lot. I put too many fucking hours into it. Don't want to see it fall apart after I'm gone. Spent a lotta time training Donnie too. He can take over now and I think him and Benny and Wanda will make out after I'm gone. I'm proud of what I've built up there.

I think my shop, the guys in the shop, wanting to get Donnie set up to run the shop, my grandkids, and that made a difference. Definitely has mellowed me.

But Not Reformed

Even now, if had a good tip, I would think of clipping the place. And if Jesse called and said, "Let's go," I'd go. I think I still have the heart for burglary but maybe getting too old for crawling in windows. Just the excitement. From knowing what is there and where it is at, having my outlets in place. Would be a kick, a spark, 'cause life is pretty boring at times. And to see if I could still do it. It would be worth it for that.

Remember the building next to mine in Boonesboro that had a safe in it? An old building. Nobody was using it. I am sitting in my shop one night and I'm thinking about this fucking safe. An old square box. I'm saying, I wonder what's in it. Bugging the shit out of me.

I said fuck it, I'm going to open it. So I got a couple of tools and tried to punch it. But the tumblers wouldn't roll. So I said fuck it, I going to get that motherfucker. I got screwdrivers and old chisels. Chiseled off the rivets. It peeled like a sardine can. It was still so easy. Nothing in the damn thing [ha, ha, laughter]. But it was itching at me. Just had to see if I could do it.

I didn't have the right tools, really. What you need are a couple of drip pins, that have certain thickness, certain lengths. It's like a punch with a flat end. Couldn't get the tumblers to roll. There is a kick there, a little thrill you might say, of opening a safe and seeing you can still do it. I enjoyed just pulling a job once in a while.

If a Bobby Beck or a Rocky knocked on my door right now, or came into my shop, told me they know where is good jewelry and this is a good time to clip the place, I'd say go get it. I have changed, but not that much. I would not pass up that. Money is money. I think I could be a preacher but still have my hands in the collection plate. It's not just the money. How should I say it?— I'd be a dupe to pass it up. Maybe from just doing it so long, it would be hard to walk away.

Except for the last couple of years, I never paid taxes in my whole life. Never. 'Cause you're dealing in cash much of the time. This time, after Benny and me became partners on the upholstery work, he pushed me hard to do it. Social security for the guys in my shop. And he was leery the feds would find out. So, I started doing it. Not all the way, hell no, but some.

Go look on that table over there, all the way over. Pick up one of those nigger dolls. Don't they look *old*? They aren't that old. I'm cooking them. I'm cooking them in coffee grounds right here in the oven. Same with those salt & pepper shakers, and those piggy banks. You can cook porcelain and make it age, sell them as antique pieces. This has kept me busy the past few days.

The temptation to get back into the fencing all the way was always there. I missed the good money, what you can make if you're really heavy in the dealing. It's play money, really. If I wanted something, or I wanted to gamble big, the money was there. I still love to gamble, go to Vegas or whatever. A big thing for me is to play the poker machines. Wanda has been on my case more than once on how much money I blow on those fucking machines.

I do wish Wanda was better prepared to make it after I am gone. She has been awfully good to me. Has stayed with me, day after day, through all of this. It is a fact I lost too much gambling. I wish I had that back. Could have saved more. There are things for the house she'd like to have. But still, in many ways I was good to her. Compared to the bum she was with before, I was a step up, a big step up. A fucking cop who was no good. Put on a front for the public as a hard-ass, but was very shady. And none of it went for Wanda and her kids but spent it on himself. What an asshole.

Many times I have wished I was back in it, like the way it was before [in American City]. To tell you the truth, I would've liked to have gotten a younger guy to be the fence but I would be in the background, more supervising. Say Rocky or Kevin 'cause he has a good head on his shoulders. My knowledge to somebody is worth quite a bit. I put a lot of hours in getting the contacts, running to the auctions and meeting people. Just like if you'd say, "Fuck it, I'm gonna quit teaching. I want to be a fence." Well, I'd be a great help to you. The contacts, knowing how to get the confidence of someone, to read people. Who's buying, what's the stuff going for. It takes hours and hours, a lot of time consumed to get all that.

I didn't want the hassles but I still wanted to keep my fingers in it. If I had gotten back in big, I'm talking about right after I got out of the penitentiary this last time, I don't think I would have slowed down. Then my shop gets going so good and I am supporting five, six families—that is holding me back. The grandkids, Wanda, talking to your class—that has all mellowed me. *In a way I got to liking the legit side and having other people see me that way.*

Remorse or Regrets?

I do not feel sad about my life. I did what I thought I had to do at the time. I would always tell your students, "No, I don't feel bad for what I done. If I had to live my life over, I would not change it. Except get into the fencing sooner. And not get caught." [Ha, ha, Sam chuckles.] The big time in the penitentiary after I escaped—whew, I do regret that. *But I would not wish my life on somebody else. I made that very god damn plain to your students—"a life in crime can be a bitch."*

I done wrong, pulled some rank shit. Some very rank shit. But I do know I done a lot of good, too. Anybody that came in my shop that was on the level, got a fair shake from me. I'd see a needy person, I would help that person out. Somebody needed a refrigerator but was broke, "Take it buddy, pay me when you get the money." I'm no Robin Hood, but I don't feel as though I took bread out of anybody's mouth. No. I do feel I put a lot of bread *in* people's mouth. Same with the Red Cross or the charities that wanted to help out some families, they would come to me for furniture and the household supplies. They trusted me. All I had to do was send them the bill. They never even looked at the furniture. I treated them fair, more than fair. More or less gave the stuff away. It was known I had a soft heart, is in my nature to lend a hand if someone's in a jam.

I was honest with people. Treated them fair. Anyone that worked for me, I dealt with fairly. Got paid a good dollar and helped them out in little ways.

Benny would get on my case that I was too easy on my help, that I would keep a deadbeat around and pay his wages. I have had to tell this or that guy, "Hey, we don't need you anymore" but that was 'cause they weren't doing things the right way. The guys in my shop, the different ones who've worked for me, if you were to ask them, they would not badmouth me. No, they will say I'm a pretty good guy.

If a mother with a couple of kids came into my shop and I saw she needed something, they had the run of the store. I was always tops with kids. A real pushover, maybe because adults know what they're doing but a kid is never really bad that way. I gave a lot of stuff to kids—kids from the neighborhood, Puerto Rican kids, black kids. I would hire some of them to wash windows, do odd jobs. It was more trouble than it was worth but it gave them a chance to work and make a few bucks. I felt that was good for them. A lotta businessmen and shop owners are greedy and don't want to be bothered with those kinds of people [e.g., Puerto Ricans, blacks, poor whites]. Would just as soon throw dirt in their face or chisel them.

Looking back, I think I was too soft to make the big bucks in fencing or from my legit business, too. Same with the auction people and the other dealers, I think I let them get the stuff too cheap. Maybe I wanted to be a big shot more than I should have. I don't know how to say it but having the thieves come by, rapping with them, their looking up to me—this was important to me. Why, who the fuck knows?

I can't say if people looked up to me but they respected me for what I was. That I built up a business from scratch, that I always fended for myself. Not once, but twice I did that. My shop in American City was like no other shop in town. I feel personally for the ordinary joe blow it was the best shop in town— had the cheapest prices and the most choice of merchandise, and everybody got a square deal. This time around, my upholstery business is one of the biggest in the area. Five, six guys are working in my shop, supporting families. It makes me feel good what I have built up.

I was never just a thief. See, most thieves don't work. I always worked. Was always building up my shop. Investing what I made from the burglary and the fencing in my business. I was a businessman as much as a thief. Really more. *I would not call myself a thief, not all the way. A hustler, a conman, yes. And a businessman.* Really the two was hand in hand.

Being seen as a good burglar, as good people, I don't know how to explain it—was a good feeling. It's like somebody saying about you, he is one helluva a teacher, one helluva a professor. The fact that I was trusted, that my word was good, that I would handle my end of the deal. With the thieves and the dealers, their knowing that once the goods were in my hands, they didn't have to worry about it. It was my worry. If something happened I wouldn't take anybody down with me.

I never cared how the cops saw me but I always wanted the public to see me in a different light. Not as a guy who did time, not as a burglar, not even as a fence. But as a businessman. *As a good joe.* In that way I knew what I done was wrong. I knew this. I wanted the people to think more highly of me, not see me as a bum. *If they saw me as crook, that I could handle. But not a fucking bum. I wanted the people to respect me as me. As a businessman taking care of business in my shop.*

Doing what I done, buying hot stuff and selling it doesn't bother me. What bothers me is to take somebody's possessions out of their house that they really needed or that meant something very special to them, and then resell it. That would bother me. I never stole from somebody that needed something.

I do feel bad about some of the stuff that came out of private homes that were keepsake pieces. One time seventeen guns came my way. Old guns including a German Luger, which the guy got while in Germany in World War II, off a dead German officer. This was very special to him. I was in a club one night and he was there, complaining about it. Didn't give a damn about the other guns but that one was a keepsake. So I put the gun in his mailbox one night. Couple of nights later he was in the club and was talking about the gun. Whoever done it he really appreciated it. It made me feel good knowing he felt good.

But it was funny to hear him talk about it. To hear him, it was some kind of gun. Worth so much. Shit, it was a piece of junk. Same way with other people. They build up their story to make it look good in front of others. It might have been a .22, but they tell it like it was an antique 30/30.

I feel bad about very few things. Maybe the one old guy who I hit. Put him in la la land. He was never right after that. Me and Jesse got this tip, that this guy had all kinds of money in his house. Kept it under the bed in a metal box. But he never left the house. This is a seventy-year-old man. So we decided to pull the job at Halloween. I would dress up as Batman, do the trick or treat bit. I knocked at the door and when he opened it, I said, "Ho, ho, ho," and hit him. Boom. Wanted to put his lights out for a little while. Jesse goes in and gets the box. Some bills but not big money. Then when the guy wakes up, he tells the police that Batman hit him. Batman got in the window and robbed him. In a way it was funny, 'cause Jesse gets a kick out of telling that story. But the guy was always weird after that. That I do feel bad about.

I do not feel bad for snuffing that guy out. There is murder and there is murder. That guy could've ratted and put me away for years and years. Not all murders are the same. Snuffing out your wife just because she is causing you grief, you should get big time. I'm not saying the death penalty, not necessarily. For a baby rapist, yes. He deserves the chair. I'd pull the switch myself. I am a strong believer in the death penalty for that.

I do feel bad for hurting my mom as far as my going to the penitentiary. Even more my grandma and grandpop. Could see the hurt in their eyes after

I was sent to the juvenile reformatory. After that, we would talk but no real conversation.

Seven, eight years ago, my brother called, said Mom was in the hospital. Was in bad shape, wasn't going to live long. Said she asked about me. So, I stopped by to see her the next time I was in the area. I remember sitting there with her, seeing how she had aged. We talked but there was no closeness. I stopped by a couple of times after that. I felt an obligation. Why, I don't know. I went to her funeral but not to the viewing and that. No tears, no nothing. Her lights were out, that was it. There was very little feeling there.

I was never that close to my mother. I don't think she stood up for me. I can't remember her ever doing that. If my stepdad was a hard-ass, my mom would not interfere. It wasn't that I hated him but I certainly wasn't in love with him, put it that way.

Getting popped for the gas station burglary and my mom not showing up for the hearings, not coming to visit me in jail, that was a final straw. I would not want to admit it at that time, but there was a pain there. Some of my friends came to visit but not my mom. Not a letter, not a peep.

Looking back I think this is a big reason I like kids, try to help them. Stand up for them, really. Make them feel good about themselves. In her eye, yes, she is probably thinking she did. But, in my eye, no, my mom was not really a mother to me. I don't give a fuck if life has dealt one a good hand or a bad hand, a mother should be there for her kids, not take the easy way out. My daughter, even my grandkids, I am going to go to bat for them. No matter what. My mom did not do that. For my half-brothers, yes. For me, no.

I'm not saying my mom should answer for the rank shit I've done. Not saying that at all. I did what I did. But was she a good mom? Did she do right by me? Not in my eye. She had her head in the sand.

Was Sam a Fagin, Corrupting Others?

Looking back, I don't believe I led people into crime. That I don't believe. But, yes, I did help bring that out, more or less, what was there natural. Did help people realize the larceny in their heart, you might say. Like Woody, was not a crook like me or Louie. But he could be shady. Was a free spirit. I played on that. But did I make him do it? That is bullshit.

I do admit I gave tips to different ones on places to hit. Running to the auctions all the time, I'm hearing things. Just driving to them, I am spotting wicker or I see a place that is ripe, you might say. I gave Rocky a lot of tips on places to hit. And the Beck boys and ones like Andy. A few to Steelbeams and Bowie, but Rocky more than anybody.

Couple of them, like Rocky, I showed how to crack a safe. If it won't punch, then peel it. It was no big deal. Same with Bowie, he learnt safes from me. He is one of the very best around. Punch, peel, and good with the torch. Or can drill it. Bowie can do it all.

I more or less financed thieves. A few. Not all the way but put up bail and that. A few bills here and there to hold them over until they could clip again. Nothing big. Did a lot of coaching, you might say, on antiques and jewelry. What is a good piece, what ain't. You let them know what you are looking for, what will bring a good dollar. With some of them, sure, I'd go over how to spot places to hit, how to check it out. Don't leave a car parked near where you're clipping. If you get popped, keep your mouth shut. Don't let the fucking police buffalo you, play head games on you to get you talking.

It is only natural that this will happen. 'Cause your thieves are curious and will ask, "Why isn't this worth more? What are you looking for?" Same with breaking into places, you hear them doing dumb things. You say, hey, you're being a dumb motherfucker. Don't leave your car nearby, don't be high on dope, take your time and check the place out. Shit like that.

Take the Beck boys, you heard me chew their asses a couple of times for the dumb things they would do. I did put up bail for them 'cause that is covering your ass, too. A thief is more likely to roll over if he's sitting in jail. The cops know that too, so they will push for higher bail.

Chubby pulled a lot of shit for me. He did it as a favor to me and 'cause he wanted to be part of something, just to blow out of his ass what he had done around Rocky or Jesse. If you could guide him closely, very closely, he was okay. He didn't really have the heart for it. Would be too shaky unless it was an easy place and you guided him. Am I right? You have seen me working on Chubby, to get him to follow through. He can really fuck it up.

This is a funny one. I don't know if I ever told you. I knew of an older couple that moved away, retired to Florida. Left a ton of antique furniture in a big barn on their place. Were planning to have a big auction in the spring. I would pass the place on a back road to the auctions, so one time I stopped by. Nobody around. Place is back in the woods. The barn had no security at all. Just crawl in a window and open up the doors from the inside. I spent an hour just looking around, putting a mark on some of the better pieces. Like antique high chairs and cribs, even a French antique crib worth a very good dollar. Then I send Chubby to clip the place. But he takes the wrong turn, ends up at the wrong barn, and drives the truck into a silage pit. Surprised the truck didn't roll over. So, I get this call. It is Chubby. "Hey, Sam, you didn't tell me about this hole in the ground." I get Donnie to go with me. Take my truck and pull him out. It was lucky this place was vacant. About a month later, I check out the place again. Antiques are still there. So, I send him back—but I had to draw very careful directions. This time he pulled it off. Goddamn Chubby, he is really something.

Who is leading and who is following? *I don't think I ever made anybody do something he himself didn't want to do.* Know what I mean? I could point to this or that which made me a burglar or a fence. Blame it on my mother or that I didn't get a fair shake from the judge who sent me to the juvenile reformatory. That Angelo and the local clique were pushing on me to do the fencing. You hear this bullshit, so and so came from a broken family, he was raised poor, blah, blah, blah. See this in prison—guys whining, crying it wasn't their fault. That is blowing wind out your ass. What I did, I did because I wanted to. Nobody got me to steal, nobody made me be a fence. All the rank shit I pulled—I, Sam Goodman, did it.

Who's a Thief? There are Others (Nearly) as Bad or Worse

To me the people who buy [stolen goods] are as guilty as the ones who steal. The public and the ordinary businessman is buying from me, surmising the stuff is hot. The cops are shopping at my store, looking for bargains and asking me to keep my eyes open for something they needed. The cops I have known in my life were always looking for a handout. There are some very crooked cops who have pulled a lotta rank shit.

The guy who runs a store, legit now, is buying from a dealer like me—who is buying direct from the thieves. His [store guy's] chances of hassles with the police are small, and he doesn't have to put up with the thieves. To me, this store guy is a businessman looking for an easy buck. Is he a crook? Sure as hell doesn't see himself that way. But comes down to it, some of them were pretty shady.

Especially if they are in a pinch, the shit people will pull. The exceptions to this are very, very few. The line is narrow between the do-gooders and the ordinary joe blow who will take an edge, and even between the do-gooders and people like myself. In my eye the do-gooders are not more moral. They are more leery. Whereas I went through a lot of risk and wasn't fearful of taking a chance. The average person would be afraid, leery of his old lady finding out, or maybe his kids and the people he knows, and scared of the cops, too.

I am lying in my hospital bed, right? Who comes to visit me? Paul, the contractor guy. Builds a few houses from scratch but mostly does remodeling. Have known him a long time, from him putting a roof on my shop and my doing some upholstery work for him. Bumping into him here and there. Tells me his wife is running around on him. He is thinking of getting a divorce. Turns out he has been siphoning off her jewelry and is coming to me to unload it. She has a helluva collection from her parents and from him buying for her over all these years. Is carrying a couple of pieces with him. One is a set—necklace, bracelet, earrings with little diamonds in them. Very nice. He is leery about peddling the stuff to an ordinary jeweler. Is figuring I might know where he could take them. Told him, we should keep in touch. Would call him when

I got out of the damn hospital. Got a hold of him this last week. He should meet me at my shop, bring in what he has. In the meantime, I am calling Skip [a jewelry fence]. Yeah, he is interested but will be tricky to do on account I can't run the stuff to his place. Is not the way Skip does business, to have to arrange a meeting place. Wants to know, "Am I sure these are good pieces?"

Has been a pisser to pull off. On account I can't drive. Can't even walk is what it comes down to. Donnie or somebody from the shop has been picking me up and driving me around. Worked it out that Paul would come by my shop. Have the jewelry in a toolbox. Pay him so much now, pay the rest later. Paul leaves, then have Skip's daughter stop by later. She should pick up some fabric samples and look over the jewelry. But may have to take some pieces back to their shop, to Skip, to give a closer look.

This was done on Tuesday. Paul is edgy as a son of a bitch and Skip's daughter is antsy. With different people coming and going, I'm surprised the whole thing wasn't fucked up. Talked to Skip on Wednesday and is coming by Monday to settle up and to visit 'cause we haven't seen each other since I went to the hospital. Then I will settle up with Paul. Is a good dollar for all of us but this is not the way you want to handle things.

I have no qualms from doing this. What is between Paul and his wife is their business. Still, it has crossed my mind. Here I am, I do not think I will make it, yet I am messing around with this. Very little hesitation on my part. In a way I am thinking this will be extra cushion for Wanda 'cause it will be tough for her to make it when I'm gone. Maybe too, I am not wanting to back out on Paul, that he was counting on me to do this. Or, am I doing it to get away with something? I don't know—maybe from doing it so long, it gets to where it is hard to walk away from the easy dollar.

Everybody is out for the easy dollar. Not so much on account of they want to have stacks and stacks of money or want to buy everything they see. No, 'cause making money and having money is the way things are. What you have to do get by, what you are looked up to or looked down for. I made a lotta money in my life. A lot. Not to put it away or save for a rainy day. Maybe put a little aside to invest in my business or just to have a little cushion. But no, I made it to spend it, to come and go as I wanted and not be dependent on somebody else. I think most people are that way.

I'm not saying I done no wrong. I know I done wrong. Not saying the good I done undoes the wrong. But *the line is thin—this I truly believe, that everybody has some larceny in his heart. One way or another, has his own racket. Is getting over on somebody or is chiseling in some other way. Is some rank shit in everyone and a good side too. A good joe and an asshole joe in everybody.*

I'm a smoker, right? That's how I got the cancer. Nobody made me do it. I bought the Camels, I lighted the match, right? But still, the tobacco people are pushing me. Tried quitting but then I was very nasty. Irritable as a son of a bitch. I'm not making excuses. Don't feel sorry for me, but what about all the kids that are lighting up? They are being hustled, conned is what it comes down to. To become dope heads, only it isn't called that. The hell many of these kids will be going through, 'cause it's a bitch [the cancer] that I can tell you. All the rank shit I pulled, who should find it harder to look at himself in the mirror?

You ever watch the preachers on TV? Being in that goddamn hospital I got my fill. Is a good racket, playing on old ladies and people on their deathbed. I don't think I'm blowin' wind outta my ass when I say, they are the ones that ought to be locked up.

If I Had Live to Life Over

If I had the chance to live my live again, do it all over, I would find it hard to pass up the fencing. The money is good. There is the satisfaction in knowing you can do it, knowing you can handle whatever comes up.

Maybe be a con man. A good confidence man. That is something I have a knack for. To get over on somebody who is wanting to get something for nothing, who is more or less shady himself. That is part of fencing, too, so maybe do both.

I doubt I would get into burglary. For one, it is harder today. With the safes and security systems, and harder to find a good partner. There are fewer decent thieves to clip with. I would not be content just to be thief. It wouldn't be me. The burglar is out crawling in windows, breaking into cars. The risk and the money can be there, but the scheming and dealing with people from different walks of life isn't. Even being known as a "good burglar" by the thieves and different ones wouldn't mean as much. The satisfaction is not the same as being a dealer.

Maybe even go strictly legit, a legit businessman. There is a status there I can honestly say I enjoy. That people look up to you if you run a business. That you have people working for you, are supporting their families you might say. That is a good feeling. It has grown on me the past five or six years especially, that I would want to be known as a businessman. Maybe on account of my daughter and my grandkids, and for Wanda and her kids. Maybe on account of you, too.

If go legit, then work with kids on the side. Be a juvenile counselor. I think I have a knack with kids, know where they are coming from. If have to knock them down, leave room to build them back up. I know that sounds like I'm blowing wind outta my ass but I would enjoy doing that.

It can be a bitch to be a fence, can get to you. But the satisfaction and the recognition. That's why I liked the fencing. That and the good money. Fencing made me a smarter person. Gave me an understanding of people and how to relate. Fencing showed me I could be a leader. Knew I had the business ability but gave me more confidence. If I had it to do again, I would not be as wide open as in American City. Not as cautious as in Tylersville and have a better spider web. Shoot for somewhere in between.

Or be a guy in the rackets, if the opportunity was there. Like Angelo or Phil, who mostly stay in the background. Are pulling the strings and bringing in good money, and are keeping a layer in between. Are shady but legit, too. Operate where the line is thin between the two. In their eye and in the public's eye, they are more a businessman than a thief or a crook. That is what you want.

About "The Professor"

You were naive—very, very naive—when we first met. But I never tried to pull the wool over your eyes. Never said, "Let me shake this guy's fucking cage." 'Cause to me, I liked you right off the bat. Don't ask me why, 'cause I don't know that. I believe it was because you were honest with me. Yeah, you went around the block questioning me—ask questions different ways. I knew you were doing that. No problem. But you were always honest with me.

There is nothing that I did not tell you or try to conceal from you. Nothing. I have been honest with you. If you asked, I told you. Some rank things I may have not thought about when you asked. But intentionally, no.

Remember my shop in Boonesboro? That place was pretty nice. Was very cozy. You came there often 'cause we used to sit around the fireplace. Really peaceful. Jesse, Bernice, Rocky, and different ones used to come and meet with you there. Even Woody dropped by a couple of times. You would go around the block with questions, egg us to bullshit about the past. You would tape sometimes and play it back. We all got a kick out of that.

Rocky told me you gave him a headache sometimes 'cause you kept going around the block with the questions. "Fucking headache," Rocky would say. But I never got a headache. If you would look at the many times you went over the same territory, I think I would be consistent. I always told it like I remembered it. Now, I might forget some things and you could jog my memory. I told you the truth as I saw it.

Now, one time I did check you out but the stuff wasn't hot. I was heading for an auction in my van, full of wicker. You were along. I tells you, "Hey, this stuff is a little warm." I wanted to see how you would act, if you got scared or what. You didn't act scared or nothing. You acted natural. No reaction. You didn't show me nothing. You didn't sweat no blood. It surprised me you acted as calmly as you acted. No wind blowing out of your ass.

See, I have a theory that if you weren't a teacher that you would like to be a thief. That was my feeling. Jesse and Rocky felt the same way. 'Cause we talked about it. "Hey, what's with the Professor?" This is what I feel. You would have loved to be in it. Say, I was younger and you were younger. I told you, "Hey, this is really safe. We can clip it." You would have gone along. You would've loved to play the part.

Doing the part of a driver or the man casing the place, getting the information, you would have been okay at. You could have put on a very good front. If the pressure was there—hey, man, twenty fucking years—I personally don't think you would have held up. Not many do. Now, I never worried about you talking or ratting on me. I trusted you that far. Besides, I would have just denied it. Who in the fuck is this guy? Would just be hearsay. Never worried about you turning this stuff over or gossiping.

The penitentiary would be hard time for you. But the other cons would accept you as a square. Would want to use you for your brains, to help them in little ways. Maybe be a jailhouse lawyer. You could find a niche doing that.

Now Bernice [Jesse's wife] did worry some. Remember when we was sitting around the fire, just talking, you asked Bernice how she felt about being the dropoff for me and Jesse. She got very emotional, cried and everything. Not like Bernice to do that. All the stuff she pulled with Jesse as his dropoff driver and that—did it for him but didn't like it. How she got scared, very scared, the one night when he nearly got popped and she has to wait several hours for him. That was the last time she dropped Jesse off. Said she always wanted Jesse to quit but also admitted she liked the extra money. Bernice was skittish about talking to you after that. More revelation than she wanted. I could tell you shook her.

I think I went out of my way to educate you. I did do some of that. Like going to the auctions. Just wanted to show you how easy it can be done to unload warm stuff. Or the hustling part, the buying part. Then the selling, getting rid of it. Wanted to show you for your own benefit. I just didn't want you to know from me saying it or another joe blow telling. Wanted you to be able to say, "I seen it done." I'm a firm believer in learning by seeing. Telling you is not like showing you. I did try to educate you.

I did get a kick out of one of the times you came with me to the auction, met Jesse and Rocky and Steelbeams there. Chubby came along too. Around Thanksgiving. Got there early in the morning. Rained the day before, then froze. Very chilly. You were dressed in a cowboy shirt and work shoes. New outfit. We razzed you about making yourself look like the auction crowd. Your shoes weren't insulated, cheap K-Mart shoes, so your feet were freezing. We got a helluva kick out of that. The Professor, trying to look like the auction crowd, is freezing his dick off. We got a helluva kick out it. Jesse and them razzed you pretty good.

There were a few times, I had warm stuff in storage and wanted to unload at the auction and you were riding with me. You could not have gotten popped—

cause you had no way of knowing. I didn't do it for a charge, to rattle your cage. You were there, the stuff was there and I trusted you enough to do that.

I think I'm a good judge of people, of being able to analyze them and see which way they're coming from. If I'm with somebody a couple of hours, I can tell if they are bullshit or not. Right off the bat I felt comfortable with you. Why, I don't know. Your students would ask me that, too. "Why do you do this for Dr. Steffensmeier?" I told them I thought you was "good people." That you had always done right by me. If I could help you out, I would do that. But I always got a kick out of their asking, "Why do you do this for the Professor?"[1]

Not that you pulled any strings but I do think your knowing the assistant DA played a part in my getting off the time I was popped for buying from Bobby Beck and his buddies. That was a bad rap anyway. Just the word of a couple of kids claiming they sold me warm stuff. But I still had to be leery 'cause of my record. Assistant was from Penn State and knew you. I feel that made a difference.

I do know you helped with Becky after the [furlough] trip to American City. I am staying with her that weekend and she overhears me on the phone talking to Steelbeams. Finds out later I have been hooking up with him, Phil, and different ones during the weekend. Get back to the penitentiary, boom, says we should split, that I haven't reformed. Had a major bug up her ass. I gave Becky your phone number and she talked to you. Your vouching for me I feel really helped 'cause the letters and the visits from Becky were very regular after that. But she was keeping her distance, too, mostly was going through the motions.

But we have always stayed in touch. She has even been calling me at the hospital and now at the house. This really pisses Wanda. She is very leery of Becky, that there is still something between us. I get a kick out of it.

That the book [*The Fence*] turned out good is a good feeling for me. Different ones have told me, "Hey, Sam, that book is you." Not that they read all of it but enough to know. A lotta hours spent going over things, lotta work for you. Whichever way a question could be asked, you asked it. It is a good feeling for me that the book helped you get ahead, that it even got an award.

"If Only I Could Lick This Thing . . ."

Rocky is the only thief to come by fairly regular. Is clean now for a couple of years. Do think Rocky has packed it in and all the way this time. Seeing me lying in that damn hospital bed shook him. Not that he won't still chisel a little.

Jesse has come by only that one time. Didn't stay long. "Hey, Sam, how the fuck you doing?" Blah, blah, and he was gone. Bernice will call but Jesse doesn't get on the phone. I think it is too hard for Jesse to see me this way. That is what Bernice told Wanda, "Jesse doesn't want to remember Sam that way." I can see Jesse's thinking. But still, if it was Jesse lying here like this, I think I would stop by. We go back a long ways, have been through a lot together.

Same as Jesse going on with the burglary but telling me he has packed it in. More than once I have thought about that [these past weeks]. In a way I was hurt 'cause we was awfully close. That time he came to the hospital, I could tell he was uncomfortable. But in truthfulness it has hurt, his not coming by.

It is funny, lying in that hospital bed, how many times Jesse has run through my mind. The clipping we did, what we got away with, the close calls—even shot at a couple of times. This goes way back, Jesse and me clipped this house. Broke into a safe. We're taking off, I spot this porcelain dishware. Whole set, very beautiful. Jesse is edgy, wants to get out of the place. But goes along we should carry it out. Turns out it is registered. Worth top dollar. But we can't unload it. Even Scottie in Ocean City couldn't help us. We are leery of hanging onto it and having to shop around. Was even some suspicion we had done it. So, we're stuck. Jesse says, hell with it, we're gonna dump it. Broke it up and buried the pieces. No way they could trace it to us. But to have to get rid of it that way, I can still feel the tears [Sam laughs].[2]

A few others [crime associates] have stopped once or twice, maybe because you brought them. Now, the Beck boys will stop by the shop and ask how I am doing. That is what I am told. But, no, I have not heard from Steelbeams or Bowie. Except that Chubby ran into Steelbeams at one of the auctions, and he said to say hello.

The other ones you ask about—like Phil or someone from the local clique in American City—I don't feel bad about their not coming. I was pals with some of them but there was no real closeness there. I can't say nothing bad about them. Ones like Angelo and Phil, sure they are gonna fuck some individuals like the shitass thieves. But treated me right.

The main ones who come by are people I know from my business. Benny, my partner, comes by couple of times a week. Tommy and George, and the other guys who work in my shop, will stop by. Different antique dealers would come by the hospital and sit with me, to give Wanda a break. Like Nicki and Log Cabin, the antique guy. And Cooper, the auctioneer I've known all these years comes by. Puddy has visited pretty regular. Some of my regular customers, people I've done upholstery work for, would come by. Marge, the one neighbor lady would come. Is very religious. Would watch my booth sometimes at the big flea market in Hampton Square. Some of Wanda's friends would come by. Hard for me to know who all came to visit 'cause my lights were pretty dim. Wasn't eating and the dope would put me to sleep. Just from what Wanda tells me, that there was always people stopping by.

Norm comes very regular. Is a main one for handling good antiques. This is something else I do regret, that I would have to say I feel bad about. Remember my telling you about clipping Norm's place. Norm is good people. We have stayed pals all these years. I stopped by his shop to see him after I got out of the penitentiary this last time. He was friendly as hell. Has always sent a lot of work my way, would recommend me to other antique dealers—that I knew my business, could upholstery and doctor up pieces. I only used him that one time for the warm stuff, for the Louis XIV cabinet. Helped me make the contact but wasn't comfortable doing it. Did it as a favor for me. Then, a year or so later, I'm at his shop and worked into our conversation that I ran across some dolls that go back fifty, seventy-five years. Described to Norm what I had, they had real hair and everything. He flat out told me, "Sam, I don't want to get involved that way again." Solid, it was no big deal.

He stopped by the house this last week. Is wanting to come by on Monday. To see you, too, if you can stay that long. It has never come up but I think he surmises, at least a little, I had his place robbed that time. Included a collection of dolls and a china tea set. Very nice. Found out later Norm was planning on giving the china to his wife for their anniversary. Did cross my mind to get it back but it was too late for that. Is this rank shit or not? We were pals already then. We'd stop at each other's shop—oh, hell, maybe once or twice a week. This is one of the few things I am sorry about. Not that I am shedding tears or losing sleep over it but, yeah, I do feel bad about it.

I tease Wanda that she has a crush on him. He is a very kind man, very respectful towards women. You would want your daughter to marry him. He wouldn't hurt a flea, that is how he is.

Connie [Sam's ex-wife] comes a lot. Will usually come with my daughter. Other times she comes with her minister and they will pray over me. I go along with it. Wanted to come over today to pray with me. Told them you'd be here. Would have to wait until Monday. All these years, I still can't get away from her. Really, I appreciate her coming. She is a good woman, a good mother to Amy. I helped financially and that but I wasn't really a part of Amy's life. Not like I shoulda been. Might stop by Connie's house and take Amy for a ride in my truck, say, if I was delivering something. Other times, she'd come to my shop and I'd take her across the street for ice cream. The fact that I done time in the penitentiary was hard for her. Was some hurt there 'cause her friends knew and would ask questions. Her mother did some bad-mouthing, too, which I probably deserved. Looking back, I was an okay dad but could of done better.

Different ones have prayed with me. Elaine, Elaine's minister, Connie and her minister. But when Log Cabin's wife prayed with me, I felt something. There was some strength there. She was the hot wire. Same with Elaine's minister. They gave me strength. I felt it. Just this last week, after Mrs. Log Cabin had prayed with me. She had left. Listen to me, I'm laying in bed. We had prayed. Boy, I tell you what. It was hard for me to pull my fucking hand away. I said to myself, boy, if only this could be possible, if this could be true, that I could beat this fucking thing.

Maybe there is something to this. One night, everybody left. I can't go to sleep. I'm laying there, my fucking shoulder is hurting like you wouldn't believe. I'm in pain like you wouldn't fucking believe. I prayed. It was like a big fucking black cloud came over me. Boy it scared me. It fucking scared me. I start getting better after that. Started eating. Was that an omen from up there? Or wasn't it? I don't know what it was. Supernatural or what. I cannot tell you what to make of it.

Do I pray now? No. I prayed a couple of times at the hospital. I more or less shun it. I really should pray 'cause that is the only answer there is. It is over unless there is some miracle. But I don't really believe in it. I don't want to make a mockery out of it. I wouldn't believe my own mockery. It is a hairy subject, very hairy. If there is a God, I don't want to take any chances. Don't want to knock the praying. But for me it would be a mockery.

I didn't realize the cancer would go this fast, that it would end up this way. 'Cause life means a whole lot to me now—the shop, my grandkids, Wanda being there all the way through this. What I've built up. I would really get a kick out of doing that study of American City [follow-up study of Sam's criminal network Steffensmeier had considered doing]. If only I could lick this fucking thing.

I would help you all the way. Has it changed? Are the same people operating? In my eye, there are some new faces, but many of the same ones are still operating. The penny-ante thief and the ordinary burglar will be the ones that have packed it in. May sell a little dope or chisel here and there, but nothing major. The big ones are still at in American City, or they are dead. I hope I'm not blowing wind outta my ass 'cause I would really enjoy doing that.

If it were only possible to lick this.

Notes

1. Sam also told the students that Steffensmeier liked to talk about his daughter, that his wallet was mostly pictures of her—"this is a connection between us, my knowing he is a 'soft touch' for kids."
2. Jesse points out Sam's reluctance to destroy the porcelain. "Sam didn't want to. Should shop around, he has some contacts. I said, 'No way.' Sam was more willing to take the risk, harder for him to walk away from a dollar. That is why he gets jammed up more than me."

Epilogue

Steffensmeier attended Sam's funeral a couple of days later. The forty-seven people in attendance included family members (e.g., Wanda, Sam's ex-wife Connie, Sam's daughter Amy, and Sam's half-brother, Herb), some workers from his shop, Sam's business partner Benny, a few neighbors, an assortment of antique dealers and auction people, and Chubby, a long-time hanger-on at Sam's shop. Noticeably absent were Sam's key criminal associates (e.g., Jesse, Steelbeams, Rocky). Jesse later told Steffensmeier, he "didn't want to remember Sam that way" (i.e., in a casket and as a shell of the man he once was). Rocky said he planned on attending but his truck broke down. Connie's minister officiated and, in clear reference to Sam's waywardness, sermonized about sin and "judgment day" and prayed for the Lord's forgiveness toward the "departed." During the "eulogy" Puddy (Sam's bookmaker friend) passed a note to Steffensmeier, with the scribbling: "If Sam could speak, he would say let's get the [expletive] out of here." Afterwards Connie, clutching both of Steffensmeier's hands, commented about Sam: "You couldn't help but like Sam. He was very likable. I did my best. I really did. But he wasn't responsible. At least familywise, he wasn't. I think he was made that way." Nicki, (Log Cabin's wife) hugged nearly everyone in attendance, sharing her view that "Sam was really a pretty good guy. Sure will miss him."

Steffensmeier stayed in Tylersville that evening. He went to The Lounge and reminisced there about Sam with some patrons who knew Sam, and had breakfast the next morning with Puddy, who shared his sadness and favorite stories about Sam. On the return trip to State College, Steffensmeier mulled over their times together-the homecoming trip to American City from prison, the auction outings, the varied meetings with a colleague or crime associate, Sam's occasional get-togethers with Steffensmeier's students, the news that Sam had cancer, and the deathbed interviews. Sam had impacted a great deal on Steffensmeier's life and, as he put it, "educated" him, including in some ways that he prefers to leave unsaid.

Steffensmeier returned a few times over the years to Tylersville and American City to follow up. The shop Sam left behind struggled for a year or so before going out of business. According to Donnie, "We kept losing customers and no one to keep on our ass the way Sam could. The spark [i.e., Sam] wasn't there anymore." Benny added, "It was like losing an old shirt that fit well."

References

Abadinsky, Howard. 1994. *Organized Crime*. Chicago: Nelson-Hall.

Adler, Patricia. 1993. *Wheeling and Dealing: An Ethnography of an Upper Level Drug Dealing and Smuggling Community*, 2nd edition. New York: Columbia University Press.

Adler, Patricia and Peter Adler. 1983. "Relations between Dealers: The Social Organization of Illicit Drug Transactions." *Sociology and Social Research* 67:260–78.

Akers, Ronald. 1998. *Social Learning and Social Structure: A General Theory of Crime and Deviance*. Boston: Northeastern University Press.

Akers, Ronald, Marvin Krohn, Lonn Lanza-Kaduce, and Maria Radosevich. 1979. "Social Learning and Deviant Behavior: A Specific Test of a General Theory." *American Sociological Review* 44:635–55.

Akers, Ronald and Christine Sellers. 2004. *Criminological Theories*. Los Angeles: Roxbury.

Akerstrom, Malin. 1985. *Crooks and Squares: Lifestyles of Thieves and Addicts in Comparison to Conventional People*. New Brunswick, NJ: Transaction.

Albini, Joseph. 1971. *The American Mafia: Genesis of a Legend*. New York: Appleton Century Crofts.

Anderson, Elijah. 1990. *Streetwise: Race, Class, and Change in an Urban Community*. Chicago: University of Chicago Press.

Athens, Lonnie. 1995. "Dramatic Self Change." *Sociological Quarterly* 36(3):571–87.

Athens, Lonnie. 1997. *Violent Criminal Acts and Actors Revisited*. Urbana: University of Illinois Press.

Becker, Howard. 1960. "Notes on the Concept of Commitment." *American Journal of Sociology* 66:32–40.

Becker, Howard. 1963. *Outsiders*. New York: Macmillan.

Beirne, Piers and James Messerschmidt. 1995. *Criminology*. Boulder, CO: Westview.

Bennett, John J. DiIulio, Jr., and John P. Walters. 1996. *Body Count: Moral Poverty and How to Win America's War against Crime and Drugs*. New York: Simon & Schuster

Benson, Michael. 2002. *Crime and the Life Course*. Los Angeles: Roxbury.

Bernard, Thomas. 1987. "Structure and Control: Reconsidering Hirschi's Concept of Commitment." *Justice Quarterly* 4:409–24.

Best, Joel and David Luckenbill. 1994. *Organizing Deviance*. Englewood Cliffs, NJ: Prentice-Hall.

Blumstein, Alfred, Jaqueline Cohen, J. Roth, and Christy Visher. 1986. *Criminal Careers and "Career Criminals,"* Vols. 1 and 2. Washington, DC: National Academy Press.

Bordua, David. 1961. "Delinquent Subcultures: Sociological Interpretations of Gang Delinquency." *Annals of American Academy of Political and Social Science* 338: 119-136.

Bourdieu, Pierre. 1977. *Outline of a Theory of Practice.* London: Cambridge University Press.

———. 1985. "The Social Space and the Genesis of Groups." *Theory and Society* 14:723-744.

Braithwaite, John. 1989. *Crime, Shame, and Reintegration.* Cambridge: Cambridge University Press.

Bryant, Clifton (Ed.). 1974. *Deviant Behavior: Occupational and Organizational Bases.* Chicago: Rand McNally.

Burawoy, Michael. 2003. "Revisits: An Outline of a Theory of Reflexive Ethnography." *American Sociological Review* 68(5):645–80.

Burke, Peter and Donald Reitzes. 1991. "An Identity Theory Approach to Commitment." *Social Psychology Quarterly* 54(3):239–51.

Chambliss, William. 1972. *Box Man: A Professional Thief's Journey.* New York: Harper and Row.

Chubb, Judith. 1989. "The Mafia and Politics: The Italian State Under Siege." Western Societies Program Paper Series, Cornell University, Ithaca, New York.

Clinard, Marshall. 1952. *The Black Market.* New York: Rinehart.

Cloward, Richard and Lloyd Ohlin. 1960. *Delinquency and Opportunity.* Glencoe, IL: Free Press.

Cohen, Albert. 1955. *Delinquent Boys.* New York: Free Press.

Cohen, Albert. 1966. *Deviance and Control.* Englewood Cliffs, NJ: Prentice Hall.

Colquhoun, P. 1800. *A Treatise on the Commerce and Police of the River Thames.* London: Joseph Mawman.

Conklin, John. 1994. *Art Theft.* Westport, Conn.: Praeger.

Cressey, Donald. 1953. *Other People's Money.* NY: Free Press.

Cressey, Donald. 1967. *Theft of a Nation.* New York: Harper and Row.

Cromwell, Paul, James Olson, and D'Aunn Avary. 1996. "Who Buys Stolen Property? A New Look at Criminal Receiving." Pp. 47–56 in *In Their Own Words: Criminal on Crime,* edited by P. Cromwell. Los Angeles: Roxbury.

Cullen, Francis. 1983. *Rethinking Crime and Deviance Theory: The Emergence of a Structuring Tradition.* Totowa, NJ: Roman Allanheld.

Cusson, Maurice. 1983. *Why Delinquency?* Toronto: University of Toronto Press.

D'Unger, Amy, Kenneth Land, Patricia McCall, and Daniel Nagin. 1998. "How Many Latent Classes of Delinquent/Criminal Careers? Results from Mixed Poisson Regression Analyses." *American Journal of Sociology* 103:1593–1630.

Delisi, Matt. 2003. "Conservatism and Common Sense: The Criminological Career of James Q. Wilson." *Justice Quarterly* 20(3):661-674.

Durkheim, Emile. [1897] 1951. *Suicide.* Glencoe, IL: Free Press.

Etzioni, Amitai. 1964. *Modern Organizations.* Englewood Cliffs, NJ: Prentice-Hall.

Farrington, David. 2003. "Developmental and Life Course Criminology: Key Theoretical and Empirical Issues." *Criminology* 41(2):221–56.

Felson, Marcus. 1998. *Crime and Everyday Life.* 2d ed. Thousand Oaks, CA: Pine Forge.

Fleisher, Mark. 1995. *Beggars & Thieves.* Madison, Wisconsin: University of Wisconsin Press.

Gibbs, John and Peggy Shelly. 1982. "Life in the Fast Lane: A Retrospective View by Commercial Thieves." *Journal of Research in Crime and Delinquency"* 19: 299–330.

Giordano, Peggy, Stephen Cernkovich, and Donna Holland. 2003. "Changes in Friendship Relations Over the Life Course: Implications for Desistence from Crime." *Criminology* 41(2):293-329.

Glaser, Daniel. 1956. "Criminality Theories and Behavioral Images." *American Journal of Sociology* 61:440–41.

Glaser, Daniel. 1972. *Adult Crime and Social Policy.* Englewood Cliffs, NJ: Prentice-Hall.

Glaser, Barney and Anselm Strauss. 1967. *The Discovery of Grounded Theory.* New York: Aldine de Gruyter.

Goffman, Erving. 1959. *The Presentation of Self in Everyday Life.* New York: Doubleday.

Goffman, Erving. 1961. *Encounters.* Indianapolis: Bobbs-Merrill.

Goffman, Erving. 1967. *Interaction Ritual: Essays on Face-to-Face Behavior.* Garden City, NY: Anchor.

Goffman, Erving. 1972. *Strategic Interaction.* New York: Ballantine.

Gottfredson, Michael and Travis Hirschi. 1990. *A General Theory of Crime.* Stanford, CA: Stanford University Press.

Greenberg, David, Robin Tamarelli, and Margaret Kelly. 2002. "The Generality of the Self-Control Theory of Crime." Pp. 49–94 in *Crime and Social Organization,* edited by Elin Waring and David Weisburd. New Brunswick, NJ: Transaction.

Hagan, John. 1991. "Destiny and Drift: Subcultural Preferences, Status Attainments, and the Risks and Rewards of Youth." *American Sociological Review* 56:567–81.

Hagan, John. 1994. *Crime and Disrepute.* Thousand Oaks, CA: Pine Forge.

Hagan, John and Bill McCarthy. 1997. *Mean Streets: Youth Crime and Homelessness.* New York: Cambridge University Press.

Hall, Jerome. 1952. *Theft, Law, and Society.* Indianapolis, IN: Bobbs-Merrill.

Hall, Peter M. 1997. "Meta-Power, Social Organization, and the Shaping of Social Action." *Symbolic Interaction* 20(4):397-418.

Haller, Mark. 1990. "Illegal Enterprise: A Theoretical and Historical Interpretation." *Criminology* 28:207–35.

Hirschi, Travis. 1969. *Causes of Delinquency.* Berkeley, CA: Free Press.

Hirschi, Travis. 1996. "Theory without Ideas: Reply to Akers." *Criminology* 34(2): 249–56.

Hochstetler, Andy. 2001. "Opportunities and Decisions: Interactional Dynamics in Robbery and Burglary Groups." *Criminology* 39(3):737–63.

Ianni, Francis. 1975. *Black Mafia: Ethnic Succession in Organized Crime.* New York: Pocket Books.

Inciardi, James. 1975. *Careers in Crime.* Skokie, IL: Rand McNally.

Irwin, John. 1970. *The Felon.* Englewood Cliffs, NJ: Prentice Hall.

Jacobs, Bruce. 1999. *Dealing Crack: The Social World of Streetcorner Selling.* Boston: Northeastern University Press.

Jensen, Gary and Ronald Akers. 2003. "Taking Social Learning Theory Global:" Micro-Macro Transitions in Criminological Theory." Pp. 9–38 in *Social Learning Theory and the Explanation of Crime: A Guide for the New Century* (Advances in Criminological Theory, Volume 11), edited by R. Akers and G. Jensen. New Brunswick, NJ: Transaction.

Johnson, Michael P. 1991. "Commitment to Personal Relationships." Pp. 117–43 in *Advances in Personal Relationships,* Vol. 3, edited by William Jones and Dan Perlman. London: Jessica Kingsley.

Jones, Marshall and Donald Jones. 2000. "The Contagious Nature of Antisocial Behavior." *Criminology* 38:25-46.

Jones, Richard and Thomas Schmid. 2000. *Doing Time: Prison Experience and Identity among First Time Inmates.* Greenwich, CT: JAI.

Kanter, Rosabeth Moss. 1972. *Commitment and Community*. Cambridge, MA: Harvard University Press.

Kanter, Rosabeth Moss. 1977. *Men and Women of the Corporation*. New York: Basic Books.

Katz, Jack. 1988. *Seductions of Crime: Moral and Sensual Attractions of Doing Evil*. New York: Basic Books.

Klockars, Carl. 1974. *The Professional Fence*. New York: Free Press.

Kornhauser, Ruth. 1978. *Social Sources of Delinquency*. Chicago: University of Chicago Press.

Lemert, Edwin. 1951. *Social Pathology*. New York: McGraw-Hill.

Lemert. Edwin. 1958. "The Behavior of the Systematic Check Forger." *Social Problems* 6:141-148.

Lemert, Edwin. 1967. *Human Deviance, Social Problems, and Social Control*. Englewood Cliffs, NJ: Prentice Hall.

Lemert, Edwin. 1972. *Human Deviance, Social Problems, and Social Control*, 2nd ed. Englewood Cliffs, NJ: Prentice Hall.

Letkemann, Peter. 1973. *Crime as Work*. Englewood Cliffs, NJ: Prentice-Hall.

Lewontin, Richard. 2000. *The Triple Helix: Gene, Organism, and Environment*. Cambridge, Mass.: Harvard University Press.

Liebow, Elliot. 1967. *Tally's Corner*. Boston: Little, Brown.

Lindesmith, Alfred. 1941. "Organized Crime." *Annals of the American Academy of Political and Social Science* 217:119-127.

Lipsey, Mark and James Derzon. 1998. "Predictors of Violent or Serious Delinquency in Adolescence and Early Adulthood: A Synthesis of Longitudinal Research." In *Serious & Violent Juvenile Offenders: Risk Factors and Successful Interventions*, edited by Rolf Loeber and David Farrington. Thousand Oaks, CA: Sage.

Lofland, John. 1969. *Deviance and Identity*. Englewood Cliffs, NJ: Prentice-Hall.

Mack, John. 1975. *The Crime Industry*. London, UK: Saxon House.

Maguire, Mike. 1982. *Burglary in a Dwelling*. London: Heinemann.

Maher, Lisa, and Kathleen Daly. 1996. "Women in the Street Level Drug Economy: Continuity or Change?" Criminology 34(4):465-492.

Malcolm X. 1965. *The Autobiography of Malcolm X*. New York: Grove Press.

Maines, David R. 2001. *The Faultline of Consciousness: A View of Interactionism in Sociology*. Hawthorne, NY: Aldine de Gruyter.

March, James and Herbert Simon. 1958. *Organizations*. New York: John Wiley and Sons.

Martin, John Levi. 2003. "What Is Field Theory?" *American Journal of Sociology* 109(1):1–49.

Matsueda, Ross, Rosemary Gartner, Irving Piliavin, and Michael Polakowski. 1992. "The Prestige of Criminal and Conventional Occupations: A Subcultural Model of Criminal Activity." *American Sociological Review* 57(6):752–70.

Matsueda, Ross and Karen Heimer. 1997. "Developmental Theories of Crime." Pp. 174–86 in *Advances in Criminological Theory*, edited by T. Thornberry. New Brunswick, NJ: Transaction.

Matza, David. 1964. *Delinquency and Drift*. New York: Wiley.

Maurer, David. 1964. *The Whiz Mob: A Correlation of the Technical Argot of Pickpockets with Their Behavior Pattern*. New Haven, CT: College and University Press.

Maurer, David. 1974. *The American Confidence Man*. Springfield, IL: Charles C. Thomas.

McCarthy, Bill and John Hagan. 1992. "Mean Streets: The Theoretical Significance of Situational Delinquency among Homeless Youths." *American Journal of Sociology* 98(3):597–627

Merton, Robert. 1938. "Social Structure and Anomie." *American Sociological Review* 3:672–82.

Merton, Robert. 1997. "On the Evolving Synthesis of Differential Association and Anomie Theory: A Perspective from the Sociology of Science." *Criminology* 35:517–25.

Miller, Gale. 1978. *Odd Jobs: The World of Deviant Work.* Englewood Cliffs, NJ: Prentice-Hall.

Miller, Jody. 1998. "Up It Up: Gender and the Accomplishment of Street Robbery." Criminology 36(1):37-66.

Miller, Jerome. 1991. *The Last One Over the Wall: The Massachusetts Experiment in Closing Reform Schools.* Columbus, OH: Ohio State University Press.

Miller, Walter. 1958. "Lower Class Culture as a Generating Milieu of Gang Delinquency." *Journal of Social Issues* 14:5-19.

Mills, C. Wright. 1940. "Situated Actions and Vocabularies of Motive." *American Sociological Review* 5:904–13.

Moffitt, Terrie. 1997. "Adolescence-Limited and Life-Course Persistent Offending: A Complementary Pair of Developmental Theories." Pp. 11–54 in *Developmental Theories of Crime and Delinquency,* edited by T. Thornberry. New Brunswick, NJ: Transaction.

Naylor, R. T. 2003. "Towards a General Theory of Profit-Driven Crimes." *British Journal of Criminology* 43:81–101.

Nisan, Mordechai. 1991. "The Moral Balance Model: Theory and Research Extending Our Understanding of Moral Choice and Deviation." In *Handbook of Moral Behavior and Development,* Vol. 3, edited by W. Kurtines and J. Gewirtz. Hillsdale, NJ: Erlbaum.

Nisan, Mordechai and Gaby Horenczyk. 1990. "Moral Balance: The Effect of Prior Behavior on Decision in Moral Conflict." *British Journal of Social Psychology* 29:29–42.

Parsons, Talcott. 1937. *The Structure of Social Action.* New York: Free Press.

Pennsylvania Crime Commission. 1991. *Organized Crime in Pennsylvania: A Decade of Change: The 1990 Decade Report.* Conshohocken, PA: Commonwealth of Pennsylvania.

Pistone, Joseph. 1987. *Donnie Brasco.* New York: Penguin.

Podolny, Joe and Karen Page. 1998. "Network Forms of Organizations." *Annual Review of Sociology* 24: 57–140. Palo Alto, CA: Annual Reviews.

Polsky, Ned. 1967. *Hustlers, Beats, and Others.* Chicago: Aldine de Gruyter.

Prus, Robert and Styllianoss Irini. 1980. *Hookers, Rounders, and Desk Clerks.* Toronto: Gage.

Prus, Robert and C. R. D. Sharper. 1977. *Road Hustler.* Toronto: Gage.

Prus, Robert and C. R. D. Sharper. 1991. *Road Hustler,* 2nd ed. Toronto: Gage.

Reckless, Walter. 1973. *The Crime Problem.* New York: Appleton, Century, Crofts.

Rosenfeld, Richard, Bruce Jacobs, and Richard Wright. 2003. "Snitching and the Code of the Street." *British Journal of Criminology* 43:291–309.

Ruggiero, Vincenzo. 2000. *Crime and Markets.* London: Oxford University Press.

Sampson, Robert and John Laub. 1993. *Crime in the Making: Pathways and Turning Points through Life.* Cambridge, MA: Harvard University Press.

Sampson, Robert and John Laub. 1997. "A Life-Course Theory of Cumulative Disadvantage and the Stability of Delinquency." Pp. 133–61 in *Developmental Theories of Crime and Delinquency,* edited by Terence Thornberry. New Brunswick, NJ: Transaction.

Schatzberg, Rufus and Robert Kelly. 1996. *African American Organized Crime: A Social History.* New Brunswick, NJ: Rutgers University Press.

Scott, Marvin and Stanford Lyman. 1968. "Accounts." *American Sociological Review* 33:46–62.

Shapiro, Susan. 1984. *Wayward Capitalists: Target of the Securities and Exchange Commission.* New Haven, CT: Yale University Press.

Sherman, Lawrence. 1993. "Defiance, Deterrence, and Irrelevance: A Theory of the Criminal Sanction." *Journal of Research in Crime and Delinquency* 30:445–73.

Shover, Neal. 1972. "Structures and Careers in Burglary." *Journal of Criminal Law, Criminology, and Police Science* 63:540–49.

Shover, Neal. 1983. "The Later Stages of Ordinary Property Offender Careers." *Social Problems* 31:208–18.

Shover, Neal. 1996. *Great Pretenders: Pursuits and Careers of Persistent Thieves.* Boulder, CO: Westview.

Stebbins, Robert A. 1971. *Commitment to Deviance.* Westport, CT: Greenwood.

Steffensmeier, Darrell. 1978. "Crime and the Contemporary Woman: An Analysis of Changing Levels of Female Property Crime, 1960-1975." *Social Forces* 57:566–584.

Steffensmeier, Darrell. 1980. "A Review and Assessment of Sex Differences in Adult Crime, 1965-1977." *Social Forces* 58:1080-1108.

Steffensmeier, Darrell. 1983. "Organization Properties and Sex-Segregation in the Underworld: Building a Sociological Theory of Sex Differences in Crime." *Social Forces* 6:1010–32.

Steffensmeier, Darrell. 1986. *The Fence: In the Shadow of Two Worlds.* Totowa, NJ: Rowman and Littlefield.

Steffensmeier, Darrell. 1993. "Fencing Stolen Property." In *Encyclopedia of Police Science,* edited by W. Bailey. Oxford, UK: Elsevier Sciences.

Steffensmeier, Darrell and Emilie Allan. 1995. "Gender, Age, and Crime." Pp. 67–94 in *Criminology,* edited by Joseph Sheley. Belmont, CA: Sage.

Steffensmeier, Darrell and Robert Terry. 1986. "Institutional Sexism in the Underworld: A View from the Inside." *Sociological Inquiry* 56:304–23.

Steffensmeier, Darrell and Frederick Martens 2002. "Organized Crime." in International Encyclopedia of the Social and Behavioral Sciences, Vol. 3, edited by N. Smelser and P. Baltes. Oxford, UK: Elsevier Sciences.

Steffensmeier, Darrell and Jeffery T. Ulmer. 2003. "Confessions of a Dying Thief: A Tutorial on Differential Association/Social Learning Theory." pp. 227–64 in *Social Learning Theory and the Explanation of Crime: A Guide for the New Century* (Advances in Criminological Theory, Volume 11), edited by Ronald Akers and Gary Jensen. New Brunswick, NJ: Transaction.

Strauss, Anselm. 1969. *Mirrors and Masks.* San Francisco: Sociology.

Strauss, Anselm. 1993. *Continual Permutations of Action.* Hawthorne, NY: Aldine de Gruyter.

Sutherland, Edwin. 1937. *The Professional Thief.* Chicago: University of Chicago Press.

Sutherland, Edwin. 1940. "White Collar Criminality." *American Sociological Review* 5:1–12.

Sutherland, Edwin. 1947. *Principles of Criminology.* Philadelphia: Lippincott.

Sutherland, Edwin. 1949. *White Collar Crime*. New York: Holt, Rinehart and Winston.

Sutherland, Edwin and Donald Cressey. 1966. *Principles of Criminology*. Philadelphia: Lippincott.

Sutton, M. 1998. *Handling Stolen Goods and Theft: A Market Reduction Approach*. London: British Home Office Research Publications.

Suttles, Gerald. 1968. *The Social Order of the Slum*. Chicago: University of Chicago Press.

Sykes, Gresham and David Matza. 1957. "Techniques of Neutralization: A Theory of Delinquency." *American Sociological Review* 22:664–70.

Tremblay, Pierre. 1993. "Searching for Suitable Co-offenders." In Ronald Clarke and Marcus Felson (eds.). *Advances in Criminological Theory: Routine Activity and Rational Choice*. Vol. 5. NY: Transaction.

Tremblay, Peter and C. Morselli. 2000. "Patterns in Criminal Achievement: Wilson and Abrahamse Revisited." *Criminology 38:633–60.*

Tunnell, Kenneth. 2000. *Living Off Crime*. Chicago: Burham.

Uggen, Christopher and Melissa Thompson. 2003. "The Socioeconomic Determinants of Ill-Gotten Gains: Within Person Changes in Drug Use and Illegal Earnings." *American Journal of Sociology* 109(1):146–85.

Ulmer, Jeffery T. 1994. "Revisiting Stebbins: Labeling and Commitment to Deviance." *Sociological Quarterly* 35:135–57.

Ulmer, Jeffery T. 2000. "Commitment, Deviance, and Social Control." *Sociological Quarterly* 41:315–36.

Ulmer, Jeffery T. and J. William Spencer. 1999. "The Contributions of an Interactionist Approach to Research and Theory on Criminal Careers." *Theoretical Criminology* 3:95–124.

Veblen, Thorstein. 1934. *The Theory of the Leisure Class*. New York: Viking.

Vold, George, Thomas Bernard, and T. Snipes. 1998. *Theoretical Criminology*. New York: Oxford University Press.

Walsh, Marilyn. 1977. *The Fence: A New Look at the World of Property Theft*. Westport, CT: Greenwood.

Warr, Mark. 2002. *Companions in Crime: The Social Aspects of Criminal Conduct*. New York: Cambridge University Press.

Weerman, Frank. 2003. "Co-offending as Social Exchange: Explaining Characteristics of Co-offending." *British Journal of Criminology* 43:398–416.

Weisburd, David and Elin Waring. 2001. *White-Collar Crime and Criminal Careers*. Cambridge: Cambridge University Press.

Weisburd, David, Stanton Wheeler, Elin Waring, and Nancy Bode. 1991. *Crimes of the Middle Classes: White Collar Offenders in the Federal Courts*. New Haven, CT: Yale University Press.

Williams, Ryan. 1998. "Offense Specialization Among Juvenile Offenders During the Early Stages of Criminal Careers." Masters Thesis. Department of Sociology, University of Calgary (Alberta).

Wilson, James Q. and Richard Herrnstein. 1985. *Crime and Human Nature*. New York: Simon and Schuster.

Wright, Richard and Scott Decker. 1994. *Burglars on the Job: Street Life and Residential Break-Ins*. Boston: Northeastern University Press.

Wright, Richard and Scott Decker. 1997. *Armed Robbers in Action*. Boston: Northeastern University Press

Index

Abadinsky, Howard, 269
Adler, Patricia, 35, 172, 303
Akers, Ronald, 26, 77, 294, 298, 302, 361
Akerstom, Malin, 56, 129, 132
Albini, Joseph, 266-267
Anderson, Elijah, 309
Apologia pro vita, 347-348, 352-358. See also Neutralizations/accounts.
Athens, Lonnie, 36
Attractions of crime. See Rewards.

Becker, Howard, 33-34, 36, 173, 363
Beirne, Piers, 68, 181
Benson, Michael, 24, 117, 306
Bernard, Thomas, 34
Best, Joel, 37, 61-64, 68
Bordua, David, 11
Bourdieu, Pierre, 8, 38, 181, 213, 265
Braithwaite, John, 36
Burglars/burglary, 43-47, 59-67, 69 and passim; skills and pecking order, 46, 71-77,147; crew roles, 71-82; stages in committing burglary, 60-64; conditions for success at, 64-68; types of 46, 67-68, 71, 74. See also Change/stability; Crime skills; Professional criminal.

Change/stability in crime/underworld, 223-228, 252-263; in identity theft/fraud, 224-225, 262; in Internet crime, 225; in drug trade, 224-227, 258, 318; new crime syndicates, 277; shifts in law enforcement, 226-227, 257; in burglary, 224, 256; in stolen goods market, 260-262
Cloward, Richard, 25, 28-29, 211, 214
Commitment, 26, 33-35, 171-181, 348-351, 356-358; cumulative

commitment processes, 309-310; commitment portfolio, 174 and passim. See also Structural commitment; Personal commitment; Moral commitment; Learning-opportunity-commitment framework.
Contacts/networking, 137-146, 155-169; types of, 138-141; as spider-web, 141-144; as mafia networks, 266-267; for burglary, 64-67; for fencing, 117, 122, 137 and passim; as element of opportunity theory, 26-28; as criminal capital, 127, 145. See also Crime opportunities; Criminal social capital; Homosocial reproduction; Racism; Sexism; Underworld stratification.
Cressey, Donald, 266
Crime as work, a business, 87-91, 125-127. See also Criminal/illegal enterprise; Fencing stolen goods; Professional criminal.
Crime opportunity, 24-29, 36 and passim, 59, 80-86, 96-99, 166 and passim, 202-205, 229; typology of, 24-29, 211-212; as criminal capital, 40-44; as structural commitment, 31-32; motivational side of, 31, 67, 212, 299; incarceration effects, 51-52, 300, 330-332; in differential association/social learning, 20-24; in labeling theory, 36-37; in learning-opportunity-commitment perspective, 180. See also Changes/stability in crime/ underworld; Commitment [structural]; Contacts/networking; Incarceration; Organization of crime; Racism; Sexism; Skills/attributes.

397